David Henry Montgomery

The Leading Facts of English History

David Henry Montgomery

The Leading Facts of English History

ISBN/EAN: 9783337397210

Printed in Europe, USA, Canada, Australia, Japan

Cover: Foto ©ninafisch / pixelio.de

More available books at **www.hansebooks.com**

The Leading Facts of History Series.

THE
LEADING FACTS OF ENGLISH HISTORY.

BY

D. H. MONTGOMERY.

Nothing in the past is dead to the man who would learn how the present came to be what it is." — STUBBS: *Constitutional History of England.*

SECOND EDITION, REVISED.

BOSTON, U.S.A.:
GINN & COMPANY, PUBLISHERS.
1894.

PREFACE.

MOST of the materials for this book were gathered by the writer during several years' residence in England.

The attempt is here made to present them in a manner that shall illustrate the great law of national growth, in the light thrown upon it by the foremost English historians.

The authorities for the different periods will be found in the List of Books on page 434; but the author desires to particularly acknowledge his indebtedness to the works of Gardiner, Guest, and Green, and to the excellent constitutional histories of Taswell-Langmead and Ransome.

SECOND EDITION.

The present edition has been very carefully revised throughout, and numerous maps and genealogical tables have been added.

The author's hearty thanks are due to G. Mercer Adam, Esq., of Toronto, Canada; Prof. W. F. Allen, of The University of Wisconsin; President Myers, of Belmont College, Ohio; Prof. George W. Knight, of Ohio State University; and to Miss M. A. Parsons, teacher of history in the High School, Winchester, Mass., for the important aid which they have kindly rendered.

DAVID H. MONTGOMERY,

CAMBRIDGE, MASS.

CONTENTS.

SECTION	PAGE
I. Britain before History begins.	1
II. The Relation of the Geography of England to its History.	12
III. A Civilization which did not civilize; Roman Britain.	18
IV. The Coming of the Saxons; Britain becomes England[1].	31
V. The Coming of the Normans.	58
VI. The Angevins, or Plantagenets; Rise of the English Nation.	87
VII. The Self-Destruction of Feudalism.	150
VIII. Absolutism of the Crown; the Reformation; the New Learning.	179
IX. The Stuart Period; the Divine Right of Kings *vs.* the Divine Right of the People	229
X. The American Revolution; the House of Commons the Ruling Power; the Era of Reform.	306
XI. A General Summary of English Constitutional History.	391
Table of Principal Dates	421
Descent of the English Sovereigns	432
List of Books	434
Statistics	438
Index	440

[1] Each section or period is followed by a general view of that period.

CONTENTS.

MAPS.

MAP		PAGE
I.	County Map of England and Wales (in colors). Frontispiece.	
II.	Britain before its Separation from the Continent	4
III.	Roman Britain	24
IV.	The Continental Home of the English, with their Successive Invasions of Britain	34
V.	The English Settlements and Kingdoms	38
VI.	Danish England	42
VII.	The Four Great Earldoms	44
VIII.	The Dominions of the Angevins, or Plantagenets.	88
IX.	The English Possessions in France, 1360 (in colors)	130
X.	England during the Wars of the Roses	174
XI.	The World as known in 1497, Reign of Henry VII., showing Voyages of Discovery by the Cabots and Others	186
XII.	Drake's Circumnavigation of the Globe, with the First English Colonies planted in America	218
XIII.	England during the Civil Wars of the Seventeenth Century	244
XIV.	Clive's Conquests in India	318
XV.	The British Empire at the Present Time	382
XVI.	Plan of a Manor	80

THE

LEADING FACTS OF ENGLISH HISTORY.

I.

> "This fortress built by Nature for herself
> Against infection and the hand of war;
> This happy breed of men, this little world,
> This precious stone set in the silver sea,
> Which serves it in the office of a wall,
> Or as a moat defensive to a house,
> Against the envy of less happier lands;
> This blessed plot, this earth, this realm, this England."
> SHAKESPEARE, *Richard II.*

BRITAIN BEFORE WRITTEN HISTORY BEGINS.

THE COUNTRY.

1. Britain once a Part of the Continent. — The island of Great Britain has not always had its present form. Though separated from Europe now by the English Channel and the North Sea, yet there is abundant geological evidence that it was once a part of the continent.

2. Proofs. — The chalk cliffs of Dover are really a continuation of the chalk of Calais, and the strait dividing them, which is nowhere more than thirty fathoms deep,[1] is simply the result of a

---

[1] The width of the Strait of Dover at its narrowest point is twenty-one miles. The bottom is a continuous ridge of chalk. If St. Paul's Cathedral were placed in the strait, midway between England and France, more than half of the building would be above the surface of the water.

slight and comparatively recent depression in that chalk. The waters of the North Sea are also shallow, and in dredging, great quantities of the same fossil remains of land animals are brought up which are found buried in the soil of England, Belgium, and France. It would seem, therefore, that there can be no reasonable doubt that the bed of this sea, where these creatures made their homes, must once have been on a level with the countries whose shores it now washes.

3. Appearance of the Country. — What we know to-day as England, was at that time a western projection of the continent, wild, desolate, and without a name.[1] The high hill ranges show unmistakable marks of the glaciers which once ploughed down their sides, and penetrated far into the valleys, as they still continue to do among the Alps.

4. The Climate. — The climate then was probably like that of Greenland now. Europe was but just emerging, if, indeed, it had begun to finally emerge, from that long period during which the upper part of the northern hemisphere was buried under a vast field of ice and snow.

5. Trees and Animals. — The trees and animals corresponded to the climate and the country. Forests of fir, pine, and stunted oak, such as are now found in latitudes much farther north, covered the lowlands and the lesser hills. Through these roamed the reindeer, the mammoth, the wild horse, the bison or "buffalo," and the cave-bear.

MAN. — THE ROUGH-STONE AGE.

6. His Condition. — Man seems to have taken up his abode in Britain before it was severed from the mainland. His condition was that of the lowest and most brutal savage. He probably stood apart, even from his fellow-men, in selfish isolation; if so, he was

---

[1] See Map No. 2, page 4.

bound to no tribe, acknowledged no chief, obeyed no law. All his interests were centred in himself and in the little group which constituted his family.

7. How he lived. — His house was the first empty cave he found, or a rude rock-shelter made by piling up stones in some partially protected place. Here he dwelt during the winter. In summer, when his wandering life began, he built himself a camping place of branches and bark, under the shelter of an overhanging cliff by the sea, or close to the bank of a river. He had no tools. When he wanted a fire he struck a bit of flint against a lump of iron ore, or made a flame by rubbing two dry sticks rapidly together. His only weapon was a club or a stone. As he did not dare encounter the larger and fiercer animals, he rarely ventured into the depths of the forests, but subsisted on the shell-fish he picked up along the shore, or on any chance game he might have the good fortune to kill, to which, as a relish, he added berries or pounded roots.

8. His First Tools and Weapons. — In process of time he learned to make rough tools and weapons from pieces of flint, which he chipped to an edge by striking them together. When he had thus succeeded in shaping for himself a spear-point, or had discovered how to make a bow and to tip the arrows with a sharp splinter of stone, his condition changed. He now felt that he was a match for the beasts he had fled from before. Thus armed, he slew the reindeer and the bison, used their flesh for food, their skins for clothing, while he made thread from their sinews, and needles and other implements from their bones. Still, though he had advanced from his first helpless state, his life must have continued to be a constant battle with the beasts and the elements.

9. His Moral and Religious Nature. — His moral nature was on a level with his intellect. No questions of conscience disturbed him. In every case of dispute might made right.

His religion was the terror inspired by the forces and convulsions of nature, and the dangers to which he was constantly exposed. Such, we have every reason to believe, was the condition of the Cave-Man who first inhabited Britain, and the other countries of Europe and the East.

10. Duration of the Rough-Stone Age. — The period in which he lived is called the Old or Rough-Stone Age, a name derived from the implements then in use.

When that age began, or when it came to a close, are questions which at present cannot be answered. But we may measure the time which has elapsed since man appeared in Britain by the changes which have taken place in the country. We know that sluggish streams like the Avon, with whose channel the lapse of many centuries has made scarcely any material difference, have, little by little, cut their way down through beds of gravel till they have scooped out valleys sometimes a hundred feet deep. We know also the climate is wholly unlike now what it once was, and that the animals of that far-off period have either wholly disappeared from the globe or are found only in distant regions.

The men who were contemporary with them have vanished in like manner. But that they were contemporary we may feel sure from two well-established grounds of evidence.

11. Remains of the Rough-Stone Age. — First, their flint knives and arrows are found in the caves, mingled with ashes and with the bones of the animals on which they feasted; these bones having been invariably split in order that they might suck out the marrow.[1] Next, we have the drawings they made of those very creatures scratched on a tusk or on a smooth piece of slate with a bit of sharp-pointed quartz.[2] Nearly everything else has perished;

---

[1] Very few remains of the Cave-Men themselves have yet been found, and these with the most trifling exceptions have been discovered on the continent, especially in France and Switzerland. The first rough-stone implement found in England was dug up in Gray's Inn Road, London, in 1690. It is of flint, and in shape and size resembles a very large pear. It forms the nucleus of a collection in the British Museum.

[2] These drawings have been found in considerable number on the continent.

BRITAIN BEFORE ITS SEPARATION FROM THE CONTINENT OF EUROPE

To face page 4.

The dark lines represent land, now submerged.
The dotted area, that occupied by animals.
The white land area, portions once covered by glaciers.
The figures show the present depth of sea in fathoms.
F. (France), T. (Thames), W. (Wales), S. (Scotland), I. (Ireland).
?, doubtful area, but probably glacial.

Univ.

even their burial places, if they had any, have been swept away by the destroying action of time. Yet these memorials have come down to us, so many fragments of imperishable history, made by that primeval race who possessed no other means of recording the fact of their existence and their work.

THE AGE OF POLISHED STONE.

12. The Second Race; Britain an Island. — Following the Cave-Men, there came a higher race who took possession of the country; these were the men of the New or Polished-Stone Age. When they reached Britain, it had probably become an island. Long before their arrival the land on the east and south had been slowly sinking, till at last the waters of the North Sea crept in and made the separation complete. The new-comers appear to have brought with them the knowledge of grinding and polishing stone, and of shaping it into hatchets, chisels, spears, and other weapons and utensils.[1] They did not, like the race of the Rough-Stone Period, depend upon such chance pieces of flint as they might pick up, and which would be of inferior quality, but they had regular quarries for digging their supplies. They also obtained polished-stone implements of a superior kind from the inhabitants of the continent, which they in turn got by traffic with Asiatic countries.

13. Government and Mode of Life. — These people were organized into tribes or clans under the leadership of a chief. They lived in villages or "pit circles" consisting of a group of holes dug in the ground, each large enough to accommodate a family. These pits were roofed over with branches covered with

---

Thus far the only one discovered in England is the head of a horse scratched or cut in bone. It came from the upper cave-earth of Robin Hood Cave, in the Cresswell Crags, Derbyshire. See Dawkins' Early Man in Britain, page 185.

[1] Grinding or polishing stone: this was done by rubbing the tools or weapons, after they had been chipped into shape, on a smooth, flat stone. The natives of Australia still practise this art.

slabs of baked clay. The entrance to them was a long, inclined passage, through which the occupants crawled on their hands and knees.

Armed with their stone hatchets, these men were able to cut down trees and to make log canoes in which they crossed to the mainland. They could also undertake those forest clearings which had been impossible before. The point, however, of prime difference and importance was their mode of subsistence.

14. Farming and Cattle-Raising. — Unlike their predecessors, this second race did not depend on hunting and fishing alone, but were herdsmen and farmers as well. They had brought from other countries such cereals as wheat and barley, and such domestic animals as the ox, sheep, hog, horse, and dog. Around their villages they cultivated fields of grain, while in the adjacent woods and pastures they kept herds of swine and cattle.

15. Arts. — They had learned the art of pottery, and made dishes and other useful vessels of clay, which they baked in the fire. They raised flax and spun and wove it into coarse, substantial cloth. They may also have had woollen garments, though no remains of any have reached us, perhaps because they are more perishable than linen. They were men of small stature, with dark hair and complexion, and it is supposed that they are represented in Great Britain to-day by the inhabitants of Southern Wales.

16. Burial of the Dead. — They buried their dead in long mounds, or barrows, some of which are upward of three hundred feet in length. These barrows were often made by setting up large, rough slabs of stone so as to form one or more chambers which were afterward covered with earth. In some parts of England these burial mounds are very common, and in Wiltshire, several hundred occur within the limits of an hour's walk.

During the last twenty years many of these mounds have been opened and carefully explored. Not only the remains of the builders have been discovered in them, but with them their tools and weapons. In addition to these, earthen dishes for holding food and drink have been found, placed there it is supposed, to supply the wants of the spirits of the departed, as the American Indians still do in their interments. When a chief or great man died, it appears to have been the custom of the tribe to hold a funeral feast, and the number of cleft human skulls dug up in such places has led to the belief that prisoners of war may have been sacrificed and their flesh eaten by the assembled guests in honor of the dead. Be that as it may, there are excellent grounds for supposing that these tribes were constantly at war with each other, and that their battles were characterized by all the fierceness and cruelty which uncivilized races nearly everywhere exhibit.

THE BRONZE AGE.

17. The Third Race. — But great as was the progress which the men of the New or Polished-Stone Age had made, it was destined to be surpassed. A people had appeared in Europe, though at what date cannot yet be determined, who had discovered how to melt and mingle two important metals, copper and tin.

18. Superiority of Bronze to Stone. — The product of that mixture, named bronze, perhaps from its brown color, had this great advantage : a stone tool or weapon, though hard, is brittle; but bronze is not only hard, but tough. Stone, again, cannot be ground to a thin cutting edge, whereas bronze can. Here, then, was a new departure. Here was a new power. From that period the bronze axe and the bronze sword, wielded by the muscular arms of a third and stronger race, became the symbols of a period appropriately named the Age of Bronze. The men thus equipped invaded Britain. They drove back or enslaved the possessors of the soil. They conquered the island, settled it, and held it as their own until the Roman legions, armed with swords of steel, came in turn to conquer them.

19. Who the Bronze-Men were, and how they lived. — The Bronze-Men may be regarded as offshoots of the Celts, a large-limbed, fair-haired, fierce-eyed people, that originated in Asia, and overran Central and Western Europe. Like the men of the Age of Polished Stone, they lived in settlements under chiefs and possessed a rude sort of government. Their villages were built above ground and consisted of circular houses somewhat resembling Indian wigwams. They were constructed of wood, chinked in with clay, having pointed roofs covered with reeds, with an opening to let out the smoke and let in the light. Around these villages the inhabitants dug a deep ditch for defence, to which they added a rampart of earth surmounted by a palisade of stout sticks, or by felled trees piled on each other. They kept sheep and cattle. They raised grain, which they deposited in subterranean storehouses for the winter. They not only possessed all the arts of the Stone-Men, but in addition, they were skilful workers in gold, of which they made necklaces and bracelets. They also manufactured woollen cloth of various textures and brilliant colors.

They buried their dead in round barrows or mounds, making for them the same provision that the Stone-Men did. Though divided into tribes and scattered over a very large area, yet they all spoke the same language; so that a person would have been understood if he had asked for bread and cheese in Celtic anywhere from the borders of Scotland to the southern boundaries of France.

20. Greek Account of the Bronze-Men of Britain. — At what time the Celts came into Britain is not known, though some writers suppose that it was about 500 B.C. However that may be, we learn something of their mode of life two centuries later from the narrative of Pytheas,[1] a learned Greek navigator and geographer who made a voyage to Britain at that time. He says he saw plenty of grain growing, and that the farmers gathered the sheaves at harvest into large barns, where they threshed it under cover, the fine weather being so uncertain in the island that they could not do it out of doors, as in countries farther south. Here, then, we

---

[1] See Pytheas, in Rhys' Celtic Britain or Elton's Origins of English History.

have proof that the primitive Britons saw quite as little of the sun as their descendants do now. Another characteristic discovery made by Pytheas was that the farmers of that day had learned to make beer and liked it. So that here, again, the primitive Briton was in no way behind his successors.

21. Early Tin Trade of Britain. — Of their skill in mining Pytheas does not speak, though from that date, and perhaps many centuries earlier, the inhabitants of the southern part of the island carried on a brisk trade in tin ore with merchants of the Mediterranean. Indeed, if tradition can be depended upon, Hiram, king of Tyre, who reigned over the Phœnicians, a people particularly skilful in making bronze, and who aided Solomon in building the Jewish temple, may have obtained his supplies of tin from the British Isles. At any rate, about the year 300 B.C., a certain Greek writer speaks of the country as then well known, calling it Albion, or the "Land of the White Cliffs."

22. Introduction of Iron. — About a century after that name was given, the use of bronze began to be supplemented to some extent by the introduction of iron. Cæsar tells us that rings of it were employed for money; if so, it was probably by tribes in the north of the island, for the men of the south had not only gold and silver coins at that date, but what is more, they had learned how to counterfeit them.

Such were the inhabitants the Romans found when they invaded Britain in the first century before the Christian era. Rude as these people seemed to Cæsar as he met them in battle array clad in skins, with their faces stained with the deep blue dye of the woad plant, yet they proved no unworthy foemen even for his veteran troops.

23. The Religion of the Primitive Britons; the Druids. — We have seen that they held some dim faith in an overruling power and in a life beyond the grave, since they offered human sacrifices to the one, and buried the warrior's spear with him, that he might be provided for the other. Furthermore, the Britons when Cæsar invaded the country had a regularly organized priesthood, the Druids, who appear to have worshipped the heavenly bodies. They dwelt in the depths of the forests, and venerated the oak and the mistletoe. There in the gloom and secrecy of the woods they raised their altars; there, too, they offered up criminals to propitiate their gods. They acted not only as interpreters of the divine will, but they held the savage passions of the people in check, and tamed them as wild beasts are tamed. Besides this, they were the repositories of tradition, custom, and law. They were also prophets, judges, and teachers. Lucan, the Roman poet, declared he envied them their belief in the indestructibility of the soul, since it banished that greatest of all fears, the fear of death. Cæsar tells us that "they did much inquire, and hand down to the youth concerning the stars and their motions, concerning the magnitude of the earth, concerning the nature of things, and the might and power of the immortal gods."[1] They did more; for they not only transmitted their beliefs and hopes from generation to generation, but they gave them architectural power and permanence in the massive columns of hewn stone, which they raised in that temple open to the sky, the ruins of which are still to be seen on Salisbury Plain. There, on one of those fallen blocks, Carlyle and Emerson sat and discussed the great questions of the Druid philosophy when they made their pilgrimage to Stonehenge[2] more than forty years ago.

24. What we owe to Primitive or Prehistoric Man. — The

---

[1] See Cæsar's Gallic War, Books IV. and V. (for these and other references, see list of books in Appendix).

[2] Stonehenge (literally, the "Hanging Stones"): this is generally considered to be the remains of a Druid temple. It is situated on a plain near Salisbury, Wiltshire, in the south of England. It consists of a number of immense upright stones arranged in two circles, an outer and an inner, with a row of flat stones partly connecting them at the top. The temple had no roof. An excellent description of it may be found in R. W. Emerson's English Traits.

Romans, indeed, looked down upon these people as barbarians; yet it is well to bear in mind that all the progress which civilization has since made is built on the foundations which they slowly and painfully laid during unknown centuries of toil and strife. It is to them that we owe the taming of the dog, horse, and other domestic animals, the first working of metals, the beginning of agriculture and mining, and the establishment of many salutary customs which help not a little to bind society together to-day.

II.

> "Father Neptune one day to Dame Freedom did say,
> 'If ever I lived upon dry land,
> The spot I should hit on would be little Britain.'
> Says Freedom, 'Why, that's my own island.'
> O, 'tis a snug little island,
> A right little, tight little island!
> Search the world round, none can be found
> So happy as this little island."
>
> T. DIBDIN.

THE GEOGRAPHY OF ENGLAND IN RELATION TO ITS HISTORY.[1]

25. Geography and History. — As material surroundings strongly influence individual life, so the physical features — situation, surface, and climate — of a country have a marked effect on its people and its history.

26. The Island Form; Race Settlements — the Romans. — The insular form of Britain gave it a certain advantage over the continent during the age when Rome was subjugating the barbarians of Northern and Western Europe. As their invasions could only be by sea, they were necessarily on a comparatively small scale. This perhaps is one reason why the Romans did not succeed in establishing their language and laws in the island. They conquered and held it for centuries, but they never destroyed its individuality; they never Latinized it as they did France and Spain.

---

[1] As this section necessarily contains references to events in the later periods of English history, it may be advantageously reviewed after the pupil has reached a somewhat advanced stage in the course.

27. The Saxons. In like manner, when the power of Rome fell and the northern tribes overran and took possession of the Empire, they were in a measure shut out from Britain. Hence the Saxons, Angles, and Jutes could not pour down upon it in countless hordes, but only by successive attacks. This had two results: first, the native Britons were driven back only by degrees — thus their hope and courage were kept alive and transmitted; next, the conquerors settling gradually in different sections built up independent kingdoms. When in time the whole country came under one sovereignty the kingdoms, which had now become shires or counties, retained through their chief men an important influence in the government, thus preventing the royal power from becoming absolute.

28. The Danes and Normans. — In the course of the ninth, tenth, and eleventh centuries, the Danes invaded the island, got possession of the throne, and permanently established themselves in the northern half of England, as the country was then called. They could not come, however, with such overwhelming force as either to exterminate or drive out the English, but were compelled to unite with them, as the Normans did later in their conquest under William of Normandy. Hence, every conquest of the island ended in a compromise, and no one race got complete predominance. Eventually all mingled and became one people.

29. Earliest Names: Celtic. — The steps of English history may be traced to a considerable extent by geographical names. Thus the names of most of the prominent natural features, the hills, and especially the streams, are British or Celtic, carrying us back to the Bronze Age, and perhaps even earlier. Familiar examples of this are found in the name, Malvern Hills, and in the word Avon ("the water"), which is repeated many times in England and Wales.

30. Roman Names. — The Roman occupation of Britain is shown by the names ending in "cester," or "chester" (a corruption of *castra*, a camp). Thus Leicester, Worcester, Dorchester, Colchester, Chester, indicate that these places were walled towns and military stations.

31. Saxon Names. — On the other hand, the names of many of the great political divisions, especially in the south and east of England, mark the Saxon settlements, such as Essex (the East Saxons), Sussex (the South Saxons), Middlesex (the Middle or Central Saxons). In the same way the settlement of the two divisions of the Angles on the coast is indicated by the names Norfolk (the North folk) and Suffolk (the South folk)[1].

32. Danish Names. — The conquests and settlements of the Danes are readily traced by the Danish termination "by" (an abode or town), as in Derby, Rugby, Grimsby. Names of places so ending, which may be counted by hundreds, occur with scarce an exception north of London. They date back to the time when Alfred made the treaty of Wedmore,[2] by which the Danes agreed to confine themselves to the northern half of the country.

33. Norman Names. — The conquest of England by the Normans created but few new names. These, as in the case of Richmond and Beaumont, generally show where the invading race built a castle or an abbey, or where, as in Montgomeryshire, they conquered and held a district in Wales.

While each new invasion left its mark on the country, it will be seen that the greater part of the names of counties and towns are of Roman, Saxon, or Danish origin; so that, with some few and comparatively unimportant exceptions, the map of England remains to-day in this respect what those races made it more than a thousand years ago.

34. Eastern and Western Britain. — As the southern and eastern coasts of Britain were in most direct communication with the continent and were first settled, they continued until modern

---

[1] See Map No. 7, page 44.
[2] Treaty of Wedmore. See Map No. 6, page 42.

times to be the wealthiest, most civilized, and progressive part of the island. Much of the western portion is a rough, wild country. To it the East Britons retreated, keeping their primitive customs and language, as in Wales and Cornwall. In all the great movements of religious or political reform, up to the middle of the seventeenth century, we find the people of the eastern half of the island on the side of a larger measure of liberty; while those of the western half, were in favor of increasing the power of the king and the church.

35. The Channel in English History. — The value of the Channel to England, which has already been referred to in its early history, may be traced down to our own day.

In 1264, when Simon de Montfort was endeavoring to secure parliamentary representation for the people, the king (Henry III.) sought help from France. A fleet was got ready to invade the country and support him, but owing to unfavorable weather it was not able to sail in season, and Henry was obliged to concede the demands made for reform.[1]

Again, at the time of the threatened attack by the Spanish Armada, when the tempest had dispersed the enemy's fleet and wrecked many of its vessels, leaving only a few to creep back, crippled and disheartened, to the ports whence they had so proudly sailed, Elizabeth fully recognized the value of the "ocean-wall" to her dominions.

So a recent French writer,[2] speaking of Napoleon's intended expedition, which was postponed and ultimately abandoned on account of a sudden and long-continued storm, says, "A few leagues of sea saved England from being forced to engage in a war, which, if it had not entirely trodden civilization under foot, would have certainly crippled it for a whole generation." Finally, to quote the words of Prof. Goldwin Smith, "The English Channel, by exempting England from keeping up a large standing army

---

[1] Stubbs, Select Charters, 401.
[2] Madame de Rémusat.

[though it has compelled her to maintain a powerful and expensive navy], has preserved her from military despotism, and enabled her to move steadily forward in the path of political progress."

36. Climate. — With regard to the climate of England, — its insular form, geographical position, and especially its exposure to the warm currents of the Gulf Stream, give it a mild temperature particularly favorable to the full and healthy development of both animal and vegetable life. Nowhere is found greater vigor or longevity. Charles II. said that he was convinced that there was not a country in the world where one could spend so much time out of doors comfortably as in England; and he might have added that the people fully appreciate this fact and habitually avail themselves of it.

37. Industrial Division of England. — From an industrial and historical point of view, the country falls into two divisions. Let a line be drawn from Whitby, on the northeast coast, to Leicester, in the midlands, and thence to Exmouth, on the southwest coast.[1] On the upper or northwest side of that line will lie the coal and iron, which constitute the greater part of the mineral wealth and manufacturing industry of England; and also all the large places except London. On the lower or southeast side of it will be a comparatively level surface of rich agricultural land, and most of the fine old cathedral cities[2] with their historic associations; in a word, the England of the past as contrasted with modern and democratic England, that part which has grown up since the introduction of steam.

38. Commercial Situation of England. — Finally, the position of England with respect to commerce is worthy of note. It is not only possessed of a great number of excellent harbors, but it is situated in the most extensively navigated of the oceans, between the two continents having the highest civilization and the most

---

[1] Whitby, Yorkshire; Exmouth, near Exeter, Devonshire.
[2] In England the cathedral towns only are called cities.

constant intercourse. Next, a glance at the map[1] will show that geographically England is located at about the centre of the land masses of the globe. It is evident that an island so placed stands in the most favorable position for easy and rapid communication with every quarter of the world. On this account England has been able to attain and maintain the highest rank among maritime and commercial powers.

It is true that since the opening of the Suez Canal, in 1869, the trade with the Indies and China has changed. Many cargoes of teas, silks, and spices, which formerly went to London, Liverpool, or Southampton, and were thence reshipped to different countries of Europe, now pass by other channels direct to the consumer. But aside from this, England still retains her supremacy as the great carrier and distributer of the productions of the earth — a fact which has had and must continue to have a decided influence on her history and on her relations with other nations, both in peace and war.

---

[1] See Maps Nos. 11 and 14, pages 186, 382.

III.

" Force and Right rule the world: Force, till Right is ready."
— JOUBERT.

ROMAN BRITAIN, 55 B.C. 43–410 A.D.
A CIVILIZATION WHICH DID NOT CIVILIZE.

39. Europe at the Time of Cæsar's Invasion of Britain. — Before considering the Roman invasion of Britain let us take a glance at the condition of Europe. We have seen that the Celtic tribes of the island, like those of Gaul (France), were not mere savages. On the contrary, we know that they had taken more than one important step in the path of progress; still, the advance should not be overrated. For, north of the shores of the Mediterranean, there was no real civilization. Whatever gain the men of the Bronze Age had made, it was nothing compared to what they had yet to acquire. They had neither organized legislatures, written codes of law, effectively trained armies, nor extensive commerce. They had no great cities, grand architecture, literature, painting, music, or sculpture. Finally, they had no illustrious and imperishable names. All these belonged to the Republic of Rome, or to the countries to the south and east, which the arms of Rome had conquered.

40. Cæsar's Campaigns. — Such was the state of Europe when Julius Cæsar, who was governor of Gaul, but who aspired to be ruler of the world, set out on his first campaign against the tribes north of the Alps. (58 B.C.)

In undertaking the war he had three objects in view: first, he wished to crush the power of those restless hordes that threatened the safety, not only of the Roman provinces, but of the Republic itself. Next, he sought military fame as a stepping-stone to supreme political power. Lastly, he wanted money to maintain his army and to bribe the party leaders of Rome. To this end every tribe which he conquered would be forced to pay him tribute in cash or slaves.

41. Cæsar reaches Boulogne; resolves to cross to Britain. — In three years Cæsar had subjugated the enemy in a succession of victories, and Europe lay virtually helpless at his feet. Late in the summer of 55 B.C. he reached that part of the coast of Gaul where Boulogne is now situated, opposite which one may see on a clear day the gleaming chalk cliffs of Dover, so vividly described in Shakespeare's "Lear." While encamped on the shore he "resolved," he says, "to pass over into Britain, having had trustworthy information that in all his wars with the Gauls the enemies of the Roman Commonwealth had constantly received help from thence."[1]

42. Britain not certainly known to be an Island. — It was not known then with certainty that Britain was an island. Many confused reports had been circulated respecting that strange land in the Atlantic on which only a few adventurous traders had ever set foot. It was spoken of in literature as "another world," or, as Plutarch called it, "a country beyond the bounds of the habitable globe."[2] To that other world the Roman general, impelled by ambition, by curiosity, by desire of vengeance, and by love of gain, determined to go.

43. Cæsar's First Invasion, 55 B.C. — Embarking with a force of between eight and ten thousand men[3] in eighty small vessels, Cæsar crossed the Channel and landed not far from Dover, where he overcame the Britons, who made a desperate resistance. After

---

[1] Cæsar's Gallic War, Book IV.

[2] Plutarch's Lives (Julius Cæsar).

[3] Cæsar is supposed to have sailed about the 25th of August, 55 B.C. His force consisted of two legions, the 7th and 10th. A legion varied at different times from 3000 foot and 200 horse soldiers to 6000 foot and 400 horse.

a stay of a few weeks, during which he did not leave the coast, he returned to Gaul.

44. Second Invasion, 54 B.C. — The next year, a little earlier in the season, Cæsar made a second invasion with a much larger force, and penetrated the country to a short distance north of the Thames. Before the September gales set in, he re-embarked for the continent, never to return. The total result of his two expeditions was, a number of natives, carried as hostages to Rome, a long train of captives destined to be sold in the slave-markets, and some promises of tribute which were never fulfilled. Tacitus remarks, "He did not conquer Britain; he only showed it to the Romans."

Yet so powerful was Cæsar's influence, that his invasion was spoken of as a splendid victory, and the Roman Senate ordered a thanksgiving of twenty days, in gratitude to the gods and in honor of the achievement.

45. Third Invasion of Britain, 43 A.D. — For nearly a hundred years no further attempt was made, but in 43 A.D., after Rome had become a monarchy, the Emperor Claudius ordered a third invasion of Britain, in which he himself took part.

This was successful, and after nine years of fighting, the Roman forces overcame Caractacus, the leader of the Britons.

46. Caractacus carried Captive to Rome. — In company with many prisoners, Caractacus was taken in chains to Rome. Alone of all the captives, he refused to beg for life or liberty. "Can it be possible," said he, as he was led through the streets, "that men who live in such palaces as these envy us our wretched hovels!"[1] "It was the dignity of the man, even in ruins," says Tacitus, "which saved him." The Emperor, struck with his bearing and his speech, ordered him to be set free.

47. The First Roman Colony planted in Britain. — Meanwhile the armies of the Empire had firmly established themselves in the

---

[1] Tacitus, Annals.

southeastern part of the island. There they formed the colony of Camulodunum, the modern Colchester. There, too, they built a temple and set up the statue of the Emperor Claudius, which the soldiers worshipped, both as a protecting god and as a representative of the Roman state.

48. Llyn-din.[1] — The army had also conquered other places, among which was a little native settlement on one of the broadest parts of the Thames. It consisted of a few miserable huts and a row of entrenched cattle-pens. This was called in the Celtic or British tongue Llyn-din or the Fort-on-the-lake, a word which, pronounced with difficulty by Roman lips, became that name which the world now knows wherever ships sail, trade reaches, or history is read, — London.

49. Expedition against the Druids. — But in order to complete the conquest of the country, the Roman generals saw that it would be necessary to crush the power of the Druids, since their passionate exhortations kept patriotism alive. The island of Mona, now Anglesea, off the coast of Wales, was the stronghold to which the Druids had retreated. As the Roman soldiers approached to attack them, they beheld the priests and women standing on the shore, with uplifted hands, uttering "dreadful prayers and imprecations." For a moment they hesitated, then urged by their general, they rushed upon them, cut them to pieces, levelled their consecrated groves to the ground, and cast the bodies of the Druids into their own sacred fires. From this blow, Druidism as an organized faith never recovered, though traces of its religious rites still survive in the use of the mistletoe at Christmas and in May-day festivals.

50. Revolt of Boadicea. — Still the power of the Latin legions was only partly established, for while Suetonius was absent with his troops at Mona, a formidable revolt had broken out in the east. The cause of the insurrection was Roman rapacity and cruelty. A native chief, Prasutagus, in order to secure half of his

---

[1] Llyn-din (lĭn-dĭn).

property to his family at his death, left it to be equally divided between his daughters and the Emperor; but the governor of the district, under the pretext that his widow Boadicea had concealed part of the property, seized the whole. Boadicea protested. To punish her presumption she was stripped, bound, and scourged as a slave, and her daughters given up to still more brutal and infamous treatment. Maddened by these outrages, Boadicea roused the tribes by her appeals. They fell upon London and other cities, burned them to the ground, and slaughtered many thousand inhabitants. For a time it looked as though the whole country would be restored to the Britons; but Suetonius heard of the disaster, hurried from the north, and fought a final battle, so tradition says, on ground within sight of where St. Paul's Cathedral now stands. The Roman general gained a complete victory, and Boadicea, the Cleopatra of the North, as she has been called, took her own life, rather than, like the Egyptian queen, fall into the hands of her conquerors. She died, let us trust, as the poet has represented, animated by the prophecy of the Druid priest that, —

> "Rome shall perish — write that word
> In the blood that she has spilt; —
> Perish, hopeless and abhorred,
> Deep in ruin, as in guilt." [1]

51. Christianity introduced into Britain. — Perhaps it was not long after this that Christianity made its way to Britain; if so, it crept in so silently that nothing certain can be learned of its advent. Our only record concerning it is found in monkish chronicles filled with bushels of legendary chaff, from which a few grains of historic truth may be here and there picked out. The first church, it is said, was built at Glastonbury.[2] It was a long, shed-like structure of wicker-work. "Here," says Fuller, "the converts watched, fasted, preached, and prayed, having high meditations under a low roof and large hearts within narrow walls."

---

[1] Cowper, Boadicea. [2] Glastonbury, Somersetshire.

Later there may have been more substantial edifices erected at Canterbury by the British Christians, but at what date, it is impossible to say. At first, no notice was taken of the new religion. It was the faith of the poor and the obscure, hence the Roman generals regarded it with contempt; but as it continued to spread, it caused alarm. The Roman Emperor was not only the head of the state, but the head of religion as well. He represented the power of God on earth: to him every knee must bow; but the Christian refused this homage. He put Christ first; for that reason he was dangerous to the state: if he was not already a traitor and rebel, he was suspected to be on the verge of becoming both.

52. Persecution of British Christians; St. Alban. — Toward the last of the third century the Roman Emperor Diocletian resolved to root out this pernicious belief. He began a course of systematic persecution which extended to every part of the Empire, including Britain. The first martyr was Alban. He refused to sacrifice to the Roman deities, and was beheaded. "But he who gave the wicked stroke," says Bede,[1] with childlike simplicity, "was not permitted to rejoice over the deed, for his eyes dropped out upon the ground together with the blessed martyr's head." Five hundred years later the abbey of St. Albans[2] rose on the spot to commemorate him who had fallen there, and on his account that abbey stood superior to all others in power and privilege.

53. Agricola explores the Coast and builds a Line of Forts. — In 78 A.D. Agricola, a wise and equitable ruler, became governor of the country. His fleets explored the coast, and first discovered Britain to be an island. He gradually extended the limits of the government, and, in order to prevent invasion from the north, he built a line of forts across Caledonia, or Scotland, from the river Firth to the Clyde.

54. The Romans clear and cultivate the Country. — From this date the power of Rome was finally fixed. During the period of

---

[1] Bede, Ecclesiastical History of Britain, completed about the year 731.
[2] St. Albans, Hertfordshire, about twenty miles northwest of London.

three hundred years which follows, the entire surface of the country underwent a great change. Forests were cleared, marshes drained, waste lands reclaimed, rivers banked in and bridged, and the soil made so productive that Britain became known in Rome as the most important grain-producing and grain-exporting province in the Empire.

55. Roman Cities; York. — Where the Britons had had a humble village enclosed by a ditch, with felled trees, to protect it, there rose such walled towns as Chester, Lincoln, London, and York, with some two score more, most of which have continued to be centres of population ever since. Of these, London early became the commercial metropolis, while York was acknowledged to be both the military and civil capital of the country. There the Sixth Legion was stationed. It was the most noted body of troops in the Roman army, and was called the "Victorious Legion." It remained there for upward of three hundred years. There, too, the governor resided and administered justice. For these reasons York got the name of "another Rome." It was defended by walls flanked with towers, some of which are still standing. It had numerous temples and public buildings, such as befitted the first city of Britain. There, also, an event occurred in the fourth century which made an indelible mark on the history of mankind. For at York, Constantine, the subsequent founder of Constantinople, was proclaimed emperor, and through his influence Christianity became the established religion of the Empire.[1]

56. Roman System of Government; Roads. — During the Roman possession of Britain the country was differently governed at different periods, but eventually it was divided into five provinces. These were intersected by a magnificent system of paved roads running in direct lines from city to city, and having London as a common centre. Across the Strait of Dover, they connected with a similar system of roads throughout France,

---

[1] Constantine was the first Christian emperor of Rome. The preceding emperors had generally persecuted the Christians.

No. 3.

ROMAN BRITAIN.

Spain, and Italy, which terminated at Rome. Over these roads bodies of troops could be rapidly marched to any needed point, and by them officers of state mounted on relays of fleet horses could pass from one end of the Empire to the other in a few days' time. So skilfully and substantially were these highways constructed, that modern engineers have been glad to adopt them as a basis for their work, and the four leading Roman roads[1] continue to be the foundation, not only of numerous turnpikes in different parts of England, but also of several of the great railway lines, especially those from London to Chester and from London to York.

57. Roman Forts and Walls. — Next in importance to the roads were the fortifications. In addition to those which Agricola had built, later rulers constructed a wall of solid masonry entirely across the country from the shore of the North to that of the Irish Sea. This wall, which was about seventy-five miles south of Agricola's work, was strengthened by a deep ditch and a rampart of earth. It was further defended by castles built at regular intervals of one mile. These were of stone, and from sixty to seventy feet square. Between them were stone turrets or watch-towers which were used as sentry-boxes; while at every fourth mile there was a fort, covering from three to six acres, occupied by a large body of troops.

58. Defences against Saxon Pirates. — But the northern tribes were not the only ones to be guarded against; bands of pirates prowled along the east and south coasts, burning, plundering, and kidnapping. These marauders came from Denmark and the adjacent countries. The Britons and Romans called them Saxons, a most significant name if, as is generally supposed, it refers to the short, stout knives which made them a terror to every land on which they set foot. To repel them a strong chain of forts was erected on the coast, extending from the mouth of the river Blackwater, in Essex, to Portsmouth on the south.

---

[1] The four chief roads were: 1. Watling Street; 2. Icknield Street; 3. Ermine Street; and 4. The Fosse Way. See Map No. 3, page 24.

Of these great works, cities, walls, and fortifications, though by far the greater part have perished, yet enough still remain to justify the statement that "outside of England no such monuments exist of the power and military genius of Rome."

59. Roman Civilization False.—Yet the whole fabric was as hollow and false as it was splendid. Civilization, like truth, cannot be forced on minds unwilling or unable to receive it. Least of all can it be forced by the sword's point and the taskmaster's lash. In order to render his victories on the continent secure, Cæsar had not hesitated to butcher thousands of prisoners of war or to cut off the right hands of the entire population of a large settlement to prevent them from rising in revolt. The policy pursued in Britain, though very different, was equally heartless and equally fatal. There was indeed an occasional ruler who endeavored to act justly, but such cases were rare. Galgacus, a leader of the North Britons, said with truth of the Romans, "They give the lying name of Empire to robbery and slaughter; they make a desert and call it peace."

60. The Mass of the Native Population Slaves.—It is true that the chief cities of Britain were exempt from oppression. They elected their own magistrates and made their own laws, but they enjoyed this liberty because their inhabitants were either Roman soldiers or their allies. Outside these cities the great mass of the native population were bound to the soil, while a large proportion of them were absolute slaves. Their work was in the brick fields, the quarries, the mines, or in the ploughed land, or the forest. Their homes were wretched cabins plastered with mud, thatched with straw, and built on the estates of masters who paid no wages.

61. Roman Villas.—The masters lived in stately villas adorned with pavements of different colored marbles and beautifully painted walls. These country-houses, often as large as palaces, were warmed in winter, like our modern dwellings, with currents of heated air, while in summer they opened on terraces ornamented with vases and statuary, and on spacious gardens of fruits and flowers.[1]

62. Roman Taxation and Cruelty. — Such was the condition of the laboring classes. Those who were called free were hardly better off, for nearly all that they could earn was swallowed up in taxes. The standing army of Britain, which the people of the country had to support, rarely numbered less than forty thousand. The population was not only scanty, but it was poor. Every farmer had to pay a third of all that his farm could produce, in taxes. Every article that he sold had also to pay duty, and finally there was a poll-tax on the man himself. On the continent there was a saying that it was better for a property-owner to fall into the hands of savages than into those of the Roman assessors. When they went round, they counted not only every ox and sheep, but every plant, and registered them as well as the owners. "One heard nothing," says a writer of that time, speaking of the days when revenue was collected, "but the sound of flogging and all kinds of torture. The son was compelled to inform against his father, and the wife against her husband. If other means failed, men were forced to give evidence against themselves and were assessed according to the confession they made to escape torment."[2] So great was the misery of the land that it was not an uncommon thing for parents to destroy their children, rather than let them grow up to a life of suffering. This vast system of organized oppression, like all tyranny, "was not so much an institution as a destitution," undermining and impoverishing the country. It lasted until time brought its revenge, and Rome, which had crushed so many nations of barbarians, was in her turn threatened with a like fate, by bands of barbarians stronger than herself.

63. The Romans compelled to abandon Britain. — When Cæsar returned from his victorious campaigns in Gaul in the first

---

[1] About one hundred of these villas or country-houses, chiefly in the South and Southwest of England, have been exhumed. Some of them cover several acres.

[2] Lactantius. See Elton's Origins of English History.

century B.C., Cicero exultingly exclaimed, "Now, let the Alps sink! the gods raised them to shelter Italy from the barbarians; they are no longer needed." For nearly five centuries that continued true; then the tribes of Northern Europe could no longer be held back. When the Roman emperors saw that the crisis had arrived, they recalled the legions from Britain. The rest of the colonists soon followed. In the year 409 we find this brief but expressive entry in the Anglo-Saxon Chronicle,[1] "After this the Romans never ruled in Britain." A few years later this entry occurs: "418. This year the Romans collected all the treasures in Britain; some they hid in the earth, so that no one since has been able to find them, and some they carried with them into Gaul."

64. Remains of Roman Civilization. — In the course of the next three generations whatever Roman civilization had accomplished in the island, politically and socially, had disappeared. A few words, indeed, such as "port" and "street," have come down to us. Save these, nothing is left but the material shell, — the roads, forts, arches, gateways, altars, and tombs, which are still to be seen scattered throughout the land.

The soil, also, is full of relics of the same kind. Twenty feet below the surface of the London of to-day lie the remains of the London of the Romans. In digging in the "city,"[2] the laborer's shovel every now and then brings to light bits of rusted armor, broken swords, fragments of statuary, and gold and silver ornaments. So, likewise, several towns, long buried in the earth, and the foundations of upwards of a hundred country-houses, have been discovered; but these seem to be all. If Rome left any traces

---

[1] Anglo-Saxon Chronicle: the earliest English history. It was probably begun in the ninth century, in the reign of Alfred. It extends, in different copies, from Cæsar's invasion until the beginning of the reign of Henry II., 1154. It is supposed that the work was written in Canterbury, Peterborough, and other monasteries. The first part of it is evidently based on tradition; but the whole is of great value, especially from the time of Alfred.

[2] The "city" — that part of London formerly enclosed by Roman walls, together with a small outlying district. Its limit on the west is the site of Temple Bar; on the east, the Tower of London.

of her literature, law, and methods of government, they are so doubtful that they serve only as subjects for antiquarians to wrangle over.[1] Were it not for the stubborn endurance of ivy-covered ruins like those of Pevensey, Chester, and York, and of that gigantic wall which still stretches across the bleak moors of Northumberland, we might well doubt whether there ever was a time when the Cæsars held Britain in their relentless grasp.

65. Good Results of the Roman Conquest of Britain. — Still, it would be an error to suppose that the conquest and occupation of the island had no results for good. Had Rome fallen a century earlier, the world would have been the loser by it, for during that century the inhabitants of Gaul and Spain were brought into closer contact than ever with the only power then existing which could teach them the lesson they were prepared to learn. Unlike the Britons, they adopted the Latin language for their own; they made themselves acquainted with its literature and aided in its preservation; they accepted the Roman law and the Roman idea of government; lastly, they acknowledged the influence of the Christian church, and, with Constantine's help, they organized it on a solid foundation. Had Rome fallen a prey to the invaders in 318 instead of 410,[2] it is doubtful if any of these results would have taken place, and it is almost certain that the last and most important of all could not.

Britain furnished Rome with abundant food supplies, and sent thousands of troops to serve in the Roman armies on the continent. Britain also supported the numerous colonies which were constantly emigrating to her from Italy, and thus kept open the lines of communication with the mother-country. By so doing she helped to maintain the circulation of the life-currents in the remotest branches of the Roman Empire. Because of this, that

---

[1] Scarth, Pearson, Guest, Elton, and Coote believe that Roman civilization had a permanent influence; while Lappenburg, Stubbs, Freeman, Green, Wright, and Gardiner deny it.

[2] Rome was plundered by the Goths, under Alaric, in 410. The empire finally fell in 476.

empire was able to resist the barbarians until the seeds of the old civilization had time to root themselves and to spring up with promise of a new and nobler growth. In itself, then, though the island gained practically nothing from the Roman occupation, yet through it mankind was destined to gain much. During these centuries the story of Britain is that which history so often repeats — a part of Europe was sacrificed that the whole might not be lost.

IV.

"The happy ages of history are never the productive ones." — HEGEL.

THE COMING OF THE SAXONS, OR ENGLISH, 449 A.D.

THE BATTLES OF THE TRIBES. — BRITAIN BECOMES ENGLAND.

66. Condition of the Britons after the Romans left the Island. — Three hundred and fifty years of Roman law and order had so completely tamed the fiery aborigines of the island that when the legions abandoned it, the complaint of Gildas,[1] "the British Jeremiah," as Gibbon calls him, may have been literally true, when he declared that the Britons were no longer brave in war or faithful in peace.

Certainly their condition was both precarious and perilous. On the north they were assailed by the Picts, on the northwest by the Scots,[2] on the south and east by the Saxons. What was perhaps worst and most dangerous of all, they quarrelled among themselves over points of theological doctrine. They had, indeed, the love of liberty, but not the spirit of unity; and the consequence was, that their enemies, bursting in on all sides, cut them down, Bede says, as "reapers cut down ripe grain."

67. Letter to Aëtius. — At length the chief men of the country joined in a piteous and pusillanimous letter begging help from

---

[1] Gildas: a British monk, 516(?)-570(?). He wrote an account of the Saxon conquest of Britain.

[2] Picts: ancient tribes of the North and Northeast of Scotland; Scots: originally inhabitants of Ireland, some of whom settled in the West of Scotland, and gave their name to the whole country.

Rome. It was addressed as follows: "To Aëtius, Consul[1] for the third time, the groans of the Britons"; and at the close their calamities were summed up in these words, "The barbarians drive us to the sea, the sea drives us back to the barbarians; between them we are either slain or drowned." Aëtius, however, was fighting the enemies of Rome at home, and left the Britons to shift for themselves.

68. Vortigern's Advice. — Finally, in their desperation, they adopted the advice of Vortigern, a chief of Kent, who urged them to fight fire with fire, by inviting a band of Saxons to form an alliance with them against the Picts and Scots. The proposal was very readily accepted by a tribe of Jutes. They, with the Angles and Saxons, occupied the peninsula of Jutland, or Denmark, and the seacoast to the south of it. All of them were known to the Britons under the general name of Saxons.

69. Coming of the Jutes. — Gildas records their arrival in characteristic terms, saying that "in 449 a multitude of whelps came from the lair of the barbaric lioness, in three *keels*, as they call them."[2] We get a good picture of what they were like from the exultant song of their countryman, Beowulf,[3] who describes with pride "the dragon-prowed ships," filled with sea-robbers, armed with "rough-handled spears and swords of bronze," which under other leaders sailed for the shining coasts of Britain.

These three *keels*, or war-ships, under the command of the chieftains Hengist and Horsa, were destined to grow into a kingdom. Settling at first, according to agreement, in the island of

---

[1] Consul: originally one of two chief magistrates governing Rome; later the consuls ruled over the chief provinces, and sometimes commanded armies. Still later they became wholly subject to the emperors, and had little, if any, real power of their own.

[2] See Map No. 4, page 34.

[3] Beowulf: the hero of the earliest Anglo-Saxon or English epic poem. It is uncertain whether it was written on the continent or in England. Some authorities refer it to the ninth century, others to the fifth.

Thanet, near the mouth of the Thames, the Jutes easily fulfilled their contract to free the country from the ravages of the Picts, and quite as easily found a pretext afterward for seizing the fairest portion of Kent for themselves and their kinsmen and adherents, who came, vulture-like, in ever-increasing multitudes.

70. Invasion by the Saxons. — The success of the Jutes incited their neighbors, the Saxons, who came under the leadership of Ella, and Cissa, his son, for their share of the spoils. They conquered a part of the country bordering on the Channel, and, settling there, gave it the name of Sussex, or the country of the South Saxons. We learn from two sources how the land was wrested from the native inhabitants. On the one side is the account given by the British monk Gildas; on the other, that of the Saxon or English Chronicle. Both agree that it was gained by the edge of the sword, with burning, pillaging, massacre, and captivity. "Some," says Gildas, "were caught in the hills and slaughtered; others, worn out with hunger, gave themselves up to lifelong slavery. Some fled across the sea; others trusted themselves to the clefts of the mountains, to the forests, and to the rocks along the coast." By the Saxons, we are told that the Britons fled before them "as from fire."

71. Siege of Anderida. — Again, the Chronicle tersely says: "In 490 Ella and Cissa besieged Anderida (the modern Pevensey)[1] and put to death all who dwelt there, so that not a single Briton remained alive in it." When, however, they took a fortified town like Anderida, they did not occupy, but abandoned it. So the place stands to-day, with the exception of a Norman castle, built there in the eleventh century, just as the invaders left it. Accustomed as they were to a wild life, they hated the restraint and scorned the protection of stone walls. It was not until after many generations had passed that they became reconciled to live within them. In the same spirit, they refused to appropriate

---

[1] Pevensey: see coast of Sussex, Map No. 5, page 38.

anything which Rome had left. They burned the villas, killed or enslaved the serfs who tilled the soil, and seized the land to form rough settlements of their own.

72. Settlement of Wessex, Essex, and Middlesex. — In this way, after Sussex was established, bands came over under Cerdic in 495. They conquered a territory to which they gave the name of Wessex, or the country of the West Saxons. About the same time, or possibly a little later, we have the settlement of other invaders in the country north of the Thames, which became known as Essex and Middlesex, or the land of the East and the Middle Saxons.

73. Invasion by the Angles. — Finally, there came from a little corner south of the peninsula of Denmark, between the Baltic and an arm of the sea called the Sley (a region which still bears the name of Angeln), a tribe of Angles, who took possession of all of Eastern Britain not already appropriated. Eventually they came to have control over the greater part of the land, and from them all the other tribes took the name of Angles, or English.

74. Bravery of the Britons. — Long before this last settlement was complete, the Britons had plucked up courage, and had, to some extent, joined forces to save themselves from utter extermination. They were naturally a brave people, and the fact that the Saxon invasions cover a period of more than a hundred years shows pretty conclusively that, though the Britons were weakened by Roman tyranny, yet in the end they fell back on what pugilists call their "second strength." They fought valiantly and gave up the country inch by inch only.

75. King Arthur checks the Invaders. — In 520, if we may trust tradition, the Saxons received their first decided check at Badbury, in Dorsetshire, from that famous Arthur, the legend of whose deeds has come down to us, retold in Tennyson's "Idylls of the King." He met them in their march of insolent triumph,

THE CONQUEST OF BRITAIN BY TRIBES FROM THE LOW OR NORTHERN AND FLATTER PARTS OF GERMANY.

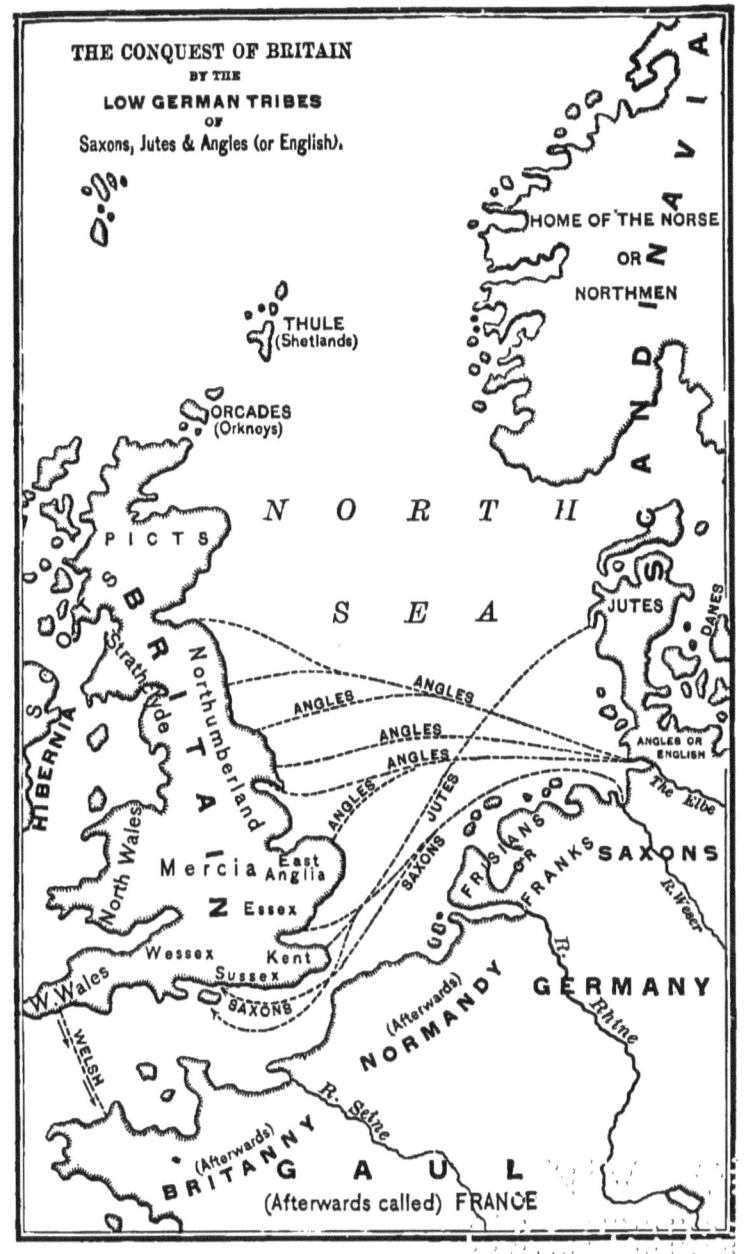

Why.

and with his irresistible sword "Excalibur" and his stanch Welsh spearsmen, proved to them, at least, that he was not a myth, but a man,[1] able "to break the heathen and uphold the Christ."

76. The Britons driven into the West. — But though temporarily brought to a stand, the heathen were neither to be expelled nor driven back. They had come to stay. At last the Britons were forced to take refuge among the hills of Wales, where they continued to abide unconquered and unconquerable by force alone. In the light of these events, it is interesting to see that that ancient stock never lost its love of liberty, and that more than eleven centuries later, Thomas Jefferson, and several of the other fifty-five signers of the Declaration of American Independence were either of Welsh birth or of direct Welsh descent.

77. Gregory and the English Slaves. — The next period, of nearly eighty years, until the coming of Augustine, is a dreary record of constant bloodshed. Out of their very barbarism, however, a regenerating influence was to arise. In their greed for gain, some of the English tribes did not hesitate to sell their own children into bondage. A number of these slaves exposed in the Roman forum, attracted the attention, as he was passing, of a monk named Gregory. Struck with the beauty of their clear, ruddy complexions and fair hair, he inquired from what country they came. "They are Angles," was the dealer's answer. "No, not Angles, but angels," answered the monk, and he resolved that, should he ever have the power, he would send missionaries to convert a race of so much promise.[2]

78. Coming of Augustine, 597. — In 590 he became the head of the Roman church. Seven years later he fulfilled his resolution, and sent Augustine with a band of forty monks to Britain. They landed on the very spot where Hengist and Horsa had disembarked

---

[1] The tendency at one time was to regard Arthur as a mythical or imaginary hero, but later investigation seems to prove that he was a vigorous and able British leader.

[2] Bede.

nearly one hundred and fifty years before. Like Cæsar and his legions, they brought with them the power of Rome; but this time it came not as a force from without to crush men in the iron mould of submission and uniformity, but as a persuasive voice to arouse and cheer them with new hope. Providence had already prepared the way. Ethelbert, king of Kent, had married Bertha, a French princess, who in her own country had become a convert to Christianity. The Saxons, or English, at that time were wholly pagan, and had, in all probability, destroyed every vestige of the faith for which the British martyrs gave their lives.

79. Augustine converts the King of Kent and his People. — Through the queen's influence, Ethelbert was induced to receive Augustine. He was afraid, however, of some magical practice, so he insisted that their meeting should take place in the open air and on the island of Thanet. The historian Bede represents the monks as advancing to salute the king, holding a tall silver cross in their hands and a picture of Christ painted on an upright board. Augustine delivered his message, was well received, and invited to Canterbury, the capital of Kent. There the king became a convert to his preaching, and before the year had passed ten thousand of his subjects had received baptism; for to gain the king was to gain his tribe as well.

80. Augustine builds the First Monastery. — At Canterbury Augustine became the first archbishop over the first cathedral. There, too, he erected the first monastery in which to train missionaries to carry on the work which he had begun, a building still in use for that purpose, and that continues to bear the name of the man who founded it. The example of the ruler of Kent was not without its effect on others.

81. Conversion of the North. — The North of England, however, owed its conversion chiefly to the Irish monks of an earlier age. They had planted monasteries in Ireland and Scotland from which colonies went forth, one of which settled at Lindisfarne, in Durham. Cuthbert, a Saxon monk of that monastery in the seventh century, travelled as a missionary throughout Northumbria, and was afterward recognized as the saint of the North. Through his influence that kingdom was induced to accept Christianity. Others, too, went to other districts. In one case, an aged chief arose in an assembly of warriors and said, "O king, as a bird flies through this hall in the winter night, coming out of the darkness and vanishing into it again, even such is our life. If these strangers can tell us aught of what is beyond, let us give heed to them." But Bede informs us that, notwithstanding their success, some of the new converts were too cautious to commit themselves entirely to the strange religion. One king, who had set up a large altar devoted to the worship of Christ, very prudently set up a smaller one at the other end of the hall to the old heathen deities, in order that he might make sure of the favor of both.

82. Christianity organized; Labors of the Monks. — Gradually, however, the pagan faith was dropped. Christianity organized itself under conventual rule. Monasteries either already existed or were now established at Lindisfarne,[1] Wearmouth, Whitby and Jarrow in the north, and at Peterborough and St. Albans in the east. These monasteries were educational as well as industrial centres. Part of each day was spent by the monks in manual toil, for they held that "to labor is to pray." They cleared the land, drained the bogs, ploughed, sowed, and reaped. Another part of the day they spent in religious exercises, and a third in writing, translating, and teaching. A school was attached to each monastery, and each had besides its library of manuscript books as well as its room for the entertainment of travellers and pilgrims. In these libraries important charters and laws relating to the kingdom were also preserved.

83. Literary Work of the Monks. — It was at Jarrow that Bede wrote in rude Latin the church-history of England. It was at

---

[1] Lindisfarne, or Holy Island, off the coast of Northumberland — see Scott's Marmion, Canto II., 9-10. Wearmouth and Jarrow are in Durham, Whitby in Yorkshire, and Peterborough in Northamptonshire.

Whitby that the poet Cædmon[1] composed his poem on the Creation, in which, a thousand years before Milton, he dealt with Milton's theme in Milton's spirit. It was at Peterborough and Canterbury that the Anglo-Saxon Chronicle was probably begun, a work which stands by itself, not only as the first English history, but the first English book, and the one from which we derive much of our knowledge of the time from the Roman conquest down to a period after the coming of the Normans. It was in the abbeys of Malmesbury[2] and St. Albans that, at a later period, that history was taken up and continued by William of Malmesbury and Matthew Paris. It was also from these monasteries that an influence went out which eventually revived learning throughout Europe.

84. Influence of Christianity on Society. — But the work of Christianity for good did not stop with these things. The church had an important social influence. It took the side of the weak, the suffering, and the oppressed. It shielded the slave from ill usage. It secured for him Sunday as a day of rest, and it constantly labored for his emancipation.

85. Political Influence of Christianity. — More than this, Christianity had a powerful political influence. In 664 a synod, or council, was held at Whitby to decide when Easter should be observed. To that meeting, which was presided over by the Archbishop of Canterbury, delegates were sent from all parts of the country. After a protracted debate the synod decided in favor of the Roman custom, and thus all the churches were brought into agreement. In this way, at a period when the country was divided into hostile kingdoms of Angles, Saxons, and Jutes, each struggling fiercely for the mastery, there was a spirit of true religious unity growing up. The bishops, monks, and priests, gathered at Whitby, were from tribes at open war with each other. But in that, and other conferences which followed, they felt that they had a common interest, that they were fellow-country-

---

[1] Cædmon (Kădmon).   [2] Malmesbury, Wiltshire.

No. 5.

men, and that they were all members of the same church and laboring for the same end.

86. Egbert. — But during the next hundred and fifty years the chief indication outside the church of any progress toward consolidation was in the growing power of the kingdom of Wessex. In 787 Egbert, a direct descendant of Cerdic, the first chief and king of the country, laid claim to the throne. Another claimant arose, who gained the day, and Egbert, finding that his life was in danger, fled the country.

87. Egbert at the Court of Charlemagne. — He escaped to France, and there took refuge at the court of King Charlemagne, where he remained thirteen years. Charlemagne had conceived the gigantic project of resuscitating the Roman Empire. To accomplish that, he had engaged in a series of wars, and in the year 800 had so far conquered his enemies that he was crowned Emperor of the West by the Pope at Rome.

88. Egbert becomes "King of the English." — That very year the king of Wessex died, and Egbert was summoned to take his place. He went back impressed with the success of the French king and ambitious to imitate him. Twenty-three years after that, we hear of him fighting the tribes in Mercia, or Central Britain. His army is described as "lean, pale, and long-breathed"; but with those cadaverous troops he conquered and reduced the Mercians to subjection. Other victories followed, and in 828 he had brought all the sovereignties of England into vassalage. He now ventured to assume the title, which he had fairly won, of "King of the English."[1]

89. Britain becomes England. — The Celts had called the land Albion; the Romans, Britain:[2] the country now called itself Angle-Land, or ENGLAND. Three causes had brought about this consoli-

---

[1] In a single charter, dated 828, he called himself "Egbert, by the grace of God, King of the English."

[2] Britain: nothing definite is known respecting the origin or meaning of this word.

dation, to which each people had contributed part. The Jutes of Kent encouraged the foundation of the national church; the Angles gave the national name, the West Saxons furnished the national king. From him as a royal source, every subsequent English sovereign, with the exception of Harold II., and a few Danish rulers, has directly or indirectly descended down to the present time.

90. Alfred the Great. — Of these the most conspicuous during the period of which we are writing was Alfred, grandson of Egbert. He was rightly called Alfred the Great, since he was the embodiment of whatever was best and bravest in the English character. The key-note of his life may be found in the words which he spoke at the close of it, "So long as I have lived, I have striven to live worthily."

91. Danish Invasion. — When he came to the throne in 871, through the death of his brother Ethelred, the Danes were sweeping down on the country. A few months before that event Alfred had aided his brother in a desperate struggle with them. In the beginning, the object of the Danes was to plunder, later, to possess, and finally, to rule over the country. In the year Alfred came to the throne, they had already overrun a large portion and invaded Wessex. Wherever their raven-flag appeared, there destruction and slaughter followed.

92. The Danes destroy the Monasteries. — The monasteries were the especial objects of their attacks. Since their establishment many of them had accumulated wealth and had sunk into habits of idleness and luxury. The Danes, without intending it, came to scourge these vices. From the thorough way in which they robbed, burned, and murdered, there can be no doubt that they enjoyed what some might think was their providential mission. In their helplessness and terror, the panic-stricken monks added to their usual prayers, this fervent petition: "From the fury of the Northmen, good Lord deliver us!" The power raised up to answer that supplication was Alfred.

93. Alfred's Victories over the Danes; The White Horse. — After repeated defeats, he, with his brother, finally drove back these savage hordes, who thought it a shame to earn by sweat what they could win by blood; whose boast was that they would fight in paradise even as they had fought on earth, and would celebrate their victories with foaming draughts of ale drunk from the skulls of their enemies. In these attacks, Alfred led one-half the army, Ethelred the other. They met the Danes at Ashdown, in Berkshire. While Ethelred stopped to pray for success, Alfred, under the banner of the "White Horse," — the common standard of the Anglo-Saxons at that time, — began the attack and won the day. Tradition declares that after the victory he ordered his army to commemorate their triumph by carving that colossal figure of a horse on the side of a neighboring chalk-hill, which still remains so conspicuous an object in the landscape. It was shortly after this that Alfred became king; but the war, far from being ended, had in fact but just begun.

94. The Danes compel Alfred to retreat. — The Danes, reinforced by other invaders, overcame Alfred s forces and compelled him to retreat. He fled to the wilds of Somersetshire, and was glad to take up his abode for a time, so the story runs, in a peasant's hut. Subsequently he succeeded in rallying part of his people, and built a stronghold on a piece of rising ground, in the midst of an almost impassable morass. There he remained during the winter.

95. Great Victory by Alfred; Treaty of Wedmore, 878. — In the spring he marched forth and again attacked the Danes. They were entrenched in a camp at Edington, Wiltshire. Alfred surrounded them, and starved them into submission so complete that Guthrum, the Danish leader, swore a peace, called the Peace or Treaty of Wedmore, and sealed the oath with his baptism — an admission that Alfred had not only beaten, but converted him as well.

96. Terms of the Treaty. — By the Treaty of Wedmore[1] the Danes bound themselves to remain north and east of a line drawn from London to Chester, following the old Roman road called Watling-street. All south of this line, including a district around London, was recognized as the dominions of Alfred, whose chief city, or capital, was Winchester. By this treaty the Danes got much the larger part of England, on the one hand, though they acknowledged Alfred as their over-lord, on the other. He thus became nominally what his predecessor, Egbert, had claimed to be, — the king of the whole country.[2]

97. Alfred's Laws; his Translations. — He proved himself to be more than mere ruler; for he was law-giver and teacher as well. Through his efforts a written code was compiled, prefaced by the Ten Commandments and ending with the Golden Rule; and, as Alfred added, referring to the introduction, "He who keeps this shall not need any other law-book." Next, that learning might not utterly perish in the ashes of the abbeys and monasteries which the Danes had destroyed, the king, though feeble and suffering, set himself to translate from the Latin the Universal History of Orosius, and also Bede's History of England. He afterward rendered into English the Reflections of the Roman senator, Boethius, on the Supreme Good, an inquiry written by the latter while in prison, under sentence of death.

98. Alfred's Navy. — Alfred, however, still had to combat the Danes, who continued to make descents upon the coast, and even sailed up the Thames to take London. He constructed a superior class of fast-sailing war-vessels from designs made by himself, and with this fleet, which may be regarded as the beginning of the English navy, he fought the enemy on their own element. He thus effectually checked a series of invasions which, had they continued, might have eventually reduced the country to primitive barbarism.

---

[1] Wedmore (the Wet-Moor), near Wells, Somersetshire: here, according to tradition, Alfred had a palace in which the treaty was consummated.

[2] See Map No. 6, page 42.

No. 6.

ENGLAND TOWARD THE CLOSE OF THE NINTH CENTURY.

To face page 42.

The shaded district on the northeast shows the part obtained by the Danes by the

99. Estimate of Alfred's Reign. — Considered as a whole, Alfred's reign is the most noteworthy of any in the annals of the early English sovereigns. It was marked throughout by intelligence and progress. His life speaks for itself. The best commentary on it is the fact that, in 1849, the people of Wantage,[1] his native place, celebrated the thousandth anniversary of his birth — another proof that "what is excellent, as God lives, is permanent."[2]

100. Dunstan's Reforms. — Two generations after Alfred's death, Dunstan, Archbishop of Canterbury, the ablest man in an age when all statesmen were ecclesiastics, came forward to take up and push onward the work begun by the great king. He labored for higher education, for strict monastic rule, and for the celibacy of the monks.

101. Regular and Secular Clergy. — At that time the clergy of England were divided into two classes, — the "regulars," or monks, and the "seculars," or parish priests and other clergy not bound by monastic vows. The former lived in the monasteries apart from the world; the latter lived in it. By their monastic vows,[3] the "regulars" were bound to remain unmarried, while the "seculars" were not. Notwithstanding Alfred's efforts at reform, many monasteries had relaxed their rules, and were again filled with drones. In violation of their vows, large numbers of the monks were married. Furthermore, many new churches had been endowed and put into the hands of the "seculars."

102. Danger to the State from Each Class of Clergy. — The danger was that this laxity would go on increasing, so that in time the married clergy would monopolize the clerical influence and clerical wealth of the kingdom for themselves and their families. They would thus become an hereditary body, a close corporation, transmitting their power and possessions from father to son through generations. On the other hand, the tendency of the unmarried

---

[1] Wantage, Berkshire.   [2] R. W. Emerson.

[3] The monastic vows required poverty, chastity, and obedience to the rules of their order.

clergy would be to become wholly subservient to the church and the Pope, though they must necessarily recruit their ranks from the people. In this last respect they would be more democratic than the opposite class. They would also be more directly connected with national interests and the national life, while at the same time they would be able to devote themselves more exclusively to study and to intellectual culture than the "seculars."

103. Dunstan as a Statesman and Artisan. — In addition to these reforms, Dunstan proved himself to be as clever a statesman as theologian. He undertook, with temporary success, to reconcile the conflicting interests of the Danes and the English. He was also noted as a mechanic and worker in metals. The common people regarded his accomplishments in this direction with superstitious awe. Many stories of his skill were circulated, and it was even whispered that in a personal contest with Beelzebub, it was the devil and not the monk who got the worst of it and fled from the saint's workshop, howling with dismay.

104. New Invasions; Danegeld. — With the close of Dunstan's career, the period of decline sets in. Fresh inroads began on the part of the Northmen,[1] and so feeble and faint-hearted grew the resistance that at last a royal tax, called Danegeld, or Dane-money, was levied on all landed property in order to raise means to buy off the invaders. For a brief period this cowardly concession answered the purpose. But a time came when the Danes would no longer be bribed to keep away.

105. The Northmen invade France. — The Danish invasion was really a part of a great European movement. The same Northmen who had obtained so large a part of England, had also, in the tenth century, under the leadership of Rollo, established themselves in France. There they were known as Normans, a softened form of the word "Northmen," and the district where they settled came to be called from them Normandy. They founded

---

[1] This name was given to Norsemen, Swedes, Danes, and all northern tribes.

No. 7.

To face page 44.

10

a line of dukes, or princes, who were destined, in the course of the next century, to give a new aspect to the events of English history.

106. Sweyn conquers England; Canute.[1] — In 1013 Sweyn, the Dane, conquered England, and "all the people," says the Chronicle, "held him for full king." He was succeeded by his son Canute, who, though from beyond sea, could hardly be called a foreigner, since he spoke a language and set up a government differing but little from that of the English. After his first harsh measures were over he sought the friendship of both church and people. He rebuked the flattery of courtiers by showing them that the in-rolling tide is no respecter of persons; he endeavored to rule justly, and his liking for the monks found expression in his song: —

"Merrily sang the monks of Ely
As Cnut the King was passing by."

107. Canute's Plan; the Four Earldoms. — Canute's plan was to establish a great northern empire embracing Denmark, Norway, Sweden, and England. To facilitate the government of so large a realm, he divided England into four districts, Wessex, Mercia, East Anglia, and Northumbria, which, with their dependencies, embraced the entire country. Each of these districts was ruled by an earl[2] invested with almost royal power. For a time the arrangement worked well, but eventually discord sprang up between the rulers, and the unity of the country was imperilled by their individual ambition and their efforts to obtain supreme authority.

108. Prince Edward. — On the accession of the Danish conqueror Sweyn, Ethelred II., the Saxon king, sent his French wife Emma back to Normandy for safety. She took with her her son Prince Edward, then a lad of nine. He remained at the French

---

[1] Also spelled Cnut and Knut.
[2] Earl ("chief" or "leader"): a title of honor, and of office. The four earldoms established by Canute remained nearly unchanged until the Norman Conquest, 1066. See Map No. 7, page 44.

court nearly thirty years, and among other friends to whom he became greatly attached was his second cousin, William, Duke of Normandy.

109. Restoration of the English Kings; Edward the Confessor. — In 1042 the oppressive acts of Canute's sons excited insurrection, and both Danes and Saxons joined in the determination to restore the Saxon line. Edward was invited to accept the crown. He returned to England and obtained the throne. By birth he was already half Norman; by education and tastes he was wholly so. It is very doubtful whether he could speak a word of English, and it is certain that from the beginning he surrounded himself with French favorites, and filled the church with French priests. Edward's piety and blameless life gained for him the title of "the Confessor," or, as we should say to-day, "the Christian." He married the daughter of Godwin, Earl of Wessex, the most powerful noble in England. Godwin really ruled the country in the king's name until his death in 1053, when his son Harold succeeded him as earl. The latter continued to exercise his father's influence to counteract the French.

110. Edward builds Westminster Abbey. — During a large part of his reign, Edward was engaged in building an abbey at the west end of London, and hence called the West-minster.[1] He had just completed and consecrated this great work when he died, and was buried there. We may still see a part of his building in the crypt or basement of the abbey, while the king's tomb above is the centre around which lies a circle of royal graves. To it multitudes made pilgrimage in the olden time, and once every year a little band of devoted Roman Catholics still gather about it in veneration of virtues that would have adorned a cloister, but had not breadth and vigor to fill a throne.

With Edward, save for the short interlude of Harold, the last of the Saxon kings and the "ablest man of an unprogressive race," the period closes.

---

[1] Minster: a name given originally to a monastery; next, to a church connected with a monastery; and now often, though incorrectly, applied to a cathedral.

111. Harold becomes King, 1066. — On his death-bed, Edward, who had no children, recommended Harold, Earl of Wessex, as his successor, though, according to the Normans, he had promised that their Duke William, who, as we have seen, was a distant kinsman, should reign after him. The Witan,[1] or National Council, chose Harold, who was crowned Jan. 16, 1066.

112. What the Saxon Conquest did for Britain. — Saxons, Jutes, and Angles invaded Britain at a period when its original inhabitants had become cowed and enervated by the despotism and worn-out civilization forced on them by a foreign power.

The new-comers brought that healthy spirit of barbarism, that irrepressible love of personal liberty, which the country stood most in need of. The conquerors were rough, ignorant, cruel; but they were fearless and determined. These qualities were worth a thousand times more to Britain than the gilded corruption of Rome. In time the English themselves lost spirit. Their besetting sin was a stolidity which degenerated into animalism and sluggish content.

113. Elements contributed by the Danes. — Then came the Danes, bringing with them that new spirit of still more savage independence which so well expressed itself in their song, "I trust my sword, I trust my steed, but most I trust myself at need." They conquered the land, and in conquering regenerated it. So strong was their love of independence, that even the peasants were quite generally free. More small independent landholders were found among the Danish population than anywhere else; and it is said that the number now existing in the region they settled is still much larger than in the south. Finally, the Danes and English, both of whom sprang from the same parent stock, mingled and became in all respects one people.

114. Summary: What the Anglo-Saxons accomplished. — Thus Jutes, Saxons, Angles, and Danes, whom together we may

---

[1] Witan: literally the "Wise men," the chief men of the realm.

call the Anglo-Saxons,[1] laid the corner-stone of the English nation. However much it has changed since, it remains, nevertheless, in its solid and fundamental qualities, what these first peoples made it.

They gave first the language, simple, strong, direct, and plain, — the familiar, every-day speech of the fireside and the street, the well-known words of both the newspaper and the Bible.

Next, they established the government in its main outlines as it still exists; that is, a king, a legislative body representing the people, and the germ, at least, of a judicial system embodying trial by jury.[2]

Last, and best, they furnished that conservative patience, that calm, steady, persistent effort, that indomitable tenacity of purpose, and cool, determined courage, which have won glorious battle-fields on both sides the Atlantic, and which in peace, as well as in war, are destined to win still greater victories in the future.

GENERAL VIEW OF THE SAXON, OR EARLY ENGLISH, PERIOD — 449-1066.[3]

I. GOVERNMENT. — II. RELIGION. — III. MILITARY AFFAIRS. — IV. LITERATURE, LEARNING, AND ART. — V. GENERAL INDUSTRY AND COMMERCE. — VI. MODE OF LIFE, MANNERS, AND CUSTOMS.

GOVERNMENT.

115. Beginning of the English Monarchy. — During the greater part of the first four centuries after the Saxon conquest Britain was divided into a number of tribal settlements, or petty kingdoms, held by Jutes, Angles, and Saxons, constantly at war with each other. In the

---

[1] Anglo-Saxons: some authorities insist that this phrase means the Saxons of England in distinction from those of the continent. It is used here, however, in the sense given by Mr. Freeman as a term describing the people formed in England by the union of all the Germanic tribes.

[2] See Paragraph No. 125.

[3] This section contains a summary of much of the preceding period, with considerable additional matter. It is believed that it will be found useful both for review and for reference. When a continuous narrative history is desired, this, and similar sections following, may be omitted.

ninth century, the West Saxons, or inhabitants of Wessex, succeeded, under the leadership of Egbert, in practically conquering and uniting the country. Egbert now assumed the title of "King of the English," and Britain came to be known, from the name of its largest division, as Angle-Land, or England. Later, the Danes obtained possession of a large part of the country, but eventually united with the English and became one people.

116. The King and the Witan. — The government of England was vested in an elective sovereign, assisted by the council of the Witan, or Wise Men. Every freeman had the right to attend this national council, but, in practice, the right became confined to a small number of the nobles and clergy.

117. What the Witan could do. — 1. The Witan elected the king (its choice being confined to the royal family). 2. In case of misgovernment, it deposed him. 3. It made or confirmed grants of public lands. 4. It acted as a supreme court of justice both in civil and criminal cases.

118. What the King and Witan could do. — 1. They enacted the laws, both civil and ecclesiastical. (In most cases this meant nothing more than stating what the custom was, the common law being merely the common custom.) 2. They levied taxes. 3. They declared war and made peace. 4 They appointed the chief officers and bishops of the realm.

119. Land-Tenure before the Conquest. — Before they invaded Britain the Saxons and kindred tribes appear to have held their estates in common. Each had a permanent homestead, but that was all.[1] "No one," says Cæsar, "has a fixed quantity of land or boundaries to his property. The magistrates and chiefs assign every year to the families and communities who live together, as much land and in such spots as they think suitable. The following year they require them to take up another allotment.

"The chief glory of the tribes is to have their territory surrounded with as wide a belt as possible of waste land. They deem it not only a special mark of valor that every neighboring tribe should be driven to a distance, and that no stranger should dare to reside in their vicinity,

---

[1] "The houses were not contiguous, but each was surrounded by a space of its own." — TACITUS, *Germania*.

but at the same time they regard it as a precautionary measure against sudden attacks."[1]

120. Folkland. — Each tribe, in forming its settlement, seized more land than it actually needed. This excess was known as Folkland (the People's land), and might be used by all alike for pasturing cattle or cutting wood. With the consent of the Witan, the king might grant portions of this Folkland as a reward for services done to himself or to the community. Such grants were usually conditional and could only be made for a time. Eventually, they returned to the community. Other grants, however, might be made in the same way, which conferred full ownership. Such grants were called Bocland (Book land), because conveyed by writing, or registered in a charter or book. In time, the king obtained the power of making these grants without having to consult the Witan, and at last the whole of the Folkland came to be regarded as the absolute property of the crown.

121. Duties of Freemen. — Every freeman was obliged to do three things: 1. He must assist in the maintenance of roads and bridges. 2. He must aid in the repair of forts. 3. He must serve in case of war. Whoever neglected or refused to perform this last and most important of all duties was declared to be a *Nithing*, or infamous coward.[2]

122. The Feudal System. — In addition to the Eorls (earls)[3] or nobles by birth, there gradually grew up a class known as Thanes (companions or servants of the king), who in time outranked the hereditary nobility. To both these classes the king would have occasion to give rewards for faithful service and for deeds of valor. As his chief wealth consisted in land, he would naturally give that. At first no conditions seem to have been attached to the gift; but later the king might require the receiver to agree to furnish a certain number of fully equipped sol-

---

[1] Cæsar, Gallic War, Book VI.

[2] Also written *Niding*. The English, as a rule, were more afraid of this name than of death itself.

[3] The Saxons, or Early English, were divided up into three classes, — Eorls (earls), who were noble by birth; Ceorls (churls), or simple freemen, and slaves. The slaves were either the absolute property of the master, or were bound to the soil and sold with it. This latter class, under the Norman name of *villeins*, became numerous after the Norman Conquest in the eleventh century. The chieftains of the first Saxon settlers were called either Ealdormen (aldermen) or Heretogas, the first being civil or magisterial, the latter military officers. The Thanes were a later class, who, from serving the king or some powerful leader, became noble by military service.

diers to fight for him. These grants were originally made for life only, and on the death of the recipient they returned to the crown.

The nobles and other great landholders following the example of the king, granted portions of their estates to tenants on similar conditions, and these again might grant portions to those below them in return for satisfactory military or other service.

In time, it came to be an established principle, that every freeman below the rank of a noble must be attached to some superior whom he was bound to serve, and who, on the other hand, was his legal protector and responsible for his good behavior. The lordless man was, in fact, a kind of outlaw, and might be seized like a robber. In that respect, therefore, he would be worse off than the slave, who had a master to whom he was accountable and who was accountable for him. Eventually it became common for the small landholders, especially during the Danish invasions, to seek the protection of some neighboring lord who had a large band of followers at his command. In such cases the freeman gave up his land and received it again on certain conditions. The usual form was for him to kneel, and, placing his hands within those of the lord, to swear an oath of homage, saying, "I become your man for the lands which I hold of you, and I will be faithful to you against all men, saving only the service which I owe to my lord the King." On his side, the lord solemnly promised to defend his tenant or vassal in the possession of his property, for which, he was to perform some service to the lord.

In these two ways, first, by grant of lands from the king or a superior, and second, by the act of homage (known as *commendation*), the feudal system (a name derived from *feodum*, meaning land or property), grew up in England. Its growth, however, was irregular and incomplete; and it should be distinctly understood that it was not until after the Norman Conquest in the eleventh century that it became fully established.

123. Advantages of Feudalism. — This system had at that time many advantages. 1. The old method of holding land in common was a wasteful one, since the way in which the possessor of a field might cultivate it would perhaps spoil it for the one who received it at the next allotment. 2. In an age of constant warfare, feudalism protected all classes better than if they had stood apart, and it enabled the king to raise a powerful and well-armed force in the easiest and quickest manner. 3. It cultivated two important virtues, — fidelity on the part of the vassal, protection on that of the lord. Its corner-stone was the faithfulness of man to man. Society has outgrown feudalism, which like every system had its dark side, but it can never outgrow the feudal principle.

124. Political Divisions; the Sheriff. — Politically, the kingdom was divided into townships, hundreds (districts furnishing a hundred warriors, or supporting a hundred families), and shires or counties, the shire having been originally, in some cases, the section settled by an independent tribe, as Sussex, Essex, etc.

In each shire the king had an officer, called a shire-reeve or sheriff,[1] who represented him, collected the taxes due the crown, and saw to the execution of the laws. In like manner, the town and the hundred had a head-man of its own choosing to see to matters of general interest.

125. The Courts. — As the nation had its assembly of wise men acting as a high court, so each shire, hundred, and town had its court, which all freemen might attend. There, without any special judge, jury, or lawyers, cases of all kinds were tried and settled by the voice of the entire body, who were both judge and jury in themselves.

126. Methods of Procedure; Compurgation. — In these courts there were two methods of procedure: first, the accused might clear himself of the charge brought against him by compurgation;[2] that is, by swearing that he was not guilty and getting a number of reputable neighbors to swear that they believed his oath. If their oaths were not satisfactory, witnesses might be brought to swear to some particular fact. In every case the value of the oath was graduated according to the rank of the person, that of a man of high rank being worth as much as that of twelve common men.

127. The Ordeal. — If the accused could not clear himself in this way, he was obliged to submit to the ordeal.[3] This usually consisted in carrying a piece of hot iron a certain distance, or in plunging the arm up to the elbow in boiling water. The person who underwent the ordeal appealed to God to prove his innocence by protecting him from harm. Rude as both these methods were, they were better than the old tribal method, which permitted every man or every man's family to be the avenger of his wrongs.

---

[1] Reeve: a man in authority, or having charge of something.
[2] Compurgation: the act of wholly purifying or clearing a person from guilt.
[3] Ordeal: judgment.

128. The Common Law. — The laws by which these cases were tried were almost always ancient customs, few of which had been reduced to writing. They formed that body of common law[1] which is the foundation of the modern system of justice both in England and America.

129. Penalties. — The penalties inflicted by these courts consisted chiefly of fines. Each man's life had a certain pecuniary value. The punishment for the murder of a man of very high rank was 2400 shillings; that of a simple freeman was only one-twelfth as much.

A slave could neither testify in court nor be punished by the court. For the man in that day who held no land had no rights. If a slave was convicted of crime, his master paid the fine and then took what he considered an equivalent with the lash. Treason was punished with death, and common scolds were ducked in a pond until they were glad to hold their tongues.

RELIGION.

130. The Ancient Saxon Faith. — Before their conversion to Christianity, the Saxons worshipped Woden and Thor, names preserved in Wednesday (Woden's day) and Thursday (Thor's day). The first appears to have been considered the creator and ruler of heaven and earth; the second was his son, the god of thunder, slayer of evil spirits, and friend of man. The essential element of their religion was the deification of strength, courage, and fortitude. It was a faith well suited to a warlike people. It taught that there was a heaven for the brave, and a hell for cowards.

131. What Christianity did. — Christianity, on the contrary, laid emphasis on the virtues of self-sacrifice and sympathy. It took the side of the weak and the helpless. It labored to emancipate the slave. It built monasteries, and encouraged industry and education. The church edifice was a kind of open Bible. Very few who entered it could spell out a single word of either Old or New Testament, but all, from the poorest peasant or meanest slave up to the greatest noble, could read the meaning of the Scripture histories painted on wall and window.

The church, furthermore, was a peculiarly sacred place. It was powerful to shield those who were in danger. If a criminal, or a person flee-

---

[1] So called, in distinction from the later statute laws made by Parliament and other legislative bodies.

ing from vengeance, took refuge in it, he could not be seized until forty days had expired, during which time he had the privilege of leaving the kingdom and going into exile. This "right of sanctuary" was often a needful protection in an age of violence. It became, however, in time, an intolerable nuisance, since it enabled robbers and desperadoes of all kinds to defy the law. The right was modified at different times, but was not wholly abolished until 1624, in the reign of James I.

MILITARY AFFAIRS.

132. The Army.—The organization of the army has already been spoken of under Land-Tenure. It consisted of a national and a feudal militia. From the earliest times all freemen were obliged to fight in the defence of the country. Under the feudal system, every large landholder had to furnish the king a stipulated number of men, fully equipped with armor and weapons. As this method was found more effective than the first, it gradually superseded it.

The Saxons always fought on foot. They wore helmets and rude, flexible armor, formed of iron rings, or of stout leather covered with small plates of iron and other substances. They carried oval-shaped shields. Their chief weapons were the spear, javelin, battle-axe, and sword. The wars of this period were those of the different tribes seeking supremacy, or of the English with the Danes.

133. The Navy.—Until Alfred's reign, the English had no navy. From that period they maintained a fleet of small war-ships to protect the coast from invasion. Most of these vessels appear to have been furnished by certain ports on the south coast.

LITERATURE, LEARNING, AND ART.

134. Runes.—The language of the Saxons was of Low-German origin. Many of the words resemble the German of the present day. When written, the characters were called *runes*, mysteries or secrets. The chief use of these runes was to mark a sword-hilt, or some article of value, or to form a charm against evil and witchcraft.

It is supposed that one of the earliest runic inscriptions is the following, which dates from about 400 A.D. It is cut on a drinking-horn,[1] and (reproduced in English characters) stands thus:—

---

[1] The golden horn of Gallehas, found on the Danish-German frontier.

EK HLEWAGASTIR . HOLTINGAR . HORNA . TAWIDO.

I, Hlewgastir, son of Holta, made the horn.

With the introduction of Christianity, the Latin alphabet, from which our modern English alphabet is derived, took the place of the runic characters, which bore some resemblance to Greek, and English literature began with the coming of the monks.

135. The First Books. — One of the first English books was the Anglo-Saxon Chronicle, a history covering a period of about twelve hundred years, beginning with the Roman invasion and ending in the year 1154.

Though written in prose, it contains various fragments of poetry, of which the following (rendered into modern English), on the death of Edward the Confessor, 1066, may be quoted as an example: —

> "Then suddenly came
> Death the bitter
> And that dear prince seized.
> Angels bore
> His steadfast soul,
> Into heaven's light,
> But the wise King,
> Bestowed his realm
> On one grown great,
> On Harold's self,
> A noble Earl!
> Who in all times
> Faithfully hearkened
> Unto his lord,
> In word and deed,
> Nor ever failed
> In aught the King
> Had needed of him!"

Other early books were Cædmon's poem of the Creation, also in English, and Bede's church history of Britain, written in Latin, a work giving a full and most interesting account of the coming of Augustine and his first preaching in Kent. All of these books were written by the monks.

136. Art. — The English were skilful workers in metal, especially in gold and silver, and also in the illumination of manuscripts.[1] Alfred's Jewel, a fine specimen of the blue enamelled gold of the ninth century, is preserved in the Ashmolean Museum, Oxford. It bears the inscription: "Alfred me heht gewurcan," *Alfred caused me to be worked* [*or made*].

The women of that period excelled in weaving fine linen and woollen cloth and in embroidering tapestry.

---

[1] These illuminations get their name from the gold, silver, and bright colors used in the pictures, borders, and decorated letters with which the monks ornamented these books. For beautiful specimens of the work, see Silvestre's Paléographie.

137. Architecture. — In architecture no advance took place until very late. Up to the year 1000 the general belief that the world would end with the close of the year 999 prevented men from building for permanence. The Saxon stone work exhibited in a few buildings like the church-tower of Earl's Barton, Northamptonshire, is an attempt to imitate timber with stone, and has been called "stone carpentry."[1] Edward the Confessor's work in Westminster Abbey was not Saxon, but Norman, he having obtained his plans, and probably his builders, from Normandy.

GENERAL INDUSTRY AND COMMERCE.

138. Farms; Slave-Trade. — The farming of this period, except on the church lands, was of the rudest description. Grain was ground by the women and slaves in stone hand-mills. Later, the mills were driven by wind or water power. The principal commerce was in wool, lead, tin, and slaves. A writer of that time says he used to see long trains of young men and women tied together, offered for sale, "for men were not ashamed," he adds, "to sell their nearest relatives, and even their own children."

MODE OF LIFE, MANNERS, AND CUSTOMS.

139. The Town. — The first Saxon settlements were quite generally on the line of the old Roman roads. They were surrounded by a rampart of earth set with a thick hedge or with rows of sharp stakes. Outside this was a deep ditch. These places were called towns from "tun," meaning a fence, hedge, or other enclosure.[2]

140. The Hall. — The buildings in these towns were of wood. Those of the lords or chief men were called "halls" from the fact that they consisted mainly of a hall, or large room, used as a sitting, eating and, often as a sleeping room, — a bundle of straw or some skins thrown on the floor serving for beds. There were no chimneys, but a hole in the roof let out the smoke. If the owner was rich, the walls would be decorated with bright-colored tapestry, and with suits of armor and shields hanging from pegs.

---

[1] See Parker's Introduction to Gothic Architecture for illustrations of this work.
[2] One or more houses might constitute a town. A single farmhouse is still so called in Scotland.

141. Life in the Hall.—Here in the evening the master supped on a raised platform at one end of the "hall," while his followers ate at a lower table.

The Saxons were hard drinkers as well as hard fighters. After the meal, while horns of ale and mead were circulating, the minstrels, taking their harps, would sing songs of battle and ballads of wild adventure.

Outside the "hall" were the "bowers," or chambers for the master and his family, and, perhaps, an upper chamber for a guest, called later by the Normans a *sollar*, or sunny room.

If a stranger approached a town, he was obliged to blow a horn; otherwise, he might be slain as an outlaw.

Here, in the midst of rude plenty the Saxons or Early English lived a life of sturdy independence. They were rough, strong, outspoken, and fearless. Theirs was not the nimble brain, for that was to come with another people, though a people originally of the same race. Their mission was to lay the foundation; or, in other words, to furnish the muscle, grit, and endurance, without which the nimble brain is of little permanent value.

142. Guilds.—The inhabitants of the towns and cities had various associations called guilds (from *gild*, a payment or contribution). The object of these was mutual assistance. The most important were the Peace-guilds[1] and the Merchant-guilds. The former constituted a voluntary police-force to preserve order, and bring thieves to punishment. Each member contributed a small sum to form a common fund which was used to make good any losses incurred by robbery or fire. The association held itself responsible for the good behavior of its members, and kept a sharp eye on strangers and stragglers, who had to give an account of themselves or leave the country. The Merchant-guilds were organized, apparently at a late period, to protect and extend trade. After the Norman Conquest they came to be very wealthy and influential. In addition to the above there were social and religious guilds which made provision for feasts, for the maintenance of religious services, and for the relief of the poor and the sick.

---

[1] Frithgilds.

V.

"In other countries, the struggle has been to gain liberty; in England, to preserve it." — ALISON.

THE COMING OF THE NORMANS.

THE KING versus THE BARONS.

BUILDING THE NORMAN SUPERSTRUCTURE. — THE AGE OF FEUDALISM.

NORMAN SOVEREIGNS.

William I., 1066-1087.	Henry I., 1100-1135.
William II., 1087-1100.	Stephen (House of Blois), 1135-1154

143. Duke William hears of Harold's Accession; message to Harold. — Duke William of Normandy was in his park near Rouen, the capital of his dukedom, getting ready for a hunting expedition, when the news was brought to him of Harold's accession. The old chronicler says "he stopped short in his preparations; he spoke to no man, and no man dared speak to him."

At length he resolved to send a message to the king of England. His demand is not known; but whatever it was, Harold appears to have answered with a rough refusal.

144. William prepares to invade England. — Then William determined to appeal to the sword. During the spring and summer of that year, the duke was employed in fitting out a fleet for the invasion, and his smiths and armorers were busy making lances, swords, and coats of mail. The Pope favored the expedition, and presented a banner blessed by himself, to be carried in the attack; "mothers, too, sent their sons for the salvation of their souls."

145. The Expedition sails. — After many delays, at length all was ready, and at daybreak, Sept. 27, 1066, William sailed with a fleet of several hundred ships and a large number of transports, his own vessel leading the van, with the consecrated banner at the mast-head. His army consisted of archers and cavalry, and may have numbered between fifty and sixty thousand. They were partly his own subjects, and partly hired soldiers, or those who joined for the sake of plunder. He also carried a large force of smiths and carpenters, with timber ready cut and fitted for a wooden castle.

146. William lands at Pevensey. — The next day the fleet anchored at Pevensey,[1] under the walls of that old Roman fortress of Anderida, which had stood, a vacant ruin, since the Saxons stormed it nearly six hundred years before. As William stepped on shore he stumbled and fell. "God preserve us!" cried one of his men, "this is a bad sign." But the duke, grasping the pebbles of the beach with both his outstretched hands, exclaimed, "Thus do I seize the land!"

147. Harold in the North. — There was, in fact, no power to prevent him from establishing his camp, for King Harold was in the north quelling an invasion headed by the king of the Norwegians and his brother Tostig, who hoped to secure the throne for himself. Harold had just sat down to a victory-feast, after the battle of Stamford Bridge,[2] when news was brought to him of the landing of William. It was this fatal want of unity in England which made the Norman conquest possible. Had not Harold's own brother Tostig turned traitorously against him, or had the north country stood squarely by the south, Duke William might have found his fall on the beach an omen indeed full of disaster.

---

[1] Pevensey: see Map No. 7, page 44.
[2] Stamford Bridge, Yorkshire.

148. What William did after landing. — As there was no one to oppose him, William made a fort in a corner of the old Roman wall of Anderida, and then marched on to Hastings, a few miles farther east, where he set up his wooden castle on that hill where the ruins of a later stone castle may still be seen. Having done this, he pillaged the country in every direction, until the fourteenth of October, the day of the great battle.

149. Harold marches to meet William. — Harold, having gathered what forces he could, marched to meet William at Senlac, a place midway between Pevensey and Hastings, and about five miles back from the coast. Here, on the evening of the thirteenth, he entrenched himself on a hill, and there the battle was waged. Harold had the advantage of the stockaded fort he had built; William, that of a body of cavalry and archers, for the English fought on foot with javelins and battle-axes mainly. The Saxons spent the night in feasting and song; the Normans, in prayer and confession.

150. The Battle (Oct. 14, 1066). — On the morning of the fourteenth the fight began. It lasted until dark, with heavy loss on both sides. At length William's strategy carried the day, and Harold and his brave followers found to their cost that then, as now, it is "the thinking bayonet" which conquers. The English king was slain and every man of his chosen troops with him. A monkish chronicler, in speaking of the Conquest, says that "the vices of the Saxons had made them effeminate and womanish, wherefore it came to pass that, running against Duke William, they lost themselves and their country with one, and that an easy and light, battle."[1] Doubtless the English had fallen off in many ways from their first estate; but the record at Senlac (or Hastings) shows that they had lost neither strength, courage, nor endurance, and a harder battle or a longer was never fought on British soil.

151. The Abbey of Battle; Harold's Grave. — A few years later, the Norman conqueror built the Abbey of Battle on the

---

[1] William of Malmesbury.

spot to commemorate the victory by which he gained his crown, and to have perpetual prayers chanted by the monks over the Norman soldiers who had fallen there. Here, also, tradition represents him as having buried Harold's body, just after the fight, under a heap of stones by the seashore. Some months later, it is said that the friends of the English king removed the remains to Waltham, near London, and buried them in the church which he had built and endowed there.[1] Be that as it may, his grave, wherever it is, is the grave of the old England, for henceforth a new people (though not a new race) and a somewhat modified form of government appear in the history of the island.

152. The Bayeux Tapestry. — Several contemporary accounts of the battle exist by both French and English writers, but the best history is one wrought in colors by a woman's hand, in the scenes of the famous strip of canvas known from the French cathedral where it is still preserved, as the Bayeux Tapestry.[2]

153. William marches on London. — Soon after the battle, William advanced on London, and set fire to the Southwark suburbs.[3] The Londoners, terrified by the flames, and later cut off from help from the north by the Conqueror's besieging army, opened their gates and surrendered without striking a blow.

154. William grants a Charter to London. — In return, William granted the city a charter, or formal and solemn written pledge, by which he guaranteed the inhabitants the liberties which they had enjoyed under Edward the Confessor. That document may still be seen among the records in Guildhall,[4] in London. It is a bit of parchment, hardly bigger than a man's hand, containing a few lines in English, and is signed with William's mark; for he who wielded the sword so effectually either could not or would

---

[1] This church became afterward Waltham Abbey.
[2] See Paragraph No. 205.
[3] Southwark, on the right bank of the Thames. It is now connected with London proper by London Bridge.
[4] Guildhall: the City-Hall, the place where the guilds, or different corporations of the city proper, meet to transact business.

not handle the pen. By that mark all the past privileges and immunities of the city were confirmed and protected.

155. The Coronation; William returns to Normandy. — On the following Christmas Day (1066) William was anointed and crowned in Westminster Abbey. In the spring he sailed for Normandy, where he had left his queen, Matilda, to govern in his absence. While on the continent he intrusted England to the hands of his half-brother, Odo, Bishop of Bayeux, and his friend, William Fitz-Osbern, having made the former, Earl of Kent, and the latter, of Hereford. During the next three years there were outbreaks and uprisings in the lowlands of Cambridgeshire and the moors of Yorkshire, besides incursions of both Danes and Scots.

156. William quells Rebellion in the North. — The oppressive rule of the regents soon caused a rebellion; and in December William found it expedient to return to England. In order to gain time, the king bought off the Danes. Little by little, however, the land was brought to obedience. By forced marches in midwinter, by roads cast up through bogs, and by sudden night attacks, William accomplished the end he sought. But in 1069, news came of a fresh revolt in the north, accompanied by another invasion of foreign barbarians. Then William, roused to terrible anger, swore by the "splendor of God" that he would lay waste the land. He made good his oath. For a hundred miles beyond the river Humber he ravaged the country, firing villages, destroying houses, crops, and cattle, and reducing the wretched people to such destitution that many sold themselves for slaves to escape starvation. Having finished his work in the north, he turned toward Chester, in the west, and captured that city.

157. Hereward. — Every part of the land was now in William's power except an island in the swamps of Ely,[1] in the east, where the Englishman Hereward, with his resolute little band of fellow-

---

[1] Ely, Cambridgeshire.

countrymen, continued to defy the power of the conqueror. "Had there been three more men like him in the island," said one of William's own men, "the Normans would never have entered it." But as there were not three more such, the conquest was at length completed.

158. Necessity of William's Severity. — Fearful as the work of death had been, yet even these pitiless measures were better than that England should sink into anarchy, or into subjection to hordes of Norsemen who destroyed purely out of love of destruction and hatred to civilization and its works. For whatever William's faults or crimes, his great object was the upbuilding of a government better than any England had yet seen. Hence his severity, hence his elaborate safeguards, by which he made sure of retaining his hold upon whatever he had gained.

159. He builds the Tower of London. — We have seen that he gave London a charter; but overlooking the place in which that charter was kept, he built the Tower of London to hold the turbulent city in wholesome restraint. That tower, as fortress, palace, and prison, stands as the dark background of most of the great events in English history. It was the forerunner, so to speak, of the multitude of castles which soon after rose on the banks of every river, and on the summit of every rocky height from the west hill of Hastings to the peak of Derbyshire, and from the banks of the Thames to those of the Tweed. Side by side with these strongholds there also rose an almost equal number of monasteries, churches and cathedrals.

160. William confiscates the Land; Classes of Society. — Hand in hand with the progress of conquest, the confiscation of land went on. William had seized the estates of Harold and all the chief men associated with him, to grant them to his followers. In this way, Bishop Odo, Fitz-Osbern, and Roger of Montgomery became possessed of immense estates in various parts of England. Other grants were made by him, until by the close of his reign, no great landholder was left among the English, with the exception of a very few who were thoroughly Norman in their sympathies and in their allegiance.

Two great classes of society now existed in England. First, the Norman conquerors, who as chief tenants or landholders under the king were called barons. Second, the English who had been reduced to a subordinate condition. Most of these now held their land under the barons, and a majority of them were no longer free.

This latter class were called villeins.[1] They were bound to the soil, and could be sold with it, but not, like slaves, separately from it. They could be compelled to perform any menial service, but usually held their plots of land and humble cottages on condition of ploughing a certain number of acres or doing a certain number of days' work in each year for their lord. In time they often obtained the privilege of paying a fixed money rent in place of labor, and then their condition gradually though very slowly improved.

161. How he granted Estates.—Yet it is noticeable that in these grants, William was careful not to give large possessions to any one person in any one shire. His experience in Normandy had taught him that it was better to divide than to concentrate the power of the great nobles, who were only too ready to plot to get the crown for themselves. Thus William developed and extended the feudal system of land tenure, already in existence in outline among the Saxons, until it covered every part of the realm. He, however, kept it strictly subordinate to himself, and before the close of his reign made it absolutely so.

162. The Three Counties Palatine.—The only exceptions to these grants were the three Counties Palatine,[2] which defended

---

[1] Villein: a name derived from the Latin *villa*, a country-house, or farm, because originally the villein was a laborer who had a share in the common land. Our modern word "villain" comes from the same source, though time has given it a totally different meaning.

[2] Palatine (from *palatium*, palace), having rights equal with the king in his palace. Shropshire was practically a fourth county palatine until Henry I. Later, Lancaster was added to the list.

the border country in the north and west, and the coast on the south. To the earls of these counties, Chester, Durham, and Kent, William gave almost royal power, which descended in their families, thus making the title hereditary.

163. How William stopped Assassination. — The hard rule of the Norman nobles caused many secret assassinations. To put a stop to these, William ordered that the people of the district where a murder was perpetrated should pay a heavy fine for every Norman so slain, it being assumed that unless they could prove to the contrary, every man found murdered was a Norman.[1]

164. Pope Gregory VII. — While these events were taking place in England, Hildebrand, the archdeacon who had urged Pope Alexander to favor William's expedition, had ascended the papal throne, under the title of Gregory VII. He was the ablest, the most ambitious, and, in some respects, the most far-sighted man who had made himself the supreme head of the church.

165. State of Europe; Gregory's Scheme of Reform. — Europe was at that time in a condition little better than anarchy. A perpetual quarrel was going on between the barons. The church, too, as we have seen, had lost much of its power for good in England, and was rapidly falling into obscurity and contempt. Pope Gregory conceived a scheme of reform which should be both wide and deep. Like Dunstan, he determined to correct the abuses which had crept into the monasteries. He would have an unmarried priesthood, who should devote themselves body and soul to the interests of the church. He would bring all society into submission to that priesthood, and finally he would make the priesthood itself acknowledge him as its sole master. His purpose in this gigantic scheme was a noble one; it was to establish the unity and peace of Europe.

166. The Pope and the Conqueror. — Gregory looked to William for help in this matter. The Conqueror was ready to give it,

---

[1] This was known as the Law of Englishry.

but with limitations. He promised to aid in reforming the English church, to remove inefficient men from its high places, to establish special ecclesiastical courts for the trial of church cases, and finally, to pay a yearly tax to Rome; but he refused to take any step which should make England politically subservient to the Pope. On the contrary, he emphatically declared that he was and would remain an independent sovereign, and that the English church must obey him in preference to any other power.

He furthermore laid down these three rules: 1. That neither the Pope, the Pope's representative, nor letters from the Pope should be received in England without his leave. 2. That no meeting of church authorities should be called or should take any action without his leave. 3. That no baron or servant of his should be expelled from the church without his leave.

Thus William alone of all the sovereigns of Europe successfully withstood the power of Rome. Henry IV. of Germany had attempted the same, but so completely was he defeated and humbled that he had been compelled to stand barefooted in the snow before the Pope's palace waiting for three successive days for permission to enter and beg forgiveness. But William knew the independent temper of England, and that he could depend on it for support.

167. William a Stern but Just Ruler; New Forest. — Considering his love of power and strength of will, the reign of William was conspicuous for its justice. He was harsh but generally fair. His most despotic act was the seizure and devastation of a tract of over 60,000 acres in Hampshire for a hunting-ground, which received the name of the New Forest.[1] It has been said that William destroyed many churches and estates in order to form this forest, but these accounts appear to have been greatly exaggerated. The real grievance was not so much the appropriation of the land, which was sterile and of little value, but it was the

---

[1] Forest: as here used, this does not mean a region covered with woods, but simply a section of country, partially wooded and suitable for game, set apart as a royal park or hunting-ground. As William made his residence at Winchester, in Hampshire, he naturally took land in that vicinity for the chase.

enactment of the savage Forest Laws. These made the life of a stag of more value than that of a man, and decreed that any one found hunting the royal deer should have both eyes torn out.

168. The Great Survey.— Not quite twenty years after his coronation, William ordered a survey and valuation to be made of the whole realm outside of London, with the exception of certain border counties on the north. These appear to have been omitted either because they were sparsely populated by a mixed race, or for the reason that since his campaign in the north little was left to record there but heaps of ruins and ridges of grass-grown graves.

169. The Domesday Book.— The returns of that survey are known as Domesday or Doomsday Book, a name given, it is said, by the English, because, like the Day of Doom, it spared no one.

It recorded every piece of property, and every particular concerning it. As the Chronicle indignantly said, not a rood of land, not a peasant's hut, not an ox, cow, pig, or even a hive of bees, escaped. While the report showed the wealth of the country, it also showed the suffering it had passed through in the revolts against William. Many towns had fallen into decay. Some were nearly depopulated. In Edward the Confessor's reign, York had 1607 houses; at the date of the survey, it had but 967, while Oxford which had had 721 houses had then only 243.

This census and assessment proved of the highest importance to William and his successors. The people, indeed, said bitterly that the king kept the book constantly by him, in order "that he might be able to see at any time of how much more wool the English flock would bear fleecing." The object of the work, however, was not extortion, but to present a full and exact account of the financial and military condition of the kingdom which might be directly available for revenue and defence.

170. The Great Meeting, 1086.— In the midsummer following the completion of Domesday Book, William summoned all the nobles and chief landholders of the realm with their vassals, numbering, it is said, about sixty thousand, to meet him on Salisbury

Plain, Wiltshire.[1] There was a logical connection between that summons and the survey. Each man's possessions and each man's responsibility were now known. Thus Domesday Book prepared the way for the assembly, and for the action that was to be taken there. The place chosen was historic ground. On that field William had once reviewed his victorious troops, and in front of the encampment rose the hill of Old Sarum scarred with the remains of Roman entrenchments. Stonehenge was near. It was within sight of it, and of the burial mounds of those primeval races which had there had a home during the childhood of the world, that the Norman sovereign finished his work.

171. The Oath of Allegiance. — There William demanded and received the sworn allegiance not only of every lord, but of every lord's free vassal or tenant, from Cornwall to the Scottish borders. By that act, England was made one. By it, it was settled that every man in the realm, of whatever condition, was bound first of all to fight for the king, even if in doing so he had to fight against his own lord.

172. What William had done. — A score of years before, William had landed, seeking a throne to which no human law had given him any just claim, but to which Nature had elected him by preordained decree when she endowed him with power to take, power to use, and power to hold. It was fortunate for England that he came; for out of chaos, or affairs fast drifting to chaos, his strong hand, clear brain, and resolute purpose brought order, beauty, safety, and stability, so that we may say with Guizot, that "England owes her liberties to her having been conquered by the Normans."

173. William's Death. — In less than a year from that time, William went to Normandy to quell an invasion led by his eldest

---

[1] The Saxon seat of government had been at Winchester (Hampshire); under Edward the Confessor and Harold it was transferred to Westminster (London); but the honor was again restored to Winchester by William who made it his principal residence. This was perhaps the reason why he chose Salisbury Plain (the nearest open region) for the meeting. It was held where the modern city of Salisbury stands.

son, Robert. As he rode down a steep street in Mantes, his horse stumbled, and he received a fatal injury. He was carried to the priory of St. Gervase, just outside the city of Rouen. Early in the morning he was awakened by the great cathedral bell. "It is the hour of praise," his attendant said to him, "when the priests give thanks for the new day." William lifted up his hands in prayer and expired.

174. His Burial. — His remains were taken for interment to St. Stephen's Church,[1] which he had built. As they were preparing to let down the body into the grave, a man suddenly stepped forward and forbade the burial. William, he said, had taken the land, on which the church stood, from his father by violence. He demanded payment. The corpse was left on the bier, and inquiry instituted, and not until the debt was discharged was the body lowered to its last resting-place. "Thus," says the old chronicle, "he who had been a powerful king, and the lord of so many territories, possessed not then of all his lands more than seven feet of earth," and not even that until the cash was paid for it!

175. Summary. — The results of the conquest may be thus summed up: 1. It was not the subjugation of the English by a different race, but rather a victory won for their advantage by a branch of their own race.[2] It brought England into closer contact with the higher civilization of the continent, introduced fresh intellectual stimulus, and gave to the Anglo-Saxon a more progressive spirit. 2. It modified the English language by the influence of the Norman French element, thus giving it greater flexibility, refinement, and elegance of expression. 3. It substituted for the fragile and decaying structures of wood built by the Saxons, noble edifices in stone, the cathedral and the castle, both being essentially Norman. 4. It hastened consolidating influences already at work, developed and completed the feudal

---

[1] Caen, Normandy.
[2] It has already been shown that Norman, Saxon, and Dane were originally branches of the Teutonic or German race. See Paragraphs Nos. 105 and 114.

form of land tenure;[1] reorganized the church, and defined the relation of the state to the papal power. 5. It abolished the four great earldoms,[2] which had been a constant source of weakness, danger, and division; it put an end to the Danish invasions; and it established a strong monarchical government to which the nobles and their vassals were compelled to swear allegiance. 6. It made no radical changes in the English laws, but enforced impartial obedience to them among all classes.

WILLIAM RUFUS.[3] — 1087-1100.

176. William the Conqueror's Bequest. — William the Conqueror left three sons, — Robert, William Rufus, and Henry. He also left a daughter, Adela, who married a powerful French nobleman, Stephen, Count of Blois. On his death-bed, William bequeathed Normandy to Robert. He expressed a wish that William Rufus should become ruler over England, while to Henry he left five thousand pounds of silver, with the prediction that he would ultimately be the greatest of them all. Before his eyes were closed, the sons hurried away — William Rufus to seize the realm of England, Henry to get possession of his treasure. Robert was not present. His recent rebellion would alone have been sufficient reason for allotting to him the lesser portion; but even had he deserved the sceptre, William knew that it required a firmer hand than his to hold it.

177. Precarious State of England. — France was simply an aggregation of independent and mutually hostile dukedoms. The reckless ambition of the Norman leaders threatened to bring England into the same condition. During the twenty-one years of William's reign they had perpetually tried to break loose from his restraining power. It was certain, then, that the news of his death would be the signal for still more desperate attempts.

---

[1] See Paragraph No. 200.   [2] See Paragraph No. 107.
[3] William Rufus, William the Red: a nickname probably derived from his red face.

178. Character of William Rufus. — Rufus had his father's ability and resolution, but none of his father's conscience. As the historian of that time declared, "He feared God but little, man not at all." He had Cæsar's faith in destiny, and said to a boatman who hesitated to set off with him in a storm at his command, "Did you ever hear of a king's being drowned?"

179. His Struggle with the Barons. — During the greater part of the thirteen years of his reign he was at war with his barons. It was a battle of centralization against disintegration. "Let every man," said he, "who would not be branded infamous and a coward, whether he live in town or country, leave everything and come to me."

In answer to that appeal, the English rallied around their Norman sovereign, and gained the day for him under the walls of Rochester Castle, Kent. Of the two evils, the tyranny of one or the tyranny of many, the first seemed to them preferable.

180. William's Method of raising Money; he defrauds the Church. — If in some respects William the Conqueror had been a harsh ruler, his son was worse. His brother Robert had mortgaged Normandy to him in order to get money to join the first crusade.[1] The king raised it by the most oppressive and unscrupulous means.

William's most trusted counsellor was Ranulf Flambard.[2] Flambard had brains without principle. He devised a system of plundering both church and people in the king's interest. Lanfranc, Archbishop of Canterbury, died three years after William's accession. Through Flambard's advice, the king left the archbishopric

---

[1] Crusade (Latin *crux*, the cross): the crusades were a series of eight military expeditions undertaken by the Christian powers of Europe to recover Jerusalem and the Holy Land from the hands of the Mohammedans. They received their name from the badge of the cross worn by the soldiers. The first crusade was undertaken in 1095, and the last in 1270. Their effects will be fully considered under Richard I., who took part in them.

[2] Flambard: a nickname; the torch, or firebrand.

vacant, and appropriated its revenues to himself. He practised the same course with respect to every office of the church.

181. The King makes Anselm Archbishop. — While this process of systematized robbery was going on, the king fell suddenly ill. In his alarm lest death was at hand, he determined to make reparation to the defrauded and insulted priesthood. He invited Anselm, a noted French scholar, to accept the archbishopric. Anselm, who was old and feeble, declined, saying that he and the king could not work together. "It would be," said he, "like yoking a sheep and a bull." But the king would take no refusal. Calling Anselm to his bedside, he forced the staff of office into his hands. When the king recovered, he resumed his old practices and treated Anselm with such insult, that he finally left the country.

182. William's Merit. — William's one merit was that he kept England from being devoured piecemeal by the Norman barons, who regarded her, as a pack of hounds, in full chase, regard the hare about falling into their rapacious jaws. Like his father, he insisted on keeping the English church independent of the ever-growing power of Rome. In both cases his motives were purely selfish, but the result to the country was good.

183. His Death. — In 1100 his power came suddenly to an end. He had gone in the morning to hunt in the New Forest with his brother Henry. He was found lying dead among the bushes, pierced by an arrow shot by an unknown hand. William's character speaks in his deeds. It was hard, cold, despotic, yet in judging it we should consider the words of Fuller, "No pen hath originally written the life of this king but what was made with a monkish pen-knife, and no wonder if his picture seem bad, which was thus drawn by his enemy."

184. Summary. — Notwithstanding William's oppression of both church and people, his reign checked the revolt of the baronage and prevented the kingdom from falling into anarchy like that existing on the continent.

HENRY I. — 1100-1135.

185. Henry's Charter. — Henry, third son of William the Conqueror, was the first of the Norman kings who was born and educated in England. Foreseeing a renewal of the contest with the barons, he issued a charter[1] of liberties on his accession, by which he bound himself to reform the abuses which had been practised by his brother William Rufus. The king sent a hundred copies of this important document to the leading abbots and bishops for preservation in their respective monasteries and cathedrals. As this charter was the earliest written and formal guarantee of good government ever given by the crown to the nation, it marks an important epoch in English history. It may be compared to the platforms or statements of principles issued by our modern political parties. It was a virtual admission that the time had come when even a Norman sovereign could not dispense with the support of the country. It was therefore an admission of the truth that while a people can exist without a king, no king can exist without a people. Furthermore, this charter established a precedent for those which were to follow, and which reached a final development in the Great Charter wrested from the unwilling hand of King John somewhat more than a century later. Henry further strengthened his position with his English subjects by his marriage with Maud, niece of the Saxon Edgar, a direct descendant of King Alfred.

186. The Appointment of Bishops settled. — Henry also recalled Anselm and reinstated him in his office. But the peace was of short duration. The archbishop insisted with the Pope that the power of appointment of bishops should be vested wholly

---

[1] Charter (literally, parchment or paper on which anything may be written): a royal charter is a writing bearing the king's seal by which he confers or secures certain rights and privileges to those to whom it is granted. Henry's charter guaranteed: 1. The rights of the church (which William Rufus had constantly violated), 2. The rights of the nobles and landholders against extortion. 3. The right of all classes to be governed by the old English law with William the Conqueror's improvements.

in Rome. The king was equally determined that such appointments should spring from himself. "No one," said he, "shall remain in my land who will not do me homage." The quarrel was eventually settled by compromise. The Pope was to invest the bishop with the ring and crozier, or pastoral staff of office, as emblems of the spiritual power; the king, on the other hand, was to grant the lands from which the bishop drew his revenues, and in return was to receive his homage or oath of allegiance. This acknowledgment of royal authority by the church was of great importance, since it gave the king power as feudal lord to demand from each bishop his quota of fully equipped knights or cavalry soldiers.[1]

187. Henry's Quarrel with Robert. — While this church question was in dispute, Henry had still more pressing matters to attend to. His elder brother Robert had invaded England and demanded the crown. The greater part of the Norman nobles supported this claim; but the English people held to Henry. Finally, in consideration of a heavy money payment, Robert agreed to return to Normandy and leave his brother in full possession of the realm. On his departure, Henry resolved to drive out the prominent nobles who had aided Robert. Of these, Robert of Belesme, Earl of Shrewsbury, was the leader. With the aid of the English, who hated him for his cruelty, the earl was at last compelled to leave the country. He fled to Normandy, and, in violation of a previous agreement, was received by Henry's brother Robert. Upon that, Henry declared war, and, crossing the Channel, fought the battle of Tinchebrai,[2] by which he conquered and held Normandy as completely as Normandy had once conquered England. The king carried his brother captive to Wales, and kept him in prison during his life in Cardiff Castle. This ended the contest with the nobles. By his uprightness, his decision, his

---

[1] See note on Clergy, Paragraph No. 200.
[2] Tinchebrai, Normandy, about midway between Caen and Avranches. See Map No. 8, page 88.

courage, Henry fairly won the honorable title of the "Lion of Justice"; for, as the Chronicle records, "No man durst mis-do against another in his time."

188. Summary. — The three leading points of Henry's reign are: 1. The self-limitation of the royal power embodied in the charter of liberties. 2. The settlement of old disputes between the king and the church. 3. The banishment of the chief of the mutinous barons, and the victory of Tinchebrai, with its results.

STEPHEN. — 1135-1154.

189. The Rival Candidates. — With Henry's death two candidates presented themselves for the throne, — Henry's daughter, Matilda (for he left no lawful son), and his nephew, Stephen. In France, the custom of centuries had determined that the crown should never descend to a female; and in an age when the sovereign was expected to lead his army in person, it certainly was not expedient that a woman should hold a position one of whose chief duties she could not discharge. This French custom had, of course, no force in England; but the Norman nobles must have recognized its reasonableness; or if not, the people did.[1] Four years after Stephen's accession Matilda landed in England and claimed the crown. The East of England stood by Stephen, the West by Matilda. For the sake of promoting discord, and through discord their own private ends, part of the barons gave their support to Matilda, while the rest refused, as they said, to "hold their estates under a distaff." The fatal defect in the new king was the absence of executive ability. Following the example of Henry, he issued two charters or pledges of good government;

---

[1] Before Henry's death, the baronage had generally sworn to support Matilda (commonly called the Empress Matilda, or Maud, from her marriage to the Emperor Henry V. of Germany; later, she married Geoffrey of Anjou). But Stephen, with the help of London and the church, declared himself "*elected king by the assent of the clergy and the people.*" Many of the barons now gave Stephen their support.

but without authority to carry them out, they proved simply waste paper.

190. The Battle of the Standard. — David I. of Scotland, Matilda's uncle, espoused her cause, and invaded England with a powerful force. He was met at North Allerton, in Yorkshire, by the party of Stephen, and the battle of the Standard was fought. The leaders of the English were both churchmen, who showed that on occasion they could fight as vigorously as they could pray. The standard consisted of four consecrated banners, surmounted by a cross. This was set up on a wagon, on which one of the bishops stood. The sight of this sacred standard made the English invincible. After a fierce contest, the Scots were driven from the field. It is said that this was the first battle in which the English peasants used the long-bow; they had taken the hint, perhaps, from the Normans at the battle of Hastings. Some years later, their skill in foreign war made that weapon as famous as it was effective.

191. Civil War. — For fifteen years following, the country was torn by civil war. While it raged, fortified castles, which, under William the Conqueror, had been built and occupied by the king only, or by those whom he could trust, now arose on every side. These became, as the Anglo-Saxon Chronicle declares, "very nests of devils and dens of thieves." More than a thousand of these castles, it is said, were built. The armed bands who inhabited them levied tribute on the whole country around. Not satisfied with that, they seized those who were suspected of having property, and, to use the words of the Chronicle again, "tortured them with pains unspeakable; for some they hung up by the feet and smoked with foul smoke; others they crushed in a narrow chest with sharp stones. About the heads of others they bound knotted cords until they went into the brain." "Thousands died of hunger, the towns were burned, and the soil left untilled. By such deeds the land was ruined; and men said openly that Christ and his saints were asleep." The sleep, however, was not always to last; for in the next reign, Justice, in the person of Henry II., effectually vindicated her power. The strife for the crown continued till the last year of Stephen's reign, when, by the Treaty of Wallingford,[1] it was agreed that Matilda's son Henry should succeed him.

192. Summary. — Stephen was the last of the Norman kings. Their reign had covered nearly a century. The period began in conquest and usurpation; it ended in gloom. We are not, however, to judge it by Stephen's reign alone, but as a whole. Thus considered, it shows many points of advance over the preceding period. Finally, even Stephen's reign was not all loss since we find that out of the "war, wickedness, and waste" of his misgovernment came a universal desire for peace through law. Thus indirectly, his very inefficiency prepared the way for future reforms.

GENERAL VIEW OF THE NORMAN PERIOD. — 1066-1154.

I. GOVERNMENT. — II. RELIGION. — III. MILITARY AFFAIRS. — IV. LITERATURE, LEARNING, AND ART. — V. GENERAL INDUSTRY AND COMMERCE. — VI. MODE OF LIFE, MANNERS, AND CUSTOMS.

GOVERNMENT.

193. The King. — We have seen that the Saxons, or Early English rulers, in the case of Egbert and his successors, styled themselves "Kings of the English," or leaders of a race or people. The Norman sovereigns made no immediate change in this title, but as a matter of fact, William, toward the close of his reign, claimed the whole of the country as his own by right of conquest. For this reason he and his Norman successors might properly have called themselves "Kings of England"; that is, supreme owners of the soil and rulers over it, a title which was formally assumed about fifty years later (in John's reign).

194. The National Council. — Associated with the king in government, was the Great or National Council, made up of, first, the arch-

---

[1] Wallingford, Berkshire.

bishops, bishops, and abbots; and second, the earls and barons; that is, of all the great landholders holding directly from the crown. The National Council usually met three times a year, — at Christmas, Easter, and Whitsuntide. All laws were held to be made by the king, acting with the advice and consent of this council, but practically, the king alone often enacted such laws as he saw fit. When a new sovereign came to the throne, it was with the consent or by the election of the National Council, but their choice was generally limited to some one of the late king's sons, and unless there was good reason for making a different selection, the oldest was chosen. Finally, the right of imposing taxes rested theoretically, at least, in the king and Council, but, in fact, the king himself frequently levied them. This action of the king was a cause of constant irritation and of frequent insurrection.

195. The Private or King's Council. — There was also a second and permanent council, called the King's Council. The three leading officers of this were, the Chief Justice, who superintended the execution of the laws, represented the king, and ruled for him during his absence from the country. Second, the Lord Chancellor (so called from *cancelli*, the screen behind which he sat with his clerks), who acted as the king's adviser and confidential secretary, and as keeper of the Great Seal, with which he stamped all important papers.[1] Third, the Lord High Treasurer, who took charge of the king's revenue, received all moneys due the crown, and kept the king's treasure in the vaults at Winchester or Westminster.

196. Tallies. — All accounts were kept by the Treasurer on tallies or small sticks, notched on the opposite sides to represent different sums. These were split lengthwise. One was given as a receipt to the sheriff, or other person paying in money to the treasury, while the duplicate of this tally was held by the Treasurer. This primitive method of keeping royal accounts remained legally in force until 1785, in the reign of George III.

197. Curia Regis,[2] or the King's Court of Justice. — The Chief

---

[1] The Chancellor was also called the "Keeper of the King's Conscience," because intrusted with the duty of redressing those grievances of the king's subjects which required royal interference. The Court of Chancery, mentioned in note 1, to Paragraph No. 197, grew out of this office.

[2] Curia Regis: this name was given, at different times, first, to the National Council; second, to the King's Private Council; and lastly, to the High Court of Justice, consisting of members of the Private Council.

THE COMING OF THE NORMANS. 79

Justice and Chancellor were generally chosen by the king from among the clergy; first, because the clergy were men of education, while the barons were not; and next, because it was not expedient to intrust too much power to the barons. These officials, with the other members of the Private Council, constituted the King's High Court of Justice. It followed the king as he moved from place to place, to hear and decide cases carried up by appeal from the county courts, together with other questions of importance.[1] In local government, the country remained under the Normans essentially the same that it had been before the conquest. The king continued to be represented in each county by an officer called the sheriff, who collected the taxes and enforced the laws.

198. Trial by Battle. — In the administration of justice, Trial by Battle was introduced in addition to the Ordeal of the Saxons. This was a duel in which each of the contestants appealed to Heaven to give him the victory, it being believed that the right would vanquish. Noblemen[2] fought on horseback in full armor, with sword, lance, and battle-axe; common people fought on foot with clubs. In both cases the combat was in the presence of judges and might last from sunrise until the stars appeared. Priests and women had the privilege of being represented by champions, who fought for them. Trial by battle was claimed and allowed by the court (though the combat did not come off) as late as 1817, reign of George III. This custom was finally abolished in 1819.[3]

199. Divisions of Society. — The divisions of society remained after the conquest nearly as before, but the Saxon orders of nobility,

---

[1] The King's High Court of Justice (Curia Regis) was divided about 1215 into three distinct courts. 1. The Exchequer Court (so called from the chequered cloth which covered the table of the court, and which was probably made useful in counting money), which dealt with cases of finance and revenue. 2. The Court of Common Pleas, which had jurisdiction in civil suits between subject and subject. 3. The Court of King's Bench, which transacted the remaining business, both civil and criminal, and had special jurisdiction over all inferior courts and civil corporations.

Later, a fourth court, that of Chancery (see Paragraph No. 195, and note), over which the Lord Chancellor presided, was established as a court of appeal and equity, to deal with cases where the common law gave no relief.

[2] See Shakespeare's Richard II., Act I. scenes 1 and 3; also Scott's Ivanhoe, Chapter XLIII.

[3] Trial by battle might be demanded in cases of chivalry or honor, in criminal actions and in civil suits. The last were fought not by the disputants themselves but by champions.

with a few very rare exceptions, were deprived of their rank, and their estates were given to the Normans.

It is important to notice here the marked difference between the new or Norman nobility and that of France.

In England, a man was considered noble because, under William and his successors, he was a member of the National Council, or, in the case of an earl, because he represented the king in the government of a county or earldom.

His position did not exempt him from taxation, nor did his rank descend to more than one of his children. In France, on the contrary, the aristocracy were noble by birth, not office; they were generally exempt from taxation, thus throwing the whole of that burden on the people, and their rank descended to all their children.

During the Norman period a change was going on among the slaves, whose condition gradually improved. On the other hand many who had been free now sank into that state of villeinage which, as it bound them to the soil, was but one remove from actual slavery.

The small, free landholders who still existed were mostly in the old Danish territory north of Watling-street, or in Kent in the South.

200. Tenure of Land (Military Service, Feudal Dues, National Militia). — All land was held directly or indirectly from the king on condition of military or other service. The number of chief-tenants who derived their title from the crown, including ecclesiastical dignitaries, was probably about 1500. These constituted the Norman barons. The under-tenants were about 8000, and consisted chiefly of the English who had been driven out from their estates. Every holder of land was obliged to furnish the king a fully armed and mounted soldier, to serve for forty days during the year for each piece of land bringing £20 annually, or about $2000 in modern money[1] (the pound of that day probably representing twenty times that sum now). All chief-tenants were also bound to attend the king's Great Council three times a year, — at Christmas, Easter, and Whitsuntide.

Feudal Dues or Taxes. Every free tenant was obliged to pay a sum of money to the king or baron from whom he held his land, on three special occasions. 1. To ransom his lord from captivity in case he was made a prisoner of war. 2. To defray the expense of making

---

[1] This amount does not appear to have been fully settled until the period following the Norman kings, but the principle was recognized by William.

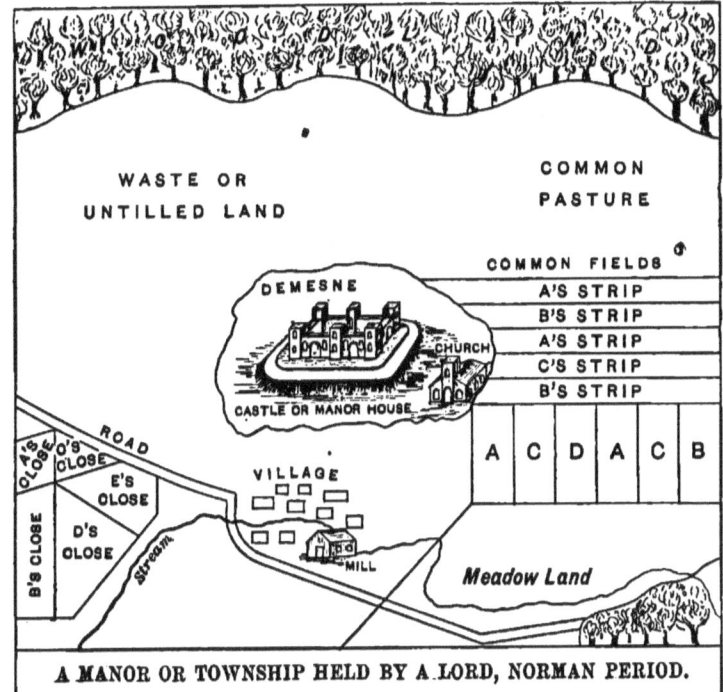

A MANOR OR TOWNSHIP HELD BY A LORD, NORMAN PERIOD.

The inhabitants of a manor, or the estate of a lord, were: 1. The lord himself, or his representative, who held his estate on condition of furnishing the king a certain number of armed men. (See Paragraphs 160 and 200.) 2. The lord's personal followers, who lived with him, and usually a parish priest or a number of monks. 3. The villeins, bound to the soil, who could not leave the manor, were not subject to military duty, and who paid rent in labor or produce; there might also be a few slaves, but this last class gradually rose to the partial freedom of villeinage. 4. Certain soke-men or free tenants, who were subject to military duty, but were not bound to remain on the manor, and who paid a fixed rent in money, or otherwise.

Next to the manor-house (where courts were also held) the most important buildings were the church (used sometimes for markets and town meetings); the lord's mill (if there was a stream), in which all tenants must grind their grain and pay for the grinding; and finally, the cottages of the tenants, gathered in a village near the mill.

The land was divided as follows: 1. The demesne (or domain) surrounding the manor-house. This was strictly private — the lord's ground. 2. The land outside the demesne, suitable for cultivation. This was let in strips, usually of thirty acres, but was subject to certain rules in regard to methods of tillage and crops. 3. A piece of land which was divided into fenced fields, called closes (because enclosed), and which tenants might hire and use as they saw fit. 4. Common pasture, open to all tenants to pasture their cattle on. 5. Waste or untilled land, where all tenants had the right to cut turf for fuel, or gather plants or shrubs for fodder. 6. The forest or woodland, where all tenants had the right to turn their hogs out to feed on acorns, and where they might also collect a certain amount of small wood for fuel. 7. Meadow-land on which tenants might hire the right to cut grass and make hay. On the above plan the fields of tenants — both those of villeins and of soke-men — are marked by the letters A, B, C, etc.

If the village grew to be a thriving manufacturing or trading town, the tenants might, in time, purchase from the lord the right to manage their own affairs in great measure, and so become a free town in a considerable degree. (See Paragraph 234.)

his lord's eldest son a knight. 3. To provide a suitable marriage portion on the marriage of his lord's eldest daughter.

In addition to these taxes, or "aids," as they were called, there were other demands which the lord might make, such as, 1. A year's profits of the land from the heir, on his coming into possession of his father's estate.[1] 2. The income from the lands of orphan heirs not of age. 3. Payment for privilege of disposing of land.[2]

In case of an orphan heiress not of age, the feudal lord became her guardian and might select a suitable husband for her. Should the heiress reject the person selected, she forfeited a sum of money equal to the amount the lord expected to receive by the proposed marriage. Thus we find one woman in Ipswich giving a large fee for the privilege of "not being married except to her own good liking." In the collection of these "aids" and "reliefs" great extortion was often practised both by the king and the barons.

In addition to the feudal troops there was a national militia, consisting of peasants and others not provided with armor, who fought on foot with bows and spears. These could also be called on as during the Saxon period. In some cases of revolt of the barons, for instance, under William Rufus, this national militia proved of immense service to the crown. The great landholders let out part of their estates to tenants on similar terms to those on which they held their own, and in this way the entire country was divided up. The lowest class of tenants were villeins or serfs, who held small pieces of land on condition of performing labor for it. These were bound to the soil and could be sold with it, but were not wholly destitute of legal rights. Under William I. and his successors, all free tenants, of whatever grade, were bound to uphold the king, and in case of insurrection or civil war to serve under him. In this most important respect, the great landholders of England differed from those of the continent, where the lesser tenants were bound only to serve their masters, and might, and in fact often did, take up arms against the king. William removed this serious defect. By do-

---

[1] Technically called a *relief*.
[2] The clergy being a corporate, and hence an ever-living body, were exempt from these last demands. Not satisfied with this, they were constantly endeavoring, with more or less success, to escape *all* feudal obligations, on the ground that they rendered the state divine service. In 1106, reign of Henry I., it was settled, for the time, that the bishops were to do homage to the king, *i.e.*, furnish military service, for the lands they received from him as their feudal lord. See Paragraph No. 186.

ing so he did the country an incalculable service. He completed the organization of *feudal land-tenure*, but he never established *the continental system* of feudal government.

RELIGION.

201. The Church. — With respect to the organization of the church, no changes were made under the Norman kings. They, however, generally deposed the English bishops and substituted Normans or foreigners, who, as a class, were superior in education to the English. It came to be pretty clearly understood at this time that the church was subordinate to the king, and that in all cases of dispute about temporal matters, he, and not the Pope, was to decide. During the Norman period great numbers of monasteries were built. The most important action taken by William was the establishment of ecclesiastical courts in which all cases relating to the church and the clergy were tried by the bishops according to laws of their own. Under these laws persons wearing the dress of a monk or priest, or who could manage to spell out a verse of the Psalms, and so pass for ecclesiastics, would claim the right to be tried, and, as the punishments which the church inflicted were notoriously mild, the consequence was that the majority of criminals escaped the penalty of their evil doings. So great was the abuse of this privilege, that, at a later period, Henry II. made an attempt to reform it; but it was not finally done away with until the beginning of the present century.

MILITARY AFFAIRS.

202. The Army. — The army consisted of cavalry, or knights, and foot-soldiers. The former were almost wholly Normans. They wore armor similar to that used by the Saxons. It is represented in the pictures of the Bayeux Tapestry (see 205), and appears to have consisted of leather or stout linen, on which pieces of bone or scales or rings of iron were securely sewed. Later, these rings of iron were set up edgewise, and interlinked, or the scales made to overlap. The helmet was pointed, and had a piece in front to protect the nose. The shield was long and kite-shaped. The weapons of this class of soldiers consisted of a lance and a double-edged sword. The foot-soldiers wore little or no armor and fought principally with long-bows. In case of need, the king could probably muster about 10,000 knights, or armed horsemen, and a much larger force of foot-soldiers. Under the Norman kings the principal wars were insurrections against William I., the various revolts of the barons, and the civil war under Stephen.

203. Knighthood.[1] — Candidates for knighthood were usually obliged to pass through a long course of training under the care of some distinguished noble. The candidate served first as a page, then as a squire or attendant, following his master to the wars. After seven years in this capacity, he prepared himself for receiving the honors of knighthood by spending several days in a church, engaged in solemn religious rites, fasting, and prayer. The young man, in the presence of his friends and kindred, then made oath to be loyal to the king, to defend religion, and to be the champion of every lady in danger or distress. Next, a high-born dame or great warrior buckled on his spurs, and girded the sword, which the priest had blessed, to his side. This done, he knelt to the prince or noble who was to perform the final ceremony. The prince struck him lightly on the shoulder with the flat of the sword, saying, " In the name of God, St. Michael,[2] and St. George [the patron saint of England], I dub thee knight. Be brave, hardy, and loyal." Then the young cavalier leaped into the saddle and galloped up and down, brandishing his weapons in token of strength and skill. In case a knight proved false to his oaths, he was publicly degraded. His spurs were taken from him, his shield reversed, his armor broken to pieces, and a sermon preached upon him in the neighboring church, proclaiming him dead to the order.

LITERATURE, LEARNING, AND ART.

204. Education. — The learning of this period was confined almost wholly to the clergy. Whatever schools existed were connected with the monasteries and nunneries. Very few books were written. Generally speaking, the nobility considered fighting the great business of

---

[1] Knighthood: Originally the knight (cniht) was a youth or attendant. Later the word came to mean an armed horse-soldier or cavalier who had received his weapons and title in a solemn manner. Those whom the English called knights the Normans called chevaliers (literally, horsemen), and as only the wealthy and noble could, as a rule, afford the expense of a horse and armor, chivalry or knighthood came in time to be closely connected with the idea of aristocracy. Besides the method described above, soldiers were sometimes made knights on the battle-field as a reward for valor.

[2] St. Michael, as representative of the triumphant power of good over evil.

life and cared nothing for education. To read or write was beneath their dignity. Such accomplishments they left to monks, priests, and lawyers. For this reason seals or stamps having some device or signature engraved on them came to be used on all papers of importance.

205. Historical Works. — The chief books written in England, under the Norman kings, were histories. Of these, the most noteworthy were the continuation of the Anglo-Saxon Chronicle in English and the chronicles of William of Malmesbury and Henry of Huntingdon in Latin.[1] William's book and the Saxon Chronicle still continue to be of great importance to students of this period. Mention has already been made of the Bayeux Tapestry, a history of the Norman Conquest worked in colored worsteds, on a long strip of narrow canvas. It consists of a series of seventy-two scenes, or pictures, done about the time of William's accession. Some have supposed it to be the work of his queen, Matilda. The entire length is two hundred and fourteen feet and the width about twenty inches. It represents events in English history from the last of Edward the Confessor's reign to the battle of Hastings. As a guide to a knowledge of the armor, weapons, and costume of the period, it is of very great value.

206. Architecture. — Under the Norman sovereigns there was neither painting, statuary, nor poetry worthy of mention. The spirit that creates these arts found expression in architecture introduced from the continent. The castle, cathedral, and minster, with here and there an exceptional structure like London Bridge and the Great Hall at Westminster, built by William Rufus, were the buildings which mark the time. Aside from Westminster Abbey, which, although the work of Edward the Confessor, was really Norman, a fortress or two, like Coningsborough in Yorkshire, and a few churches, the Saxons erected nothing worthy of note. On the continent, stone had already come into general use for churches and fortresses. William was no sooner firmly established on his throne than he began to employ it for similar purposes in England. The characteristic of the Norman style of architecture was its massive grandeur. The churches were built in the form of a cross, with a square, central tower, the main entrance being at the

---

[1] Among the historical works of this period may be included Geoffrey of Monmouth's History of the Britons, in Latin, a book whose chief value is in the curious romances with which it abounds, especially those relating to King Arthur. It is the basis of Tennyson's Idylls of the King.

west. The interior was divided into a nave, or central portion, with an aisle on each side for the passage of religious processions. The windows were narrow, and rounded at the top. The roof rested on round arches supported by heavy columns. The cathedrals of Peterborough, Ely, Durham, Norwich, the church of St. Bartholomew, London, and St. John's Chapel in the Tower of London are fine examples of Norman work. The castles consisted of a square keep, or citadel, with walls of immense thickness having a few slit-like windows in the lower story and somewhat larger ones above. In these everything was made subordinate to strength and security. They were surrounded by a high stone wall and deep ditch, generally filled with water. The entrance to them was over a draw-bridge through an archway protected by an iron grating, or portcullis, which could be raised and lowered at pleasure. The Tower of London, Rochester Castle, Carisbrook Keep, New Castle on the Tyne, and Tintagel Hold were built by William or his Norman successors. Although, with the exception of the first, all are in ruins, yet these ruins bid fair to stand as long as the pyramids. They were mostly the work of churchmen, who were the best architects of the day, and knew how to plan a fortress as well as to build a minster.

GENERAL INDUSTRY AND COMMERCE.

207. Trade.— No very marked change took place in respect to agriculture or trade during the Norman period. The Jews who came in with the Conqueror got the control of much of the trade, and were the only capitalists of the time. They were protected by the kings in money-lending at exorbitant rates of interest. In turn, the kings extorted immense sums from them. The guilds, or associations for mutual protection among merchants, now became prominent, and came eventually to have great political influence.

MODE OF LIFE, MANNERS, AND CUSTOMS.

208. Dress.— The Normans were more temperate and refined in their mode of living than the Saxons. In dress they made great display. In Henry I.'s reign it became the custom for the nobility to wear their hair very long, so that their curls resembled those of women. The clergy thundered against this effeminate fashion, but with no effect. At last, a priest preaching before the king on Easter Sunday, ended his sermon by taking out a pair of shears and cropping the entire congregation, king and all.

By the regulation called the curfew,[1] a bell rang at sunset in summer and eight in winter, which was the government signal for putting out lights and covering up fires. This law, which was especially hated by the English, as a Norman innovation and act of tyranny, was a necessary precaution against fire, at a time when London and other cities were masses of wooden hovels.

Surnames came in with the Normans. Previous to the conquest, Englishmen had but one name; and when, for convenience, another was needed, they were called by their occupation or from some personal peculiarity, as Edward the Carpenter, Harold the Dauntless. Among the Normans the lack of a second, or family name, had come to be looked upon as a sign of low birth, and the daughter of a great Lord (Fitz-Haman) refused to marry a nobleman who had but one, saying, "My father and my grandfather had each two names, and it were a great shame to me to take a husband who has less."

The principal amusements were hunting and hawking (catching small game with trained hawks).

The church introduced theatrical plays, written and acted by the monks. These represented scenes in Scripture history, and, later, the career of the Vices and the Virtues personified.

Tournaments, or mock combats between knights, were not encouraged by William I. or his immediate successors, but became common in the period following the Norman kings.

---

[1] Curfew: *couvre-feu*, cover-fire.

VI.

"Man bears within him certain ideas of order, of justice, of reason, with a constant desire to bring them into play . . . ; for this he labors unceasingly." — GUIZOT, *History of Civilization*.

THE ANGEVINS, OR PLANTAGENETS, 1154-1399.

THE BARONS versus THE CROWN.

CONSOLIDATION OF NORMAN AND SAXON INTERESTS. — RISE OF THE NEW ENGLISH NATION.

Henry II., 1154-1189. Edward I., 1272-1307.[1]
Richard I., 1189-1199. Edward II., 1307-1327.
John, 1199-1216. Edward III., 1327-1377.
Henry III., 1216-1272. Richard II., 1377-1399.

209. Accession and Dominions of Henry II. — Henry was just of age when the death of Stephen called him to the throne.

From his father, Count Geoffrey of Anjou, came the title of Angevin. The name Plantagenet, by which the family was also known, was derived from the count's habit of wearing a sprig of the golden-blossomed broom-plant, or Plante-genét, as the French called it, in his helmet.

Henry received from his father the dukedoms of Anjou and Maine, from his mother, Normandy and the dependent province of Brittany, while through his marriage with Eleanor, the divorced queen of France, he acquired the great southern dukedom of Aquitaine.

Thus on his accession he became ruler over England and more than half of France, his realms extending from the borders of Scotland to the base of the Pyrenees.[2] To these extensive posses-

---

[1] Not crowned until 1274. [2] See Maps Nos. 8 and 9, pages 88 and 130.

sions Henry added the eastern half of Ireland,[1] which was but partially conquered and never justly ruled, so that the English power there has remained ever since like a spear-point embedded in a living body, inflaming all around it.[2]

210. Henry's Charter and Reforms. — On his mother's side Henry was a descendant of Alfred the Great; for this reason he was hailed with enthusiasm by the native English. He at once began a system of reforms worthy of his illustrious ancestor. His first act was to issue a charter confirming the promises of good government made by his grandfather, Henry I. His next was to begin levelling to the ground the castles illegally built in Stephen's reign, which had caused such widespread misery to the country.[3] He continued the work of demolition until it is said he had destroyed no less than eleven hundred of these strongholds of oppression. Having accomplished this work, the king turned his attention to the coinage. During the civil war the barons had issued money debased in quality and deficient in weight. Henry abolished this currency and issued in its place silver pieces of full weight and value.

---

[1] Ireland: the population of Ireland at this time consisted mainly of descendants of the Celtic and other prehistoric races which inhabited Britain at the period of the Roman invasion. When the Saxons conquered Britain, many of the natives, who were of the same stock and spoke essentially the same language as the Irish, fled to that country. Later, the Danes formed settlements on the coast, especially in the vicinity of Dublin. The conquest of England by the Normans was practically a victory gained by one branch of a German race over another (Saxons and Normans having originally sprung from the same stock), and the two soon mingled; but the partial conquest of Ireland by the Normans was a radically different thing. They and the Irish had really nothing in common. The latter refused to accept the feudal system, and continued split up into savage tribes or clans under the rule of petty chiefs always at war with each other. Thus for centuries after England had established a settled government Ireland remained, partly through the battles of the clans, and partly through the aggressions of a hostile race, in a state of anarchic confusion which prevented all true national growth.

[2] Lecky's England.

[3] Under William the Conqueror and his immediate successors no one was allowed to erect a castle without a royal license. During Stephen's time the great barons constantly violated this salutary regulation.

No. 8.

To face page 88.

211. War with France; Scutage. — Having completed these reforms, the king turned his attention to his continental possessions. Through his wife, Henry claimed the county of Toulouse in Southern France. To enforce this claim he declared war. Henry's barons, however, refused to furnish troops to fight outside of England. The king wisely compromised the matter by offering to accept from each knight a sum of money in lieu of service, called scutage, or shield-money.[1] The proposal was agreed to, and means were thus furnished to hire soldiers for foreign wars.

Later in his reign Henry supplemented this tax by the passage of a law[2] which revived the national militia and placed it at his command for home-service. By these two measures the king made himself practically independent of the barons, and thus gained a greater degree of power than any previous ruler had possessed.

212. Thomas Becket.[3] — There was, however, one man in Henry's kingdom — his chancellor, Thomas Becket — who was always ready to serve him. At his own expense he now equipped seven hundred knights, and, crossing the Channel, fought valiantly for the suppression of the rebellion in Toulouse.

An old but unfortunately a doubtful story represents Becket as the son of an English crusader, Gilbert Becket, who was captured in the Holy Land, and who in turn succeeded in captivating the heart of an Eastern princess. She helped him to escape to his native land, and then followed. The princess knew but two words of English, — "Gilbert" and "London." By constantly repeating these, as she wandered from city to city, she at length

---

[1] Scutage: from the Latin *scutum*, a shield; the understanding being that he who would not take his shield and do battle for the king, should pay enough to hire one who would.

The scutage was assessed at two marks. Later, the assessment varied. The mark was two-thirds of a pound of silver by weight, or thirteen shillings and four pence ($3.20). Reckoned in modern money, the tax was probably at least twenty times two marks, or about $128. The only coin in use in England up to Edward I.'s reign, 1272, was the silver penny, of which twelve made a shilling.

[2] The Assize or Law of Arms.   [3] Also spelled À Becket and Beket.

found both, and the long search for her lover ended in a happy marriage.

213. Becket made Archbishop. — Shortly after Becket's return from the continent Henry resolved to appoint him archbishop of Canterbury. Becket knew that the king purposed beginning certain church reforms with which he was not in sympathy, and declined the office. But Henry would take no denial. At last, wearied with his importunity, Becket consented, but warned the king that he should uphold the rights of the clergy. He now became the head of the church, and was the first Englishman called to that exalted position since the Norman Conquest. With his assumption of the sacred office, Becket seemed to wholly change his character. He had been a man of the world, fond of pomp and pleasure. He now gave up all luxury and show. He put on sackcloth, lived on bread and water, and spent his nights in prayer, tearing his flesh with a scourge.

214. The First Quarrel. — The new archbishop's presentiment of evil soon proved true. Becket had hardly taken his seat when a quarrel broke out between him and the king. In his need for money Henry had levied a tax on all lands, whether belonging to the barons or churchmen.

Becket opposed this tax.[1] He was willing, he said, that the clergy should contribute, but not that they should be assessed.

The king declared with an oath that all should pay alike; the archbishop vowed with equal determination that not a single penny should be collected from the church. What the result was we do not know, but from that time the king and Becket never met again as friends.

215. The Second Quarrel. — Shortly after, a much more serious quarrel broke out between the two. Under the law of William the Conqueror, the church had the right to try in its own courts all offences committed by monks and priests. This privilege had led to great abuses. Men whose only claim to sanctity was that

---

[1] See Paragraph 200, note on Clergy.

they wore a black gown or had a shaven head claimed the right of being judged by the ecclesiastical tribunal. The heaviest sentence the church could give was imprisonment in a monastery, with degradation from the clerical office. Generally, however, offenders got off with flogging and fasting. On this account many criminals who deserved to be hanged escaped with a slight penalty. Such a case now occurred. A priest named Brois had committed an unprovoked murder. Henry commanded him to be brought before the king's court; Becket interfered, and ordered the case to be tried by the bishop of the diocese. That functionary sentenced the murderer to lose his place for two years.

216. The Constitutions of Clarendon (1164). — The king, now thoroughly roused, determined that such flagrant disregard of justice should no longer go on. He called a council of his chief men at Clarendon,[1] and laid the case before them. He demanded that in future the state or civil courts should be supreme, and that in every instance their judges should decide whether a criminal should be tried by the common law of the land or handed over to the church courts. He required furthermore that the clergy should be held strictly responsible to the crown, so that in case of dispute the final appeal should be to neither the archbishop nor the Pope, but to himself. After protracted debate the council passed these measures, which, under the name of the Constitutions of Clarendon, now became law.

Becket, though bitterly opposed to this enactment, finally assented and swore to obey it. Afterward, feeling that he had conceded too much, he retracted his oath and refused to be bound by the Constitutions. The other church dignitaries became alarmed at the prospect, and left Becket to settle with the king as best he might. Henceforth it was a battle between one man and the whole power of the government.

217. The King enforces the Law; Becket leaves the Country. — Henry at once proceeded to put the Constitutions into execution without fear or favor.

---

[1] Clarendon Park, Wiltshire, near Salisbury.

"Then was seen the mournful spectacle," says a champion of the church of that day, "of priests and deacons who had committed murder, manslaughter, robbery, theft, and other crimes, carried in carts before the commissioners and punished as though they were ordinary men."[1]

Not satisfied with these summary procedures, the king, who seems now to have resolved to either ruin Becket or drive him from the kingdom, summoned the archbishop before a royal council at Northampton. The charges brought against him appear to have had little, if any, foundation. Becket, though he answered the summons, refused to acknowledge the jurisdiction of the council, and appealed to the Pope. "Traitor!" cried a courtier, as he picked up a bunch of muddy rushes from the floor and flung them at the archbishop's head.

Becket turned, and looking him sternly in the face, said, "Were I not a churchman, I would make you repent that word."

Realizing, however, that he was now in serious danger, he soon after left Northampton and fled to France.

218. Banishment versus Excommunication. — Henry, finding Becket beyond his reach, next proceeded to banish his kinsmen and friends, without regard to age or sex, to the number of nearly four hundred. The miserable exiles, many of whom were nearly destitute, were forced to leave the country in midwinter, and excited the pity of all who saw them. Becket indignantly retaliated by hurling at the king's counsellors that awful anathema of excommunication which declares those against whom it is directed accursed of God and man, deprived of help in this world, and shut out from hope in the world to come. In this manner the quarrel went on with ever-increasing bitterness for the space of six years.

219. Prince Henry crowned; Reconciliation. — In 1170, Henry, who had long wished to associate his son Prince Henry with him in the government, had him crowned at Westminster by

---

[1] William of Newburgh.

the Archbishop of York, the bishops of London and Salisbury taking part.

By custom, if not indeed by law, Becket alone, as Archbishop of Canterbury, had the right to perform this ceremony.

When Becket heard of the coronation, he declared it an outrage both against Christianity and the church. So great an outcry now arose that Henry believed it expedient to recall the absent archbishop, especially as the king of France was urging the Pope to take up the matter. Henry accordingly went over to the continent, met Becket and persuaded him to return.

220. Renewal of the Quarrel; Murder of Becket. — But the reconciliation was on the surface only; underneath, the old hatred smouldered, ready to burst forth into flame.

As soon as he reached England, Becket invoked the thunders of the church against those who had officiated at the coronation of the boy Henry. He excommunicated the archbishop of York with his assistant bishops. The king took their part, and in an unguarded moment exclaimed, in an outburst of passion, "Will none of the cowards who eat my bread rid me of that turbulent priest?" In answer to his angry cry for relief, four knights set out without Henry's knowledge for Canterbury, and brutally murdered the archbishop within the walls of his own cathedral.

221. Results of the Murder. — The crime sent a thrill of horror throughout the realm. The Pope proclaimed Becket a saint. The English people, feeling that he had risen from their ranks and was of their blood, now looked upon the dead ecclesiastic as a martyr who had died in the defence of the church, and of all those around whom the church cast its protecting power. The cathedral was hung in mourning; Becket's shrine became the most famous in England, and the stone pavement, with the steps leading to it, both show by their deep-worn hollows where thousands of pilgrims coming from all parts of the kingdom, and from the continent even, used to creep on their knees to the saint's tomb to pray for his intercession. Henry himself was so far vanquished by the reaction in Becket's favor, that he gave up any further attempt to enforce the Constitutions of Clarendon, by which he had hoped to establish a uniform system of administration of justice. But the attempt, though baffled, was not wholly lost; like seed buried in the soil, it sprang up and bore good fruit in later generations.

222. The King makes his Will; Civil War. — Some years after the murder the king bequeathed England and Normandy to Prince Henry.[1] He at the same time provided for his sons Geoffrey and Richard. To John, the youngest of the brothers, he gave no territory, but requested Henry to grant him several castles, which the latter refused to do.

"It is our fate," said one of the sons, " that none should love the rest; that is the only inheritance which will never be taken from us."

It may be that that legacy of hatred was the result of Henry's unwise marriage with Eleanor, an able but perverse woman, or it may have sprung from her jealousy of "Fair Rosamond" and other favorites of the king.[2]

Eventually this feeling burst out into civil war. Brother fought against brother, and Eleanor, conspiring with the king of France, turned against her husband.

223. The King's Penance. — The revolt against Henry's power began in Normandy. While he was engaged in quelling it, he re-

---

[1] After his coronation Prince Henry had the title of Henry III.; but as he died before his father, he never properly became king in his own right.

[2] "Fair Rosamond" [Rosa mundi, the Rose of the world (as *then* interpreted)] was the daughter of Lord Clifford. According to tradition the king formed an attachment for this lady before his unfortunate marriage with Eleanor, and constructed a place of concealment for her in a forest in Woodstock, near Oxford. Some accounts report the queen as discovering her rival and putting her to death. She was buried in the nunnery of Godstow near by. When Henry's son John became king, he raised a monument to her memory with the inscription in Latin: —

> "This tomb doth here enclose
> The world's most beauteous Rose —
> Rose passing sweet erewhile,
> Now nought but odor vile."

ceived intelligence that Earl Bigod of Norfolk[1] and the Bishop of Durham, both of whom hated the king's reforms, since they curtailed their authority, had risen against him.

Believing that this new trouble was a judgment of Heaven for Becket's murder, Henry resolved to do penance at his tomb. Leaving the continent with two prisoners in his charge — one his son Henry's queen, the other his own, — he travelled with all speed to Canterbury. There kneeling abjectly before the grave of his former chancellor and friend, the king submitted to be beaten with rods by the priests, in expiation of his sin.

224. End of the Rebellion. — Henry then moved against the rebels in the north. Convinced of the hopelessness of holding out against his forces, they submitted. With their submission the struggle of the barons against the crown came to an end. It had lasted just one hundred years (1074-1174). It settled the question, once for all, that England was not like the rest of Europe, to be managed in the interest of a body of great baronial landholders always at war with each other; but was henceforth to be governed by one central power, restrained but not overridden by that of the nobles and the church.

225. The King again begins his Reforms. — As soon as order was restored, Henry once more set about completing his legal and judicial reforms. His great object was to secure a uniform system of administering justice which should be effective and impartial. Henry I. had undertaken to divide the kingdom into districts or circuits, which were assigned to a certain number of judges, who travelled through them at stated times collecting the royal revenue and administering the law. Henry II. revised and perfected this plan.[2] Not only had the barons set up private courts on their estates, but they had in many cases got the entire control of the

---

[1] Hugh Bigod: the Bigods were among the most prominent and also the most turbulent of the Norman barons. On the derivation of the name, see Webster's Dictionary, "Bigot."

[2] Grand Assize and Assize of Clarendon (not to be confounded with the Constitutions of Clarendon).

town and other local courts, and dealt out such justice or injustice as they pleased. The king's judges now presided over these tribunals, thus bringing the common law of the realm to every man's door.

226. Grand Juries. — The Norman method of settling disputes was by trial of battle, in which the contestants or their champions fought the matter out with either swords or cudgels. There were those who objected to this club-law. To them the king offered the privilege of leaving the case to the decision of twelve knights, chosen from the neighborhood, who were supposed to know the facts.

In like manner, when the judges passed through a circuit, a grand jury of not less than sixteen was to report to them the criminals of each district. These the judges forthwith sent to the church to be examined by the ordeal.[1] If convicted, they were punished; if not, the judges ordered them as suspicious characters to leave the country within eight days. In that way the rascals of that generation were summarily disposed of.

227. Origin of the Modern Trial by Jury. — In 1215 (reign of Henry's son John) the church abolished the ordeal throughout Christendom. It then became the custom in England to choose a petty jury, acquainted with the facts, who confirmed or denied the accusations brought by the grand jury. When this petty jury could not agree, the decision of a majority was sometimes accepted.

Owing to the difficulty of securing justice in this way, it gradually became the custom to summon witnesses, who gave their testimony before the petty jury in order to thereby obtain a unanimous verdict. The first mention of this change occurs in the reign of Edward III. (1350); and from that time, perhaps, may be dated the true beginning of our modern method, by which the jury bring in a verdict, not from what they personally know, but from evidence sworn to by those who do. Henry II. may rightfully be regarded as the true founder of the system which England, and

---

[1] Ordeal: See Paragraph No. 127.

England alone, fully matured, and which has since been adopted by every civilized country of the globe.

228. The King's Last Days. — Henry's last days were full of bitterness. Ever since his memorable return from the continent, he had been obliged to hold the queen a prisoner lest she should undermine his power. His sons were discontented and rebellious. Toward the close of his reign they again plotted against him with King Philip of France. War was then declared against that country. When peace was made, Henry, who was lying ill, asked to see a list of those who had conspired against him. At the head of it stood the name of his youngest son John, whom he trusted. At the sight of it the old man turned his face to the wall, saying, "I have nothing left to care for; let all things go their way." Two days afterward he died of a broken heart.

229. Summary. — Henry II. left his work only half done; yet that half was permanent and its beneficent mark may be seen on the English law and the English constitution at the present time. When he ascended the throne he found a people who had long been suffering the miseries of a protracted civil war. He established a stable government. He redressed their wrongs. He punished the mutinous barons. He compelled the church, at least for a time, to acknowledge the supremacy of the state. He reformed the administration of law; established methods of judicial inquiry which were to gradually develop into trial by jury; and made all men feel that a king sat on the throne who believed in justice and was able to make justice respected.

RICHARD I. (Cœur de Lion).[1] — 1189-1199.

230. Accession and Character of Richard. — Henry II. was succeeded by his second son Richard, his first having died during

---

[1] Richard Cœur de Lion (keŭr dĕ le' ōn), Richard the Lion-hearted. An old chronicler says the king got the name from his adventure with a lion. The beast attacked him, and as the king had no weapons, he thrust his hand down his throat and "tore out his heart!!"

the civil war of 1183, in which he and his brother Geoffrey had fought against Prince Richard and their father. Richard was born at Oxford, but he spent his youth in France. The only English sentence that he was ever known to speak was when in a raging passion he vented his wrath against an impertinent Frenchman, in some broken but decidedly strong expressions of his native tongue. Richard's bravery in battle and his daring exploits gained for him the flattering surname of Cœur de Lion. He had a right to it, for with all his faults he certainly possessed the heart of a lion. He might, however, have been called, with equal truth, Richard the Absentee, since out of a nominal reign of ten years he spent but a few months in England, the remaining time being consumed in wars abroad.

231. Condition of Society. — No better general picture of society in England during this period can be found than that presented by Sir Walter Scott's novel, "Ivanhoe." There every class appears — the Saxon serf and swineherd, wearing the brazen collar of his master Cedric; the pilgrim wandering from shrine to shrine, with the palm branch in his cap to show that he has visited the Holy Land; the outlaw, Robin Hood, lying in wait to strip rich churchmen and other travellers who were on their way through Sherwood Forest; the Norman baron in his castle torturing the aged Jew to extort his hidden gold; and the steel-clad knights, with Ivanhoe at their head, splintering lances in the tournament, presided over by Richard's brother, the traitorous Prince John.

232. Richard's Coronation. — Richard was on the continent at the time of his father's death. His first act was to liberate his mother from her long imprisonment at Winchester; his next, to place her at the head of the English government until his arrival from Normandy. Unlike Henry II., Richard did not issue a charter, or pledge of good government. He, however, took the usual coronation oath to defend the church, maintain justice, make salutary laws, and abolish evil customs; such an oath might well be considered a charter in itself.

THE ANGEVINS, OR PLANTAGENETS. 99

233. The Crusade; Richard's Devices for raising Money. — Immediately after his coronation, Richard began to make preparations to join the king of France and the emperor of Germany in the third crusade. To get money for the expedition, the king extorted loans from the Jews, who were the creditors of half England, and had almost complete control of the capital and commerce of every country in Europe. The English nobles who joined Richard also borrowed largely from the same source; and then, suddenly turning on the hated lenders, they tried to extinguish the debt by extinguishing the Jews. A pretext against the unfortunate race was easily found. Riots broke out in London, York, and elsewhere, and hundreds of Israelites were brutally massacred. Richard's next move to obtain funds was to impose a heavy tax; his next, to dispose of titles of rank and offices in both church and state, to all who wished to buy them. Thus, to the aged and covetous bishop of Durham he sold the earldom of Northumberland for life, saying, as he concluded the bargain, "Out of an old bishop I have made a new earl." He sold, also, the office of chief justice to the same prelate for an additional thousand marks,[1] while the king of Scotland purchased freedom from subjection to the English king for ten thousand marks. Last of all, Richard sold charters to towns. One of his courtiers remonstrated with him for his greed for gain. He replied that he would sell London itself if he could but find a purchaser.

234. The Rise of the Free Towns. — Of all these devices for raising money, the last had the most important results. From the time of the Norman Conquest the large towns of England, with few exceptions, were considered part of the king's property; the smaller places generally belonged to the great barons. The citizens of these towns were obliged to pay rent and taxes of various kinds to the king or lord who owned them. These dues were collected by an officer appointed by the king or lord (usually the sheriff), who was bound to obtain a certain sum, whatever more

---

[1] Mark: see note to Paragraph No. 211.

he could get being his own profit. For this reason it was for his interest to exact from every citizen the uttermost penny. London, as we have seen, had secured a considerable degree of liberty through the charter granted to it by William the Conqueror. Every town was now anxious to obtain a similar pledge. The three great objects aimed at by the citizens were (1) to get the right of paying their taxes (a fixed sum) directly to the king, (2) to elect their own magistrates, and (3) to administer justice in their own courts in accordance with laws made by themselves. The only way to gain these privileges was to pay for them. Many of the towns were rich; and, when the king or lord needed money, they bargained with him for the favors they desired. When the agreement was made, it was drawn up in Latin, stamped with the king's seal, and taken home in triumph by the citizens, who locked it up as the safeguard of their liberties. If they could not get all they wanted, they bought a part. Thus, the people of Leicester, in the next reign, purchased from the earl, their master, the right to decide their own disputes. For this they paid a yearly tax of three pence on every house having a gable on the main street. These concessions may seem small; but they prepared the way for greater ones. What was still more important, they educated the citizens of that day in a knowledge of self-government. It was the tradesmen and shopkeepers of these towns who preserved free speech and equal justice. Richard granted a large number of such charters, and thus unintentionally made himself a benefactor to the nation.

235. Failure of the Third Crusade. — The object of the third crusade was to drive the Turks from Jerusalem. In this it failed. Richard got as near Jerusalem as the Mount of Olives. When he had climbed to the top, he was told that he could have a full view of the place; but he covered his face with his mantle, saying, "Blessed Lord, let me not see thy holy city since I may not deliver it from the hands of thine enemies!"

236. Richard taken Prisoner; his Ransom. — On his way home the king fell into the hands of the German emperor, who held him captive. His brother John, who had remained in England, plotted with Philip of France to keep Richard in prison while he got possession of the throne. Notwithstanding his efforts, Richard regained his liberty,[1] on condition of raising a ransom so enormous that it compelled every Englishman to contribute a fourth of his personal property, and to strip the churches of their jewels and silver plate even. When the king of France heard of this, he wrote to John notifying him that his brother was free, saying, "Look out for yourself; the devil has broken loose." Richard pardoned him; and when the king was killed in France in 1199, John gained and disgraced the throne he coveted.

237. Purpose of the Crusades. — Up to the time of the crusades, the English wars on the continent had been actuated either by ambition for military glory or desire for conquest. The crusades, on the contrary, were undertaken from motives of religious enthusiasm. Those who engaged in them fought for an idea. They considered themselves soldiers of the cross. Moved by this feeling, "all Christian believers seemed ready to precipitate themselves in one united body upon Asia." Thus the crusades were "the first European event."[2] They gave men something to battle for, not only outside their country, but outside their own selfish interests. Richard, as we have seen, was the first English king who took part in them. Before that period, England had stood aloof, — " a world by itself." The country was engaged in its own affairs or in its contests with France. Richard's expedition to Palestine brought England into the main current of history, so

---

[1] It is not certainly known how the news of Richard's captivity reached England. One story says that it was carried by Blondel, a minstrel who had accompanied the king to Palestine. He, it is said, wandered through Germany in search of his master, singing one of Richard's favorite songs at every castle he came to. One day, as he was thus singing at the foot of a tower, he heard the well-known voice of the king take up the next verse in reply.

[2] Guizot, History of Civilization.

that it was now moved by the same feeling which animated the continent.

238. The Results of the Crusades: Educational, Social, Political. — In many respects the civilization of the East was far in advance of the West. One result of the crusades was to open the eyes of Europe to this fact. When Richard and his followers set out, they looked upon the Mohammedans as barbarians; before they returned, many were ready to acknowledge that the barbarians were chiefly among themselves. At that time England had few Latin and no Greek scholars. The Arabians, however, had long been familiar with the classics, and had translated them into their own tongue. Not only did England gain its first knowledge of the philosophy of Plato and Aristotle from Mohammedan teachers, but it received from them also the elements of arithmetic, algebra, geometry, and astronomy. This new knowledge gave an impulse to education, and had a most important influence on the growth of the universities of Cambridge and Oxford, though these did not become prominent until more than a century later. Had these been the only results, they would perhaps have been worth the blood and treasure spent in vain attempts to recover possession of the sepulchre of Christ; but these were by no means all. The crusades brought about a social and political revolution. They conferred benefits and removed evils. When they began, the greater part of the inhabitants of Europe, including England, were chained to the soil. They had neither freedom, property, nor knowledge.

There were in fact but two classes, the churchmen and the nobles, who really deserved the name of citizens and men. We have seen that the crusades compelled kings like Richard to grant charters of freedom to towns. The nobles conferred similar privileges on those in their power. Thus their great estates were, in a measure, broken up and from this period the common people began to acquire rights, and, what is more, to defend them.[1]

---

[1] Gibbon's Rome.

239. Summary.—We may say in closing that the central fact in Richard's reign was his embarking in the crusades. From them, directly or indirectly, England gained two important results: first, a greater degree of political liberty, especially in the case of the towns; second, a new intellectual and educational impulse.

JOHN.—1199-1216.

240. John Lackland.—When Henry II. in dividing his realm left his youngest son John dependent on the generosity of his brothers, he jestingly gave him the surname of "Lackland." As John never received any principality, the nickname continued to cling to him even after he had become king through the death of his brother Richard.

241. The Quarrels of the King.—The reign of the new king was taken up mainly with three momentous quarrels: first, with France; next, with the Pope; lastly, with the barons. By his quarrel with France he lost Normandy and the greater part of the adjoining provinces, thus becoming in a new sense John Lackland. By his quarrel with the Pope he was humbled to the earth. By his quarrel with the barons he was forced to grant England the Great Charter.

242. Murder of Prince Arthur.—Shortly after John's accession the nobles of a part of the English possessions in France expressed their desire that John's nephew, Arthur, a boy of twelve, should become their ruler. John refused to grant their request. War ensued, and Arthur fell into his uncle's hands, who imprisoned him in the castle of Rouen. A number of those who had been captured with the young prince were starved to death in the dungeons of the same castle, and not long after Arthur himself mysteriously disappeared. Shakespeare represents John as ordering the keeper of the castle to put out the lad's eyes, and then tells us that he was killed in an attempt to escape. The earlier belief, however, was that the king murdered him.

243. John's Loss of Normandy. — Philip of France accused John of the crime, and ordered him as Duke of Normandy, and hence as a feudal dependant, to appear at Paris for trial.[1] He refused. The court was convened, John was declared a traitor and sentenced to forfeit all his lands on the continent. For a long time he made no attempt to defend his dominions, but left his Norman nobles to carry on a war against Philip as best they could. At last, after much territory had been lost, the English king made an attempt to regain it. The result was a humiliating and crushing defeat, in which Philip seized Normandy and followed up the victory by depriving John of all his possessions north of the river Loire.

244. Good Results of the Loss of Normandy. — From that period the Norman nobles were compelled to choose between the island of England and the continent for their home. Before that time the Norman contempt for the Saxon was so great, that his most indignant exclamation was, "Do you take me for an Englishman?" Now, however, shut in by the sea, with the people he had hitherto oppressed and despised, he gradually came to regard England as his country, and Englishmen as his countrymen. Thus the two races so long hostile found at last that they had common interests and common enemies.[2]

245. The King's Despotism. — Hitherto our sympathies have been mainly with the kings. We have watched them struggling against the lawless nobles, and every gain which they have made in power we have felt to be so much for the cause of good government; but we are coming to a period when our sympathies will be the other way. Henceforth the welfare of the nation will depend largely on the resistance of these very barons to the despotic encroachments of the crown.[3]

---

[1] It is proper to state in this connection that a recent French writer on this period — M. Bémont — is satisfied that John's condemnation and the forfeiture of Normandy took place before Arthur's death, for tyranny in Poitou.

[2] Macaulay.

[3] Ransome's Constitutional History of England.

246. Quarrel of the King with the Church. — Shortly after his defeat in France, John entered upon his second quarrel. Pope Innocent III. had commanded a delegation of the monks of Canterbury to choose Stephen Langton archbishop in place of a person whom the king had compelled them to elect. When the news reached John, he forbade Langton's landing in England, although it was his native country. The Pope forthwith declared the kingdom under an interdict, or suspension of religious services. For two years the churches were hung in mourning, the bells ceased to ring, the doors were shut fast. For two years the priests denied the sacraments to the living and funeral prayers for the dead. At the end of that time the Pope, by a bull of excommunication,[1] cut off the king as a withered branch from the church. John laughed at the interdict, and met the decree of excommunication with such cruel treatment of the priests, that they fled terrified from the land. The Pope now took a third step; he deposed John, and ordered Philip of France to seize the English crown. Then John, knowing that he stood alone, made a virtue of necessity. He kneeled at the feet of the Pope's legate, or representative, accepted Stephen Langton as Archbishop of Canterbury, and promised to pay a yearly tax to Rome of 1000 marks (about $64,000 in modern money) for permission to keep his crown. The Pope was satisfied with the victory he had gained over his ignoble foe, and peace was made.

247. The Great Charter. — But peace in one direction did not mean peace in all. John's tyranny, brutality, and disregard of his subjects' welfare had gone too far. He had refused the church both the right to fill its offices and to enjoy its revenues. He had extorted exorbitant sums from the barons. He had violated the charters of London and other cities. He had compelled merchants to pay large sums for the privilege of carrying on their business unmolested. He had imprisoned men on false or frivolous charges, and refused to bring them to trial. He had unjustly

---

[1] Bull (Latin *bulla*, a leaden seal) : a decree issued by the Pope, bearing his seal.

claimed heavy sums from serfs and other poor men; and when they could not pay, had seized their carts and tools, thus depriving them of their means of livelihood. Those who had suffered these and greater wrongs were determined to have reformation, and to have it in the form of a written charter or pledge bearing the king's seal. The new archbishop was not less determined. He no sooner landed than he demanded of the king that he should swear to observe the laws of Edward the Confessor,[1] a phrase in which the whole of the national liberties was summed up.

248. Preliminary Meeting at St. Albans. — In the summer of 1213, a council was held at St. Albans, near London, composed of representatives from all parts of the kingdom. It was the first assembly of the kind on record. It convened to consider what claims should be made on the king in the interest of the nobles, the clergy, and the country. Their deliberations took shape probably under Langton's guiding hand. He had obtained a copy of the charter granted by Henry I.[2] This was used as a model for drawing up a new one of similar character, but in every respect fuller and stronger in its provisions.

249. Second Meeting. — Late in the autumn of the following year, the barons met in the abbey church of Bury St. Edmund's, in Suffolk, under their leader, Robert Fitz-Walter, of London. Advancing one by one up the church to the high altar, they solemnly swore that they would oblige John to grant the new charter, or they would declare war against him.

250. The King grants the Charter. — At Easter, 1215, the same barons, attended by two thousand armed knights, met the king at Oxford, and made known to him their demands. John tried to evade giving a direct answer. Seeing that to be impossible, and finding that London was on the side of the barons, he yielded, and requested them to name the day and place for the

---

[1] Laws of Edward the Confessor: not necessarily the laws made by that king, but rather the customs and rights enjoyed by the people during his reign.

[2] See Paragraph No. 185, and note.

ratification of the charter. "Let the day be the 15th of June, the place Runnymede,"[1] was the reply. In accordance therewith, we read at the foot of the shrivelled parchment preserved in the British museum, "Given under our hand * * in the meadow called Runnymede, between Windsor and Staines, on the 15th June, in the 17th year of our reign."

251. Terms and Value of the Charter. — By the terms of that document, henceforth to be known as Magna Carta,[2] or the Great Charter, — a term used to emphatically distinguish it from all previous and partial charters, — it was stipulated that the following grievances should be redressed: first, those of the church; second, those of the barons and their vassals or tenants; third, those of citizens and tradesmen; fourth, those of freemen and serfs. This, then, was the first agreement entered into between the king and all classes of his people. Of the sixty-three articles which constituted it, the greater part, owing to the changes of time, are now obsolete; but three possess imperishable value. These provide first, that no free man shall be imprisoned or proceeded against except by his peers, or the law of the land;[3] second, that justice shall neither be sold, denied, nor delayed; third, that all dues from the people to the king, unless otherwise distinctly specified, shall be imposed only with the consent of the National Council — an expedient which converted the power of taxation into the shield of liberty.[4] Thus, for the first time, the interests of all classes were protected, and for the first time the English people appear in the constitutional history of the country as a united body. So highly was this charter esteemed, that in the course of the next two centuries it was confirmed no less than thirty-seven

---

[1] Runnymede: about twenty miles southwest of London, on the south bank of the Thames, in Surrey.

[2] Magna Carta: *carta* is the spelling in the mediæval Latin of this and the preceding charters.

[3] Peers (from Latin *pares*), equals. This secures trial by jury.

[4] Mackintosh. This provision was, however, dropped in the next reign; but later the principle it laid down was firmly established.

times: and the very day that Charles II. entered London, after the civil wars of the seventeenth century, the House of Commons asked him to confirm it again.

252. John's Efforts to break the Charter. — But John had no sooner set his hand to this document than he determined to repudiate it. He hired bands of soldiers on the continent to come to his aid. The Pope also used his influence, and threatened the barons with excommunication if they persisted in enforcing the provisions of the charter.

253. The Barons invite Louis of France to aid them. — In their desperation, — for the king's mercenaries were now ravaging the country, — the barons despatched a messenger to John's sworn enemy, Philip of France, inviting him to send over his son, Louis, to free them from tyranny, and become ruler of the kingdom. He came with all speed, and soon made himself master of the southern counties.

254. The King's Death. — John had styled himself on his great seal "King of England"; thus formally claiming the actual ownership of the realm. He was now to find that the sovereign who has no place in his subjects' hearts has small hold of their possessions.

The rest of his ignominious reign was spent in war against the barons and Louis of France. "They have placed twenty-four kings over me!" he shouted, in his fury, referring to the twenty-four leading men who had been appointed to see that the charter did not become a dead letter. But the twenty-four did their duty, and the battle went on. In the midst of it John suddenly died, as the old record said, "a knight without truth, a king without justice, a Christian without faith." He was buried in Worcester Cathedral, wrapped in a monk's gown, and placed, for further protection, between the bodies of two Saxon saints.

255. Summary. — John's reign may be regarded as a turning-point in English history.

1. Through the loss of Normandy, the Norman nobility found it for their interest to make the welfare of England and of the English race one with their own. Thus the two peoples became more and more united, until finally all differences ceased.

2. In demanding and obtaining the Great Charter, the church and the nobility made common cause with the people. That document represents the victory, not of a class, but of the nation. The next eighty years will be mainly taken up with the effort of the nation to hold fast what it has gained.

HENRY III. — 1216-1272.

256. Accession and Character. — John's eldest son Henry was crowned at the age of nine. During his long and feeble reign England's motto might well have been the words of Ecclesiastes, "Woe to thee, O land, when thy king is a child!" since a child he remained to the last; for if John's heart was of millstone, Henry's was of wax. In one of his poems, written perhaps not long after Henry's death, Dante represents him as he sees him in imagination just on the borderland of purgatory. The king is not in suffering, for as he has done no particular good, so he has done no great harm; he appears, therefore, "as a man of simple life, spending his time singing psalms in a narrow valley."[1]

That shows one side of his negative character; the other was love of extravagance and vain display joined to instability of purpose.

257. Reissue of the Great Charter. — Louis, the French prince who had come to England in John's reign as an armed claimant to the throne, finding that both the barons and the church preferred an English to a foreign king, now retired. During his minority Henry's guardians twice reissued the great charter: first, with the omission of the article which reserved the power of taxation to the National Council, and finally with an addition declaring that no man should lose life or limb for hunting in the royal forests.

---

[1] Dante's Purgatory, vii. 131.

On the last occasion the council granted the king in return a fifteenth of their movable or personal property. This tax, as it reached a large class of people like merchants in towns, who were not landholders, had a decided influence in making them desire to have a voice in the National Council, or Parliament, as it began to be called in this reign (1246). It thus helped, as we shall see later on, to prepare the way for an important change in that body.[1]

258. Henry's Extravagance. — When Henry became of age he entered upon a course of extravagant expenditure. This, with unwise and unsuccessful wars, finally piled up debts to the amount of nearly a million of marks, or, in modern money, upwards of £13,000,000 ($65,000,000). To satisfy the clamors of his creditors he mortgaged the Jews, or rather the right of extorting money from them, to his brother Richard. He also violated charters and treaties in order to compel the nation to purchase their reissue. On the birth of his first son, Prince Edward, he showed himself so eager for congratulatory gifts, that one of the nobles present at court said, "Heaven gave us this child, but the king sells him to us."

259. His Church Building. — Still, not all of the king's extravagance was money thrown away. Everywhere on the continent magnificent churches were rising. The heavy and sombre Norman architecture, with its round arches and square, massive towers, was giving place to the more graceful Gothic style, with its pointed arch and lofty, tapering spire. The king shared the religious enthusiasm of those who built the grand cathedrals of Salisbury, Lincoln, and Ely. He himself rebuilt the greater part of Westminster Abbey as it now stands. A monument so glorious ought to make us willing to overlook some faults in the builder. Yet the expense and taxation incurred in erecting the great minster

---

[1] The first tax on movable or personal property appears to have been levied by Henry II., in 1188, for the support of the crusades. Under Henry III. the idea began to become general that no class should be taxed without their consent; out of this grew the representation of townspeople in Parliament.

must be reckoned among the causes that bred discontent and led to civil war.

260. Religious Reformation; the Friars; Roger Bacon. — While this movement, which covered the land with religious edifices, was in progress, religion itself was undergoing a change. The old monastic orders had grown rich, indolent, and corrupt. The priests had well-nigh ceased to do missionary work; preaching had almost died out. At this period a reform sprang up within the church itself. A new order of monks had arisen calling themselves in Norman French Frères,[1] or Brothers, a word which the English turned into Friars. These Brothers bound themselves to a life of self-denial and good works. From their living on charity they came to be known as Mendicant Friars. They went from place to place exhorting men to repentance, and proclaiming the almost forgotten Gospel of Christ. Others, like Roger Bacon at Oxford, took an important part in education, and endeavored to rouse the sluggish monks to make efforts in the same direction. Bacon's experiments in physical science, which was then neglected and despised, got him the reputation of being a magician. He was driven into exile, imprisoned for many years, and deprived of books and writing materials. But, as nothing could check the religious fervor of his mendicant brothers, so no hardship or suffering could daunt the intellectual enthusiasm of Bacon. When he emerged from captivity he issued his Opus Majus,[2] an "inquiry" as he called it "into the roots of knowledge." It was especially devoted to mathematics and the sciences, and deserves the name of the encyclopædia of the thirteenth century.

261. The Provisions of Oxford. — But the prodigal expenditure and mismanagement of Henry kept on increasing. At last the burden of taxation became too great to bear. Bad harvests had caused a famine, and multitudes perished even in London.

---

[1] Frères (frâr).

[2] Opus Majus: Greater Work, to distinguish it from a later summary entitled the Opus Minus, or Lesser Work.

Confronted by these evils, Parliament met in the Great Hall at Westminster. Many of the barons were in complete armor. As the king entered there was an ominous clatter of swords. Henry, looking around, asked timidly, "Am I a prisoner?"

"No, sire," answered Earl Bigod; "but we must have reform." The king agreed to summon a Parliament to meet at Oxford and consider what should be done. Their enemies nicknamed the assembly the "Mad Parliament"; but there was both method and determination in their madness, for which the country was grateful. With Simon de Montfort, the king's brother-in-law, at their head, they drew up a set of articles or provisions to which Henry gave an unwilling assent, which practically took the government out of his inefficient hands and vested it in the control of three committees, or councils.

262. Renewal of the Great Charter. — Even this was not enough. The king was now compelled to reaffirm that Great Charter which his father had unwillingly granted at Runnymede. Standing in St. Catherine's Chapel within the partially finished church of Westminster Abbey, Henry, holding a lighted taper in his hand, in company with the chief men of the realm, swore to observe the provisions of the covenant. At the close he exclaimed, as he dashed the taper on the pavement, while all present repeated the words and the action, "So go out with smoke and stench the accursed souls of those who break or pervert this charter." There is no evidence that the king was insincere in his oath; but unfortunately his piety was that of impulse, not of principle. The compact was soon broken, and the land again stripped by taxes extorted by violence, partly to cover Henry's own extravagance, but largely to swell the coffers of the Pope, who had promised to make his son Prince Edward ruler over Sicily.

263. Growing Feeling of Discontent. — During this time the barons were daily growing more mutinous and defiant, saying that they would rather die than be ruined by the "Romans," as they called the papal power. To a fresh demand for money Earl

Bigod gave a flat refusal. "Then I will send reapers and reap your fields for you," cried the king to him. "And I will send you back the heads of your reapers," retorted the angry earl.

It was evident that the nobles would make no concessions. The same spirit was abroad which, at an earlier date, made the parliament of Merton declare, when asked to alter the customs of the country to suit the ordinances of the church of Rome, "We will not change the laws of England." So now they were equally resolved not to pay the Pope money in behalf of the king's son.

264. Civil War; Battle of Lewes. — In 1264 the crisis was reached, and war broke out between the king and his brother-in-law, Simon de Montfort, Earl of Leicester, better known by his popular name of Sir Simon the Righteous.

With fifteen thousand Londoners, and a number of the barons, he met Henry, who had a stronger force, on the heights above the town of Lewes, in Sussex. The result of the great battle fought there, was as decisive as that fought two centuries before by William the Conqueror, not many miles distant on the same coast.[1]

265. De Montfort's Parliament; the House of Commons (1265). — Bracton, the foremost jurist of that day, said in his comments on the dangerous state of the times, "If the king were without a bridle, — that is, the law, — his subjects ought to put a bridle on him."

Earl Simon had that bridle ready, or rather he saw clearly where to get it. The battle of Lewes had gone against Henry, who had fallen captive to De Montfort. As head of the state the earl now called a parliament, which differed from all its predecessors in the fact that for the first time two citizens from each city, and two townsmen from each borough, or town, together with two knights, or country gentlemen, from each county, were summoned to London to join the barons and clergy in their deliberations. Thus, in the winter of 1266, that House of Commons, or legislative

---

[1] The village of Battle, which marks the spot where the battle of Hastings was fought, 1066, is less than twenty miles east of Lewes.

assembly of the people, originated, which, when fully established in the next reign, was to sit for more than three hundred years in the chapter-house[1] of Westminster Abbey. At last those who had neither land nor rank, but who paid taxes on personal property only, had obtained representation. Henceforth the king had a bridle which he could not shake off. Henceforth Magna Carta was no longer to be a dead parchment promise of reform, rolled up and hidden away, but was to become a living, ever-present, effective truth.

From this date the Parliament of England began to lose its exclusive character and to become a true representative body standing for the whole nation, and hence the model of every such assembly which now meets, whether in the old world or the new; the beginning of what President Lincoln called, "government of the people, by the people, for the people."

266. Earl Simon's Death. — Yet the same year brought for the earl a fatal reaction. The barons, jealous of his power, fell away from him. Edward, the king's eldest son, gathered them round the royal standard to attack and crush the man who had humiliated his father. De Montfort was at Evesham;[2] from the top of the church tower he saw the prince approaching. "Commend your souls to God," he said to the faithful few who stood by him; "for our bodies are the foes'!" There he fell. In the north aisle of Westminster Abbey, not far from Henry's tomb, may be seen the emblazoned arms of the brave earl. England, so rich in effigies of her great men, so faithful, too, in her remembrance of them, has not yet set up in the vestibule of the House of Commons among the statues of her statesmen, the image of him who was in many respects the leader of them all, and the real originator and founder of the House itself.

267. Summary. — Henry's reign lasted over half a century. During that period England, as we have seen, was not standing

---

[1] Chapter-house: the building where the chapter or governing body of an abbey or cathedral meet to transact business.

[2] Evesham, Worcestershire.

still. It was an age of reform. In religion, the Mendicant Friars were exhorting men to better lives. In education, Roger Bacon and other devoted scholars were laboring to broaden knowledge and deepen thought. In political affairs the people through the House of Commons now first obtained a voice. Henceforth the laws will be in a measure their work, and the government will reflect in an ever-increasing degree their will.

EDWARD I.—1272-1307.[1]

268. Edward I. and the Crusades.—Henry's son, Prince Edward, was in the East, fighting the battles of the crusades, at the time of his father's death. According to an account given in an old Spanish chronicle, his life was saved by the devotion of his wife Eleanor, who, when her husband was assassinated with a poisoned dagger, heroically sucked the poison from the wound.

269. Edward's First Parliament.—Shortly after his return to England, he convened a parliament, to which the representatives of the people were summoned. This body declared that all previous laws should be impartially executed, and that there should be no interference with elections.[2] Thus it will be seen that though Earl Simon was dead, his work went on. Edward had the wisdom to adopt and perfect the example his father's conqueror had left. By him, though not until near the close of his reign (1295), Parliament was firmly established, in its twofold form, of Lords and Commons,[3] and became "a complete image of the nation."

270. Conquest of Wales; Birth of the first Prince of Wales. —Henry II. had labored to secure unity of law for England. Edward's aim was to bring the whole island of Britain under one ruler. On the West, Wales only half acknowledged the power of the English king, while on the north, Scotland was practically an

---
[1] Edward I. was not crowned until 1274.
[2] The First Statute of Westminster.
[3] Lords: this term should be understood to include the higher clergy.

independent sovereignty. The new king determined to begin by annexing the first-named country to the crown. He accordingly led an army thither, and, after several victorious battles, considered that he had gained his end. To make sure of his new possessions, he erected the magnificent castles of Conway, Beaumaris, Harlech, and Caernarvon, all of which were permanently garrisoned with bodies of troops ready to check revolt.

In the last-named stronghold, tradition still points out a little dark chamber, more like a state-prison cell than a royal apartment, where Edward's son, the first Prince of Wales, was born. The Welsh had vowed that they would never accept an Englishman as king; but the young prince was a native of their soil, and certainly in his cradle, at least, spoke as good Welsh as their own children of the same age. No objection, therefore, could be made to him; by this happy compromise, it is said, Wales became a principality joined to the English crown.[1]

271. Conquest of Scotland; the Stone of Scone. — An opportunity now presented itself for Edward to assert his power in Scotland. Two claimants, both of Norman descent, had come forward demanding the crown.[2] One was John Baliol; the other, Robert Bruce, an ancestor of the famous king and general of that name, who comes prominently forward some years later. Edward

---

[1] Wales was not wholly incorporated with England until two centuries later, in the reign of Henry VIII. It then obtained local self-government and representation in Parliament.

[2] Scotland: At the time of the Roman conquest of Britain, Scotland was inhabited by a Celtic race nearly akin to the primitive Irish, and more distantly so to the Britons. In time, the Saxons from the continent invaded the country, and settled on the lowlands of the East, driving back the Celts to the western highlands. Later, many English emigrated to Scotland, especially at the time of the Norman Conquest, where they found a hearty welcome. In 1072, William the Conqueror compelled the Scottish king to acknowledge him as overlord; and eventually so many Norman nobles established themselves in Scotland, that they constituted the chief landed aristocracy of the country. The modern Scottish nation, though it keeps its Celtic name (Scotland), is made up in great measure of inhabitants of English descent, the pure Scotch being confined mostly to the Highlands, and ranking in population only as about one to three of the former.

was invited by the contestants to settle the dispute. He decided in Baliol's favor, but insisted, before doing so, that the latter should acknowledge the overlordship of England, as the king of Scotland had done to William I. Baliol made a virtue of necessity, and agreed to the terms; but shortly after formed a secret alliance with France against Edward, which was renewed from time to time, and kept up between the two countries for three hundred years. It is the key to most of the wars in which England was involved during that period. Having made this treaty, Baliol now openly renounced his allegiance to the English king. Edward at once organized a force, attacked Baliol, and compelled the country to acknowledge him as ruler. At the Abbey of Scone, near Perth, the English seized the famous "Stone of Destiny," the palladium of Scotland, on which her kings were crowned. Carrying the trophy to Westminster Abbey, Edward enclosed it in that ancient coronation chair which has been used by every sovereign since, from his son's accession down to that of Victoria.

272. Confirmation of the Charters. — Edward next prepared to attack France. In great need of money, he demanded a large sum from the clergy, and seized a quantity of wool in the hands of the merchants. The barons, alarmed at these arbitrary measures, insisted on the king's reaffirming all previous charters of liberties, including the Great Charter, with certain additions expressly providing that no money or goods should be taken by the crown except by the consent of the people. Thus out of the war, England "gained the one thing it needed to give the finishing touch to the building-up of Parliament; namely, a solemn acknowledgment by the king that the nation alone had power to levy taxes."[1]

273. Revolt and Death of Wallace. — Scotland, however, was not wholly subdued. The patriot, William Wallace rose and led his countrymen against the English — led them with that impetuous valor which breathes in Burns' lines: —

---

[1] Rowley, Rise of the English People.

"Scots wha ha'e wi' Wallace bled."

But fate was against him. After eight years of desperate fighting, the valiant soldier was captured, executed on Tower Hill as a traitor, and his head, crowned in mockery with a wreath of laurel, set on a pike on London Bridge.

But though the hero who perished on the scaffold could not prevent his country from becoming one day a part of England, he did hinder its becoming so on unfair and tyrannical terms. "Scotland is not Ireland. No; because brave men arose there, and said, 'Behold, ye must not tread us down like slaves,—and ye shall not,—and ye cannot!'"[1]

274. Expulsion of the Jews. — The darkest stain on Edward's reign was his treatment of the Jews. Up to this period that unfortunate race had been protected by the kings of England as men protect the cattle which they fatten for slaughter. So long as they accumulated money, and so long as the sovereign could rob them of their accumulations when he saw fit, they were worth guarding. A time had now come when the populace demanded their expulsion from the island, on the ground that their usury and extortion were ruining the country. Edward yielded to the clamor, and first stripping the Jews of their possessions, he prepared to drive them into exile. It is said that even their books were taken from them and given to the libraries of Oxford. Thus pillaged, they were forced to leave the realm — a miserable procession, numbering some sixteen thousand. Many perished on the way, and so few ventured to return, that for four centuries and a half, until Cromwell came to power, they practically disappear from English history.

275. Death of Queen Eleanor. — Shortly after this event, Queen Eleanor died. The king showed the love he bore her in the crosses he raised to her memory, three of which still stand.[2]

---

[1] Carlyle, Past and Present.

[2] Originally there were thirteen of these crosses. Of these, three remain; viz., at Northampton, at Geddington, near by, and at Waltham, about twelve miles northeast of London.

These were erected at the places where her body was set down, in its transit from Grantham, in Lincolnshire, where she died, to the little village of Charing (now Charing Cross, the geographical centre of London), its last station before reaching its final resting-place, in that abbey at Westminster, which holds such wealth of historic dust. Around her tomb wax-lights were kept constantly burning, until the Protestant Reformation extinguished them, three hundred years later.

276. Edward's Reforms; Statute of Winchester. — The condition of England when Edward came to the throne was far from settled. The country was overrun with marauders. To suppress these, the Statute of Winchester made the inhabitants of every district punishable by fines for crimes committed within their limits. Every walled town had to close its gates at sunset, and no stranger could be admitted during the night unless some citizen would be responsible for him.

To clear the roads of the robbers that infested them, it was ordered that all highways between market towns should be kept free of underbrush for two hundred feet on each side, in order that desperadoes might not lie in ambush for travellers.

Every citizen was required to keep arms and armor, according to his condition in life, and to join in the pursuit and arrest of criminals.

277. Land Legislation. — Two important statutes were passed during this reign, respecting the free sale or transfer of land.[1]

Their effect was to confine the great estates to the hands of their owners and direct descendants, or, when land changed hands, to keep alive the claims of the great lords or the crown upon it. These laws rendered it difficult for landholders to evade, as they hitherto frequently had, their feudal duties to the king by the sale

---

[1] These laws may be regarded as the foundation of the English system of landed property: they completed the feudal claim to the soil established by William the Conqueror. They are known as the Second Statute of Westminster (De Donis, or Entail, 1285) and the Third Statute of Westminster (Quia Emptores, 1290).

or subletting of estates. While they often built up the great families, they also operated to strengthen the power of the crown at the very time when that of Parliament and the people was increasing as a check upon its authority.

278. Legislation respecting the Church. — A third enactment checked the undue increase of church property. Through gifts and bequests the clergy had become owners of a very large part of the most fertile soil of the realm. No farms, herds of cattle, or flocks of sheep compared with theirs. These lands were said to be in mortmain, or "dead hands"; since the church, being a corporation, never let go its hold, but kept its property with the tenacity of a dead man's grasp. The clergy constantly strove to get these church lands exempted from furnishing soldiers, or paying taxes to the king. Instead of men or money they offered prayers. Practically, the government succeeded from time to time in compelling them to do considerably more than this, but seldom without a violent struggle, as in the case of Henry II. and Becket. On account of these exemptions it had become the practice with many persons who wished to escape bearing their just share of the support of the government, to give their lands to the church, and then receive them again as tenants of some abbot or bishop. In this way they evaded their military and pecuniary obligations to the crown. To put a stop to this practice, and so make all landed proprietors do their part, a law was passed[1] requiring the donor of an estate to the church to obtain a royal license; which it is perhaps needless to say was not readily granted.[2]

279. Death of Edward. — Edward died while endeavoring to subdue a revolt in Scotland, in which Robert Bruce, grandson of the first of that name, had seized the throne. His last request was that his son Edward should continue the war. "Carry my bones before you on your march," said the dying king, "for the rebels will not be able to endure the sight of me, alive or dead!"

---

[1] Statute of Mortmain, 1279.
[2] See note on Clergy, Paragraph No. 200.

280. Summary. — During Edward I.'s reign, the following changes took place: —

1. Wales and Scotland were conquered, and the first remained permanently a part of the English kingdom.

2. The landed proprietors of the whole country were made more directly responsible to the crown.

3. The excessive growth of church property was checked.

4. Laws for the better suppression of acts of violence were enacted and rigorously enforced.

5. The Great Charter, with additional articles for the protection of the people, was confirmed by the king, and the power of taxation expressly acknowledged to reside in Parliament only.

6. Parliament, a legislative body now representing all classes of the nation, was permanently organized, and for the first time regularly and frequently summoned by the king.[1]

EDWARD II. — 1307-1327.

281. Accession and Character. — The son to whom Edward left his power was in every respect his opposite. The old definition of the word "king," was "the man who *can*," or the able man. The modern explanation usually makes him "the chief or head of a people." Edward II. would satisfy neither of these definitions. He lacked all disposition to do anything himself; he equally lacked power to incite others to do. By nature he was a jester, trifler, and waster of time. Being such, it is hardly necessary to say that he did not push the war with Scotland. Robert Bruce did not expect that he would; that valiant fighter, indeed, held the new English sovereign in utter contempt, saying that he feared the dead father much more than the living son.

---

[1] It will be remembered that De Montfort's Parliament, in 1265, was not regularly and legally summoned, since the king (Henry III.) was at that time a captive. The first Parliament (including a House of Commons, Lords, and Clergy) which was convened by the crown, was that called by Edward I. in 1295.

282. Piers Gaveston; the Lords Ordainers. — During the first five years of his reign, Edward did little more than lavish wealth and honors on his chief favorite and adviser, Piers Gaveston, a Frenchman who had been his companion and playfellow from childhood. While Edward I. was living, Parliament had with his sanction banished Gaveston from the kingdom, as a man of corrupt practices, but Edward II. was no sooner crowned, than he recalled him, and gave him the government of the realm during his absence in France, on the occasion of his marriage. On his return, the barons protested against the monopoly of privileges by a foreigner, and the king was obliged to consent to his banishment. He soon came back, however, and matters went on from bad to worse. Finally, the indignation of the nobles rose to such a pitch, that at the council held at Westminster the government was virtually taken from the king's hands and vested in a body of barons and bishops. The head of this committee was the king's cousin, the Earl of Lancaster; and from the ordinance which they drew up for the management of affairs they got the name of the Lords Ordainers. Gaveston was now sent out of the country for a third time; but the king persuaded him to return, and gave him the office of secretary of state. This last insult — for so the Lords Ordainers regarded it — was too much for the nobility to bear. They resolved to exile the hated favorite once more, but this time to send him "to that country from which no traveller returns." Edward taking the alarm, placed Gaveston in Scarborough Castle[1] for safety. The barons besieged it, starved Gaveston into surrender, and beheaded him forthwith. Thus ended the first favorite.

283. Scotland regains its Independence. — Seeing Edward's lack of manly fibre, Robert Bruce, who had been crowned king of the Scots, determined to make himself ruler in fact as well as in name. He had suffered many defeats; he had wandered a fugitive in forests and glens; he had been hunted with bloodhounds like a wild beast; but he had never lost courage or hope. On the field

---

[1] Scarborough: on the coast of Yorkshire.

of Bannockburn he once again met the English, and in a bloody and decisive battle drove them back like frightened sheep into their own country. By this victory, Bruce re-established the independence of Scotland — an independence which continued until the rival kingdoms were peaceably united under one crown, by the accession of a Scotch king to the English throne.[1]

284. The New Favorites; the King made Prisoner. — For the next seven years the Earl of Lancaster had his own way in England. During this time Edward, whose weak nature needed some one to lean on, had got two new favorites, — Hugh Despenser and his son. They were men of more character than Gaveston; but as they cared chiefly for their own interests, they incurred the hatred of the baronage.

The king's wife, Isabelle of France, now turned against him. She had formerly acted as a peacemaker, but from this time did all in her power to the contrary. Roger Mortimer, one of the leaders of the barons, was the sworn enemy of the Despensers. The queen had formed a guilty attachment for him. Together they plotted the ruin of Edward and his favorites. They raised a force, seized and executed the Despensers, and then took the king prisoner.

285. Deposition and Murder of the King. — Having imprisoned Edward in Kenilworth Castle,[2] the barons now resolved to remove him from the throne. Parliament drew up articles of deposition against him, and appointed commissioners to demand his resignation of the crown. When they went to the castle, Edward appeared before them clad in deep mourning. Presently he sank fainting to the floor. On his recovery he burst into a fit of weeping. Then, checking himself, he thanked Parliament through the commissioners for having chosen his eldest son Edward, a boy of fourteen, to rule over the nation.

Judge Trussel then stepped forward and said: "Unto thee, O

---

[1] James VI. of Scotland and I. of England, in 1603.
[2] Kenilworth Castle, Warwickshire.

king, I, William Trussel, in the name of all men of this land of England and speaker of this Parliament, renounce to you, Edward, the homage [oath of allegiance] that was made to you some time; and from this time forth I defy thee and deprive thee of all royal power, and I shall never be attendant on thee as king from this time."

Then Sir Thomas Blount, steward of the king's household, advanced, broke his staff of office before the king's face, and proclaimed the royal household dissolved.

Edward was soon after committed to Berkeley Castle,[1] in Gloucestershire. There, by the order of Mortimer, with the connivance of queen Isabelle, the "she-wolf of France," who acted as his companion in iniquity, the king was secretly and horribly murdered.

286. Summary. — The lesson of Edward II.'s career is found in its culmination. Other sovereigns had been guilty of misgovernment, others had had unworthy and grasping favorites, but he was the first whom Parliament had deposed. By that act it became evident that great as was the power of the king, there had now come into existence a greater still, which could not only make but unmake him who sat on the throne.

EDWARD III. — 1327-1377

287. Edward's Accession; Execution of Mortimer. — Edward III., son of Edward II., was crowned at fourteen. Until he became of age, the government was nominally in the hands of a council, but really in the control of Queen Isabelle and her "gentle Mortimer," the two murderers of his father. Early in his reign Edward attempted to reconquer Scotland, but failing in his efforts, made a peace acknowledging the independence of that country. At home,

---

[1] Berkeley Castle continues in the possession of the Berkeley family. It is considered one of the finest examples of feudal architecture now remaining in England. Over the stately structure still floats the standard borne in the crusades by an ancestor of the present Lord Berkeley.

however, he now gained a victory which compensated him for his disappointment in not subduing the Scots.

Mortimer was staying with Queen Isabelle at Nottingham Castle. Edward obtained entrance by a secret passage, carried him off captive, and soon after brought him to the gallows. He next seized his mother, the queen, and kept her in confinement for the rest of her life in Castle Rising, Norfolk.

288. The Rise of English Commerce. — The reign of Edward III. is directly connected with the rise of a flourishing commerce with the continent. In the early ages of its history England was almost wholly an agricultural country. At length the farmers in the eastern counties began to turn their attention to wool-growing. They exported the fleeces, which were considered the finest in the world, to the Flemish cities of Ghent and Bruges, where they were woven into cloth, and returned to be sold in the English market; for, as an old writer quaintly remarks, "the English people at that time knew no more what to do with the wool, than the sheep on whose backs it grew."[1] Through the influence of Edward's wife, Queen Philippa, who was a native of a province adjoining Flanders,[2] which was also extensively engaged in the production of cloth, woollen factories were now established at Norwich and other towns in the East of England. Skilled Flemish workmen were induced to come over, and by their help England successfully laid the foundation of one of her greatest and most lucrative industries. From that time wool was considered a chief source of the national wealth. Later, that the fact might be kept constantly in mind, a square crimson bag filled with it — the "Woolsack" — became, and still continues to be, the seat of the Lord Chancellor in the House of Lords.

---

[1] Fuller. This remark applies to the production of fine woollens only. The English had long manufactured common grades of woollen cloth, though not in any large quantity.

[2] Flanders: a part of the Netherlands or Low Countries. The latter then embraced Holland, Belgium, and a portion of Northern France.

289. The Beginning of the Hundred Years' War (1338).—
Indirectly, this trade between England and Flanders helped to bring on a war of such duration, that it received the name of the Hundred Years' War. Flanders was at that time a dependency of France; but the great commercial towns were rapidly rising in power, and were restive and rebellious under the exactions and extortion of their feudal master, Count Louis. Their business interests bound them strongly to England; and they were anxious to form an alliance with Edward against Philip VI. of France, who was determined to bring the Flemish cities into absolute subjection.

Philip was by no means unwilling to begin hostilities with England. He had long looked with a greedy eye on the tract of country south of the Loire,[1] which remained in possession of the English kings; and only wanted a pretext for annexing it. Through his alliance with Scotland, he was threatening to attack Edward's kingdom on the north, while for some time his war-vessels had been seizing English ships laden with wool, so that intercourse with Flanders was maintained with difficulty and peril.

Edward remonstrated in vain against these outrages. At length, having concluded an alliance with Ghent, the chief Flemish city, he boldly claimed the crown of France as his lawful right,[2] and

---

[1] Aquitaine (with the exception of Poitou). At a later period the province got the name of Guienne, which was a part of it. See Map No. 8, page 88.

[2] CLAIM OF EDWARD III. TO THE FRENCH CROWN.

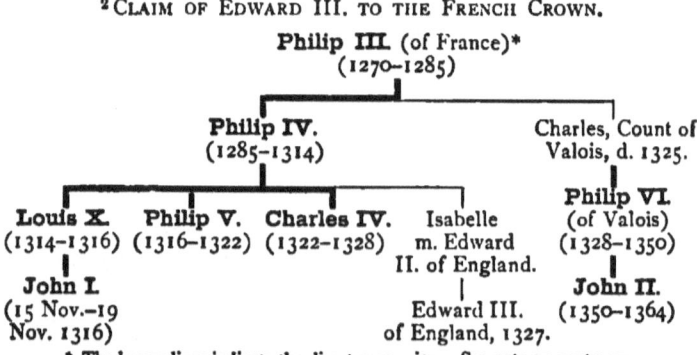

* The heavy lines indicate the direct succession. See note on next page.

followed the demand with a declaration of war. Edward based his claim on the fact that through his mother Isabelle he was nephew to the late French king, Charles IV., whereas the reigning monarch was only cousin. Nothing in the law of France justified the English sovereign in his extravagant pretensions, though, as we have seen, he had good cause for attacking Philip on other grounds.

290. Battle of Crécy[1] (1346). — For the next eight years, fighting between the two countries was going on pretty constantly on both land and sea, but without decisive results. Edward was pressed for money, and had to resort to all sorts of expedients to get it, even to pawning his own and the queen's crown, to raise enough to pay his troops. At last he succeeded in equipping a strong force, and with his son Edward, a lad of fifteen, invaded Normandy.[2]

His plan seems to have been to attack the French army in the South of France; but after landing he changed his mind, and determined to ravage Normandy, and then march north to meet his Flemish allies, who were advancing to join him. At Crécy, near the coast, on the way to Calais, a desperate battle took place. The French had the larger force, but Edward the better position. Philip's army included a number of hired Genoese cross-bowmen, on whom he placed great dependence; but a thunder-storm had wet their bowstrings, which rendered them nearly useless, and, as they advanced toward the English, the

---

When, in 1328, Charles IV. of France died without leaving a son, his cousin, Philip of Valois, succeeded him as Philip VI. (the French law excluding females from the throne). Edward III. of England claimed the crown, because through his mother Isabelle he was nephew to the late king, Charles IV. The French replied, with truth, that his claim was worthless, since he could not inherit from one who could not herself have ascended the throne.

[1] Crécy (kray-see).

[2] He landed near Cherbourg, opposite the Isle of Wight, crossed the Seine not very far below Paris, — the bridges having been destroyed up to that point, — and then marched for Calais by way of Crécy, a village near the mouth of the river Somme. See Map No. 9, page 130.

afternoon sun shone so brightly in their eyes, that they could not take accurate aim. The English archers, on the other hand, had kept their long-bows in their cases, so that the strings were dry and ready for action.

In the midst of the fight, the Earl of Warwick, who was hard pressed by the enemy, became alarmed for the safety of young Prince Edward. He sent to the king, asking reinforcements. "Is my son killed?" asked the king. "No, sire, please God!" "Is he wounded?" "No, sire." "Is he thrown to the ground?" "No, sire; but he is in great danger." "Then," said the king, "I shall send no aid. Let the boy win his spurs;[1] for I wish, if God so order it, that the honor of the victory shall be his." The father's wish was gratified. From that time the "Black Prince," as the French called him, from the color of his armor, became a name renowned throughout Europe. The battle, however, was gained, not by his bravery or that of the nobles who supported him, but by the sturdy English yeomen, who shot their keen white arrows so thick and fast, and with such deadly aim, that a writer who was present on the field compared them to a shower of snow. It was that fatal snow-storm which won the day.[2]

291. Use of Cannon; Chivalry. — At Crécy small cannon appear to have been used for the first time, though gunpowder was probably known to the English monk, Roger Bacon, many years before. The object of the cannon was to frighten and annoy the

---

[1] Spurs were the especial badge of knighthood. It was expected of every one who attained that honor that he should do some deed of valor; this was called "winning his spurs."

[2] The English yeomen, or country people, excelled in the use of the long-bow. They probably learned its value from their Norman conquerors, who employed it with great effect at the battle of Hastings. Writing at a much later period Bishop Latimer said: "In my tyme my poore father was as diligent to teach me to shote as to learne anye other thynge. * * * He taught me how to drawe, how to laye my bodye in my bowe, and not to drawe wyth strength of armes as other nacions do, but with strength of the bodye. I had bowes boughte me accordyng to my age and strength; as I encreased in them, so my bowes were made bigger, and bigger, for men shal neuer shot well, excepte they be broughte up in it." The advantage of this weapon over the steel cross-bow (used by the Genoese) lay in the fact that it could

horses of the French cavalry. They were laughed at as ingenious toys; but in the course of the next two centuries those toys revolutionized warfare and made the steel-clad knight little more than a tradition and a name.

In its day, however, knighthood did the world good service. Chivalry aimed to make the profession of arms a noble instead of a brutal calling. It gave it somewhat of a religious character. It taught the warrior the worth of honor, truthfulness, and courtesy, as well as valor — qualities which still survive in the best type of the modern gentleman. We owe, therefore, no small debt to that military brotherhood of the past, and may join the English poet in his epitaph on the order: —

> "The Knights are dust,
> Their good swords rust;
> Their souls are with the saints, we trust." [1]

292. Calais taken. — Edward now marched against Calais. He was particularly anxious to take the place, since its situation as a fortified port on the Strait of Dover, within sight of the chalk cliffs of England, would, if he captured it, give him at all times "an open doorway into France."

After besieging it for nearly a year, the garrison was starved into submission and prepared to open the gates. Edward was so exasperated with the stubborn resistance the town had made, that he resolved to put the entire population to the sword, but consented at last to spare them, on condition that six of the chief men should give themselves up to be hanged.

---

be discharged much more rapidly; the latter being a cumbrous affair, which had to be wound up with a crank for each shot. Hence the English long-bow was to that age what the revolver is to ours. It sent an arrow with such force that only the best armor could withstand it. The French peasantry at that period had no skill with this weapon; and about the only part they took in a battle was to stab horses and despatch wounded men.

Scott, in the Archery Contest in Ivanhoe (Chap. XIII.) has given an excellent picture of the English bowman.

[1] Coleridge (altered by Scott?), The Knight's Tomb.

A meeting was called, and St. Pierre, the wealthiest citizen of the place, volunteered, with five others, to go forth and die.

Bareheaded, barefooted, with halters round their necks, they silently went out, carrying the keys of the city. When they appeared before the English king, he ordered the executioner, who was standing by, to seize them and carry out the sentence forthwith; but Queen Philippa, who had accompanied her husband, now fell on her knees before him, and with tears, begged that they might be forgiven. For a long time Edward was inexorable, but finally, unable to resist her entreaties, he granted her request, and the men who had dared to face death for others, found life both for themselves and their fellow-citizens.[1]

293. Victory of Poitiers[2] **(1356).** — After a long truce, war again broke out. Philip VI. had died, and his son, John II., now sat on the French throne. Edward, during this campaign, ravaged Northern France. The next year his son, the Black Prince, marched from Bordeaux into the heart of the country.

Reaching Poitiers[3] with a force of ten thousand men, he found himself nearly surrounded by a French army of sixty thousand. He so placed his troops amidst the narrow lanes and vineyards, that the enemy could not attack him with their full strength. Again the English archers gained the day, and King John himself was taken prisoner and carried in triumph to England.

294. Peace of Brétigny[4] **(1360).** — The victory of Poitiers was followed by another truce; then war began again. Edward intended besieging Paris, but was forced to retire to obtain provisions for his troops. Negotiations were now opened by the French. While they were going on, a terrible thunder-storm destroyed great numbers of men and horses in Edward's camp. Edward, believing it a sign of the displeasure of Heaven against his expedition, fell on his knees, and within sight of the Cathedral of Chartres

---

[1] See Froissart's Chronicles.
[2] Poitiers (Pwă-te-ā'), nearly like Pwĭ-te-ā'.
[3] Poitiers, near a southern branch of the Loire. See Map No. 9, page 130.
[4] Brétigny (bray-teen-yee').

No. 9.

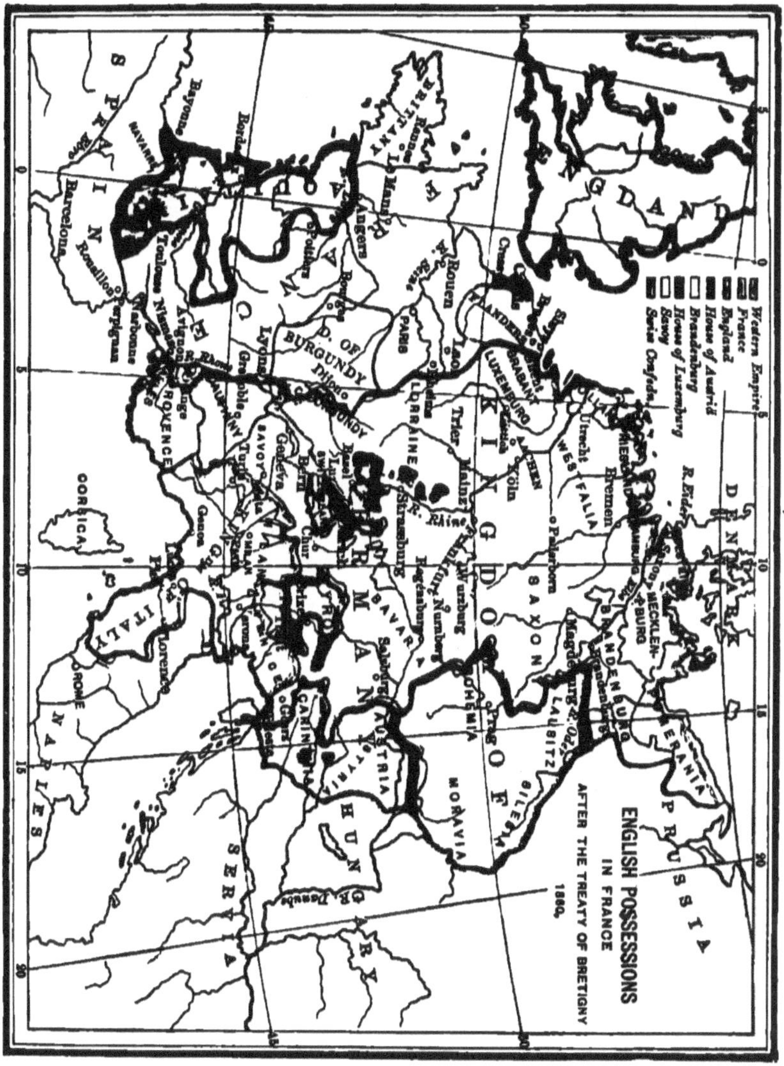

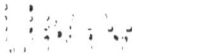

To face page 130.

vowed to make peace. A treaty was accordingly signed at Brétigny near by. By it, Edward renounced all claim to Normandy and the French crown.[1] France, on the other hand, acknowledged the right of England, in full sovereignty, to the country south of the Loire, together with Calais, and agreed to pay an enormous ransom in gold for the restoration of King John.

295. Effects of the French Wars in England. — The great gain to England from these wars was not in the territory conquered, but in the new feeling of unity they aroused among all classes. For generations afterward, the memory of the brave deeds achieved in those fierce contests on a foreign soil made the glory of the Black Prince, whose rusty helmet and dented shield still hang above his tomb in Canterbury Cathedral,[2] one with the glory of the plain bowmen, whose names are found only in country churchyards.

Henceforth, whatever lingering feeling of jealousy and hatred had remained in England, between the Norman and the Englishman, now gradually melted away in an honest patriotic pride, which made both feel that at last they had become a united and homogeneous people.

The second effect of the wars was political. In order to carry them on, the king had to apply constantly to Parliament for money. Each time that body granted a supply, they insisted on some reform which increased their strength, and brought the crown more and more under the influence of the nation.

Thus it came to be clearly understood, that though the king held the sword, the people held the purse; and that the ruler who made the greatest concessions got the largest grants.

It was also in this reign that the House of Commons, which

---

[1] But the title of "King of France" was retained by English sovereigns down to a late period of the reign of George III.

[2] These are probably the oldest accoutrements of the kind existing in Great Britain. The shield is of embossed leather stretched over a wooden frame, and is almost as hard as metal; the helmet is of iron. See Stothard's Monumental Effigies.

now sat as a separate body, and not, as at first, with the Lords,[1] obtained the important power of impeaching, or bringing to trial before the Upper House, any of the king's ministers or council guilty of misgovernment.

About this time, also, statutes were passed which forbade appeals from the king's courts of justice to that of the Pope,[2] who was then a Frenchman, and was believed to be under French political influence.

All foreign church officials were prohibited from taking money from the English church, or interfering in any way with its management.[3]

296. The Black Death. — Shortly after the first campaign in France, a frightful pestilence broke out in London, which swept over the country, destroying upwards of half the population. The disease, which was known as the Black Death,[4] had already traversed Europe, where it had proved equally fatal. "How many amiable young persons," said an Italian writer of that period,[5] "breakfasted with their friends in the morning, who, when evening came, supped with their ancestors." In Bristol and some other English cities, the mortality was so great that the living were hardly able to bury the dead; so that all business, and, for a time even war, came to a standstill.

297. Effect of the Plague on Labor. — After the pestilence had subsided, it was impossible to find laborers enough to till the soil and shear the sheep. Those who were free now demanded higher wages, while the villeins and slaves left their masters, and roamed about the country asking pay for their work, like freemen.

It was a general agricultural strike which lasted over thirty years.

---

[1] The knights of the shire, or country gentlemen, now took their seats with the House of Commons, and as they were men of property and influence, this greatly increased the power of the representatives of the people in Parliament.

[2] First Statute of Præmunire.

[3] Statute of Provisors.

[4] Black Death: so called from the black spots it produced on the skin.

[5] Boccaccio, Decameron.

It marks the beginning of that contest between capital and labor which had such an important influence in the next reign, and which, after a lapse of five hundred years, is not yet satisfactorily adjusted.

Parliament endeavored to restore order. They passed laws forbidding any freeman from asking more for a day's work than before the plague. They gave the master the right to punish a serf who persisted in running away, by branding him on the forehead with the letter "F," for fugitive. But legislation was all in vain; the movement had begun, and parliamentary statutes could no more stop it than they could stop the ocean tide. It continued to go on until it reached its climax in the peasant insurrection led by Wat Tyler under Edward's successor, Richard II.

298. Beginning of English Literature. — During Edward's reign the first work in English prose was written. It was a volume of travels by Sir John Mandeville, who had journeyed in the East for over thirty years. On his return he wrote an account of what he had heard and seen, first in Latin, that the learned might read it; next in French, that the nobles might read it; and lastly in Engglish for the common people. He dedicated the work to the king. Perhaps the most interesting and wonderful thing in it was the statement of his belief that the world is a globe, and that a ship may sail round it "above and beneath," — an assertion which probably seemed to those who read it then as less credible than any of the marvellous stories in which his book abounds.

William Langland was writing rude verses about his "vision of Piers the Plowman," contrasting "the wealth and woe" of the world, and so helping forward that democratic outbreak which was soon to take place among those who knew the woe and wanted the wealth. John Wycliffe, a lecturer at Oxford, attacked the rich and indolent churchmen in a series of tracts and sermons, while Chaucer, who had fought on the fields of France, was preparing to bring forth the first great poem in our language.[1]

---

[1] Wycliffe and Chaucer will appear more prominently in the next reign,

299. Edward's Death. — The king's last days were far from happy. His son, the Black Prince, had died, and Edward fell into the hands of selfish favorites and ambitious schemers. The worst of these was a woman named Alice Perrers, who, after Queen Philippa was no more, got almost absolute control of the king. She stayed with him until his last sickness. When his eyes began to glaze in death, she plucked the rings from his unresisting hands, and fled from the palace.

300. Summary. — During this reign the following events deserve especial notice: —

1. The acknowledgment of the independence of Scotland.
2. The establishment of the manufacture of fine woollens in England.
3. The beginning of the Hundred Years' War, with the victories of Crécy, and Poitiers, the Peace of Brétigny, and their social and political results in England.
4. The Black Death and its results on labor.
5. The partial emancipation of the English church from the power of Rome.
6. The rise of modern literature, represented by the works of Mandeville, Langland, and the early writings of Wycliffe and Chaucer.

RICHARD II. — 1377-1399.

301. England at Richard's Accession. — The death of the Black Prince left his son Richard heir to the crown. As he was but eleven years old, Parliament provided that the government during his minority should be carried on by a council; but John of Gaunt, Duke of Lancaster, speedily got the control of affairs.[1] He was an unprincipled man, who wasted the nation's money, opposed reform, and was especially hated by the laboring classes. The times were critical. War had again broken out with both Scotland and France, the French fleet was raiding the English

---

[1] John of Gaunt (a corruption of Ghent, his birthplace): he was a younger brother of Edward the Black Prince.

coast, the national treasury had no money to pay its troops, and the government debt was rapidly accumulating.

302. The New Tax; Tyler and Ball. — To raise money, it was resolved to levy a new form of tax, — a poll or head tax, — which had first been tried on a small scale during the last year of the previous reign. The attempt had been made to assess it on all classes, from laborers to lords. This imposition was now renewed in a much more oppressive form. Not only every laborer, but every member of a laborer's family above the age of fifteen, was required to pay what would be equal to the wages of an ablebodied man for at least several days' work.[1]

We have already seen that, owing to the ravages of the Black Death, and the strikes which followed, the country was on the verge of revolt. This new tax was the spark that caused the explosion. The money was roughly demanded in every poor man's cottage, and its collection caused the greatest distress. In attempting to enforce payment, a brutal collector shamefully insulted the young daughter of a workman named Wat Tyler. The indignant father, hearing the girl's cry for help, snatched up a hammer, and rushing in, struck the ruffian dead on the spot.

Tyler then collected a multitude of discontented serfs and free laborers on Blackheath Common, near London, with the determination of attacking the city and overthrowing the government.

John Ball, a fanatical priest, harangued the gathering, now sixty thousand strong, using by way of a text lines which were at that time familiar to every workingman: —

"When Adam delved and Eve span,
Who was then the gentleman?"

"Good people" he cried, "things will never go well in England so long as goods be not in common, and so long as there be

---

[1] The tax on laborers and their families varied from four to twelve pence each, the assessor having instructions to collect the latter sum, if possible. The wages of a day-laborer were then about a penny, so that the smallest tax for a family of three would represent the entire pay for nearly a fortnight's labor. See Pearson's England in the Fourteenth Century.

villeins and gentlemen. They call us slaves, and beat us if we are slow to do their bidding, but God has now given us the day to shake off our bondage."

303. The Outbreak General; Violence in London. — Twenty years before there had been similar outbreaks in Flanders and in France. This therefore was not an isolated instance of insurrection, but rather part of a general uprising. The rebellion begun by Tyler and Ball spread through the southern and eastern counties of England, taking different forms in different districts. It was violent in St. Albans, where the serfs rose against the exactions of the abbot, but it reached its greatest height in London.

For three weeks the mob held possession of the capital. They pillaged and then burned John of Gaunt's palace. They seized and beheaded the Lord Chancellor and the chief collector of the odious poll-tax, destroyed all the law papers they could lay hands on, and ended by murdering a number of lawyers; members of that profession being particularly obnoxious because they, as the rioters believed, forged the chains by which the laboring class were held in subjection.

304. Demands of the Rebels; End of the Rebellion. — The insurrectionists demanded of the king that villeinage should be abolished, that the rent of agricultural lands should be fixed by Parliament at a uniform rate in money, that trade should be free, and that a general unconditional pardon should be granted to all who had taken part in the rebellion. Richard promised redress; but while negotiations were going on, Walworth, mayor of London, struck down Tyler with his dagger, and with his death the whole movement collapsed almost as suddenly as it arose. Parliament now began a series of merciless executions, and refused to consider any of the claims which Richard had shown a disposition to listen to. In their punishment of the rebels the House of Commons vied with the Lords in severity, few showing any sympathy with the efforts of the peasants to obtain their freedom from feudal bondage. The uprising, however, was not in vain, for by it the old restrictions were in some degree loosened, so that in the course of the next century and a half villeinage was gradually abolished, and the English laborer acquired that greatest yet most perilous of all rights, the complete ownership of himself.[1] So long as he was a serf, the peasant could claim assistance from his master in sickness and old age ; in attaining independence he had to risk the danger of pauperism, which began with it — this possibility being part of the price which man must everywhere pay for the inestimable privilege of freedom.

305. The New Movement in Literature. — The same spirit which demanded emancipation on the part of the working classes showed itself in literature. We have already seen how, in the previous reign, Langland, in his poem of "Piers Plowman," gave bold utterance to the growing discontent of the times in his declaration that the rich and great destroyed the poor. In a different spirit Chaucer, "the morning-star of English song," now began to write his "Canterbury Tales," a series of stories in verse, supposed to be told by a merry band of pilgrims on their way from the Tabard-Inn, Southwark,[2] to the shrine of St. Thomas Becket in Canterbury.

There is little of Langland's complaint in Chaucer, for he was generally a favorite at court, seeing mainly the bright side of life, and sure of his yearly allowance of money and daily pitcher of wine from the royal bounty. Yet, with all his mirth, there is a vein of playful satire in his description of men and things ; and his pictures of jolly monks and easy-going churchmen, with his lines addressed to his purse "as his saviour down in this world here," show that he too was thinking, at least at times, of the manifold evils of poverty and of that danger springing from religious indifference which poor Langland had taken so much to heart.

---

[1] In Scotland villeinage lasted much longer, and so late as 1774, in the reign of George III., men working in coal and salt mines were held in a species of slavery, which was finally abolished the following year.

[2] Southwark: see note to Paragraph No. 153.

306. Wycliffe; The First English Bible. — But the real reformer of that day was John Wycliffe, rector of Lutterworth and lecturer at Oxford. He boldly attacked both the religious and political corruption of the age. The mendicant friars who at an earlier period had done such good work had now grown too rich and lazy to be of further use. Wycliffe organized a new band of brothers, known as "Poor Priests," to take up and push forward the reforms the friars had dropped. Clothed in red sackcloth cloaks, barefooted, with staff in hand, they went about from town to town[1] preaching "God's law," and demanding that church and state bring themselves into harmony with it.

The only Bible then in use was the Latin version. The people could not read a line of it, and many priests were almost as ignorant of its contents. To carry on the revival which he had begun, Wycliffe now translated the Scriptures into English. The work was copied and circulated by the "Poor Priests." But the cost of such a book in manuscript — for the printing-press had not yet come into existence — was so great that only the rich could buy the complete volume. Many, however, who had no money would give a load of farm produce for a few favorite chapters. In this way Wycliffe's translation was spread throughout the country among all classes.[2] Later, when persecution began, men hid these precious copies and read them with locked doors at night, or met in the forests to hear them expounded by preachers who went about at the peril of their lives, so that the complaint was made by Wycliffe's enemies "that common men and women who could read were better acquainted with the Scriptures than the most learned and intelligent of the clergy."

---

[1] Compare Chaucer's

"A good man ther was of religioun,
That was a poure persone [parson] of a town."
Prologue to the Canterbury Tales (479).

[2] The great number of copies sent out is shown by the fact that after the lapse of five hundred years, one hundred and sixty-five, more or less complete, are still preserved in England.

307. The Lollards; Wycliffe's Remains burned. — The followers of Wycliffe eventually became known as Lollards, or Psalm-singers.[1] From having been religious reformers denouncing the wealth and greed of a corrupt church, they would seem, at least in many cases, to have degenerated into socialists or communists, demanding, like John Ball, — who may have been one of their number, — that all property should be equally divided, and that all rank should be abolished. This fact should be borne in mind with reference to the subsequent efforts made by the government to suppress the movement. In the eye of the church, the Lollards were heretics; in the judgment of many moderate men, they were destructionists and anarchists, as unreasonable and as dangerous as the "dynamiters" of to-day.

By a decree of the church council of Constance,[2] forty-four years after Wycliffe's death the reformer's body was dug up and burned. But his influence had not only permeated England, but had passed to the continent, and was preparing the way for that greater movement which Luther was to inaugurate in the sixteenth century. Tradition says that the ashes of his corpse were thrown into a brook flowing near the parsonage of Lutterworth, the object being to utterly destroy and obliterate the remains of the arch-heretic, but, as Fuller says, "this brook did convey his ashes into the Avon, Avon into Severn, Severn into the narrow sea, and that into the wide ocean. And so the ashes of Wycliffe are the emblem of his doctrine, which is now dispersed all the world over."[3]

308. Richard's Misgovernment. — Richard's reign was unpopular with all classes. The people hated him for his extravagance;

---

[1] Or "Babblers."
[2] Constance, Southern Germany. This Council (1415) sentenced John Huss and Jerome of Prague, both of whom may be considered Wycliffites, to the stake.
[3] Fuller's Church History of Britain. Compare also Wordsworth's Sonnet to Wycliffe, and the lines, attributed to an unknown writer of Wycliffe's time: —

> "The Avon to the Severn runs,
> The Severn to the sea;
> And Wycliffe's dust shall spread abroad,
> Wide as the waters be."

the clergy, for his failing to put down the Wycliffites, with the doctrines of whose founder he was believed to sympathize; while the nobles disliked his injustice and favoritism. Some political reforms were attempted, which were partially successful; but the king soon regained his power, and took summary vengeance on the leaders, besides imposing heavy fines on the counties which had supported them. Two influential men were left, Thomas Mowbray, Duke of Norfolk, and Henry Bolingbroke, Duke of Hereford, whom he had found no opportunity to punish. After a time they openly quarrelled, and accused each other of treason. A challenge passed between them, and they were to fight the matter out in the king's presence; but when the day arrived, and they came ready for the combat, the king banished both from England. Shortly after they had left the country Bolingbroke's father, John of Gaunt, Duke of Lancaster, died. Contrary to all law, Richard now seized and appropriated the estate, which belonged by right to the banished nobleman.

309. Richard deposed and murdered. — When Bolingbroke, who was now by his father's death Duke of Lancaster, heard of the outrage, he raised a small force and returned to England, demanding the restitution of his lands.

Finding that the powerful family of the Percies were willing to aid him, and that many of the common people desired a change of government, the duke now boldly claimed the crown, on the ground that Richard had forfeited it by his tyranny, and that he stood next in succession (through his descent from Henry III.). The king now fell into Henry's hands, and events moved rapidly to a crisis. Richard had rebuilt Westminster Hall. The first Parliament which assembled there met to depose him, and to give his throne to the victorious Duke of Lancaster. Shakespeare represents the fallen monarch saying in his humiliation, —

> "With mine own tears I wash away my balm,[1]
> With mine own hand I give away my crown."

---

[1] Richard II., Act IV. Sc. 1. The balm was the sacred oil used in anointing the king at his coronation.

After his deposition Richard was confined in Pontefract Castle, Yorkshire, where he found, like his unfortunate ancestor Edward II., "that in the case of princes there is but a step from the prison to the grave." His death did not take place, however, until after Henry's accession.[1]

310. Summary. — Richard II.'s reign comprised, —

1. The peasant revolt under Wat Tyler, which led eventually to the emancipation of the villeins, or serfs.

2. Wycliffe's reformation movement; his translation of the Latin Bible, with the rise of the Lollards.

3. The publication of Chaucer's "Canterbury Tales," the first great English poem.

4. The deposition of the king, and the transfer of the crown by Parliament to Henry, Duke of Lancaster.

---

[1] Henry of Lancaster was the son of John of Gaunt, who was the fourth son of Edward III.; but there were descendants of that king's *third* son (Lionel, Duke of Clarence) living, who, of course, had a prior claim, as the following table shows.

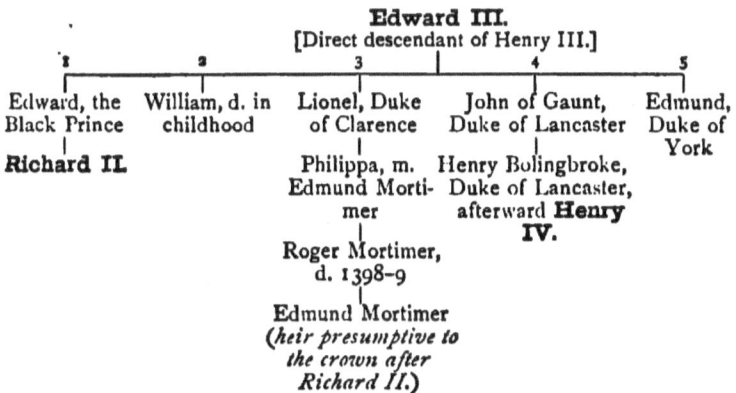

This disregard of the strict order of succession furnished a pretext for the Civil Wars of the Roses, which broke out sixty years later.

GENERAL VIEW OF THE ANGEVIN, OR PLANTAGENET, PERIOD. — 1154-1399.

I. GOVERNMENT. — II. RELIGION. — III. MILITARY AFFAIRS. — IV. LITERATURE, LEARNING, AND ART. — V. GENERAL INDUSTRY AND COMMERCE. — VI. MODE OF LIFE, MANNERS, AND CUSTOMS.

GOVERNMENT.

311. Judicial Reforms. — In 1164, Henry II. undertook, by a series of statutes called the Constitutions of Clarendon, to bring the church under the common law of the land, but was only temporarily successful. By subsequent statutes he reorganized the administration of justice, and laid the foundation of trial by jury.

312. Town Charters. — Under Richard I. many towns secured charters giving them the control of their own affairs in great measure. In this way municipal self-government arose, and a prosperous and intelligent class of merchants and artisans grew up who eventually obtained important political influence in the management of national affairs.

313. The Great, or National, Charter. — This pledge extorted from King John in 1215 put a check to the arbitrary power of the sovereign, and guaranteed the rights of all classes from the serf and the townsman to the bishop and baron. It consisted originally of sixty-three articles, founded mainly on the first royal charter (that of Henry I.), given in 1100. (See Paragraph No. 185, and note.)

It was not a statement of principles, but a series of specific remedies for specific abuses, which may be summarized as follows: —

1. The church to be free from royal interference, especially in the election of bishops.

2. No taxes except the regular feudal dues (see Paragraph No. 200), to be levied except by the consent of the National Council.

3. The Court of Common Pleas (see Paragraph No. 197, note) not to follow the king, but remain stationary at Westminster. Justice to be neither sold, denied, nor delayed. No man to be imprisoned, outlawed, punished, or otherwise molested, save by the judgment of his equals or

the law of the land. The necessary implements of all freemen, and the farming-tools of villeins or serfs, to be exempt from seizure.

4. Weights and measures to be kept uniform throughout the realm. All merchants to have the right to enter and leave the kingdom without paying exorbitant tolls for the privilege.

5. Forest laws to be justly enforced.

6. The charter to be carried out by twenty-four barons together with the mayor of London.

This document marks the beginning of a written constitution, and it proved of the highest value henceforth in securing good government. It was confirmed thirty-seven times by subsequent kings and parliaments, the confirmation of this and previous charters by Edward I. in 1297 being of especial importance.

314. Rise of the House of Commons. — In 1265, under Henry III., through the influence of Simon de Montfort, two representatives from each city and borough, or town, together with two knights of the shire, or country gentlemen, were summoned to meet with the lords and clergy in the National Council, or Parliament. From this time the body of the people began to have a voice in making the laws. Later in the period the knights of the shire joined the representatives from the towns in forming a distinct body in Parliament sitting by themselves under the name of the House of Commons. They obtained the power of levying all taxes, and also of impeaching before the House of Lords any government officer guilty of misuse of power.

315. New Class of Barons. — Under Henry III. other influential men of the realm, aside from the great landholders and barons by tenure, began to be summoned to the king's council. These were called "barons by writ." Later (under Richard II.), barons were created by open letters bearing the royal seal, and were called "barons by patent."[1]

316. Land Laws. — During this period important laws [De Donis, or Entail, and Quia Emptores] respecting land were passed, which had the effect of keeping estates in families, and also of preventing their possessors from evading their feudal duties to the king. At the same

---

[1] This is the modern method of raising a subject (*e.g.*, Lord Tennyson) to the peerage. It marks the fact that from the thirteenth century the ownership of land was no longer considered a necessary condition of nobility; and that the peerage had now developed into the five degrees, which it still maintains, of dukes, marquises, earls, viscounts, and barons.

time a restriction on the acquisition of land by the church (Statute of Mortmain), which was exempt from paying certain feudal dues, was also imposed to prevent the king's revenue from being diminished.

RELIGION.

317. Restriction of the Papal Power. — During the Angevin period the popes endeavored to introduce the canon law (a body of ordinances consisting mainly of the decisions of church councils and popes) into England, with the view of making it supreme; but Parliament, at Merton, refused to accept it, saying, " We will not change the laws of England." The Statute of Mortmain was also passed (see Paragraph No. 278) and other measures (Statute of Provisors and Statute of Præmunire), which forbade the Pope from taking the appointment of bishops and other ecclesiastics out of the hands of the clergy; and which prohibited any appeal from the king's court to the papal court. Furthermore, many hundreds of parishes, formerly filled by foreigners who could not speak English, were now given to native priests, and the sending of money out of the country to support foreign ecclesiastics was in great measure stopped.

During the crusades two religious military orders had been established, called the Knights Hospitallers and the Knights Templars. The object of the former was, originally, to provide entertainment for pilgrims going to Jerusalem; that of the latter, to protect them. Both had extensive possessions in England. In 1312 the order of Templars was broken up on a charge of heresy and evil life, and their property in England given to the Knights Hospitallers, who were also called Knights of St. John.

318. Reform. — The Mendicant Friars began a reformatory movement in the church and accomplished much good. This was followed by Wycliffe's attack on religious abuses, by his translation of the Bible, with the revival carried on by the " Poor Priests," and by the rise of the Lollards, who were eventually punished by the passage of severe laws, partly on the ground of their heretical opinions, and partly because they became in a measure identified with socialistic and communistic efforts to destroy rank and equalize property.

MILITARY AFFAIRS.

319. Scutage. — By a tax called scutage, or shield-money, levied on all knights who refused to serve the king in foreign wars, Henry II.

obtained the means to hire soldiers. By a law reviving the national militia, composed of freemen below the rank of knights, the king made himself in great measure independent of the barons, with respect to raising troops.

320. Armor; Heraldry. — The linked or mail armor now began to be superseded by that made of pieces of steel joined together so as to fit the body. This, when it was finally perfected, was called plate armor, and was both heavier and stronger than mail.

With the introduction of plate armor and the closed helmet it became the custom for each knight to wear a device, called a crest, on his helmet, and also to have one called a coat of arms (because originally worn on a loose coat over the armor). This served to distinguish him from others, and was of practical use not only to the followers of a great lord, who thus knew him at a glance, but it served in time of battle to prevent the confusion of friend and foe. Eventually, coats of arms became hereditary, and the descent, and to some extent the history, of a family can be traced by them. In this way heraldry serves as a help to the knowledge of men and events.

321. Chivalry; Tournaments. — The profession of arms was regulated by certain rules, by which each knight solemnly bound himself to serve the cause of religion and the king, and to be true, brave, and courteous to those of his own rank, to protect the ladies and succor all persons in distress. Under Edward III. chivalry reached its culmination and began to decline. One of the grotesque features of the attack on France was an expedition of English knights with one eye bandaged; this half-blind company having vowed to partially renounce their sight until they did some glorious deed. The chief amusement of the nobles and knights was the Tournament, a mock combat fought on horseback, in full armor, which sometimes ended in a real battle. At these entertainments a lady was chosen queen, who gave prizes to the victors.

322. The Use of the Long-Bow; Introduction of Cannon; Wars. — The common weapon of the yeomen, or foot-soldiers, was the long-bow. It was made of yew-tree wood, and was of the height of the user. Armed with this weapon, the English soldiers proved themselves irresistible in the French wars, the French having no native archers of any account.

Roger Bacon is supposed to have known the properties of gunpowder as early as 1250, but no practical use was made of the discovery until the battle of Crécy, 1346, when a few very small cannon are said to have been employed by the English against the enemy's cavalry. Later, they were used to throw heavy stones in besieging castles. Still later, rude hand-guns came slowly into use. From this period kings gradually began to realize the full meaning of the harmless-looking black grains, with whose flash and noise the Oxford monk had amused himself.

The chief wars of the time were the contests between the kings and the barons, Richard I.'s crusade, John's war with France, resulting in the loss of Normandy, Edward I.'s conquest of Wales and temporary subjugation of Scotland, and the beginning of the Hundred Years' War with France under Edward III.

The navy of this period was made up of small, one-masted vessels, seldom carrying more than a hundred and fifty fighting men. As the mariner's compass had now come into general use, these vessels could, if occasion required, make voyages of considerable length.

LEARNING, LITERATURE, AND ART.

323. Education. — In 1264 Walter de Merton founded the first college at Oxford, an institution which has ever since borne his name, and which really originated the English college system. During the reign of Edward III., William of Wykeham, Bishop of Winchester, gave a decided impulse to higher education by the establishment, at his own expense, of Winchester College, the first great public school founded in England. Later, he built and endowed New College at Oxford to supplement it. In Merton's and Wykeham's institutions young men of small means were instructed, and in great measure supported, without charge. They were brought together under one roof, required to conform to proper discipline, and taught by the best teachers of the day. In this way a general feeling of emulation was roused, and at the same time a fraternal spirit cultivated which had a strong influence in favor of a broader and deeper intellectual culture than the monastic schools at Oxford and elsewhere had encouraged.

324. Literature. — The most prominent historical work was that by Matthew Paris, a monk of St. Albans, written in Latin, based largely on earlier chronicles, and covering a period from the Norman Conquest, 1066, to his death, in 1259. It is a work of much value, and was continued by writers of the same abbey.

The first English prose work was a volume of travels by Sir John Mandeville, dedicated to Edward III. It was followed by Wycliffe's translation of the Bible into English from the Latin version, and by Chaucer's "Canterbury Tales," the first great English poem.

325. Architecture. — Edward I. and his successors began to build structures combining the palace with the stronghold.[1] Conway and Caernarvon Castles in Wales, Warwick Castle, Warwickshire, and a great part of Windsor Castle on the Thames, twenty-three miles west of London, are magnificent examples, the last still being occupied as a royal residence.

In churches, the massive architecture of the Normans, with its heavy columns and round arches, was followed by Early English, or the first period of the Gothic, with pointed arches, slender, clustered, columns and tapering spires like that of Salisbury Cathedral. Later the Decorated style was adopted. It was characterized by broader windows, highly ornamented to correspond with the elaborate decoration within, which gave this style its name, which is seen to best advantage in Exeter Cathedral, York Minster and Merton College Chapel.

GENERAL INDUSTRY.

326. Fairs; Guilds. — The domestic trade of the country was largely carried on during this period by great fairs held at stated times by royal license. Bunyan, in "Pilgrim's Progress," gives a vivid picture of one of these centres of trade and dissipation, under the name of "Vanity Fair." Though it represents the great fair of Sturbridge, near Cambridge, as he saw it in the 17th century, yet it undoubtedly describes similar gatherings in the time of the Plantagenets. In all large towns the merchants had formed associations for mutual protection and the advancement of trade called merchant-guilds. Artisans now instituted similar societies, under the name of craft-guilds. For a long time the merchant-guilds endeavored to shut out the craft-guilds, the men, as they said, "with dirty hands and blue nails," from having any part in the government of the towns; but eventually the latter got their full share, and in some cases, as in London, became the more

---

[1] The characteristic features of the Edwardian castles are double surrounding walls, with numerous protecting towers, and the omission of the square Norman keep.

influential party of the two. In London they still survive under the name of the "City Companies."

327. The Wool Trade. — Under Edward III. a flourishing trade in wool grew up between England and Flanders. The manufacture of fine woollen goods was also greatly extended in England. All commerce at this period was limited to certain market towns called "staples." To these places material and goods for export had to be carried in order that they might pay duty to the government before leaving the country. Imports also paid duties. If an Englishman carried goods abroad and sold them in the open market without first paying a tax to the crown, he was liable to the punishment of death.

328. The Great Strike. — The scarcity of laborers caused by the ravages of the Black Death caused a general strike for higher wages on the part of free workingmen, and also induced thousands of villeins to run away from their masters, in order to get work on their own account. The general uprising which a heavy poll-tax caused among the laboring class, though suppressed at the time, led to the ultimate emancipation of the villeins, by a gradual process extending through many generations.

MODE OF LIFE, MANNERS, AND CUSTOMS.

329. Dress; Furniture. — During most of this period great luxury in dress prevailed among the rich and noble. Silks, velvets, scarlet cloth and cloth of gold were worn by both men and women. At one time the lords and gallants at court wore shoes with points curled up like rams' horns and fastened to the knee with silver chains. Attempts were made by the government to abolish this and other ridiculous fashions, and also to regulate the cost of dress according to the rank and means of the wearer; but the effort met with small success. Even the rich at this time had but little furniture in their houses, and chairs were almost unknown. The floors of houses were strewn with rushes, which, as they were rarely changed, became horribly filthy, and were a prolific cause of sickness.

330. The Streets; Amusements; Profanity. — The streets of London and other cities were rarely more than twelve or fifteen feet wide. They were neither paved nor lighted. Pools of stagnant water and heaps of refuse abounded. There was no sewerage. The only scavengers were the crows. The houses were of timber and plaster, with projecting stories, and destructive fires were common. The chief amusements were hunting and hawking, contests at archery, and tournaments. Plays were acted by amateur companies on stages on wheels which could be moved from street to street. The subjects continued to be drawn in large measure from the Bible and from legends of the saints. They served to instruct men in Scripture history, in an age when few could read. The instruction was not, however, always taken to heart, as profane swearing was so common that an Englishman was called on the continent by his favorite oath, which the French regarded as a sort of national name before that of "John Bull" had come into use.

VII.

> "God's most dreaded instrument,
> In working out a pure intent,
> Is man — arrayed for mutual slaughter."
>
> WORDSWORTH

THE SELF-DESTRUCTION OF FEUDALISM.

BARON against BARON.

THE HOUSES OF LANCASTER AND YORK. — 1399–1485.

House of Lancaster (the Red Rose).	House of York (the White Rose).
Henry IV., 1399–1413.	Edward IV., 1461–1483.
Henry V., 1413–1422.	†Edward V., 1483.
*Henry VI., 1422–1471.	Richard III., 1483–1485.

331. Henry IV.'s Accession. — Richard II. left no children. The nearest heir to the kingdom by right of birth was the boy Edmund Mortimer, a descendant of Richard's uncle Lionel, Duke of Clarence.[1] Henry ignored Mortimer's claim, and standing before Richard's empty throne in Westminster Hall, boldly demanded the crown for himself.[2] The nation had suffered so much from the misgovernment of those who had ruled during the minor-

---

* Henry VI. deposed 1461; reinstated for a short time in 1470.
† Edward V. never crowned.
[1] See genealogical table, Paragraph No. 309.
[2] "In the name of the Father, Son, and Holy Ghost, I, Henry of Lancaster, challenge this realm of England and the crown, with all the members and the appurtenances, as that I am descended by right line of blood, coming from the good King Henry III., and through that right that God of his grace hath sent me, with help of kin and of all my friends to recover it, the which realm was in point to be undone by default of government and undoing of the good laws."

ity of Richard, that they wanted no more boy kings. Parliament, therefore, set aside the direct line of descent and accepted Henry.

332. Conspiracy in Favor of Richard. — The new king had hardly seated himself on the throne when a conspiracy was discovered, having for its object the release and restoration of Richard, still a prisoner in Pontefract Castle. The plot was easily crushed. A month later Richard was found dead. Henry had his body brought up to London and exposed to public view in St. Paul's Cathedral, in order that not only the people, but all would-be conspirators might now see that Richard's hands could never again wield the sceptre.

There was, however, one man at least who refused to be convinced. Owen Glendower, a Welshman, whom the late king had befriended, declared that Richard was still living, and that the corpse exhibited was not his body. Glendower prepared to maintain his belief by arms. King Henry mustered a force with the intention of invading Wales and crushing the rebel on his own ground; but a succession of terrible tempests ensued. The English soldiers got the idea that Glendower raised these storms, for as an old chronicle declares: "Through art magike he" [Glendower] "caused such foule weather of winds, tempest, raine, snow, and haile to be raised for the annoiance of the King's armie, that the like had not beene heard of."[1] For this reason the troops became disheartened, and the king was obliged to postpone the expedition.

333. Revolt of the Percies. — The Percy family had been active in helping Henry to obtain the throne,[2] and had spent large sums in defending the North against invasions from Scotland.[3] They expected a royal reward for these services, and were sorely disappointed because they did not get it. As young Henry Percy said of the King: —

---

[1] Holinshed's Chronicle.
[2] Thomas Percy, Earl of Worcester, with Henry Percy, Earl of Northumberland, and his son Sir Henry Percy, or "Hotspur."
[3] See the Ballad of Chevy Chase.

> "My father, and my uncle, and myself,
> Did give him that same royalty he wears;
> And,—when he was not six-and-twenty strong,
> Sick in the world's regard, wretched and low,
> A poor, unminded outlaw sneaking home,—
> My father gave him welcome to the shore:
> * * * * * * * *
> Swore him assistance and perform'd it too."[1]

But the truth is, Henry had little to give except promises. Parliament voted money cautiously, limiting its supplies to specific purposes; and men of wealth, feeling anxious about the issue of the king's usurpation,—for such many regarded it—were afraid to lend him what he required. Furthermore, the king was hampered by a council whose advice he had pledged himself to follow. For these reasons Henry's position was in every way precarious. He had no clear title to the throne, and he had no means to buy military support. In addition to these difficulties, Henry had made an enemy of Sir Henry Percy by refusing to ransom his brother-in-law, a Mortimer,[2] whom Glendower had captured, but whom the king wished well out of the way with all others of that name. Young Percy proved a dangerous foe. His hot temper and impetuous daring had got for him the title of "the Hotspur of the North." He was so fond of fighting that Shakespeare speaks of him as "he that kills me some six or seven dozen of Scots at a breakfast, washes his hands, and says to his wife, *Fie upon this quiet life! I want work.*"[3] It was this "fire-eater," who with his father, and his uncle, the Earl of Worcester, with the Scotch Earl of Douglas and Glendower, now formed an alliance to force Henry to give up the throne.

334. Battle of Shrewsbury. — At Shrewsbury, on the edge of Wales, the armies of the king and of the revolutionists met. A

---

[1] Shakespeare, Henry IV., Part I. Act IV. Sc. 3.

[2] Sir Edmund Mortimer: he was uncle to the Edmund Mortimer, Earl of March, who was heir to the crown. See Bailey's Succession to the English Crown.

[3] Shakespeare, Henry IV., Part I. Act II. Sc 4.

number of Henry's enemies had sworn to single him out in battle. The plot was divulged, and it is said thirteen knights arrayed themselves in armor resembling the king's in order to mislead the assailants. The whole thirteen perished on that bloody field, where fat Sir John Falstaff vowed he fought on Henry's behalf "a long hour by Shrewsbury clock."[1] The insurgents were utterly defeated. Douglas was taken prisoner, "Hotspur" was killed, and several of his companions were beheaded after the battle. But new insurrections arose, and the country was far from enjoying any permanent peace.

335. Persecution of the Lollards; the First Martyr. — Thus far Henry had spent much time in crushing rebels, but he had also given part of it to burning heretics. To gain the favor of the clergy, and thus render his throne more secure, the king had favored the passage of a law by the lords and bishops (for the House of Commons had no part in it), by which the Lollards and others who dissented from the doctrines of Rome would be punished with death. William Sawtrey, a London clergyman, was the first victim under the new law (1401). He had declared that he would not worship "the cross on which Christ suffered, but only Christ himself who had suffered on the cross." He had also openly denied the doctrine of transubstantiation, which teaches that the sacramental bread is miraculously changed into the actual body of the Saviour. For these and minor heresies he was burned at Smithfield, in London, in the presence of a great multitude. Some years later a second martyrdom took place. But as the English people would not allow torture to be used in the case of the Knights Templars in the reign of Edward II.,[2] so they never favored the idea that by committing the body to the flames error could thereby be burned out of the soul. The Lollards, indeed, were still cast into prison, as some of the extreme and communistic part of them doubtless deserved to be, but we hear of no more being

---

[1] Shakespeare, Henry IV., Part I. Act V. Sc. 4.
[2] See Paragraph No. 317.

put to cruel deaths during Henry's reign, though later, the utmost rigor of the law was again to some extent enforced.

336. Henry's Last Days. — Toward the close of his life the king seems to have thought of reviving the crusades for the conquest of Jerusalem, where, according to tradition, an old prediction declared that he should die. But his Jerusalem was nearer than that of Palestine. While praying at the tomb of Edward the Confessor in Westminster Abbey, he was seized with mortal illness. His attendants carried him into a room near by. When he recovered consciousness, and inquired where he was, he was told that the apartment was called the Jerusalem Chamber. "Praise be to God," he exclaimed, "then here I die!" There he breathed his last, saying to his son, young Prince Henry: —

> "God knows, my son,
> By what by-paths and indirect crook'd ways,
> I met this crown; and I myself know well
> How troublesome it sat upon my head;
> To thee it shall descend with better quiet,
> Better opinion, better confirmation;
> For all the soil of the achievement [1] goes
> With me into the earth."

337. Summary. — At the outset of his reign Parliament showed its power by changing the succession and making Henry king instead of young Edmund Mortimer, the direct hereditary heir to the crown. Though successful in crushing rebellion, Henry was obliged to submit to the guidance of a council, and was rendered more entirely dependent on Parliament, especially in the matter of supplies, than any previous king. For the first time in English history heresy was made punishable by death; yet such was the restraining influence of the people, that but two executions took place.

---

[1] "Soil of the achievement:" stain or blame by which the crown was won. Henry IV., Part II. Act IV. Sc. 4.

HENRY V. — 1413-1422.

338. Lollard Outbreak at Henry's Accession. — Henry's youth had been wild and dissolute, but the weight of the crown sobered him. He cast off poor old Jack Falstaff and his other roistering companions, and began his new duties in earnest.

Sir John Oldcastle, or Lord Cobham, was at this time the most influential man among the Lollards. He was now brought to trial and convicted of heresy. The penalty was death; but the king granted him a respite, in the hope that he might recant. Oldcastle managed to escape from prison. Immediately after, a conspiracy was detected among the Lollards for seizing the government, destroying the chief monasteries in and about London, and raising Oldcastle to power. Henry attacked the rebels unawares, killed many, and took a large number of prisoners, who were executed on a double charge of heresy and treason. Several years afterwards Oldcastle was also executed.

339. Report that Richard II. was Alive. — A strange report now began to circulate. It was said that Richard II. had been seen in Scotland, and that he was preparing to claim the throne which Henry's father had taken from him. To silence this seditious rumor, the king exhumed Richard's body from its grave in the little village of Langley, Hertfordshire. The ghastly remains were propped up in a chair of state so that all might see them. In this manner the king and his court escorted the corpse in solemn procession to Westminster Abbey, where it was re-interred among the tombs of the English sovereigns. With it he buried once for all the troublesome falsehood which had kept up insurrection, and had made the deposed king more feared after death than he had ever been during life.

340. War with France. — To divert the attention of the nation from dangerous home questions likely to cause fresh revolts, Henry now determined to act on his father's dying counsel and pick a foreign quarrel. The old grudge against France which began with the feuds of Duke William of Normandy before he conquered England, made a war with that country always popular. At this period the French were divided into fierce parties who hated each other even more, if possible, than they hated the English. This, of course, greatly increased the chances of Henry's success, as he might form an alliance with one of these factions.

The king believed it a good opportunity to get three things he wanted, — a wife, a fortune, and the French crown. The king of France and his most powerful rival, the Duke of Burgundy, had each a daughter. To make sure of one of them, Henry secretly proposed to both. After long and fruitless negotiations, the French king declined to grant the enormous dowry which the English king demanded. The latter gladly interpreted this refusal as equivalent to a declaration of war.

341. Battle of Agincourt[1] **(1415).** — Henry set to work with vigor, raised an army, and invaded France. He besieged Harfleur, near the mouth of the Seine, and took it; but his army had suffered so much from sickness that, after leaving a garrison in the place, he resolved to move north, to Calais, and await re-enforcements. After a long and perilous march he reached a little village about midway between Crécy and Calais. There he encountered the enemy in great force. Both sides prepared for battle. The French had fifty thousand troops to Henry's seven or eight thousand; but the latter had that determination which wins victories, and said to one of his nobles who regretted that he had not a larger force: —

> "No, my fair cousin;
> If we are marked to die, we are enough
> To do our country loss; and if we live,
> The fewer men, the greater share of honor."[2]

A heavy rain had fallen during the night, and the ploughed land over which the French must cross was so wet and miry that their heavily armed horsemen sank deep at every step. The English

---

[1] Agincourt (ah'zhăn'koor').
[2] Henry V., Act IV. Sc. 3.

bowmen, on the other hand, being on foot, could move with ease. Henry ordered every archer to drive a stake, sharpened at both ends, into the ground before him. This was a substitute for the modern bayonet, and presented an almost impassable barrier to the French cavalry.

As at Crécy and Poitiers, the English bowmen gained the day. The sharp stakes stopped the enemy's horses, and the blinding showers of arrows threw the splendidly armed knights into wild confusion. With a ringing cheer Henry's troops rushed forward.

> "Then down their bows they threw,
> And forth their swords they drew,
> And on the French they flew:
> No man was tardy.
> Arms from the shoulder sent;
> Scalps from the teeth they rent;
> Down the French peasants went:
> These were men hardy." [1]

When the fight was over, the king asked, "What is the name of that castle yonder?" He was told it was called Agincourt. "Then," said he, "from henceforth this shall be known as the battle of Agincourt."

342. Treaty of Troyes [2] (1420); Henry's Death. — Henry went back in triumph to England. Two years later he again invaded France. His victorious course continued. In 1420, by the Treaty of Troyes, he gained all he had planned to get. He obtained large sums of money, the French Princess Katherine in marriage, and the promise of the crown of France on the death of her father, Charles VI., who was then insane and feeble. Meantime Henry was to govern the kingdom as regent.

Henry returned to England with the bride he had won by the sword, but he was soon recalled to France by a revolt against his

---

[1] These vigorous lines, from Drayton's Ballad of Agincourt, if not quite true to the letter of history (since it is doubtful whether the French peasants were on the field), are wholly true to its spirit.

[2] Troyes (trwä).

power. He died there, leaving an infant son, Henry. Two months afterward Charles VI. died, so that by the terms of the treaty Henry's son now inherited the French crown.

343. Summary.—The one great event with which Henry V.'s name is connected is the conquest of France. It was hailed at the time as a glorious achievement, and in honor of it his tomb in Westminster Abbey was surmounted by a statue of the king having a head of solid silver. Eventually the head was stolen and never recovered. The theft was typical of Henry's short-lived victories abroad, for all the territory he had gained was soon destined to be hopelessly lost.

HENRY VI. (House of Lancaster, Red Rose).—1422-1471.[1]

344. Accession of Henry; Renewal of the French War.—The heir to all the vast dominions left by Henry V. was proclaimed king of England and France when in his cradle, and crowned, while still a child, first at Westminster and then at Paris.

But the accession to the French possessions was merely an empty form, for as the son of the late Charles VI. of France refused to abide by the Treaty of Troyes and give up the throne, war again broke out.

345. Siege of Orleans.[2]—The Duke of Bedford[3] fought vigorously in Henry's behalf. In five years the English had got possession of most of the country north of the Loire. They now determined to make an effort to drive the French prince south of that river. To accomplish this they must take the strongly fortified town of Orleans which was situated on its banks. Forts were accordingly built around the place, and cannon planted to batter down its walls. Six months later so much progress had been

---

[1] Dethroned 1461, restored for a few months in 1470, died in the Tower of London, 1471.

[2] Orleans (or' lā-on).

[3] During Henry's minority, John, Duke of Bedford, was protector of the realm. When absent in France, Humphrey, Duke of Gloucester, acted for him.

THE SELF-DESTRUCTION OF FEUDALISM.   159

made in the siege, that it was plain the city could not hold out much longer. The fortunes of France seemed to depend on the fate of Orleans. If it fell, they would go with it.

346. Joan of Arc.[1] — At this juncture, Joan of Arc, a peasant girl of eighteen, came forward to inspire her despairing countrymen with fresh courage. She believed that Heaven had called her to drive the English from the land. The troops rallied round her. Clad in white armor, mounted on a white war-horse, she led the troops from victory to victory, until she saw Prince Charles triumphantly crowned in the Cathedral of Rheims.[1] There her fortune changed. Her own people basely abandoned her. The unworthy King Charles made no attempt to protect the "Maid of Orleans," and she fell into the hands of the infuriated English, who believed she was in league with the devil. In accordance with this belief Joan was tried for witchcraft and heresy at Rouen, and sentenced to the flames. She died as bravely as she had lived, saying in her last agonies that her celestial voices had not deceived her, and that through them she had saved France.

"God forgive us," exclaimed one of Henry's courtiers who was present; "we are lost! We have burned a saint!" It was the truth; and from the martyred girl's ashes a new spirit seemed to go forth to bless her ungrateful country. The heart of France was touched. The people rose against their invaders. Before Henry VI. reached his thirtieth year the Hundred Years' War with France which Edward III. had begun, was ended, and England had lost all of her possessions on the continent, except a bare foothold at Calais.

347. Henry VI.'s Character and Marriage. — When Henry became of age he proved to be but the shadow of a king. His health and character were alike feeble. At twenty-five he married

---

[1] The name given by the English to Jeanne d'Arc, or Darc. Later, the French called her La Pucelle, "The Maid"; or La Pucelle d'Orleans, "The Maid of Orleans."
[2] Rheims (rănz).

the beautiful and unfortunate Margaret of Anjou, who was by far the better man of the two. When years of disaster came, this dauntless "queen of tears" headed councils, led armies, and ruled both king and kingdom.

348. Poverty of the Crown and Wealth of the Nobles. — One cause of the weakness of the government was its poverty. The revenues of the crown had been greatly diminished by gifts and grants to favorites. The king was obliged to pawn his jewels and the silver plate from his table to pay his wedding expenses; and it is said on high authority[1] that the royal couple were sometimes in actual want of a dinner.

On the other hand, the Earl of Warwick and other great lords had made fortunes out of the French wars,[2] and lived in regal splendor. The earl, it is said, had at his different castles and his city mansion in London, upwards of thirty thousand men in his service. Their livery, or uniform, a bright red jacket with the Warwick arms, a bear erect holding a ragged staff, embroidered on it in white, was seen, known, and feared throughout the country. Backed by such forces it was easy for the earl and other powerful lords to overawe kings, parliaments, and courts. Between these heads of the great houses quarrels were constantly breaking out. The safety of the people was endangered by these feuds, which became more and more violent, and often ended in bloodshed and murder.

349. Disfranchisement of the Commons. — With the growth of power on the part of the nobles, there was also imposed for the first time a restriction on the right of the people to vote for members of Parliament. Up to this period all freemen might take part in the election of representatives chosen by the counties to sit in the House of Commons.

---

[1] Fortescue, on the Governance of England (Plummer).

[2] First, by furnishing troops to the government, the feudal system having now so far decayed that many soldiers had to be hired; second, by the plunder of French cities; third, by ransoms obtained from noblemen taken prisoners.

A law was now passed forbidding any one to vote at these elections unless he was a resident of the county and possessed of landed property yielding an annual income of forty shillings ($200).[1] Subsequently it was further enacted that no county candidate should be eligible unless he was a man of means and social standing. These two measures were blows against the free self-government of the nation, since their manifest tendency was to make the House of Commons represent the property rather than the people of the country.

350. Cade's Rebellion. — In 1450 a formidable rebellion broke out in Kent, then, as now, one of the most independent and democratic counties in England. The leader was Jack Cade, who called himself by the popular name of Mortimer, claiming to be cousin to Richard, Duke of York, a nephew of that Edmund Mortimer, now dead, whom Henry IV. had unjustly deprived of his succession to the crown.

Cade, who was a mere adventurer, was quite likely used as a tool by plotters much higher than himself, who, by putting him forward, could thus judge whether the country was ready for a revolution and change of sovereigns.

Wat Tyler's rebellion, seventy years before, was almost purely social in its character, having for its object the emancipation of the enslaved laboring classes. Cade's insurrection was, on the contrary, almost wholly political. His chief complaint was that the people were not allowed their free choice in the election of representatives, but were forced by the nobility to choose candidates they did not want.

Other grievances for which reform was demanded were excessive taxation and the rapacity of the evil counsellors who controlled the king.

Cade entered London with a body of twenty thousand men.

---

[1] The income required by the statute was forty shillings, which, says Freeman, we may fairly call forty pounds of our present money. See Freeman's Growth of the English Constitution, p. 97.

He took formal possession of the place by striking his sword on London Stone, — a Roman monument still standing, which then marked the centre of the ancient city, — saying, as Shakespeare reports him, "Now is Mortimer lord of this city."[1] After three days of riot and the murder of the king's treasurer, the rebellion came to an end through a general pardon. Cade, however, endeavored to raise a new insurrection in the South, but was shortly after captured, and died of his wounds.

351. Wars of the Roses (1455–1485). — The real significance of Cade's insurrection is that it showed the wide-spread feeling of discontent caused by misgovernment, and that it served as an introduction to the long and dreary period of civil strife known as the Wars of the Roses. So long as the English nobles had France for a fighting-ground, French cities to plunder, and French captives to hold for heavy ransoms, they were content to let matters go on quietly at home. But that day was over. Through the bad management, if not through the positive treachery of Edmund, Duke of Somerset, the French conquests had been lost, a weak king, at times insane, sat on the English throne, while Richard, Duke of York, a really able man and a descendant of the Mortimers, was, as many believed, unlawfully excluded from it. This fact in itself would have furnished a plausible pretext for hostilities, even as far back as Cade's rising. But the birth of a son to Henry in 1453 probably gave the signal for the outbreak, since it cut off

---

[1] "Now is Mortimer lord of this city; and here, sitting upon London Stone, I charge and command, that at the city's cost, this conduit runs nothing but claret wine this first year of our reign; and now it shall be treason for any man to call me other than Lord Mortimer." Henry VI., Part II. Act IV. Sc. 6.

It is worthy of remark that here, as elsewhere in his historical plays, the great dramatist expresses little, if any, sympathy with the cause of the people. In King John he does not mention the Great Charter, in Richard II. he passes over Wat Tyler without a word, while in Henry VI. he mentions Cade only to ridicule him and his movement. The explanation of this lies, perhaps, in the fact that Shakespeare lived in an age when England was threatened by both open and secret enemies. The need of his time was a strong, steady hand at the helm; it was no season for reform or change of any sort. This may be the reason why he was silent in regard to democratic risings and demands in the past.

all hopes which Richard's friends may have had of his peaceful succession.

352. The Scene in the Temple Garden. — Shakespeare represents the smouldering feud between the rival houses of Lancaster and York (both of whom it should be remembered were descendants of Edward III.)[1] as breaking into an angry quarrel in the Temple Garden, London, when Richard, Duke of York, says: —

> "Let him that is a true-born gentleman,
> And stands upon the honor of his birth,
> If he suppose that I have pleaded truth,
> From off this brier pluck a white rose with me."

To which John Beaufort, Duke of Somerset,[2] a descendant of

---

[1] Table showing the descendants of Edward III., with reference to the claims of Lancaster and York to the crown: —

Edward III.

Lionel, Duke of Clarence (3d son)	John of Gaunt, **Duke of Lancaster** (4th son)	Edmund, **Duke of York** (5th son)
Philippa.	Henry IV.	**Richard**, Earl of Cambridge, m. **Anne Mortimer.**
Roger Mortimer.	Henry V. John, Earl of Somerset.†	
Edmund Mortimer (Earl of March), d. 1424. Anne Mortimer, m. Richard, Earl of Cambridge (s. of Edmund, Duke of York)	**Henry VI.** Prince Edward, b. 1453; killed at battle of Tewksbury, 1471.	John, Duke of Somerset, d. 1448. Edmund, Duke of Somerset.
* **Richard, Duke of York.**		

† John, Earl of Somerset, was an illegitimate half-brother of Henry IV.'s, but was, in 1397, declared legitimate by act of Parliament and a papal decree.

* Inherited the title of Duke of York from his father's eldest brother Edward, Duke of York, who died without issue.

Richard's father, the Earl of Cambridge, had forfeited his title and estates by treason; but Parliament had so far limited the sentence that his son was not thereby debarred from inheriting his uncle's rank and fortune.

Richard, Duke of York, now represented the direct hereditary line of succession to the crown, while Henry VI. and his son represented that established by Parliament through acceptance of Henry IV. Compare Table, Paragraph No. 309.

[2] John, Duke of Somerset, died 1448. He was brother of Edmund, Duke of Somerset, who was slain at St. Albans 1455.

the house of Lancaster, who has just accused Richard of being
the dishonored son of a traitor, replies: —

> "Let him that is no coward, nor no flatterer,
> But dare maintain the party of the truth,
> Pluck a red rose from off this thorn with me."

The Earl of Warwick rejoins : —

> "This brawl to-day,
> Grown t this faction in the Temple-garden,
> Shall send, between the red rose and the white,
> A thousand souls to death and deadly night."[1]

353. The Real Object of the War. — The war, however, did not directly originate in this quarrel, but rather in the strife for power between Edmund, Duke of Somerset (John's brother), and Richard, Duke of York. Each desired to get the control of the government, though at first neither appears to have openly aimed at the crown.

During Henry's attack of insanity in 1453 Richard was appointed Protector of the realm, and shortly after, the Duke of Somerset, the king's particular favorite and chief adviser, was cast into prison on the double charge of having culpably lost Normandy and embezzled public moneys.

In 1455, when Henry recovered, he released Somerset and restored him to office. Richard protested, and raising an army in the north, marched toward London. He met the royalist forces at St. Albans; a battle ensued, and Somerset was slain.

During the next thirty years the war raged with more or less fury between the parties of the Red Rose (Lancaster) and the White (York), the first maintaining the right of Parliament to choose such king as they saw fit, as in Henry IV.'s case; the second insisting on the succession being determined by strict hereditary descent, as represented in the claim of Richard.

But beneath the surface the contest was not for principle, but for place and spoils. The great nobles, who during the French

---

[1] Shakespeare's Henry VI., Part I. Act II. Sc. 4.

wars had pillaged abroad, now pillaged each other; and as England was neither big nor rich enough to satisfy the greed of all of them, the struggle gradually became a war of mutual extermination. It was, to a certain extent, a sectional war. Eastern England, then the wealthiest and most progressive part of the country, had strongly supported Wycliffe in his reforms. It now espoused the side of Richard, Duke of York, who was believed to be friendly to religious liberty, while the western counties fought for the cause of Lancaster and the church.[1]

354. The First Battles. — We have already seen that the first blood was shed at St. Albans in 1455, where the Yorkists, after half an hour's fighting, gained a complete victory. A similar result followed at Bloreheath, Staffordshire. In a third battle, at Northampton,[2] the Yorkists were again successful. Henry was taken prisoner, and Queen Margaret fled with the young Prince Edward to Scotland. Richard now demanded the crown. Henry answered with unexpected spirit : "My father was king, his father also was king. I have worn the crown forty years from my cradle; you have all sworn fealty to me as your sovereign, and your fathers did the like to my fathers. How, then, can my claim be disputed?" Finally, after a long dispute, a compromise was effected. Henry agreed that if he were left in peaceable possession of the throne during his life, Richard or his heirs should succeed him.

355. Battles of Wakefield and Towton. — But Queen Margaret refused to see her son, Prince Edward, thus tamely set aside. She raised an army and attacked the Yorkists. Richard, whose forces were inferior to hers, had entrenched himself in his castle.[3] Day after day Margaret went up under the walls and dared him to come out. At length, stung by her taunts, the duke sallied from his stronghold, and the battle of Wakefield was fought. Margaret

---

[1] It will be remembered that the persecution of Wycliffe's followers began under Henry IV., the first Lancastrian king. See Paragraph No. 335.
[2] Northampton, Northamptonshire.
[3] Sandal Castle, near Wakefield, Yorkshire. Towton, also in Yorkshire.

was victorious. Richard was slain, and the queen, in mockery of his claims to sovereignty, cut off his head, decked it with a paper crown, and set it up over the chief gate of the city of York. Fortune now changed. The next year the Lancastrians were defeated with great slaughter at Towton.[1] The light spring snow was crimsoned with the blood of thirty thousand slain, and the way strewn with corpses for ten miles up to the walls of York. The Earl of Warwick, henceforth popularly known as "the king-maker," now placed Edward, eldest son of the late Duke of York, on the throne, with the title of Edward IV. Henry and Margaret fled to Scotland. The new government summoned them to appear, and as they failed to answer, proclaimed them traitors. Four years later Henry was taken prisoner and sent to the Tower of London. He may have been happier there than battling for his throne. He was not born to reign, but rather, as Shakespeare makes him say, to lead a shepherd's life, watching his flocks, until the peacefully flowing years should —

"Bring white hairs unto a quiet grave."[2]

356. Summary. — The history of the period is one of loss. The brilliant French conquests of Henry V. slipped from the nerveless hands of his son, leaving France practically independent. The franchise had been restricted, and the House of Commons now represented property-holders mainly. Cade's rebellion was the sign of political discontent and the forerunner of civil war. The contests of the parties of the Red and the White Roses drenched England's fair fields with the best blood of her own sons. The reign ends with King Henry in prison, Queen Margaret and the prince fugitives, and the Yorkist Edward IV. placed on the throne by the help of the powerful Earl of Warwick.

---

[1] For battle-fields of the Wars of Roses, see Map No. 10, p. 174.
[2] See Henry's soliloquy on the field of Towton, beginning, —

"O God! methinks it were a happy life
To be no better than a homely swain."

SHAKESPEARE, *Henry VI*, Part III. Act II. Sc. 5.

EDWARD IV. (House of York, White Rose). — 1461–1483.

357. Continuation of the War; Death of Henry; Tewkesbury.
— During the whole of Edward's reign the war went on with varying success, but unvarying ferocity, until at last neither side would ask or give quarter. Some years after the accession of the new sovereign the Earl of Warwick quarrelled with him, thrust him down from the throne, and restored Henry. But a few months later, at the battle of Barnet, Warwick, who was "the last of the great barons," was killed, and Henry, who had been led back to the Tower[1] again, died one of those "conveniently sudden deaths" which were then so common.

The heroic Margaret, however, would not give up the contest in behalf of her son's claim to the crown. But fate was against her. A few weeks after the battle of Barnet[2] her army was utterly defeated at Tewkesbury, her son Edward slain, and the queen herself taken prisoner. She was eventually released on the payment of a large ransom, and returned to France, where she died brokenhearted in her native Anjou, prophesying that the contest would go on until the Red Rose, representing her party, should get a still deeper dye from the blood of her enemies.[3]

358. The Introduction of Printing. — But an event was at hand of greater importance than any question of crowns or parties, though then none were wise enough to see its real significance. William Caxton, a London merchant, having learned the new art of printing in Flanders, now returned to his native country and set up a small press within the precincts of Westminster Abbey.

There, "at the sign of the red pole," he advertised his wares as "good chepe." He was not only printer, but translator and editor.

---

[1] The Tower of London, built by William the Conqueror as a fortress to overawe the city, became later both a royal palace and a prison of state. It is now used as a citadel, armory, and depository for the crown jewels.

[2] Barnet: about eleven miles northwest of London, Hertfordshire. Tewkesbury: near Gloucester, Gloucestershire.

[3] See Scott's Anne of Geierstein, Chapter XXX.

Edward gave him some royal patronage, and paid liberally for work which not long before the clergy in France had condemned as a black art emanating from the devil, and which many of the English clergy still regarded with no very friendly eye, especially as it threatened to destroy the copying trade, of which the monks had well-nigh a monopoly. The first printed book which Caxton is known to have published in England was a small volume entitled "The Sayings of the Philosophers" (1477).[1] This venture was followed in due time by Chaucer's "Canterbury Tales," and whatever other poetry, history, or classics seemed worthy of preservation; in all no less than sixty-four distinct works. Up to this time a book of any kind was a luxury, laboriously "written by the few for the few"; but from this date literature of all sorts was destined to multiply and fill the earth with many leaves and some good fruit.

Caxton's patrons though few, were choice, and when one of them, the Earl of Worcester, was beheaded in the wars, he said of him, "The axe did then cut off more learning than was left in all the heads of the surviving lords." Recently a memorial window has been placed in St. Margaret's Church within the Abbey grounds, as a tribute to the man who, while England was red with slaughter, introduced "the art preservative of all arts," and preservative of liberty no less.[2]

359. Edward's Character. — The king, however, cared more for his pleasures than for literature or the welfare of the nation.

---

[1] "The dictes or sayengis of the philosophres, enprynted by me william Caxton at westmestre, the year of our lord MCCCCLxxvii."

It has no title-page, but ends as above. A copy is preserved in the British Museum. "The Game and Play of the Chess" is supposed by some to have been published a year or two earlier, but as the book has neither printer's name, place of publication, nor date, the time of its issue remains wholly conjectural.

[2] "Lord! taught by Thee, when Caxton bade
His silent words forever speak;
A grave for tyrants then was made,
Then crack'd the chain which yet shall break."

EBENEZER ELLIOTT, *Hymn for the Printers' Gathering at Sheffield, 1833.*

His chief aim was to beg, borrow, or extort money to waste in dissipation. The loans which he forced his subjects to grant, and which were seldom, if ever, repaid, went under the name of "benevolences." But it is safe to say that those who furnished them were in no very benevolent frame of mind at the time. Exception may perhaps be made of the rich and elderly widow, who was so pleased with the king's handsome face that she willingly handed him £20 (a large sum in those days); and when the jovial monarch gallantly kissed her out of gratitude for her generosity, she at once, like a true and loyal subject, doubled the donation. Edward's course of life was not conducive to length of days, even if the times had favored a long reign. He died early, leaving a son, Prince Edward, to succeed him.

360. Summary. — The reign was marked by the continuation of the Wars of the Roses, the death of King Henry VI. and of his son, with the return of Queen Margaret to France. The most important event was the introduction of the printing-press by William Caxton.

EDWARD V. (House of York, White Rose). - - 1483–1483.

361. Gloucester appointed Protector. — Prince Edward, heir to the throne, was a lad of twelve. He was placed under the guardianship of his ambitious and unscrupulous uncle, Richard, Duke of Gloucester, who had been appointed Lord Protector of the realm until the boy should become of age. Richard protected his young nephew as a wolf would a lamb. He met the prince coming up to London from Ludlow Castle, Shropshire, attended by his half-brother Sir Richard Grey, and his uncle Lord Rivers. Under the pretext that Edward would be safer in the Tower of London than at Westminster Palace, Richard sent the prince there, and soon found means for having his kinsmen Grey and Rivers executed.

362. Murder of Lord Hastings and the Two Princes. — Richard shortly after showed his object Lord Hastings was one of the council who had voted to make the duke Protector, but he was unwilling to help him in his plot to seize the crown. While at the council-table in the Tower Richard suddenly started up and accused Hastings of treason, saying, "By St. Paul I will not to dinner till I see thy head off." Hastings was dragged out of the room, and without either trial or examination was beheaded on a stick of timber on the Tower green. The way was now clear for the accomplishment of the duke's purpose. The queen-mother (Elizabeth Woodville, widow of Edward IV.) took her younger son and his sisters, one of whom was the Princess Elizabeth, of York, and fled for protection to the sanctuary[1] of Westminster Abbey, where, refusing all comfort, "she sat alone, low on the rushes."[2] Finally, Richard half persuaded and half forced the unhappy woman to give up her second son to his tender care. With bitter weeping and dread presentiments of evil she parted from him, saying, "Farewell, mine own sweet son! God send you good keeping! Let me kiss you once ere you go, for God knoweth when we shall kiss together again." That was the last time she saw the lad. He and Edward, his elder brother, were soon after murdered in the Tower, and Richard rose by that double crime to the height he coveted.

363 Summary. — Edward's nominal reign of less than three months must be regarded simply as the time during which his uncle, the Duke of Gloucester, perfected his plot for seizing the crown by the successive murders of Rivers, Grey, Hastings, and the two young princes.

RICHARD III. (House of York, White Rose). — 1483-1485.

364. Richard's Accession; he promises Financial Reform. — Richard used the preparations which had been made for the murdered Prince Edward's coronation for his own. He probably gained over an influential party by promises of financial reform.

---

[1] See Paragraph No. 131.
[2] "On the rushes": on the stone floor covered with rushes.

In their address to him at his accession Parliament said, "Certainly we be determined rather to adventure and commit us to the peril of our lives . . . than to live in such thraldom and bondage as we have lived long time heretofore, oppressed and injured by extortions and new impositions, against the laws of God and man, and the liberty, old policy and laws of this realm, wherein every Englishman is inherited."[1]

365. Richard's Character. — Several attempts have been made of late years to defend the king against the odium heaped upon him by the older historians. But these well-meant efforts to prove him less black than tradition painted him, are perhaps sufficiently answered by the fact that his memory was so thoroughly hated by those who knew him best that no one of the age when he lived thought of vindicating his character.

We must then believe, until it is clearly proved to the contrary, that the last and worst of the Yorkist kings was what common report and Shakespeare have together represented him, — distorted in figure, and with ambition so unrestrained, that the words the poet puts into his mouth may have been really his: —

"Then, since the heavens have shap'd my body so,
Let hell make crookt my mind to answer it."[2]

Personally he was as brave as he was cruel and unscrupulous. He promoted some reforms. He abolished "benevolences," at least for a time, and he encouraged Caxton in his great work.

366. Revolts; Buckingham; Henry Tudor. — During his short reign of two years, several revolts broke out, but came to nothing. The Duke of Buckingham, who had helped Richard to the throne, turned against him because he did not get the rewards he expected. He headed a revolt; but as his men deserted him, he fell into the king's hands, and the executioner speedily did the rest. Finally a more formidable enemy arose. Before he gained the crown

---

[1] Taswell-Langmead, Constitutional History of England.
[2] Henry VI., Part III. Act V. Sc. 6.

Richard had cajoled or compelled the unfortunate Anne Neville, widow of that Prince Edward, son of Henry VI., who was slain at Tewkesbury,[1] into becoming his wife. She said with truth, "Small joy have I in being England's queen." The king intended that his son should marry Elizabeth of York,[2] sister to the two princes he had murdered in the Tower. By so doing he would strengthen his position, and secure the succession to the throne to his own family. But Richard's son shortly after died, and the king, having mysteriously got rid of his wife, now made up his mind to marry Elizabeth himself.

The princess, however, was already betrothed to Henry Tudor, Earl of Richmond, the engagement having been effected during that sad winter which she and her mother spent in sanctuary at Westminster Abbey, watched by Richard's soldiers to prevent their escape. The Earl of Richmond, who was an illegitimate descendant of the house of Lancaster, had long been waiting on the continent for an opportunity to invade England and claim the crown. Owing to the enmity of Edward IV. and Richard toward him, the earl had been, as he himself said, "either a fugitive or a captive since he was five years old." He now determined to remain so no longer. In 1485 he landed with a force at Milford Haven, in Wales, where he felt sure of a welcome, since his paternal ancestors were Welsh.[3]

Advancing through Shrewsbury, he met Richard on Bosworth Field, in Leicestershire.

367. Battle of Bosworth Field (1485). — There the decisive battle was fought between the great rival houses of York and Lan-

---

[1] See Paragraph No. 357.   [2] See Paragraph No. 362.
[3] Descent of Henry Tudor, Earl of Richmond.

Henry V. (House of Lancaster) married Catharine of France, who after his death married **Owen Tudor**, a Welshman.
Henry VI.
            Edmund Tudor (Earl of Richmond) married
            Margaret Beaufort, a descendant of John of Gaunt,
            Duke of Lancaster [she was granddaughter of
            John, Earl of Somerset, see p. 163].

               Henry Tudor, Earl of Richmond (also
               called Henry of Lancaster).

caster. Richard went out the evening before to look over the ground. He found one of his sentinels slumbering at his post. Drawing his sword, he stabbed him to the heart, saying, "I found him asleep and I leave him asleep." Going back to his tent, he passed a restless night. The ghosts of all his murdered victims seemed to pass in procession before him. Such a sight may well, as Shakespeare says, have "struck terror to the soul of Richard."[1] At sunrise the battle began. Before the attack, Richard, it is said, confessed to his troops the murder of his two nephews, but pleaded that he had atoned for the crime with "many salt tears and long penance." It is probable that had it not been for the treachery of some of his adherents the king would have won the day. When he saw that he was deserted by those on whose help he had counted, he uttered the cry of "treason! treason!" and dashed forward into the thick of the fight. With the fury of despair he hewed his way into the very presence of the earl, and killing the standard-bearer, flung the Lancastrian banner to the ground. But he could go no further. Numbers overpowered him, and he fell. During the battle he had worn his crown. After all was over, it was found hanging on a hawthorn-bush[2] and handed to the victor, who placed it on his own head. The army then gathered round Henry thus crowned, and moved by one impulse joined in the exultant hymn of the Te Deum.[3] Thus ended the last of the Plantagenet line. "Whatever their faults or crimes, there was not a coward among them."[4]

368. **End of the Wars of the Roses; their Effects.** — With Bosworth Field the Wars of the Roses ceased. During the thirty years they had continued, fourteen pitched battles had been fought, in a single one of which (Towton) more Englishmen lost

---

[1] Shakespeare's Richard III., Act V. Sc. 3.
[2] An ancient stained-glass window in Henry VII.'s Chapel (Westminster Abbey) commemorates this incident.
[3] "Te Deum laudamus": We praise Thee, O God. A Roman Catholic hymn of thanksgiving, now sung in English in the Episcopal and other churches.
[4] Stubbs' Constitutional History of England.

their lives than in the whole course of the wars with France during the preceding forty years. In all, eighty princes of the blood royal and more than half of the nobility of the realm perished.

Of those who escaped death by the sword, many died on the scaffold. The remnant who were saved had hardly a better fate. They left their homes only to suffer in foreign lands. A writer of that day[1] says: "I, myself, saw the Duke of Exeter, the king of England's brother-in-law, walking barefoot in the Duke of Burgundy's train, and begging his bread from door to door." Every individual of two families of the great houses of Somerset and Warwick fell either on the field or under the executioner's axe. In tracing family pedigrees it is startling to see how often the record reads, "killed at St. Albans," "slain at Towton," "beheaded after the battle of Wakefield," and the like.[2]

When the contest closed, the feudal baronage was broken up. In a majority of cases the estates of the nobles either fell to the crown for lack of heirs, or they were fraudulently seized by the king's officers. Thus the greater part of the wealthiest and most powerful aristocracy in the world disappeared so completely that they ceased to have either a local habitation or a name. But the elements of civil discord at last exhausted themselves. Bosworth was a turning-point in English history. When the sun went down, it saw the termination of the desperate struggle between the White Roses of York and the Red of Lancaster; when it ushered in a new day, it shone also on a new king, who introduced a new social and political period.

369. Summary. — The importance of Richard's reign is that it marks the close of thirty years of civil war, the destruction of the predominating influence of the feudal barons, and leaves as the central figure Henry Tudor, the sovereign who now ascended the throne.

---

[1] See the Paston Letters.
[2] Guest's Lectures on English History.

No. 10.

The battle-fields of the Wars of the Roses are underlined thus, Towton (in Yorkshire).

vigil

THE SELF-DESTRUCTION OF FEUDALISM. 175

GENERAL VIEW OF THE LANCASTRIAN AND YORKIST PERIOD (1399-1485).

I. GOVERNMENT. — II. RELIGION. — III. MILITARY AFFAIRS. — IV. LITERATURE, LEARNING, AND ART. — V. GENERAL INDUSTRY AND COMMERCE. — VI. MODE OF LIFE, MANNERS, AND CUSTOMS.

GOVERNMENT.

370. Parliament and the Royal Succession. — The period began with the parliamentary recognition of the claim to the crown of Henry, Duke of Lancaster, son of John of Gaunt, Duke of Lancaster, fourth son of Edward III. By this act the claim of Edmund Mortimer, a descendant of Edward III. by his third son, Lionel, Duke of Clarence, was deliberately set aside, and this change of the order of succession eventually furnished an excuse for civil war.[1]

371. Disfranchisement of Electors; Benevolences. — Under Henry VI. a property qualification was established by act of Parliament which cut off all persons from voting for county members of the House of Commons who did not have an income of forty shillings (say £40, or $200, in modern money) from freehold land. County elections, the statute said, had "of late been made by a very great, outrageous, and excessive number of people . . . of which the most part were people of small substance and of no value." Later, candidates for the House of Commons from the counties were required to be gentlemen by birth, and to have an income of not less than £20 (or say £400, or $2000, in modern money). Though the tendency of such laws was to make the House of Commons represent property-holders rather than the freemen as a body,

---

[1] Before the accession of Henry III., Parliament made choice of any one of the king's sons whom they considered best fitted to rule. After that time it was understood that the king's eldest son should be chosen to succeed him; or in case of his death during the lifetime of his father, the eldest son of the eldest son, and so forward in that line. The action taken by Parliament in favor of Henry IV. was a departure from that principle, and a reassertion of its ancient right to choose any descendant of the royal family they deemed best. See genealogical table, Paragraph No. 309.

yet no apparent change seems to have taken place in the class of county members chosen.

Eventually, however, these and other interferences with free elections caused the rebellion of Jack Cade, in which the insurgents demanded the right to choose such representatives as they saw fit. But the movement appears to have had no practical result. During the civil war which ensued, the king (Edward IV.) compelled wealthy subjects to lend him large sums (seldom, if ever, repaid) called "benevolences." Richard III. abolished this obnoxious system, but afterward revived it, and it became conspicuously hateful under his successor in the next period.

Another great grievance was Purveyance. By it the king's purveyors had the right to seize provisions and means of transportation for the king and his hundreds of attendants whenever they journeyed through the country on a "royal progress." The price offered by the purveyors was always much below the real value of what was taken, and frequently even that was not paid. Purveyance, which had existed from the earliest times, was not finally abolished until 1660.

RELIGION.

372. Suppression of Heresy. — Under Henry IV. the first act was passed by lords and clergy (without assent of the House of Commons), punishing heretics, by burning at the stake, and the first martyr suffered in that reign. Later, the Lollards, or followers of Wycliffe, who appear in many cases to have been socialists as well as religious reformers, were punished by imprisonment, and occasionally with death. The whole number of martyrs, however, was but small.

MILITARY AFFAIRS.

373. Armor and Arms. — The armor of the period was made of steel plate, fitting and completely covering the body. It was often inlaid with gold and elegantly ornamented. Firearms had not yet superseded the old weapons. Cannon were in use, and also clumsy hand-guns fired with a match. The long-bow continued to be the chief arm of the foot-soldiers, and was used with great dexterity and fatal effect. Targets were set up by law in every parish, and the yeomen were required to practise at contests in archery frequently. The principal wars were the civil wars and those with France.

LITERATURE, LEARNING, AND ART.

374. Introduction of Printing; Books. — The art of printing was introduced into England about 1471 by Caxton, a London merchant. Up to that time all books had been written on either parchment or paper, at an average rate of about fifty cents per page in modern money. The age was not favorable to literature, and produced no great writers. But Caxton edited and published a large number of works, many of which he translated from the French and Latin. The two books which throw most light on the history of the times are the Sir John Paston Letters (1424-1506), and a work by Chief Justice Fortescue, on government, intended for the use of Prince Edward (slain at Tewkesbury). The latter is remarkable for its bold declaration that the king " has the delegation of power from the people, and he has no just claims to any other power than this." The chief justice also praises the courage of his countrymen, and declares with honest pride that "more Englishmen are hanged in England in one year for robbery and manslaughter than are hanged in France in seven years."

375. Education. — Henry VI. took a deep interest in education, and founded the great public school of Eton, which ranks next in age to that of Winchester. The money for its endowment was obtained by the appropriation of the revenues of alien or foreign monasteries which had been erected in England, and which were confiscated by Henry V. The king watched the progress of the building from the windows of Windsor Castle, and to supplement the course of education to be given there, he furthermore erected and endowed the magnificent King's College, Cambridge.

376. Architecture. — A new development of Gothic architecture occurred during this period, the Decorated giving place to the Perpendicular. The latter derived its name from the perpendicular divisions of the lights in the arches of the windows. It marks the final period of the Gothic or Pointed style, and is noted for the exquisite carved work of its ceilings. King's College Chapel, Cambridge, St. George's Chapel, Windsor, and Henry VII.'s Chapel (built in the next reign), connected with Westminster Abbey, are among the most celebrated examples of this style of architecture, which is peculiar to England.

The mansions of the nobility at this period exhibited great elegance. Crosby Hall, London, at one time the residence of Richard III., and still standing, is a fine specimen of the "Inns," as they were called, of the great families and wealthy knights.

GENERAL INDUSTRY AND COMMERCE.

377. Agriculture and Trade. — Notwithstanding the civil wars of the Roses, agriculture was prosperous, and foreign trade largely increased. The latter was well represented by Sir Richard Whittington, thrice mayor of London, who, according to tradition, lent Henry V. large sums of money, and then at an entertainment which he gave to the king and queen in his city mansion, generously cancelled the debt by throwing the bonds into the open sandal-wood fire.

Goldsmiths from Lombardy had now settled in London in such numbers as to give the name of Lombard Street to the quarter they occupied. They succeeded the Jews in the business of money-lending and banking, and Lombard Street still remains famous for its bankers and brokers.

MODES OF LIFE, MANNERS, AND CUSTOMS.

378. Dress. — Great sums were spent on dress by both sexes, and the courtiers' doublets, or jackets, were of the most costly silks and velvets, elaborately puffed and slashed. During the latter part of the period the pointed shoes, which had formerly been of prodigious length, suddenly began to grow broad, with such rapidity that Parliament passed a law limiting the width of the toes to six inches. At the same time the court ladies adopted the fashion of wearing horns as huge in proportion as the noblemen's shoes. The government tried legislating them down, and the clergy fulminated a solemn curse against them; but fashion was more powerful than church and Parliament combined, and horns and hoofs came out triumphant.

VIII.

> "One half her soil has walked the rest
> In heroes, martyrs, poets, sages."
>   O. W. HOLMES.

POLITICAL REACTION. — ABSOLUTISM OF THE CROWN, — THE ENGLISH REFORMATION AND THE NEW LEARNING.

CROWN or POPE?

HOUSE OF TUDOR. — 1485–1603.

Henry VII., 1485–1509.	Edward VI., 1547–1553.
Henry VIII., 1509–1547.	Mary, 1553–1558.
	Elizabeth, 1558–1603.

379. Union of the Houses of Lancaster and York. — Before leaving the continent, Henry Tudor had promised the Yorkist party that he would marry Elizabeth, eldest daughter of Edward IV., and sister to the young princes murdered by Richard III. Such a marriage would unite the rival houses of Lancaster and York, and thus put an end to the civil war. A few months after the new king's accession the wedding was duly celebrated, and in the beautiful east window of stained glass in Henry VII.'s Chapel, Westminster Abbey, the Roses are seen joined; so that, as the quaint verse of that day says: —

> "Both roses flourish — red and white —
> In love and sisterly delight;
> The two that were at strife are blended,
> And all old troubles now are ended."

Peace came from the union, but it was peace interrupted by insurrections.[1]

380. Condition of the Country; Power of the Crown. — Henry, it is said, had his claim to the throne printed by Caxton, and distributed broadcast over the country. It was the first political appeal to the people made through the press, and was a sign of the new period upon which English history had entered. Since Caxton began his work, the kingdom had undergone a most momentous change. The great nobles, like the Earl of Warwick, were, with few exceptions, dead, their estates confiscated, their thousands of followers either buried on the battle-field or dispersed throughout the land. The small number of titled families remaining was no longer to be feared. The nation itself, though it had taken comparatively little part in the war, was weary of bloodshed, and ready for peace on any terms.

The accession of the house of Tudor marks the beginning of a long period of well-nigh absolute royal power. The nobility were

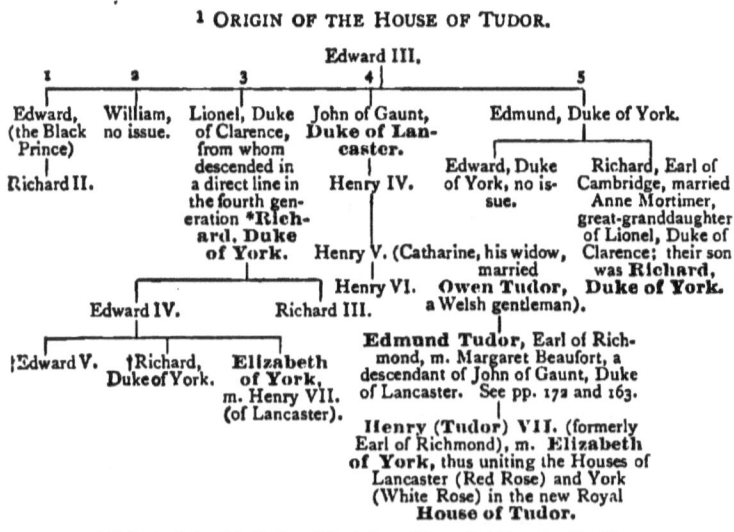

[1] ORIGIN OF THE HOUSE OF TUDOR.

* Inherited the title Duke of York from his uncle Edward. See No. 5.
† The princes murdered by Richard III.

too weak to place any check on the king; the clergy, who had not recovered from their dread of Lollardism and its attacks on their wealth and influence, were anxious for a strong conservative government such as Henry promised; as for the commons, they had no clear united policy, and though the first Parliament put certain restraints on the crown, yet they were never really enforced.[1] The truth is, that the new king was both too prudent and too crafty to give them an opportunity. By avoiding foreign wars he dispensed with the necessity of summoning frequent parliaments, and also with demands for large sums of money. By thus ruling alone for a large part of the time, Henry got the management of affairs into his own hands, and transmitted the power to those who came after him. In this way the Tudors with their successors, the Stuarts, built up that system of "personal sovereignty" which continued for a hundred and fifty years, until the outbreak of a new civil war brought it to an end forever.

381. Growth of a Stronger Feeling of Nationality. — It would be an error, however, to consider this absolutism of the crown as an unmitigated evil. On the contrary, it was in one important direction an advantage. There are times when the great need of a people is not more individual liberty, but greater national unity. Spain and France were two countries consisting of a collection of petty feudal states, whose nobility were always trying to steal each other's possessions and cut each other's throats, until the rise in each of a royal despotism forced the turbulent barons to make peace, to obey a common central law, and by this means both realms ultimately developed into great and powerful kingdoms. When the Tudors came to the throne, England was still full of

---

[1] At the accession of Henry VII., Parliament imposed the following checks on the power of the king: —

1. No new tax to be levied without consent of Parliament.
2. No new law to be made without the same consent.
3. No committal to prison without a warrant specifying the offence, and the trial to be speedy.
4. Criminal charges and questions of fact in civil cases to be decided by jury.
5. The king's officers to be held responsible to the nation.

the rankling hate engendered by the Wars of the Roses. Held down by the heavy hand of Henry VII., and by the still heavier one of his son, the country learned the same salutary lesson of growth under repression which had benefited Spain and France. Henceforth Englishmen of all classes, instead of boasting that they belonged to the Yorkist or the Lancastrian faction, came to pride themselves on their loyalty to crown and country, and their readiness to draw their swords to defend both.

382. Henry's Methods of raising Money; the Court of Star-Chamber. — Henry's reign was in the interest of the middle classes, — the farmers, tradesmen, and mechanics. His policy was to avoid heavy taxation, to exempt the poor from the burdens of state, and so ingratiate himself with a large body of the people. In order to accomplish this, he revived "benevolences," and by a device suggested by his chief minister, Cardinal Morton, and hence known and dreaded as "Morton's Fork," he extorted large sums from the rich and well-to-do.[1] The cardinal's agents made it their business to learn every man's income, and visit him accordingly. If, for instance, a person lived handsomely, the cardinal would insist on a correspondingly liberal gift; if, however, a citizen lived very plainly, the king's minister insisted none the less, telling the unfortunate man that by his economy he must surely have accumulated enough to bestow the required "benevolence."[2] Thus on one prong or the other of his terrible "fork" the shrewd cardinal impaled his writhing victims, and speedily filled the royal treasury as it had never been filled before.[3]

---

[1] Those whose income from land was less than £2, or whose movable property did not exceed £15 (say $150 and $1125 now), were exempt. The lowest rate of assessment for the "benevolences" was fixed at twenty pence on the pound on land, and half that rate on other property.

[2] Richard Reed, a London alderman, refused to contribute a "benevolence." He was sent to serve as a soldier in the Scotch wars at his own expense, and the general received government orders to "use him in all things according to sharp military discipline." The effect was such that few after that ventured to deny the king what he asked.

[3] Henry is said to have accumulated a fortune of nearly two millions sterling; an amount which would perhaps represent upwards of $150,000,000 now.

POLITICAL REACTION. 183

But Henry had other methods for raising money. He sold offices in church and state, and took bribes for pardoning rebels. When he summoned a parliament he obtained grants for putting down some real or pretended insurrection, or to defray the expenses of a threatened attack from abroad, and then quietly pocketed the appropriation, — a device not altogether unknown to modern government officials. A third and last method for getting funds was invented in Henry's behalf by two lawyers, Empson and Dudley, who were so rapacious and cut so close that they were commonly known as "the king's skin-shearers." They went about the country enforcing old and forgotten laws, by which they reaped a rich harvest. Their chief instrument for gain, however, was a revival of the Statute of Liveries, which imposed enormous fines on those noblemen who dared to equip their followers in military garb, or designate them by a badge equivalent to it, as had been their custom during the civil wars.[1]

In order to thoroughly enforce the Statute of Liveries, Henry reorganized the Court of Star-Chamber, so called from the starred ceiling where the tribunal met. This court had originally for its object the punishment of such crimes committed by the great families, or their adherents, as the ordinary law courts could not, or through intimidation dared not, deal with. It had no power to inflict death, but might impose long terms of imprisonment and ruinous fines. It, too, first made use of torture in England to extort confessions of guilt.

Henry seems to have enforced the law of Livery against friend and foe alike. Said the king to the Earl of Oxford, as he left his castle, where a large number of retainers in uniform were drawn up to do him honor, "My Lord, I thank you for your entertainment, but my attorney must speak to you." The attorney, who was the notorious Empson, brought suit in the Star-Chamber against the earl, who was fined 15,000 marks, or something like $750,000, for the incautious display he had made.

---

[1] See Paragraph No. 348.

383. The Introduction of Artillery strengthens the Power of the King. — It was easier for Henry to pursue this arbitrary course because the introduction of artillery had changed the art of war. Throughout the Middle Ages the call of a great baron had, as Macaulay says, been sufficient to raise a formidable revolt. Countrymen and followers took down their tough yew long-bows from the chimney-corner, knights buckled on their steel armor, mounted their horses, and in a few days an army threatened the throne, which had no troops save those furnished by loyal subjects.

But now that men had digged "villanous saltpetre out of the bowels of the harmless earth" to manufacture powder, and that others had invented cannon, "those devilish iron engines," as the poet Spenser called them, "ordained to kill," all was different. Without artillery, the old feudal army, with its bows, swords, and battle-axes, could do little against a king like Henry who had it. For this reason, the whole kingdom lay at his mercy; and though the nobles and the rich might groan, they saw that it was useless to fight.

384. The Pretenders Symnel and Warbeck. — During Henry's reign, two pretenders laid claim to the crown: Lambert Symnel, who represented himself to be Edward Plantagenet, nephew of the late king; and Perkin Warbeck, who asserted that he was Richard, Duke of York, generally and rightly supposed to have been murdered in the Tower by his uncle, Richard III. Symnel's attempt was easily suppressed, and he commuted his claim to the crown for the position of scullion in the king's kitchen. Warbeck kept the kingdom in a turmoil for more than five years, during which time one hundred and fifty of his adherents were executed, and their bodies exposed on gibbets along the South shore to deter their master's French supporters from landing. At length Warbeck was captured, imprisoned, and finally hanged at Tyburn.

385. Henry's Politic Marriages. — Henry accomplished more by the marriages of his children and by diplomacy than other monarchs had by their wars. He gave his daughter Margaret to King

James IV. of Scotland, and thus prepared the way for the union of the two kingdoms. He married his eldest son, Prince Arthur, to Catharine of Aragon, daughter of the king of Spain, by which he secured a very large marriage portion for the prince, and what was of equal importance, the alliance of Spain against France. Arthur died soon afterwards, and the king got a dispensation from the Pope, granting him permission to marry his younger son Henry to Arthur's widow. It was this prince who eventually became king of England, with the title of Henry VIII., and we shall hereafter see that this marriage was destined by its results to change the whole course of the country's history.

386. The World as known at Henry's Accession. — The king also took some small part in certain other events, which seemed to him, at the time, of less consequence than these matrimonial alliances, but which history has regarded in a different light from that in which the cunning and cautious monarch considered them. A glance at the map [1] will show how different our world is from that with which the English of Henry's time were acquainted. Then, the earth was not supposed to be a globe, but simply a flat body surrounded by the ocean. The only countries of which anything was certainly known, with the exception of Europe, were parts of Western Asia, together with a small strip of the northern and eastern coast of Africa. The knowledge which had once existed of India, China, and Japan appears to have died out in great measure with the travellers and merchants of earlier times who had brought it. The land farthest west of which anything was then known was Iceland.

387. First Voyages of Exploration; the Cabots. — About the time of Henry's accession a new spirit of exploration sprang up. The Portuguese had coasted along Africa as far as the Gulf of Guinea, and there established trading-posts. Stimulated by what they had done, Columbus, who believed the earth to be round,

---

[1] See Map No. 11, page 186.

determined to sail westward in the hope of reaching the Indies. In 1492 he made his first voyage, and discovered one of the West India Islands.

Five years later, John Cabot, a Venetian residing in Bristol, England, with his son Sebastian, who was probably born there, persuaded the king to aid them in a similar undertaking. On a map drawn by the father after his return we read the following lines: "In the year of our Lord 1497, John Cabot and his son Sebastian discovered that country which no one before his time had ventured to approach, on the 24th June, about 5 o'clock in the morning." That entry records the discovery of Newfoundland, which led a few days later to that of the mainland of North America, which was thus first seen by the Cabots.

As an offset to that record we have the following, taken from the king's private account-book: "10. Aug. 1497, To him that found the new isle £10."

Such was the humble beginning of a series of explorations which gave England possession of the largest part of the North American continent.

388. Henry VII.'s Reign the Beginning of a New Epoch. — A few years after Cabot's return Henry laid the corner-stone of that "solemn and sumptuous chapel" which bears his own name, and which joins Westminster Abbey on the east. There he gave orders that his tomb should be erected, and that prayers should be said over it "as long as the world lasted." Emerson remarks[1] that when the visitor to the Abbey mounts the flight of twelve black marble steps which lead from it to the edifice where Henry lies buried, he passes from the mediæval to the beginning of the modern age — a change which the architecture itself distinctly marks. The true significance of Henry's reign is, that it, in like manner, stands for a new epoch, new in modes of government, in law, in geographical discovery, in letters, art, and religion.

The century just closing was indeed one of the most remarkable

---

[1] English Traits.

No. 11.

THE WORLD SHORTLY AFTER THE ACCESSION OF HENRY VII.

Light arrows show voyages south made up to 1492; (light track, Da Gama's voyage, 1497).
Dark arrows, voyages of Columbus and Cabot.
White crosses, countries of which something was known before 1492.
White area, including western coast of Africa, the world as known shortly after Henry VII.'s accession.

in history, not only in what it had actually accomplished, but still more in the seed it was sowing for the future. The artist Kaulbach, in his fresco entitled "The Age of the Reformation,"[1] has summed up all that it was, and all that it was destined to become in its full development. Therein we see it as the period which witnessed the introduction of firearms, and the consequent overthrow of feudal warfare and feudal institutions; the growth of the power of royalty and of nationality through royalty; the sailing of Columbus and of Cabot; the revival of classical learning; the publication of the first printed book; and finally, the birth of that monk, Martin Luther, who was to emancipate the human mind from its long bondage to unmeaning tradition and arbitrary authority.

389. Summary. — Looking back, we find that with Henry the absolutism of the crown or "personal monarchy" began in England. Yet through its repressive power the country gained a prolonged peace, and, despite "benevolences" and other exactions, it grew into stronger national unity.

Simultaneously with this increase of royal authority came the discovery of a new world, in which England was to have the chief part. A century will elapse before those discoveries bear fruit. After that, our attention will no longer be confined to the British Islands, but will be fixed as well on that western continent where English enterprise and English love of liberty are destined to find a new and broader field of activity.

HENRY VIII. — 1509–1547.

390. Henry's Advantages. — Henry was not quite eighteen when he came to the throne. The country was at peace, was fairly prosperous, and the young king had everything in his favor. He was handsome, well-educated, and fond of athletic sports. His frank disposition won friends everywhere, and he had inherited

---

[1] Kaulbach's (Kowl'băk) Age of the Reformation: one of a historical series of colossal wall paintings in the Berlin Museum.

from his father the largest private fortune that had ever descended to an English sovereign. Intellectually, he was in hearty sympathy with the revival of learning, then in progress both on the continent and in England.

391. The New Learning; Colet, Erasmus, More. — During the greater part of the Middle Ages the chief object of education was to make men monks, and originally the schools established at Oxford and Cambridge were exclusively for that purpose. In their day they did excellent work; but a time came when men ceased to found monasteries, and began to erect colleges and hospitals instead.[1] In the course of the fourteenth and fifteenth centuries William of Wykeham and King Henry VI. built and endowed colleges which were specially designed to fit their pupils to live in the world and serve the state, instead of withdrawing from it to seek their own salvation. These new institutions encouraged a broader range of studies, and in Henry VI.'s time particular attention was given to the Latin classics, hitherto but little known. The geographical discoveries of Henry VII.'s reign, made by Columbus, Cabot, and others, began to stimulate scientific thought, and it was evident that the day was not far distant when questions about the earth and the stars would no longer be settled by a text from Scripture which forbade further inquiry.

With the accession of Henry VIII. education received a still further impulse. A few zealous English scholars had just returned from Italy to Oxford, full of ardor for a new study, — that of Greek. Among them was a young clergyman named John Colet. He saw that by means of that language, of which the alphabet was as yet hardly known in England, men might put themselves in direct communication with the greatest thinkers and writers of the past. Better still, they might acquire the power of reading the Gospels and the writings of St. Paul in the original, and thus reach their

---

[1] In the twelfth century 418 monasteries were founded in England; in the next century only about a third as many; in the fourteenth only 23; after that date their establishment may be said to cease.

true meaning and feel their full influence. Colet's intimate friend and fellow-worker, the Dutch scholar Erasmus, had the same enthusiasm. When in sore need of everything, he wrote in one of his letters, "As soon as I get some money I shall buy Greek books, and then I may buy some clothes." The third young man, who, with Erasmus and Colet devoted himself to the study of Greek and to the advancement of learning, was Thomas More, who later became lord chancellor. The three looked to King Henry for encouragement in the work they had undertaken; nor did they look in vain. Colet, who had become a doctor of divinity and a dean of St. Paul's Cathedral, London, encountered a furious storm of opposition on account of his devotion to the "New Learning," as it was sneeringly called. His attempts at educational reform met the same resistance. But Henry stood by him, liking the man's spirit, and saying, "Let others have what doctors they will; this is the doctor for me." The king also took a lively interest in Erasmus, who was appointed professor of Greek at Cambridge, where he began his great work of preparing an edition of the Greek Testament with a Latin translation in parallel columns. Up to this time the Greek Testament had existed in scattered manuscripts only. The publication of the work in printed form gave an additional impetus to the study of the Scriptures; helped forward the Reformation, and in a measure laid the foundation for a revised English translation of the Bible far superior to Wycliffe's. In the same spirit of genuine love of learning, Henry founded Trinity College, Cambridge, and at a later date confirmed and extended Cardinal Wolsey's endowment of Christ Church College, Oxford.

392. Henry versus Luther. — The king continued, however, to be a stanch Catholic, and certainly had no thought at this period of doing anything which should tend to undermine that ancient form of worship. In Germany, Martin Luther was making ready to begin his tremendous battle against the power and teachings of the Papacy. In 1517 he nailed to the door of the church of Wittenberg that famous series of denunciations which started the movement that ultimately protested against the authority of Rome, and gave the name of Protestant to all who joined it. A few years later Henry published a reply to one of Luther's books, and sent a copy bound in cloth of gold to the Pope. The Pope was so delighted with what he termed Henry's "angelic spirit," that he forthwith conferred on him that title of "Defender of the Faith," which the English sovereigns have persisted in retaining to the present time, though for what reason, and with what right, even a royal intellect might be somewhat puzzled to explain. With the new and flattering title the Pope also sent the king a costly two-handed sword, intended to represent Henry's zeal in smiting the enemies of Rome, but destined by fate to be the symbol of the king's final separation from the power that bestowed it.

393. Victory of Flodden; Field of the Cloth of Gold. — Politically, Henry was equally fortunate. The Scotch had ventured to attack the kingdom during the king's absence on the continent. They were defeated at Flodden by the Earl of Surrey, with great slaughter. This victory placed Scotland at Henry's feet.[1]

The king of France and the emperor Charles V. of Germany now vied with each other in seeking Henry's alliance. The emperor visited England in order to meet the English sovereign, while the king of France arranged an interview in his own dominions, known, from the magnificence of its appointments, as the "Field of the Cloth of Gold." Henry held the balance of power by which he could make France or Germany predominate as he saw fit. It was owing to his able diplomatic policy that England reaped advantages from both sides, and advanced from a comparatively low position to one that was fully abreast of the foremost nations of Europe.

394. Henry's Marriage with his Brother's Widow. — Such was the king at the outset. In less than twenty years he had become another man. At the age of twelve he had married,[2] at his

---

[1] See Scott's Marmion. [2] See Hallam; other authorities call it a solemn betrothal.

father's command, and solely for political and mercenary reasons, Catharine of Aragon, his brother Arthur's widow, who was six years his senior. Such a marriage was forbidden, except in certain cases, both by the Old Testament and by the ordinances of the Roman Catholic Church. The Pope, however, had granted his permission, and when Henry ascended the throne, the ceremony was performed a second time. Several children were the fruit of this union, all of whom died in infancy, except one daughter, Mary, unhappily fated to figure as the "Bloody Mary" of later history.

395. The King's Anxiety for a Successor; Anne Boleyn. — No woman had yet ruled in her own right, either in England or in any prominent kingdom of Europe; and so anxious was Henry to have a son to succeed him, that he had several years before sent the Duke of Buckingham to the block for casually saying, that if the king died without issue, he should consider himself entitled to receive the crown.

It was while meditating this question of the succession, that Henry became attached to Anne Boleyn, one of the queen's maids of honor, a sprightly brunette of nineteen, with long black hair and strikingly beautiful eyes.

The light that shone in those eyes, though hardly that "Gospel-light" which the poet calls it,[1] was yet bright enough to effectually clear up all difficulties in the royal mind. The king now felt conscientiously moved to obtain a divorce from the old wife, and to marry a new one. In that determination lay most momentous consequences, since it finally separated England from the jurisdiction of the church of Rome.

396. Wolsey favors the Divorce from Catharine. — Cardinal Wolsey, Henry's chief counsellor, lent his powerful aid to bring about the divorce, but with the expectation that the king would marry a princess of France, and thus form an alliance with that

---

[1] "When love could teach a monarch to be wise,
And Gospel-light first dawned from Bullen's [Boleyn's] eyes." — GRAY.

country. If so, his own ambitious schemes would be forwarded, since the united influence of the two kingdoms might elevate him to the Papacy. When Wolsey learned that the king's choice was Anne Boleyn, he fell on his knees, and begged him not to persist in his purpose; but his entreaties had no effect, and the cardinal was obliged to continue what he had begun.

397. The Court at Blackfriars. — Application had been made to the Pope to annul the marriage with Catharine on the ground of illegality; but the Pope was in the power of the emperor, Charles V., who was the queen's nephew. Vexatious delays now became the order of the day. At last, a court composed of Cardinal Wolsey and Cardinal Campeggio, an Italian, as papal legates, or representatives, was convened at Blackfriars, London, to test the validity of the marriage. Henry and Catharine were summoned. The first appeared and answered to his name. When the queen was called she declined to answer, but throwing herself at Henry's feet, begged him with tears and sobs not to put her away without cause. Finding him inflexible, she left the court, and refused to attend again, appealing to Rome for justice.

This was in the spring of 1529. Nothing was done that summer, and in the autumn, the court, instead of reaching a decision, dissolved. Campeggio, the Italian legate, returned to Italy, and Henry, to his disappointment and rage, received an order from Rome to carry the question to the Pope for settlement.

398. Fall of Wolsey. — Both the king and Anne Boleyn believed that Wolsey had played false with them. They now resolved upon his destruction. The cardinal had a presentiment of his impending doom. The French ambassador, who saw him at this juncture, said that his face had shrunk to half its size. But his fortunes were destined to shrink even more than his face. By a law of Richard II. no representative of the Pope had any rightful authority in England.[1] Though the king had given his consent to Wolsey's holding the office of legate, yet now that a

---

[1] See Paragraph No. 317.

contrary result to what he expected had been reached, he proceeded to prosecute him to the full extent of the law.

It was an easy matter to crush the cardinal. His arrogance and extravagant ostentation had excited the jealous hate of the nobility; his constant demands for money in behalf of the king had set Parliament against him; and his exactions from the common people had, as the chronicle of the time tells us, made them weep, beg, and "speak cursedly." Wolsey bowed to the storm, and to save himself gave up everything; his riches, pomp, power, all vanished as suddenly as they had come. It was Henry's hand that stripped him, but it was Anne Boleyn who moved that hand. Well might the humbled favorite say of her: —

> "There was the weight that pulled me down.
> . . . all my glories
> In that one woman I have lost forever." [1]

Thus deprived of well-nigh everything but life, Wolsey was permitted to go into retirement in the north; but a twelvemonth later he was arrested on a charge of high treason; and as the irony of fate would have it, the warrant was served by a former lover of Anne Boleyn's, whom Wolsey, it is said, had separated from her in order that she might consummate her unhappy marriage with royalty. On the way to London Wolsey fell mortally ill, and turned aside at Leicester to die in the abbey there, with the words: —

> " . . . O, Father Abbot,
> An old man, broken with the storms of state,
> Is come to lay his weary bones among ye:
> Give him a little earth for charity!" [2]

399. Appeal to the Universities. — Before Wolsey's death, Dr. Thomas Cranmer, of Cambridge, suggested that the king lay the divorce question before the universities of Europe. Henry caught eagerly at this proposition, and exclaimed, "Cranmer has the right pig by the ear." The scheme was at once adopted. Several uni-

---

[1] Shakespeare's Henry VIII., Act III. Sc. 2.
[2] Shakespeare's Henry VIII., Act IV. Sc. 2.

versities returned favorable answers. In a few instances, as at Oxford and Cambridge, where the authorities hesitated, a judicious use of bribes or threats soon brought them to see the matter in a proper light.

400. The Clergy declare Henry Head of the Church. — Armed with these decisions in his favor, Henry now charged the whole body of the English church with being guilty of the same crime of which Wolsey had been accused. In their terror they made haste to buy a pardon at a cost reckoned at nearly $5,000,000 at the present value of money. They furthermore declared Henry to be the supreme head on earth of the church of England, adroitly adding, "in so far as is permitted by the law of Christ." Thus the Reformation came into England "by a side door, as it were." Nevertheless, it came.

401. Henry marries Anne Boleyn; Act of Supremacy. — Events now moved rapidly toward a crisis. Thomas Cromwell, Wolsey's former servant and fast friend, succeeded him in the king's favor. In 1533, after having waited over five years, Henry privately married Anne, and she was soon after crowned in Westminster Abbey. When the Pope was informed of this, he ordered the king, under pain of excommunication, to put her away, and to take back Catharine. In 1534 Parliament met that demand by passing the Act of Supremacy, which declared Henry to be without reservation the sole head of the church, making denial thereof high treason.[1] As he signed the act, the king with one stroke of his pen overturned the traditions of a thousand years, and England stood boldly forth with a national church independent of the Pope.

402. Subserviency of Parliament. — But as Luther said, Henry had a pope within him. Through Cromwell's zealous aid

---

[1] Henry's full title was now " Henry VIII., by the Grace of God, King of England, France, and Ireland, Defender of the Faith and of the Church of England, and also of Ireland, on earth the Supreme Head."

he now proceeded to prove it. We have already seen that since the Wars of the Roses had destroyed the power of the barons, there was no effectual check on the despotic will of the king. The new nobility were the creatures of the crown, and hence bound to support it; the clergy were timid, the commons anything but bold, so that Parliament gradually became the servile echo and ready instrument of the throne, and empowered the king on his reaching the age of twenty-four to annul whatever legislative enactments he pleased of those which had been passed since his accession. It now humiliated itself still further by promulgating that law, in itself the destruction of all law, which enabled Henry by his simple proclamation to declare any opinions he disliked, heretical, and punishable with death.

403. Execution of More and Fisher. —Cromwell in his crooked and cruel policy had reduced bloodshed to a science. He first introduced the practice of condemning an accused prisoner without allowing him to speak in his own defence. No one was now safe who did not openly side with the king. Sir Thomas More, who had been lord chancellor, and the aged Bishop Fisher were executed because they could not affirm that they conscientiously believed that Henry was morally and spiritually entitled to be the head of the English church. Both died with Christian fortitude. More said to the governor of the Tower with a flash of his old humor, as the steps leading to the scaffold shook while he was mounting them, "Do you see me safe up, and I will make shift to get down by myself."

404. Suppression of the Monasteries; Seizure of their Property. — When the intelligence of the judicial murder of the venerable ex-chancellor reached Rome, the Pope proceeded to issue a bull of excommunication and deposition against Henry, by which he delivered his soul to the devil, and his kingdom to the first invader. The king retaliated by the suppression of the monasteries. In doing so, he simply hastened a process which had already begun. Years before, Cardinal Wolsey had not scrupled to shut up several, and take their revenues to found a college at Oxford. The truth was, that monasticism had done its work, and as a recent writer has well said, "was dead long before the Reformation came to bury it."[1]

Henry, however, had no such worthy object as Wolsey had. His pretext was that these institutions had sunk into a state of ignorance, drunkenness, and profligacy.

Their vices, however, the king had already made his own. It was their wealth which he now coveted. The smaller religious houses were speedily swept out of existence. This caused a furious insurrection in the north, but the revolt was soon put down.

Though Parliament had readily given its sanction to the extinction of the smaller monasteries, it hesitated about abolishing the greater ones. Henry, it is reported, sent for a leading member of the House of Commons, and laying his hand on the head of the kneeling representative, said, "Get my bill passed by to-morrow little man, or else to-morrow this head of yours will come off.' The next day the bill passed, and the work of destruction begai. anew. It involved the confiscation of millions of property, and the summary execution of abbots, who, like those of Glastonbury and Charter House, dared to resist.[2]

The magnificent monastic buildings throughout England were now stripped of everything of value, and left as ruins. The beautiful windows of stained glass were wantonly broken; the images of the saints were cast down from their niches; the chimes of bells were melted and cast into cannon; while the valuable libraries were torn up and sold to grocers and soap-boilers for wrapping-paper. At Canterbury, Becket's tomb was broken open, and after he had been four centuries in his grave, the saint was summoned to answer a charge of rebellion and treason. The case was tried at Westminster Abbey, the martyr's bones were

---

[1] Armitage, Childhood of the English Nation.

[2] The total number of religious houses destroyed was 645 monasteries, 2374 chapels, 90 collegiate churches, and 110 charitable institutions. Among the most famous of these ruins are Kirkstall, Furness, Netley, Tintern, and Fountains Abbeys.

sentenced to be burned, and the jewels and rich offerings of his shrine were seized by the king.

Among the few monastic buildings which escaped was the beautiful abbey church of Peterborough, where Catharine of Aragon, who died soon after the king's marriage with her rival, was buried. Henry had the grace to give orders that on her account it should be spared, saying that he would leave to her memory "one of the goodliest monuments in Christendom."

The great estates thus suddenly acquired by the crown were granted to favorites or thrown away at the gambling-table. "It is from this date," says Hallam, "that the leading families of England, both within and without the peerage, became conspicuous through having obtained possession of the monastery lands." These were estimated to comprise about one-fourth of the whole area of the kingdom.

405. Effects of the Destruction of the Monasteries. — The sweeping character of this act had a twofold effect. First, it made the king more absolute than before, for, since it removed the abbots, who had had seats in the House of Lords, that body was made just so much smaller and less able to resist the royal will.

Next, the abolition of so many religious institutions necessarily caused great misery to those who were turned out upon the world destitute of means and without ability to work. In the end, however, no permanent injury was done, since the monasteries, by their profuse and indiscriminate charity, had undoubtedly encouraged much of the very pauperism which they had relieved.

406. Distress among the Laboring Classes. — An industrial revolution was also in progress at this time which was productive of wide-spread suffering. It had begun early in Henry's reign through the great numbers of discharged soldiers, who could not readily find work. Sir Thomas More had given a striking picture of their miserable condition in his "Utopia," a book in which he urged the government to consider measures for their relief; but the evil had since become much worse. Farmers, having discovered that wool-growing was more profitable than the raising of grain, had turned their fields into sheep-pastures; so that a shepherd with his dog now took the place of several families of laborers. This change brought multitudes of poor people to the verge of starvation; and as the monasteries no longer existed to hold out a helping hand, the whole realm was overrun with beggars and thieves. Bishop Latimer, a noted preacher of that day, declared that if every farmer should raise two acres of hemp, it would not make rope enough to hang them all. Henry, however, set to work with characteristic vigor, and it is said made way with over 70,000, but without materially abating the evil.

407. Execution of Anne Boleyn; Marriage with Jane Seymour. — In 1536, less than three years after her coronation, the new queen, Anne Boleyn, for whom Henry had "turned England and Europe upside down," was accused of unfaithfulness. She was sent a prisoner to the Tower. A short time after, her head rolled in the dust, the light of its beauty gone out forever.

The next morning Henry married Jane Seymour, Anne's maid of honor. Parliament passed an act of approval, declaring that it was all done "of the king's most excellent goodness." A year later the queen died, leaving a son, Edward. She was no sooner gone than the king began looking about for some one to take her place.

408. More Marriages. — This time Cromwell had projects of his own for a German Protestant alliance. He succeeded in persuading his master to agree to marry Anne of Cleves, a German princess, whom the king had never seen, but whom the painter Holbein represented in a portrait as a woman of surpassing beauty.

When Anne reached England, Henry hurried to meet her with all a lover's ardor. To his dismay, he found that not only was she ridiculously ugly, but that she could speak — so he said — "nothing but Dutch," of which he did not understand a word. Matters, however, had gone too far to retract, and the marriage was duly solemnized. The king obtained a divorce within six months, and then took his revenge by cutting off Cromwell's head.

The same year Henry married Catharine Howard, a fascinating girl still in her teens, whose charms so moved the king that it is said he was tempted to have a special thanksgiving service prepared to commemorate the day he found her. Unfortunately, Catharine had fallen into dishonor before her marriage. She tried hard to keep the terrible secret, but finding it impossible, confessed her fault. For such cases Henry had no mercy. The queen was tried for high treason, and soon walked that road in which Anne Boleyn had preceded her.

Not to be baffled in his matrimonial experiments, the king, in 1543, took Catherine Parr for his sixth and last wife. She, too, would have gone to the block, on a charge of heresy, had not her quick wit saved her by a happily turned compliment, which flattered the king's self-conceit as a profound theologian.

409. Henry's Action respecting Religion. — Though occupied with these rather numerous domestic infelicities, Henry was not idle in other directions. By an act known as the Six Articles, or, as the Protestants called it, the "Bloody Act," the king established a new form of religion, which in words, at least, was practically the same as that upheld by the Pope, but with the Pope left out. Geographically, the country was about equally divided between Catholicism and Protestantism. The northern and western half clung to the ancient faith; the southern and eastern, including most of the large cities where Wycliffe's doctrines had formerly prevailed, was favorable to the Reformation. On the one hand, Henry prohibited the Lutheran doctrine; on the other, he caused the Bible to be translated, and ordered a copy to be chained to a desk in every parish church in England; but though all persons might now freely read the Scriptures, no one but the clergy was allowed to interpret them. Later in his reign, the king became alarmed at the spread of discussion about religious subjects, and prohibited the reading of the Bible by the "lower sort of people."

410. Heresy versus Treason. — Men now found themselves in a strange and cruel dilemma. If it was dangerous to believe too much, it was equally dangerous to believe too little. Traitor and heretic were dragged to execution on the same hurdle : for Henry burned as heretics those who declared their belief in Protestantism, and hanged as traitors those who acknowledged the authority of the Pope. Thus Anne Askew, a young and beautiful woman, was nearly wrenched asunder on the rack, in the hope of making her implicate the queen in her heresy, and afterward burned because she insisted that the bread and wine used in the communion service seemed to her to be simply bread and wine, and not in any sense the actual body and blood of Christ, as the king's statute of the "Six Articles" solemnly declared. On the other hand, the aged Countess of Salisbury suffered for treason; but with a spirit matching the king's, she refused to kneel at the block, and told the executioner he must get her gray head off as best he could.

411. Henry's Death. — But the time was at hand when Henry was to cease his hangings, beheadings, and marriages. Worn out with debauchery, he died at the age of fifty-six, a loathsome, unwieldy, and helpless mass of corruption. In his will he left a large sum of money to pay for perpetual prayers for the repose of his soul. Sir Walter Raleigh said of him, "If all the pictures and patterns of a merciless prince were lost in the world, they might all again be painted to the life out of the story of this king." It may be well to remember this, and along with it this other saying of the ablest living writer on English constitutional history, that "the world owes some of its greatest debts to men from whose memory it recoils."[1] The obligation it is under to Henry VIII. is that through his influence — no matter what the motive — England was lifted up out of the old mediæval ruts, and placed squarely and securely on the new highway of national progress.

412. Summary. — In this reign we find that though England lost much of her former political freedom, yet she gained that

---

[1] Stubbs's Constitutional History of England.

order and peace which came from the iron hand of absolute power. Next, from the suppression of the monasteries, and the sale or gift of their lands to favorites of the king, three results ensued : (1) a new nobility was in great measure created, dependent on the crown; (2) the House of Lords was made less powerful by the removal of the abbots who had had seats in it; (3) pauperism was for a time largely increased, and much distress caused. Finally, England completely severed her connection with the Pope, and established for the first time an independent national church, having the king as its head.

EDWARD VI. — 1547-1553.

413. Bad Government; Seizure of Unenclosed Lands; High Rents; Latimer's Sermon. — Edward, son of Henry VIII. by Jane Seymour, died at sixteen. In the first of his reign of six years the government was managed by his uncle, the Duke of Somerset, an extreme Protestant, whose intentions were good, but who lacked practical judgment. During the latter part of his life Edward fell under the control of the Duke of Northumberland, who was the head of a band of scheming and profligate men. They, with other nobles, seized the unenclosed lands of the country and fenced them in for sheep pastures, thus driving into beggary many who had formerly got a good part of their living from these commons. At the same time farm rents rose in some cases ten and even twenty-fold,[1] depriving thousands of the means of subsistence, and reducing many who had been in comfortable circumstances to poverty.

The bitter complaints of the sufferers found expression in Bishop Latimer's outspoken sermon preached before the king, in which he said: "My father was a yeoman [small farmer], and had no lands of his own, only he had a farm of three or four pounds

---

[1] This was owing to the greed for land on the part of the mercantile classes, who had now acquired wealth, and wished to become landed proprietors. See Froude's England.

[rent] by year, and hereupon tilled so much as kept half a dozen men; he had walk [pasture] for a hundred sheep, and my mother milked thirty kine. He was able and did find the king a harness [suit of armor] with himself and his horse, until he came to the place where he should receive the king's wages. I can remember that I buckled his harness when he went into Blackheath Field. He kept me to school, or else I had not been able to have preached before the king's majesty now. He married my sisters with five pounds . . . apiece. He kept hospitality for his poor neighbors, and some alms he gave to the poor. And all this he did off the said farm, where he that now hath it payeth sixteen pounds a year or more, and is not able to do anything for his prince, for himself, nor for his children, or give a cup of drink to the poor." But as Latimer pathetically said, "Let the preacher preach till his tongue be worn to the stumps, nothing is amended."[1]

414. Edward establishes Protestantism. — Henry had established the Church of England as an independent organization. His son took the next great step, and made it Protestant in doctrine. At his desire, Archbishop Cranmer compiled a book of Common Prayer, taken largely from the Roman Catholic Prayerbook. This collection all churches were now obliged by law to use. Edward's sister, the Princess Mary, was a firm Catholic. She refused to adopt the new service, saying to Ridley, who urged her to accept it as God's word, "I cannot tell what you call God's word, for that is not God's word now which was God's word in my father's time." It was at this period, also, that the Articles of Faith of the Church of England were first drawn up.

415. King Edward and Mary Stuart. — Henry VIII. had attempted to marry his son Edward to young Queen Mary Stuart, daughter of the king of Scotland, but the match had been broken off. Edward's guardian now insisted that it should be carried out. He invaded Scotland with an army, and attempted to effect the

---

[1] Latimer's first sermon before King Edward VI., 8th of March, 1549.

marriage by force of arms, at the battle of Pinkie. The English gained a decided victory, but the youthful queen, instead of giving her hand to young King Edward, left the country and married the son of the king of France. She will appear with melancholy prominence in the reign of Elizabeth. Had she married Edward, we should perhaps have been spared that tragedy in which she was called to play both the leading and the losing part.

416. Renewed Confiscation of Church Property; Schools founded. — The confiscation of such Roman Catholic church property as had been spared was now renewed. The result of this and of the abandonment of Catholicism was in certain respects disastrous to the country. In this general break-up, many who had been held in restraint by the old forms of faith now went to the other extreme, and rejected all religion.

Part, however, of the money thus obtained from the sale of church property was devoted, mainly through Edward's influence, to the endowment of upwards of forty grammar schools, besides a number of hospitals, in different sections of the country. But for a long time the destruction of the monastic schools, poor as they were, was a serious blow to the education of the common people.

417. Edward's London Charities; Christ's Hospital. — Just before his death Edward established Christ's Hospital, and refounded and renewed the hospitals of St. Thomas and St. Bartholomew in London. Thus "he was the founder," says Burnet, "of those houses which, by many great additions since that time, have risen to be amongst the noblest of Europe."[1]

Christ's Hospital was, perhaps, the first Protestant charity school opened in England; many more were patterned on it. It is generally known as the Blue-Coat School, from the costume of the boys — a relic of the days of Edward VI. This consists of a long blue coat, like a monk's gown, reaching to the ankles, girded with a broad leathern belt, long, bright yellow stockings, and

---

[1] Burnet: History of the Reformation in England.

buckled shoes. The boys go bareheaded winter and summer. An exciting game of foot-ball, played in the schoolyard in this peculiar mediæval dress, seems strangely in contrast with the sights of modern London streets. It is as though the spectator, by passing through a gateway, had gone back over three centuries of time. Coleridge, Lamb, and other noted men of letters were educated here, and have left most interesting reminiscences of their school life, especially the latter, in his delightful "Essays of Elia."[1]

418. Effect of Catholicism versus Protestantism. — Speaking of the Protestant Reformation, of which Edward VI. may be taken as a representative, Macaulay remarks that "it is difficult to say whether England received most advantage from the Roman Catholic religion or from the Reformation. For the union of the Saxon and Norman races, and the abolition of slavery, she is chiefly indebted to the influences which the priesthood in the Middle Ages exercised over the people; for political and intellectual freedom, and for all the blessings which they have brought in their train, she owes most to the great rebellion of the people against the priesthood."

419. Summary. — The establishment of the Protestant faith in England, and of a large number of free Protestant schools known as Edward VI.'s schools, may be regarded as the leading events of Edward's brief reign of six years.

MARY. — 1553-1558.

420. Lady Jane Grey claims the Crown. — On the death of Edward, Lady Jane Grey, a descendant of Henry VII., and a distant relative of Edward VI., was persuaded by her father-in-law, the Duke of Northumberland, to assume the crown, which had been left to her by the will of the late king. Edward's object in naming Lady Jane was to secure a Protestant successor, since

---

[1] See Lamb's Essays, "Christ's Hospital." Hospital, so called because intended for "poor, fatherless children." The word was then often used in the sense of asylum, or "home."

his elder sister, Mary, was a devout Catholic, while from his younger sister, Elizabeth, he seems for some reason to have been estranged. Mary was without doubt the rightful heir.[1] She received the support of the country, and Lady Jane Grey and her husband, Lord Dudley, were sent to the Tower.

421. Question of Mary's Marriage; Wyatt's Rebellion. — While they were confined there, the question of the queen's marriage came up. Out of several candidates for her hand, Mary gave preference to her cousin, Philip II. of Spain. Her choice was very unpopular, for it was known in England that Philip was a selfish and gloomy fanatic, who cared for nothing but the advancement of the Roman Catholic faith.

An insurrection now broke out, led by Sir Thomas Wyatt, the object of which was to place the Princess Elizabeth on the throne, and thus secure the crown to Protestantism. Lady Jane Grey's father was implicated in the rebellion. The movement ended in failure, the leaders were executed, and Mary ordered her sister

---

[1] Table showing some of the descendants of Henry VII., with the respective claims of Queen Mary and Lady Jane Grey to the crown.

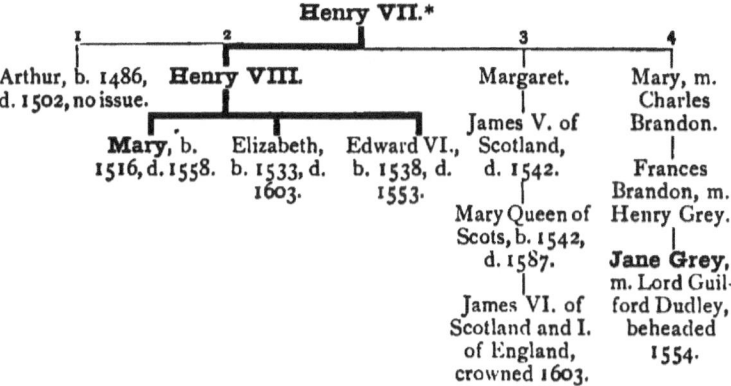

* The heavy lines indicate the direct order of succession. Next after Henry VIII.'s descendants the claim would go to the descendants of Margaret (No. 3), and lastly to those of Mary, wife of Charles Brandon (No. 4).

Elizabeth, who was thought to be in the plot, to be seized and imprisoned in the Tower.

A little later, Lady Jane Grey and her husband perished on the scaffold. The name, JANE, deeply cut in the stone wall of the Beauchamp Tower,[1] remains as a memorial of the nine days' queen. She died at the age of seventeen, an innocent victim of the greatness which had been thrust upon her.

422. Mary marries Philip II. of Spain; Efforts to restore Catholicism. — A few months afterward the royal marriage was celebrated, but Philip soon found that the air of England had too much freedom in it to suit his delicate constitution, and he returned to the more congenial climate of Spain.

From that time Mary, who was left to rule alone, directed all her efforts to the restoration of the Catholic church. She repealed the legislation of Henry VIII.'s and Edward VI.'s reign, so far as it gave support to Protestantism. The old relations with Rome were resumed. To accomplish her object in supporting her religion, the queen resorted to the arguments of the dungeon, the rack, and the fagot, and when Bishops Bonner and Gardiner slackened their work of persecution and death, Mary, half-crazed by Philip's desertion, urged them not to stay their hands.

423. Devices for reading the Bible. — The penalty for reading the English Scriptures, or for offering Protestant prayers, was death. In his autobiography, Benjamin Franklin says that one of his ancestors, who lived in England in Mary's reign, adopted the following expedient for giving his family religious instruction : He fastened an open Bible with strips of tape on the under side of a stool. When he wished to read it aloud he placed the stool upside down on his knees, and turned the pages under the tape as he read them. One of the children stood watching at the door to give the alarm if any one approached ; in that case, the stool was

---

[1] The Beauchamp Tower is part of the Tower of London. On its walls are scores of names cut by those who were imprisoned in it.

set quickly on its feet again on the floor, so that nothing could be seen.

424. Religious Toleration Unknown in Mary's Age. — Mary would doubtless have bravely endured for her faith the full measure of suffering which she inflicted. Her state of mind was that of all who then held strong convictions. Each party believed it a duty to convert or exterminate the other, and the alternative offered to the heretic was to "turn or burn."

Sir Thomas More, who gave his life as a sacrifice to conscience in Henry's reign, was eager to put Tyndale to the torture for translating the Bible. Cranmer, who perished at Oxford, had been zealous in sending to the flames those who differed from him. Even Latimer, who died bravely at the stake, exhorting his companion Ridley " to be of good cheer and play the man, since they would light such a candle in England that day as in God's grace should not be put out," had abetted the kindling of slow fires under men as honest and determined as himself but on the opposite side. In like spirit Queen Mary kept Smithfield ablaze with martyrs, whose blood was the seed of Protestantism. Yet persecution under Mary never reached the proportions that it did on the continent. At the most, but a few hundred died in England for the sake of their religion, while Philip II., during the last of his reign, covered Holland with the graves of Protestants, tortured and put to cruel deaths, or buried alive, by tens of thousands.

425. Mary's Death. — But Mary's career was short. She died in 1558, near the close of an inglorious war with France, which ended in the fall of Calais, the last English possession on the continent. It was a great blow to her pride, and a serious humiliation to the country. "After my death," she said, "you will find Calais written on my heart." Could she have foreseen the future, her grief would have been greater still. For with the end of her reign the Pope lost all power in England, never to regain it.

426. Mary deserving of Pity rather than Hatred. — Mary's name has come down to us associated with an epithet expressive of the utmost abhorrence; but she deserves pity rather than hatred. Her cruelty was the cruelty of sincerity, never, as was her father's, the result of indifference or caprice. A little book of prayers which she left, soiled by constant use, and stained with many tears, tells the story of her broken and disappointed life. Separated from her mother, the unfortunate Catharine of Aragon, when she was only sixteen, she was ill-treated by Anne Boleyn and hated by her father. Thus the springtime of her youth was blighted. Her marriage brought her no happiness; sickly, ill-favored, childless, unloved, the poor woman spent herself for naught. Her first great mistake was that she resolutely turned her face toward the past; her second, that she loved Philip of Spain with all her heart, soul, and strength, and so, out of devotion to a bigot, did a bigot's work, and earned that execration which never fails to be a bigot's reward.

427. Summary. — This reign should be looked upon as a period of reaction. The temporary check which Mary gave to Protestantism deepened and strengthened it. Nothing builds up a religious faith like martyrdom, and the next reign showed that every heretic that Mary had burned helped to make at least a hundred more.

ELIZABETH. — 1558–1603.

428. Accession of Elizabeth. — Elizabeth was the daughter of Henry VIII. and Anne Boleyn. At the time of Mary's death she was living in seclusion in Hatfield House, near London, spending most of her time in studying the Greek and Latin authors. When the news was brought to her, she was deeply moved, and exclaimed, "It is the Lord's doings; it is marvellous in our eyes." Five days afterwards she removed to London by that road over which the last time she had travelled it she was being carried a prisoner to the Tower.

429. Difficulty of Elizabeth's Position. — Her position was full of difficulty, if not absolute peril. Mary Stuart of Scotland, now by marriage queen of France,[1] claimed the English crown through descent from Henry VII., on the ground that Elizabeth, as daughter of Anne Boleyn, was not lawfully entitled to the throne, the Pope never having recognized Henry's second marriage. Both France and Rome supported this claim. On the other hand, Philip II. of Spain favored Elizabeth, but solely because he hoped to marry her and annex her kingdom to his dominions. Scotland was divided between two religious factions, and its attitude as an independent kingdom could hardly be called friendly. Ireland was a nest of desperate rebels, ready to join any attack on an English sovereign.

430. Religious Parties. — But more dangerous than all, England was divided in its religion. In the north, many noble families stood by the old faith, and hoped to see the Pope's power restored. In the towns of the southeast, a majority favored the Protestant church of England as it had been organized under Edward VI.

Besides these two great parties there were two more, who made up in zeal and determination what they lacked in numbers. One was the Jesuits; the other, the Puritans. The Jesuits were a new Roman Catholic order, banded together to support the church and to destroy heresy; openly or secretly their agents penetrated every country; it was believed that they hesitated at nothing to gain their ends. The Puritans were Protestants who, like John Calvin of Geneva, and John Knox of Edinburgh, were bent on cleansing or "*purifying*" the reformed faith from every vestige of Catholicism. Many of them were what the rack and the stake had naturally made them, — hard, fearless, narrow, bitter. In Scotland they had got entire possession of the government; in England they were steadily gaining ground. They were ready to recognize the queen as head of the state church, they even wished that all per-

---

[1] After Elizabeth, Mary stood next in order of succession. See Table, Paragraph No. 421.

sons should be compelled to worship as the government prescribed, but they protested against such a church as Elizabeth and the bishops then maintained.

431. The Queen's Choice of Counsellors. — Her policy from the beginning was one of compromise. In order to conciliate the Catholic party, she retained eleven of her sister Mary's counsellors, but added to them Sir William Cecil (Lord Burleigh), Sir Nicholas Bacon, and, later, Sir Francis Walsingham, with others who were favorable to the reformed faith.

On his appointment, Elizabeth said to Cecil, "This judgment I have of you, that you will not be corrupted with any gifts, that you will be faithful to the state, and that without respect to my private will you will give me that counsel which you think best." Cecil served the queen until his death, forty years afterward. The almost implicit obedience with which Elizabeth followed his advice sufficiently proves that he was the real power not only behind, but generally above, the throne.

432. The Coronation. — The bishops were Roman Catholic, and Elizabeth found it difficult to get one to perform the coronation services. At length the Bishop of Carlisle consented, but only on condition that the queen should take the ancient form of coronation oath, by which she virtually bound herself to support the Church of Rome.[1] To this Elizabeth agreed, and having consulted her astrologer, Dr. Dee, to fix a lucky day for the ceremony, she was crowned by his advice on Sunday, Jan. 15, 1558.

433. Changes in the Church Service; Religious Legislation. — The late Queen Mary, besides having repealed the legislation of the two preceding reigns, in so far as it was opposed to her own religious convictions, had restored the Roman Catholic Latin Prayer-Book. At Elizabeth's coronation, a petition was presented

---

[1] By this oath, every English sovereign from William the Conqueror to Elizabeth, and even as late as James II., with the single exception of Edward VI., swore to "preserve religion in the same state as did Edward the Confessor." This was changed to support Protestantism in 1688.

stating that it was the custom to release a certain number of prisoners on such occasions. The petitioners, therefore, begged her majesty to set at liberty the four evangelists, Matthew, Mark, Luke, and John, and also the apostle Paul, who had been for some time shut up in a strange language. The English Service-Book, with some slight changes, was accordingly reinstated.

A bill was soon after passed requiring all clergymen, under penalty of imprisonment for life, to use it, and it only. The same act imposed a heavy fine on all persons who failed to attend the Church of England on Sundays or holidays. At that time church and state were supposed to be inseparable. No country in Europe, not even Protestant Germany, could then conceive the idea of their existing apart. Whoever, therefore, refused to sustain the established form of worship was looked upon as a rebel against the government. To try such rebels, a special court was organized by Elizabeth, called the High Commission Court.[1] By it many Catholics were tortured and imprisoned for persisting in their allegiance to the Pope. About two hundred priests and Jesuits were put to death. A number of Puritans, also, were executed for seditious publications, while others were imprisoned or banished.

434. Act of Supremacy. — No sooner was the queen's accession announced to the Pope, than he declared her illegitimate, and ordered her to lay aside her crown and submit herself entirely to his guidance. Such a demand was a signal for battle. However much attached the larger part of the nation, especially the country people, may have been to the religion of their fathers, yet they intended to support the queen. The temper of Parliament manifested itself in the immediate re-enactment of the Act of Supremacy. It was essentially the same, "though with its edge a little blunted," as that which, under Henry, had freed England from the dominion of Rome.

To this act, every member of the House of Commons was

---

[1] High Commission Court: so called, because originally certain church dignitaries were appointed commissioners to inquire into heresies and kindred matters.

obliged to subscribe; thus all Catholics were excluded from among them. The Lords, however, not being an elective body, were excused from the obligation.

435. The Thirty-nine Articles; the Queen's Religion. — Half a year later the creed of the English church, which had been first formulated under Edward VI., was revised and reduced to the Thirty-nine Articles which constitute it at the present time. But the real value of the religious revolution which was taking place did not lie in the substitution of one creed for another, but in the new spirit of inquiry, and the new freedom of thought which that change awakened.

As for Elizabeth herself, she seems to have had no deep and abiding convictions on these matters. Her tendency was undoubtedly towards Protestantism, but to the end of her life she kept up some Catholic forms. A crucifix, with lighted candles in front of it, hung in her private chapel, before which she prayed to the Virgin as fervently as her sister Mary had ever done.

436. The Nation halting between Two Opinions. — In this double course she represented the majority of the nation, which hesitated about committing itself fully to either side. Men were not wanting who were ready to lay down their lives for conscience' sake, but they were by no means numerous. Many sympathized at heart with the notorious Vicar of Bray, who kept his pulpit under the whole or some part of the successive reigns of Henry, Edward, Mary, and Elizabeth, changing his theology with each change of rule. When taunted as a turncoat, he replied, "Not so, for I have always been true to my principles, which are to live and die Vicar of Bray."[1] Though there was nothing morally noble in such halting between two opinions, and facing both ways, yet it saved England for the time from that worst of all calamities,

---

[1] "For this as law I will maintain
Until my dying day, sir,
That whatsoever king shall reign,
I'll be Vicar of Bray, sir."

a religious civil war, such as rent France in pieces, drenched her fair fields with the blood of Catholics and Protestants, split Germany and Italy into petty states, and ended in Spain in the triumph of the Inquisition, and intellectual death.[1]

437. The Question of the Queen's Marriage. — Elizabeth showed the same tact with regard to marriage that she did with regard to religion. Her first Parliament, realizing that the welfare of the country depended largely on whom the queen should marry, begged her to consider the question of taking a husband. Her reply was that she had resolved to live and die a maiden queen. When further pressed, she returned answers that, like the ancient oracles, might be interpreted either way. The truth was, that Elizabeth saw the difficulty of her position better than any one else. The choice of her heart at that time would have been the Protestant Earl of Leicester, but she knew that to take him as consort would be to incur the enmity of the great Catholic powers of Europe. On the other hand, if she accepted a Catholic, she would inevitably alienate a large and influential number of her own subjects. In this dilemma she resolved to keep both sides in a state of hopeful expectation. Philip II. of Spain, who had married her sister Mary, made overtures to Elizabeth. She kept him waiting in uncertainty until at last his ambassador lost all patience, and declared that the queen was possessed with ten thousand devils. Later, the Duke of Anjou, a son of Henry II. of France, proposed. He was favorably received, but the country became so alarmed at the prospect of having a Catholic king, that Stubbs, a Puritan lawyer, published a coarse and violent pamphlet denouncing the marriage.[2] For this attack his right hand was cut off; as it fell, says an eye-witness,[3] he seized his hat with the other hand, and waved it, shouting, "God save Queen Elizabeth!" That act

---

[1] Gardiner's History of England.

[2] Stubbs's pamphlet was entitled "The Discovery of the Gaping Gulf, wherein England is likely to be swallowed up by another French marriage, unless the Lords forbid the bans by letting her see the sin and punishment thereof."

[3] Camden's Annals, 1581.

was an index to the popular feeling. Men stood by the crown even when they condemned its policy, determined, at all hazards, to preserve the unity of the nation.

438. The Queen a Coquette. — During all this time the court buzzed with whispered scandals. Elizabeth was by nature a confirmed coquette. The Earl of Leicester, the Earl of Essex, and Sir Walter Raleigh were by turns her favorites. Over her relations with the first there hangs the terrible shadow of the murder of his wife, the beautiful Amy Robsart.[1] Her vanity was as insatiable as it was ludicrous. She issued a proclamation forbidding any one to sell her picture, lest it should fail to do her justice. She was greedy of flattery even when long past sixty, and there was a sting of truth in the letter which Mary Queen of Scots wrote her, saying, "Your aversion to marriage proceeds from your not wishing to lose the liberty of compelling people to make love to you."

439. Violence of Temper; Crooked Policy. — In temper, Elizabeth was arbitrary, fickle, and passionate. When her blood was up, she would swear like a trooper, spit on a courtier's new velvet suit, beat her maids of honor, and box Essex's ears. She wrote abusive, and even profane, letters to high church dignitaries, and openly insulted the wife of Archbishop Parker, because she did not believe in a married clergy.

The age in which Elizabeth lived was pre-eminently one of craft and intrigue. The kings of that day endeavored to get by fraud what their less polished predecessors got by force. At this game of double dealing Elizabeth had few equals and no superior. So profound was her dissimulation that her most confidential advisers never felt quite sure that she was not deceiving them. In her diplomatic relations she never hesitated at a lie if it would serve her purpose, and when the falsehood was discovered, she always had another and more plausible one ready to take its place.

440. Her Knowledge of Men; the Monopolies. — The queen's real ability lay in her instinctive perception of the needs of the

---

[1] See the De Quadra Letter in Froude's England.

age, and in her power of self-adjustment to them. Elizabeth never made public opinion, but watched it and followed it. She knew an able man at sight, and had the happy faculty of attaching such men to her service. By nature she was both irresolute and impulsive; but her sense was good and her judgment clear. She knew when she was well advised, and although she fumed and blustered, she yielded.

It has been said that the next best thing to having a good rule is to know when to break it. Elizabeth knew when. No matter how obstinate she was, she saw the point where obstinacy became dangerous. In order to enrich Raleigh and her numerous other favorites, she granted them the exclusive right to deal in certain articles. These privileges were called "monopolies." They finally came to comprise almost everything that could be bought or sold, from French wines to second-hand shoes. The effect was to raise prices so as to make even the common necessaries of life excessively dear. A great outcry finally arose; Parliament requested the queen to abolish the "monopolies"; she hesitated, but when she saw their determined attitude she gracefully granted the petition.

441. The Adulation of the Court. — No English sovereign was so popular or so praised. The great writers and the great men of that day vied with each other in their compliments to her beauty, her wisdom, and her wit. She lived in an atmosphere of splendor, of pleasure, and of adulation. Her reign was full of pageants, progresses,[1] and feasts, like those which Scott describes in his delightful novel, "Kenilworth." Spenser composed his poem, the "Faërie Queen," as he said, to extol "the glorious person of our sovereign queen," whom he blasphemously compared to the Godhead. Shakespeare is reported to have written a play[2] for her amusement, and in his "Midsummer Night's Dream" he addresses her as the "fair vestal in the West." The common people were

---

[1] Progresses: state-journeys made with great pomp and splendor.
[2] The Merry Wives of Windsor.

equally full of enthusiasm, and loved to sing and shout the praises of their "good Queen Bess." After her death at Richmond, when her body was being conveyed down the Thames to Westminster, an extravagant eulogist declared that the very fishes that followed the funeral barge "wept out their eyes and swam blind after!"

442. Grandeur of the Age; More's "Utopia." — The reign of Elizabeth was, in fact, Europe's grandest age. It was a time when everything was bursting into life and color. The world had suddenly grown larger; it had opened toward the East in the revival of classical learning; it had opened toward the West, and disclosed a continent of unknown extent and unimaginable resources.

Shortly after the discovery of America, Sir Thomas More wrote a remarkable work of fiction, in Latin, called "Utopia"[1] (the Land of Nowhere). In it he pictured an ideal commonwealth, where all men were equal; where none were poor; where perpetual peace prevailed; where there was absolute freedom of thought; where all were contented and happy. It was, in fact, the "Golden Age" come back to earth again. Such a book, now translated into English, suited such a time, for Elizabeth's reign was one of adventure, of poetry, of luxury, of rapidly increasing wealth. When men looked across the Atlantic, their imaginations were stimulated, and the most extravagant hopes did not appear too good to be true. Courtiers and adventurers dreamed of fountains of youth in Florida, of silver mines in Brazil, of rivers in Virginia whose pebbles were precious stones.[2] Thus all were dazzled with visions of sudden riches and renewed life.

443. Change in Mode of Life. — England, too, was undergoing transformation. Once, a nobleman's residence had been simply a

---

[1] "Utopia" was published in Latin about 1518. It was first translated into English in 1551.

[2] "Why, man, all their dripping-pans [in Virginia] are pure gould; . . . all the prisoners they take are feterd in gold; and for rubies and diamonds, they goe forth on holydayes and gather 'hem by the sea-shore, to hang on their children's coates." — *Eastward Hoe*, a play by John Marston and others, "as it was playd in the Black-friers [Theatre] by the Children of her Maiesties Revels." (1603?)

square stone fortress, built for safety only; but now that the land was at peace and the old feudal barons destroyed, there was no need of such precaution. Men were no longer content to live shut up in sombre strongholds, surrounded with moats of stagnant water, or in wretched hovels, where the smoke curled around the rafters for want of chimneys by which to escape, while the wind whistled through the unglazed latticed windows. Mansions and manor-houses like Hatfield, Knowle, and the "Bracebridge Hall" of Washington Irving,[1] rose instead of castles, and hospitality, not exclusion, became the prevailing custom. The introduction of chimneys brought the cheery comfort of the English fireside, while among the wealthy, carpets,[2] tapestry, and silver plate took the place of floors strewed with rushes, of bare walls, and of tables covered with pewter or wooden dishes.

An old writer, lamenting these innovations, says: "When our houses were built of willow, then we had oaken men; but, now that our houses are made of oak, our men have not only become willow, but many are altogether of straw, which is a sore affliction."

444. An Age of Adventure and of Daring. — But they were not all of straw, for that was a period of daring enterprise. Sir Walter Raleigh planted the first English colony, which the maiden queen named Virginia, in honor of herself. It proved unsuccessful, but he said, "I shall live to see it an English nation yet"; and he did. Frobisher explored the coasts of Labrador and Greenland. Sir Francis Drake sailed into the Pacific, spent a winter in or near the harbor of San Francisco, and ended his voyage by circumnavigating the globe.[3] In the East, London merchants had founded the East India Company, the beginning of English dominion in Asia; while in Holland, Sir Philip Sydney gave his life-blood for the cause of Protestantism.

---

[1] Aston Hall, in the vicinity of Birmingham, is the original of Irving's "Bracebridge Hall."

[2] Used at first as table covers chiefly.

[3] See Map No. 12, page 218.

445. Literature. — It was an age, too, not only of brave deeds but of high thoughts. Spenser, Shakespeare, and Jonson were making English literature the noblest of all literatures. Francis Bacon, son of Sir Nicholas Bacon, of Elizabeth's council, was giving a wholly different direction to education, by teaching men in his new philosphy, that in order to use the forces of nature they must learn by observation and experiment to know nature herself; "for," said he, "knowledge is power."

446. Mary Queen of Scots claims the Crown. — For England it was also an age of great and constant peril. Elizabeth's entire reign was undermined with plots against her life and against the life of the Protestant faith. No sooner was one corspiracy detected and suppressed, than a new one sprang up. Perhaps the most formidable of these was the effort which Mary Stuart (Queen of Scots) made to supplant her English rival. Shortly after Elizabeth's accession, Mary's husband, the king of France, died. She returned to Scotland and there assumed the Scottish crown, at the same time asserting her right to the English throne.[1]

447. Mary marries Darnley; his Murder. — A few years later she married Lord Darnley, who became jealous of Mary's Italian private secretary, Rizzio, and, with the aid of accomplices, seized him in her presence, dragged him into an ante-chamber, and there stabbed him.

The next year Darnley was murdered. It was believed that Mary and the Earl of Bothwell, whom she soon after married, were guilty of the crime. The people rose and cast her into prison, and forced her to abdicate in favor of her infant son, James VI.

448. Mary escapes to England; Plots against Elizabeth and Protestantism. — Mary escaped and fled to England. Elizabeth, fearing she might pass over to France and stir up war, confined

---

[1] See Table, Paragraph No. 421. Mary's claim was based on the fact that the Pope had never recognized Henry VIII.'s marriage to Anne Boleyn, Elizabeth's mother, as lawful.

No. 12.

Showing the English discoveries in America in the 15th, 16th and 17th centuries, with a part of Drake's voyage round the globe in 1577-1579.

her in Bolton Castle.¹ During her imprisonment there and elsewhere she became implicated in a plot for assassinating the English queen, and seizing the reins of government in behalf of herself and the Jesuits.

It was a time when the Protestant faith seemed everywhere marked for destruction. In France, evil counsellors had induced the king to order a massacre of the Reformers, and on St. Bartholomew's Day thousands were slain. The Pope, misinformed in the matter, ordered a solemn thanksgiving for the slaughter, and struck a gold medal to commemorate it.* Philip of Spain, whose cold, impassive face scarcely ever relaxed into a smile, now laughed outright. Still more recently, William the Silent, who had driven out the Catholics from a part of the Netherlands,² had been assassinated by a Jesuit fanatic.

449. Elizabeth beheads Mary. — Under these circumstances, Elizabeth, aroused to a sense of her danger, reluctantly signed the Scottish queen's death warrant, and Mary, after nineteen years' imprisonment, was beheaded at Fotheringay Castle.³

As soon as the news of her execution was brought to the queen, she became alarmed at the political consequences the act might have in Europe. With her usual duplicity she bitterly upbraided the minister who had advised it, and throwing Davidson, her secretary, into the Tower, fined him £10,000, the payment of which reduced him to beggary.⁴ Not satisfied with this, Elizabeth even had the effrontery to write a letter of condolence to Mary's son (James VI.) declaring that his mother had been beheaded by mistake! Yet facts prove that not only had Elizabeth determined to put Mary to death, — a measure whose justice is still vehemently disputed, — but she had suggested to her keeper that it might be expedient to have her privately murdered.

---

¹ Bolton Castle, Yorkshire.
² Netherlands, or Low Countries: now represented in great part by Belgium and Holland.   * See The Leading Facts of French History.
³ Fotheringay Castle, Northamptonshire, demolished by James I.
⁴ £10,000: a sum probably equal to more than $300,000 now.

450. The Spanish Armada. — Mary was hardly under ground when a new and greater danger threatened the country. At her death, the Scottish queen, disgusted with her mean-spirited son James,[1] left her claim to the English throne to Philip II. of Spain, who was then the most powerful sovereign in Europe, ruling over a territory equal to that of the Roman Empire in its greatest extent. Philip resolved to invade England, conquer it, annex it to his own possessions, and restore the religion of Rome. To accomplish this, he began fitting out the "Invincible Armada,"[2] an immense fleet, intended to carry 20,000 soldiers, and to receive on its way re-enforcements of 30,000 more from the Spanish army in the Netherlands.

451. Drake's Expedition; Sailing of the Armada; Elizabeth at Tilbury. — Sir Francis Drake determined to put a check to Philip's preparations. He heard that the enemy's fleet was gathered at Cadiz. He sailed there, and in spite of all opposition effectually "singed the Spanish king's beard," as he said, by burning and otherwise destroying more than a hundred ships. This so crippled the expedition that it had to be given up for that year, but the next summer a vast armament set sail. It consisted of six squadrons carrying 2500 cannon, and having on board, it is said, shackles and instruments of torture to bind and punish the English heretics.

The impending peril thoroughly aroused England. All parties, both Catholics and Protestants, rose and joined in the defence of their country and their queen. An army of 16,000 men under the Earl of Leicester gathered at Tilbury,[3] on the Thames, to protect London. Elizabeth reviewed the troops, saying with true Tudor spirit, "Though I have but the feeble body of a woman, I have the heart of a king, and of a king of England, too."

---

[1] James had deserted his mother, and accepted a pension from Elizabeth.

[2] Armada: an armed fleet.

[3] Tilbury: a fort on the left bank of the Thames, about twenty miles below London. Some authorities make this review at Tilbury subsequent to the defeat of the Armada.

452. The Battle. — The English sea-forces under Howard, a Catholic, as admiral, and Drake, second in command, were assembled at Plymouth, watching for the enemy. When the long-looked-for fleet came in sight, beacon fires were lighted on the hills to give the alarm.

> "For swift to east and swift to west the warning radiance spread;
> High on St. Michael's mount it shone, it shone on Beachy Head.
> Far o'er the deep the Spaniard sees along each southern shire,
> Cape beyond cape in endless range those twinkling points of fire." [1]

The enemy's ships moved steadily towards the coast in the form of a crescent seven miles in length; but Howard and Drake were ready to receive them. With their fast-sailing cruisers they sailed around the unwieldy Spanish war-ships, firing four shots to their one, and "harassing them as a swarm of wasps would a bear." Several of the enemy's vessels were captured, and one blown up. At last the commander thought best to make for Calais to repair damages and take a fresh start. The English followed. As soon as night came on, Drake sent eight blazing fire-ships to drift down among the Armada as it lay at anchor. Thoroughly alarmed at the prospect of being burned where they lay, the Spaniards cut their cables and made sail for the north.

453. Pursuit and Destruction of the Armada. — They were hotly pursued by the English, who, having lost but a single vessel in the fight, might have cut them to pieces, had not the queen's suicidal economy stinted them both in powder and provisions.[2] Meanwhile the Spanish forces kept on. The wind increased to a gale, the gale to a furious storm. As in such weather the Armada could not turn back, the commander attempted to go around Scotland and return home that way; but ship after ship was driven ashore and wrecked on the wild and rocky coast. On one strand, less than five miles long, over a thousand corpses were

---

[1] Macaulay, The Armada.

[2] The English crews suffered so much for want of food through Elizabeth's parsimony, that thousands of them came home from the great victory only to die.

counted. Those who escaped the waves met death by the hands of the inhabitants. Eventually, only about a third of the fleet, half manned by crews stricken by pestilence and death, succeeded in reaching Spain. Thus ended Philip's boasted attack on England. When all was over, Elizabeth went in state to St. Paul's to offer thanks for the victory. It was afterward commemorated by a medal which the queen caused to be struck, bearing this inscription: "God blew with his winds, and they were scattered."

454. Insurrection in Ireland. — A few years later, a terrible rebellion broke out in Ireland. From its partial conquest in the time of Henry II., the condition of that island continued to be deplorable. First, the chiefs of the native tribes fought constantly among themselves; next, the English attempted to force the Protestant religion upon a people who detested it; lastly, the greed and misgovernment of the rulers put a climax to these miseries, so that the country became, as Raleigh said, "a commonwealth of common woe." Under Elizabeth a war of extermination began, so merciless that the queen herself declared that if the work of destruction went on much longer, "she should have nothing left but ashes and corpses to rule over." Then, but not till then, the starving remnant of the people submitted, and England gained a barren victory which has ever since carried with it its own curse.

455. The First Poor Law. — In 1601 the first effective English poor law was passed. It required each parish to make provision for such paupers as were unable to work, while the able-bodied were compelled to labor for their own support. This measure relieved much of the distress which had prevailed during the two previous reigns, and forms the basis of the law in force at the present time.

456. Elizabeth's Death. — The death of the great queen, in 1603, was as sad as her life had been brilliant. Her favorite, Essex, Shakespeare's intimate friend, had been beheaded for an attempted rebellion against her power. From that time she grew, as she said, "heavy-hearted." Her old friends and counsellors were dead, her people no longer welcomed her with their former enthusiasm; treason had grown so common that Hentzner, a German traveller in England, said that he counted three hundred heads of persons, who had suffered death for this crime, exposed on London Bridge. Elizabeth felt that her sun was nearly set; gradually her strength declined; she ceased to leave her palace, and sat muttering to herself all day long, "Mortua, sed non sepulta!" "Dead, but not buried!" At length she lay propped up on cushions on the floor,[1] "tired," as she said, "of reigning, and tired of life." In that sullen mood she departed to join that silent majority whose realm under earth is bounded by the sides of the grave. "Four days afterward," says a writer of that time, "she was forgotten." One may see her tomb, with her full-length, recumbent effigy, in the north aisle of Henry VII.'s Chapel, and in the opposite aisle the tomb and effigy of her old rival and enemy, Mary Queen of Scots. The sculptured features of both look placid. "After life's fitful fever they sleep well."

457. Summary. — The Elizabethan period was in every respect remarkable. It was great in its men of thought, and equally great in its men of action. It was greatest, however, in its successful resistance to the armed hand of religious oppression. The defeat of the Armada gave renewed courage to the cause of the Reformation, not only in England, but in every Protestant country in Europe. It meant that a movement had begun which, though it might be temporarily hindered, would at last secure to all civilized countries the right of private judgment and of liberty of conscience.

---

[1] See Delaroche's fine picture, "The Death of Queen Elizabeth."

GENERAL VIEW OF THE TUDOR PERIOD. — 1485-1603.

I. GOVERNMENT. — II. RELIGION. — III. MILITARY AFFAIRS. — IV. LITERATURE, LEARNING, AND ART. — V. GENERAL INDUSTRY AND COMMERCE. — VI. MODE OF LIFE, MANNERS, AND CUSTOMS.

GOVERNMENT.

458. Absolutism of the Crown; Free Trade; the Post-Office. — During a great part of the Tudor period the power of the crown was well-nigh absolute. Four causes contributed to this: 1. The destruction of a very large part of the feudal nobility by the Wars of the Roses;[1] 2. The removal of many of the higher clergy from the House of Lords;[2] 3. The creation of a new nobility dependent on the king; 4. The desire of the great body of the people for "peace at any price."

Under Henry VII. and Elizabeth the courts of Star-Chamber and High Commission exercised arbitrary power, and often inflicted cruel punishments for offences against the government, and for heresy or the denial of the religious supremacy of the sovereign.

Henry VII. established a treaty of free trade, called the "Great Intercourse," between England and the Netherlands. Under Elizabeth the first postmaster-general entered upon his duties, though the post-office was not fully established until the reign of her successor.

RELIGION.

459 Establishment of the Protestant Church of England. — Henry VIII. suppressed the Roman Catholic monasteries, seized their property, and ended by declaring the Church of England independent

---

[1] In the last Parliament before the Wars of the Roses (1454) there were 53 temporal peers; at the beginning of the reign of Henry VII. (1485) there were only 29.

[2] Out of a total of barely 90 peers, Henry VIII., by the suppression of the monasteries, removed upwards of 36 abbots and priors. He, however, added five new bishops, which made the House of Lords number about 59.

of the Pope. Thenceforth, he assumed the title of Head of the National Church. Under Edward VI. Protestantism was established by law. Mary led a reaction in favor of Romanism, but her successor, Elizabeth, reinstated the Protestant form of worship. Under Elizabeth the Puritans demanded that the national church be purified from all Romish forms and doctrines. Severe laws were passed under Elizabeth for the punishment of both Catholics and Puritans, all persons being required to conform to the Church of England.

MILITARY AFFAIRS.

460. Arms and Armor; the Navy. — Though gunpowder had been in use for two centuries, yet full suits of armor were still worn during a great part of the period. An improved match-lock gun, with the pistol, an Italian invention, and heavy cannon were introduced. Until the death of Henry VIII. foot-soldiers continued to be armed with the long-bow; but under Edward VI. that weapon was superseded by firearms. The principal wars of the period were with Scotland, France, and Spain, the last being by far the most important, and ending with the destruction of the Armada.

Henry VIII. established a permanent navy, and built several vessels of upwards of 1000 tons register. The largest men of war under Elizabeth carried forty cannon and a crew of several hundred men.

LITERATURE, LEARNING, AND ART.

461. Schools. — The revival of learning gave a great impetus to education. The money which had once been given to monasteries was now spent in building schools, colleges, and hospitals. Dean Colet established the free grammar school of St. Paul's, several colleges were endowed at Oxford and Cambridge, and Edward VI. opened upwards of forty free schools in different parts of the country, of which the Blue-Coat School, London, is one of the best known. Improved text-books were prepared for the schools, and Lilye's Latin Grammar, first published in 1513 for the use of Dean Colet's school, continued a standard work for over three hundred years.

462. Literature; the Theatre. — The latter part of the period deserves the name of the "Golden Age of English Literature." More,

Sydney, Hooker, Jewell, were the leading prose writers; while Spenser, Marlowe, Jonson, and Shakespeare represented the poets.

In 1574 a public theatre was erected in London, in which Shakespeare was a stockholder. Not very long after a second was opened. At both these (the Globe and the Blackfriars) the great dramatist appeared in his own plays, and in such pieces as King John, Richard the Third, and the Henrys, he taught his countrymen more of the true spirit and meaning of the nation's history than they had ever learned before. His historical plays are chiefly based on Holinshed and Hall, two chroniclers of the period.

463. Progress of Science; Superstitions. — The discoveries of Columbus, Cabot, Magellan, and other navigators had proved the earth to be a globe. Copernicus, a Prussian astronomer, now demonstrated the fact that it both turns on its axis and revolves around the sun, but the discovery was not accepted until many years later.

On the other hand, astrology, witchcraft, and the transmutation of copper and lead into gold were generally believed in. In preaching before Queen Elizabeth, Bishop Jewell urged that stringent measures be taken with witches and sorcerers, saying that through their demoniacal acts "your grace's subjects pine away even unto death, their color fadeth, their flesh rotteth." Lord Bacon and other eminent men held the same belief, and many persons eventually suffered death for the practice of witchcraft.

464. Architecture. — The Gothic, or Pointed, style of architecture reached its final stage (the Perpendicular) in the early part of this period. The first examples of it have already been mentioned at the close of the preceding period. See Paragraph No. 376. After the close of Henry VII.'s reign no attempts were made to build any grand church edifices until St. Paul's Cathedral was rebuilt by Wren, in the seventeenth century, in the Italian, or classical style.

In the latter part of the Tudor period many stately country houses[1] and grand city mansions were built, ornamented with carved woodwork and bay-windows. Castles were no longer constructed, and, as the country was at peace, many of those which had been built were abandoned, though a few castellated mansions like Thornbury Gloucester-

---

[1] Such as Hatfield House, Knowle and Hardwick Hall; and, in London, mansions similar to Crosby Hall.

shire were built in Henry VIII.'s time. The streets of London still continued to be very narrow, and the tall houses, with projecting stories, were so near together at the top that neighbors living on opposite sides of the street might almost shake hands from the upper windows.

GENERAL INDUSTRY AND COMMERCE.

465. Foreign Trade. — The geographical discoveries of this period gave a great impulse to foreign trade with Africa, Brazil, and North America. The wool trade continued to increase, and also commerce with the East Indies. In 1600 the East India Company was established, thus laying the foundation of England's Indian empire, and ships now brought cargoes direct to England by way of the Cape of Good Hope. Sir Francis Drake did a flourishing business in plundering Spanish settlements in America and Spanish treasure-ships, and Sir John Hawkins became wealthy through the slave trade, — kidnapping negroes on the coast of Guinea, and selling them to the Spanish West India colonies. The domestic trade of England was still carried on largely by great annual fairs. Trade, however, was much deranged by the quantities of debased money issued under Henry VIII. and Edward VI.

Elizabeth reformed the currency, and ordered the mint to send out coin which no longer had a lie stamped on its face, thereby setting an example to all future governments, whether monarchical or republican.

MODE OF LIFE, MANNERS, AND CUSTOMS.

466. Life in the Country and the City. — In the cities, this was an age of luxury; but on the farms, the laborer was glad to get a bundle of straw for a bed, and a wooden trencher to eat from. Vegetables were scarcely known, and fresh meat was eaten only by the well-to-do. The cottages were built of sticks and mud, without chimneys, and were nearly as bare of furniture as the wigwam of an American Indian.

The rich kept several mansions and country houses, but paid little attention to cleanliness; and when the filth and vermin in one became unendurable, they left it "to sweeten," as they said, and went to another of their estates. The dress of the nobles continued to be of the most costly materials and the gayest colors.

At table, a great variety of dishes were served on silver plate, but fingers were still used in place of forks. Tea and coffee were unknown, and beer was the usual drink at breakfast and supper.

Carriages were not in use, except by Queen Elizabeth, and all journeys were performed on horseback. Merchandise was also generally transported on pack-horses, the roads rarely being good enough for the passage of wagons. The principal amusements were the theatre, dancing, masquerading, bull and bear baiting (worrying a bull or bear with dogs), cock-fighting, and gambling.

IX.

"It is the nature of the devil of tyranny to tear and rend the body which he leaves." — MACAULAY.

BEGINNING WITH THE DIVINE RIGHT OF KINGS, AND ENDING WITH THE DIVINE RIGHT OF THE PEOPLE.

KING or PARLIAMENT?

HOUSE OF STUART. — 1603–1649, 1660–1714.

James I., 1603–1625.	Charles II., 1660–1685.
Charles I., 1625–1649.	James II., 1685–1688.
The Commonwealth and Protectorate, 1649–1660.	William & Mary,[1] 1689–1702.
	Anne, 1702–1714.

467. Accession of James I. — Elizabeth was the last of the Tudor family. By birth, James Stuart, only son of Mary Stuart, Queen of Scots, and great grandson of Margaret, sister of Henry VIII., was the nearest heir to the crown.[2] He was already king of Scotland under the title of James VI. He now, by choice of Parliament, became James I. of England. By his accession the two countries were united under one sovereign, but each retained its own Parliament, its own church, and its own laws.[3] The new monarch found himself ruler over three kingdoms, each professing a different religion. Puritanism prevailed in Scotland, Catholicism in Ireland, Anglicanism or Episcopacy in England.

---

[1] Orange-Stuart.
[2] See Table, Paragraph No. 421.
[3] On his coins and in his proclamations, James styled himself King of Great Britain, France, and Ireland. But the term Great Britain did not properly come into use until somewhat more than a hundred years later, when, by an act of Parliament under Anne, Scotland and England were legally united.

468. The King's Appearance and Character. — James was unfortunate in his birth. Neither his father, Lord Darnley, nor his mother had high qualities of character. The murder of Mary's Italian secretary in her own palace, and almost in her own presence,[1] gave the queen a shock which left a fatal inheritance of cowardice to her son. Throughout his life he could not endure the sight of a drawn sword. His personal appearance was by no means impressive. He had a feeble, rickety body, he could not walk straight, his tongue was too large for his mouth, and he had goggle eyes. Through fear of assassination he habitually wore thickly padded and quilted clothes, usually green in color. He was a man of considerable shrewdness, but of small mind, and of unbounded conceit. His Scotch tutor had crammed him with much ill-digested learning, so that he gave the impression of a man educated beyond his intellect. He wrote on witchcraft, kingcraft, and theology. He also wrote numerous commonplace verses, together with a sweeping denunciation of the new plant called tobacco, which Raleigh had brought from America, the smoke of which now began to perfume, or, according to James, to poison the air of England. He had all the superstitions of the age, and one of his earliest acts was the passage of a statute punishing witchcraft with death. Under that law many a wretched woman perished on the scaffold, whose only crime was that she was old, ugly, and friendless.

469. The Great Petition. — During the latter part of Elizabeth's reign, the Puritans in England had increased so rapidly that Archbishop Whitgift told James he was amazed to find how "the vipers" had multiplied. The Puritans felt that the Reformation had not been sufficiently thorough. They complained that many of the forms and ceremonies of the Church of England were by no means in harmony with the Scriptures. Many of them wished also to change the form of church government, and instead of having bishops appointed by the king, to adopt the more demo-

---

[1] See Paragraph No. 447.

cratic method of having presbyters or elders chosen by the congregation.

While James was on the way from Scotland to London to receive the crown, the Puritans presented a petition to him, signed by upwards of a thousand of their ministers, asking that they might be permitted to preach without wearing the white gown called a surplice, to baptize without making the sign of the cross on the child's forehead, and to perform the marriage ceremony without using the ring.

470. Hampton Court Conference. — The king convened a conference at Hampton Court, near London, to consider the petition, or rather to make a pedantic display of his own learning. The probability that he would grant the petitioners' request was small; for James had come to England disgusted with the violence of the Scotch Puritans, especially since one of their ministers in Edinburgh had seized his sleeve at a public meeting, and addressed him with a somewhat brutal excess of truth, as "God's silly vassal." But the new sovereign had a still deeper reason for his antipathy to the Puritans. He saw that their doctrine of equality in the church naturally led to that of equality in the state. If they objected to Episcopal government in the one, might they not presently object to royal government in the other? Hence, to all their arguments, he answered with his favorite maxim, "No bishop, no king," meaning that the two must stand or fall together. At the Hampton Court Conference no real freedom of discussion was allowed. The only good result was that the king ordered a new and revised translation of the Bible to be made. It was published in 1611, and so well was the work done that it still remains the version used in nearly every Protestant church and Protestant home where the English language is spoken. James, however, regarded the conference as a success. He had refuted the Puritans, as he believed, with much Latin and some Greek. He ended by declaiming against them with such unction that one enthusiastic bishop declared that his majesty must be specially inspired by the Holy Ghost! He closed the meeting by imprisoning the ten persons who had presented the petition, on the ground that it tended to sedition and rebellion. Henceforth, the king's attitude toward the Puritans was unmistakable. "I will make them conform," said he, "or I will harry them out of the land."

471. The Divine Right of Kings. — As if with the desire of further alienating his people, James now constantly proclaimed the doctrine of the Divine Right of Kings. This theory, which was unknown to the English constitution, declared that the king derived his power and right to rule directly from God, and in no way from the people.[1] "As it is atheism and blasphemy," he said, "to dispute what God can do, so it is presumption and a high contempt in a subject to dispute what the king can do." All this would have been amusing had it not been dangerous. James forgot that he owed his throne to that act of parliament which accepted him as Elizabeth's successor. In his exalted position as head of the nation, he boasted of his power much like the dwarf in the story, who, perched on the giant's shoulders, cries out, "See how big I am!"

Acting on this assumption, James violated the privileges of the House of Commons, rejected members who had been legally elected, and imprisoned those who dared to criticise his course. The contest was kept up with bitterness during the whole reign. Towards its close, the House again protested vigorously, and the king seized their official journal, and with his own hands tore out the record of the protest.

472. The Gunpowder Plot. — This arbitrary spirit so angered the Commons, many of whom were Puritans, that they, believing that the king secretly favored the Roman Catholics, increased the stringency of the laws against persons of that religion. The king, to vindicate himself from this suspicion, proceeded to execute the

---

[1] James's favorite saying was, "a Deo rex, a rege lex" (God makes the king, the king makes the law).

new statutes with rigor. As a rule, the Catholics were loyal subjects. When Spain threatened to invade the country, they fought as valiantly in its defence as the Protestants themselves. Many of them were now ruined by enormous fines, while the priests were driven from the realm. One of the sufferers by these unjust measures was Robert Catesby, a Catholic gentleman of good position. He, with the aid of a Yorkshire man, named Guy Fawkes, and about a dozen more, formed a plot to blow up the Parliament House, on the day the king was to open the session (Nov. 5, 1605). Their intention, after they had thus summarily disposed of the government, was to induce the Catholics to rise and proclaim a new sovereign. The plot was discovered, the conspirators executed, and the Catholics were treated with greater severity than ever.

473. American Colonies, Virginia. — In 1607 a London joint-stock company of merchants and adventurers, or speculators, established the first permanent English colony in America, on the coast of Virginia, at a place which they called Jamestown, in honor of the king.[1] The colony was wholly under the control of the crown. The religion was to be that of the Church of England. Most of those who went out were "gentlemen," that is, persons not brought up to manual labor, and had it not been for the energy and determined courage of Capt. John Smith, who was the real soul of the enterprise, it would have proved like Raleigh's undertaking, a miserable failure; in time, however, the new colony gained strength. Negro slavery, which in those days touched no man's conscience, was introduced, and by its means great quantities of tobacco were raised for export. The settlement grew in population and wealth, and in less than a dozen years it had secured the privilege of making its own laws, thus becoming practically a self-governing community.

474. The Pilgrims. — The year after this great enterprise was undertaken, another band of emigrants went out from England,

---

[1] See Map No. 12, page 218.

not West, but East; not to seek prosperity, but greater religious freedom. James's declaration that he would make all men conform to the established church, or drive them out of the land, was having its due effect.

Those who continued to refuse were fined, cast into noisome prisons, beaten, and often half-starved, so that the old and feeble soon died. Strange to say, this kind of treatment did not win over the Puritans to the side of the bishops and the king. On the contrary, it set many of them to thinking more seriously than ever of the true relations of the government to religion. The result was that not a few came to the conclusion that each body of Christians had a right to form a religious society of its own wholly independent of the state. Those of the Puritans who thus thought got the name of Independents or Separatists, because they were determined to separate from the national church and conduct their worship and govern their religious societies as they deemed best.

In the little village of Scrooby, Nottinghamshire, Postmaster William Brewster, William Bradford, John Carver, and some others, mostly farmers and poor men of the neighborhood, had organized such an independent church with John Robinson for its minister. After a time they became convinced that so long as they remained in England they would never be safe from persecution. They therefore resolved to leave their native country, and as they could not get a royal license to go to America, to emigrate to Holland, where all men were, at that time, free to establish societies for the worship of God in their own manner. With much difficulty and danger they managed to escape there. After remaining there upwards of twelve years, a part of them succeeded in obtaining from King James, after long negotiation, the privilege of emigrating to America.[1] A London trading company, which was sending out an expedition for fish and furs, agreed to furnish the Pilgrims passage by the *Mayflower*, though on terms so hard that the poor

---

[1] See "Why did the Pilgrim Fathers come to New England?" By Edwin D. Mead, in the New Englander, 1882.

exiles said the "conditions were fitter for thieves and bondslaves than honest men."

In 1620 these Pilgrims, or wanderers, set forth for that New World beyond the sea, which they hoped would redress the wrongs of the Old. Landing at Plymouth, in Massachusetts, they established a colony on the basis of "equal laws for the general good." Ten years later John Winthrop, a Puritan gentleman of wealth from Groton, Suffolk, followed with a small company and settled Salem and Boston. During the next decade no less than twenty thousand Englishmen found a home in the west, but to the little band that embarked under Bradford and Brewster in the *Mayflower*, the scene of whose landing at Plymouth is painted on the walls of the Houses of Parliament, belongs the credit of the great undertaking. Of that enterprise one of their brethren in England wrote in the time of their severest distress, with prophetic foresight, "Let it not be grievous to you that you have been instruments to break the ice for others; the honor shall be yours to the world's end." From this time forward the country was settled mainly by English emigrants, and in the course of the next century, or a little more, the total number of colonies had reached thirteen, though part of them had been gained by conquest. Thus the nation of Great Britain was beginning to expand into that *greater* Britain which it had discovered and planted beyond the sea.

475. The Colonization of Ireland. — While these events were going on in America, James was himself planning a very different kind of colony in the northeast of Ireland. The greater part of the province of Ulster, which had been the scene of the rebellion under Elizabeth, had been seized by the crown. The king now granted these lands to settlers from Scotland and England. The city of London founded a colony which they called Londonderry, and by this means Protestantism was firmly and finally established in the north of the island.

476. The New Stand taken by the House of Commons. — The House of Commons at this period began to slowly get back, with interest, the power it had lost under the Tudors. James suffered from a chronic lack of money. He was obliged to apply to Parliament to supply his wants, but Parliament was determined to grant nothing without reforms. They laid it down as a principle, to which they firmly adhered, that the king should not have the nation's coin unless he would promise to right the nation's wrongs. In order to get means to support his army in Ireland, James created a new title of rank, that of baronet,[1] which he granted to any one who would pay liberally for it. As a last resort to get funds he compelled all persons having an income of forty pounds[2] or more a year derived from landed property, to accept knighthood (thus incurring feudal obligations and payments) or purchase exemption by a heavy fine.

477. Impeachment of Lord Bacon. — In 1621 Lord Bacon was impeached by the House of Commons, and convicted by the House of Lords, for having taken bribes in lawsuits tried before him as judge. He confessed the crime, but pleaded extenuating circumstances, adding, " I beseech your worships to be merciful to a broken reed"; but Bacon had been in every respect a servile tool of James, and no mercy was granted. Parliament imposed a fine of £40,000, with imprisonment. Had it been fully executed, it would have caused his utter ruin. The king, however, interposed, and his favorite escaped with a few days' confinement in the Tower.

478. Execution of Raleigh. — With Sir Walter Raleigh the result was different. He had been a prisoner in the Tower for

---

[1] Baronet: this title does not confer the right to a seat in the House of Lords. A baronet is designated as Sir, *e.g.*, Sir John Franklin.

[2] This exaction was ridiculed by the wits of the time in these lines: —

> He that hath forty pounds per annum
> Shall be promoted from the plough;
> His wife shall take the wall of her grannum * —
> Honor's sold so dog-cheap now."

The distraint of knighthood, as it was called, began at least as far back as Edward I., 1278.

* Take precedence of her grandmother.

a number of years, on an unfounded charge of conspiracy. Influenced by motives of cupidity, James released him to go on an expedition in search of gold to replenish the royal coffers. Raleigh, contrary to the king's orders, came into collision with the Spaniards on the coast of South America.[1] He failed in his enterprise, and brought back nothing. Raleigh was especially hated by Spain, not only on account of the part he had taken in the defeat of the Armada, but also for his subsequent attacks on Spanish treasure-ships and property. The king of that country now demanded vengeance, and James, in order to get a pretext for his execution, revived the sentence which had been passed on Raleigh fifteen years before. His real motive undoubtedly was the hope that, by sacrificing Raleigh, he might secure the hand of the daughter of the king of Spain for his son, Prince Charles. Raleigh died as More did, his last words a jest at death. His deeper feelings found expression in the lines which he wrote on the fly-leaf of his Bible the night before his judicial murder: —

> "Even such is Time, that takes on trust,
> Our youth, our joys, our all we have,
> And pays us but with age and dust;
> Who in the dark and silent grave,
> When we have wandered all our ways,
> Shuts up the story of our days;
> But from this earth, this grave, this dust,
> My God shall raise me up, I trust."

479. Death of James. — As for James, when he died a few years later, a victim of confirmed drunkenness and gluttony, his fittest epitaph would have been what an eminent French statesman of that time called him, "the wisest fool in Christendom."[2]

480. Summary. — Three chief events demand our attention in this reign. First, the increased power and determined attitude of the House of Commons. Second, the growth of the Puritan and

---

[1] It is said that James had treacherously informed the Spanish ambassador of Raleigh's voyage, so that the collision was inevitable.
[2] The Duc de Sully.

Independent parties in religion. Third, the establishment of permanent, self-governing colonies in Virginia and New England, destined in time to unite with others and become a new and independent English nation.

CHARLES I. — 1625-1649.

481. Accession of Charles; Result of the Doctrine of the Divine Right of Kings. — The doctrine of the Divine Right of Kings, so zealously put forth by James, bore its full and fatal fruit in the career of his son. Unlike his father, Charles was by nature a gentleman. In his private and personal relations he was conscientious and irreproachable; in public matters he was exactly the reverse. This singular contrast — this double character, as it were — arose from the fact that as a man, Charles felt himself bound by truth and honor, but as a sovereign, he considered himself superior to such obligations. In all his dealings with the nation he seems to have acted on the principle that the people had no rights which kings were bound to respect.

482. Two Mistakes at the Outset. — He began his reign with two mistakes. First, he insisted on retaining the Duke of Buckingham, his father's favorite, as his chief adviser, though the Duke was, for good reasons, generally distrusted and disliked. Next, shortly after his accession, Charles married Henrietta Maria, a French Catholic princess, whose religion was hated by the majority of the English people, and whose extravagant habits soon got the king into trouble. To meet her incessant demands for money, and to carry on a petty war with Spain, he was obliged to ask Parliament for funds. Parliament declined to grant him a supply unless he would redress certain grievances of long standing. Charles refused and dissolved that body.

483. The Second Parliament; Hampden. — Necessity, however, compelled the king to call a new Parliament. When they met, the Commons, under the lead of Sir John Eliot and others, proceeded to draw up articles of impeachment, accusing the Duke of Buckingham of mismanagement. To save his favorite from being brought to trial, the king dissolved Parliament, and as no supply had been voted, Charles now levied illegal taxes and extorted loans.

John Hampden, a country gentleman of Buckinghamshire, who had been a member of the late House of Commons, refused to lend his majesty the sum asked for. For this refusal he was thrown into prison. This led to increased agitation and discontent. At length the king found himself again forced to summon Parliament; to this Parliament Hampden and others, who sympathized with him, were elected.

484. The Petition of Right. — Immediately on assembling, they presented to the king the Petition of Right, which was in substance a law reaffirming some of the chief provisions of the Great Charter. It stipulated in particular, that no taxes whatever should be levied without the consent of Parliament, and that no one should be unlawfully imprisoned as Hampden had been. In the petition there was not an angry word, but as a member of the Commons declared, "We say no more than what a worm trodden upon would say if he could speak: I pray thee tread upon me no more."

485. Charles revives Monopolies. — Charles refused to sign the Petition; but finding that money could be got on no other terms, he at length gave his signature. But for Charles to pledge his royal word to the nation meant its direct and open violation. The king now revived the "monopolies" which had been abolished under Elizabeth. By these he granted to certain persons, in return for large sums of money, the sole right of dealing in nearly every article of food, drink, fuel, and clothing. The Commons denounced this outrage. One member said, "The monopolists have seized everything. They sip in our cup, they sup in our dish, they sit by our fire."

486. The King rules without Parliament; "Thorough." — For the next eleven years the king ruled without a Parliament.

The obnoxious Buckingham had been assassinated. His successor was Thomas Wentworth, who, in 1640, became Earl of Strafford. Wentworth had signed the "Petition of Right," but he was now a renegade to liberty, and wholly devoted to the king. By means of the Star-Chamber and his scheme called "Thorough," by which he meant that he would stop at nothing to make Charles absolute, he labored to establish a complete despotism. Bishop Laud, who soon became head of the church, worked with him through the High Commission Court. Together, the two exercised a crushing and merciless system of political and religious tyranny; the Star-Chamber fining and imprisoning those who refused the illegal demands for money made upon them, the High Commission Court equally zealous in punishing those who could not conscientiously conform to the established church of England.

487. Eliot's Remonstrance. — Sir John Eliot drew up a remonstrance against these new acts of royal tyranny, but the speaker of the House of Commons, acting under the king's order, refused to put the measure to vote, and endeavored to adjourn. Several members sprang forward and held him in his chair while the resolutions were passed, declaring that whoever levied or paid any taxes not voted by Parliament, or attempted to make any change in religion, was an enemy to the kingdom. In revenge Charles sent Eliot to the Tower, where he died three years later.

488. Ship Money. — To obtain means with which to equip a standing army, the king forced the whole country to pay a tax known as ship money, on the pretext that it was needed to free the English coast from the depredations of Algerine pirates. During previous reigns an impost of this kind on the coast towns in time of war might have been considered legitimate, since its original object was to provide ships for the national defence. In time of peace, however, such a demand could not be rightfully made, especially as the Petition of Right expressly provided that no money should be demanded from the country without the consent of its representatives in Parliament. John Hampden again resisted payment. The case was brought to trial, and the corrupt judges decided for the king.

489. Hampden endeavors to leave the Country. — Many Puritans now emigrated to America to escape oppression. Hampden, believing that there was no safety for him in England, resolved to follow their example. With his cousin Oliver Cromwell, who was a brother-farmer, and had sat with him in the last Parliament, Hampden embarked on a vessel in the Thames, but they were prevented from sailing by the king's orders. The two friends remained to teach the despotic sovereign a lesson which neither he nor England ever forgot.*

490. The Difficulty with the Scottish Church. — In 1637 the king determined to force the use of a prayer-book, similar to that used in the English church, on the Scotch Puritans. But no sooner had the Dean of Edinburgh opened the book, than a general cry arose in the church, "A Pope, a Pope! Antichrist! stone him!" When the bishops endeavored to appease the tumult, the enraged congregation clapped and yelled.

Again the dean tried to read prayer from the hated book, when an old woman hurled her stool at his head, shouting, "D'ye mean to say mass[1] at my lug [ear]?" Riots ensued, and eventually the Scotch solemnly bound themselves by a covenant to resist all attempts to change their religion. The king resolved to force his liturgy on the Covenanters at the point of the bayonet. But he had no money to pay his army, and the "Short Parliament" which he summoned refused to grant any unless the king would redress the nation's grievances. As a last resort, he summoned that memorable Parliament in 1640, which, because it sat almost continuously for thirteen years, got the name of the "Long Parliament."[2]

491. The Long Parliament (1640). — The new Parliament was made up of three parties: the Church of England party, the Pres-

---

[1] Mass: here used for the Roman Catholic church service.

[2] Long Parliament: it was not finally dissolved until 1660, twenty years from its first meeting. * Guizot's Eng. Revol.; recent authorities deny the Cromwell incident.

byterian party, and the Independents. The spirit of this body soon showed itself. They impeached Strafford for his many years of despotic oppression, and sentenced him to execution. The king refused to sign the death warrant, but Strafford himself urged him to do so in order to appease the people. Charles, frightened at the tumult that had arisen, and entreated by his wife, finally put his hand to the paper, and thus sent his most faithful servant to the block. Parliament next charged Laud with attempting to overthrow the Protestant religion. They condemned him to prison, and ultimately to death. Next, they abolished the Star-Chamber and the High Commission Court. They then passed a bill requiring Parliament to be summoned once in three years. They followed this by drawing up the Grand Remonstrance, which they caused to be printed and circulated throughout the country. The Remonstrance set forth the faults of the king's government, while it declared their distrust of his policy. Finally, they enacted a law forbidding the dissolution of the present Parliament except by its own consent.

492. The Attempted Arrest of the Five Members. — It was now rumored, and perhaps with truth, that the parliamentary leaders were about to take a still bolder step and impeach the queen for having conspired with the Catholics and the Irish to destroy the liberties of the country. No one knew better than Charles how strong a case could be made out against his frivolous and unprincipled consort. Driven to extremities, he determined to seize the five members, Hampden, Pym, and three others, who headed the opposition, on a charge of high treason.[1] The House of Commons was requested to give them up for trial. The request was not complied with. The queen urged him to take them by force, saying, "Go, coward, pull those rogues out by the ears." Thus taunted, the king, attended by an armed force, went on the

---

[1] The full list was Hampden, Pym, Hollis, Haselrig, and Strode, to which a sixth, Mandeville, was added later. See Copley's fine picture in the Art Room of the Boston Public Library.

next day to the House of Parliament, purposing to seize the members. They had been forewarned, and had left the House, taking refuge in the city, which showed itself then, as always, on the side of liberty. Leaving his soldiers at the door, the king entered the House. Seeing that the members were absent, the king turned to the speaker and asked him where they were. The speaker kneeling, begged the king's pardon for not answering, saying, "that he could neither see nor speak but by command of the House." Vexed that he could learn nothing further, Charles left the hall amid ominous cries of "Privilege! privilege!"[1]

493. Civil War. — The king, baffled in his purpose, resolved to coerce Parliament by military force. He left London in 1642, never to return until he came as a prisoner, and was delivered into the custody of that legislative body which he had insulted and defied. Parliament now attempted to come to an understanding with the king. There was then no standing army in England, but each county and large town had a body of militia, formed of citizens who were occasionally mustered for drill. This militia was under the control of the king. Parliament now insisted on his resigning that control to them. The king refused to give up his undoubted constitutional right in the matter, raised the royal flag at Nottingham, and the war began.

494. Cavaliers and Roundheads. — It opened in the autumn of that year with the battle of Edgehill, Warwickshire, and was at first favorable to the king. On his side were a majority of the nobility, the clergy, and the country gentlemen, known collectively as Cavaliers, from their dashing and daring horsemanship. Their leader was Prince Rupert, a nephew of Charles.[2] On the side of Parliament were the shop-keepers, small farmers, and a few men of high rank; they were called in ridicule the Roundheads, from

---

[1] Privilege: the privilege of Parliament to debate all questions exempt from royal interference.

[2] See "A Charge with Prince Rupert," Atlantic Magazine (T. W. Higginson), Vol. III. 725.

their fashion of wearing their hair closely cropped, so that it showed the shape of the head. Their leaders were first Essex and Fairfax, and later, Oliver Cromwell.

495. How the Country was divided. — Taking England as a whole, we may say that the eastern half, with London, was against the king, and that the western half was for him.[1] Each side made great sacrifices in carrying on the war. The queen sold her crown jewels, and the Cavaliers melted down their silver plate to provide money to pay the troops. On behalf of the people, Parliament imposed heavy taxes, and levied now for the first time a duty on domestic products, especially on ales and liquors, known as the excise tax. They also required each household to fast once a week, and give the price of a dinner to support the army. Parliament also passed what was called the Self-denying Ordinance, which required all members who held any civil or military office to resign, and as Cromwell said, "deny themselves and their private interests for the public good." The real object of this measure was to get rid of incompetent commanders, and give the army the vigorous men that the times demanded.

With the outbreak of the war great numbers of little local newspapers sprang into short-lived existence in imitation of the first publication of that sort, the "Weekly News," which was issued not quite twenty years before in the reign of James I.[2] Each of the rival armies, it is said, carried a printing-press with it, and waged furious battles in type against the other. The whole country was inundated with floods of pamphlets discussing every conceivable religious and political question.[3]

496. The "New Model"; the Solemn League and Covenant. — At the first battle fought (Edgehill, Warwickshire) Cromwell

---

[1] See Map No. 13, and Paragraph No. 34.
[2] The first number of the "Weekly News," published by Nathaniel Butter and associates, appeared May 22, 1622. Previous to that there had been occasional papers published in London; this was the first regular sheet.
[3] About 30,000 pamphlets came out between 1640-1660.

No. 13.

To face page 244.

The country west of the broad dotted line supported the cause of Charles I.; that on the east supported Parliament.

saw that the Cavaliers had the advantage, and told Hampden that "a set of poor tapsters [drawers of liquor] and town apprentices would never fight against men of honor." He forthwith proceeded to organize his regiment of "Ironsides," a "lovely company," as he said, none of whom swore or gambled. After the Self-denying Ordinance was passed, Cromwell and Fairfax formed a new army of "God-fearing men" on the same pattern, almost all of whom were Independents. This was called the "New Model," and was placed under the joint command of the men who organized it. Very many of its officers were kinsmen of Cromwell's, and it speedily became the most formidable body of soldiers of its size in the world — always ready to preach, pray, exhort, or fight.[1]

Meanwhile Parliament endeavored to persuade the Scotch to join them against the king. They finally agreed to do so on condition that Parliament should sign the Solemn League and Covenant, establishing the Scotch Presbyterian form of worship as the state religion of England and Ireland; to this all were obliged to conform.

497. Marston Moor and Naseby. — On the field of Marston Moor in 1644, the North of England was conquered by Cromwell with his invincible little army. The following year Cromwell's "Ironsides," who "trusted in God and kept their powder dry," gained the decisive victory of Naseby (1645). This practically ended the war. After the fight, papers belonging to the king were picked up on the battle-field which proved that Charles intended betraying those who were negotiating with him for peace, and that he was planning to bring foreign troops to England. This discovery was more damaging to the royal cause than the defeat itself.

498. The King and Parliament. — Shortly after this, Charles was surrendered to Parliament by the Scotch, to whom he had

---

[1] "The common soldiers, as well as the officers, did not only pray and preach among themselves, but went up into the pulpits in all churches and preached to the people." Clarendon's History of the Rebellion, Book X. p. 79.

fled, and taken to Holmby House, Northamptonshire. There Cromwell and the army made overtures to him, but without effect. He was then brought by the army to Hampton Court, near London. Here, and elsewhere, the army again attempted to come to some definite understanding with the king, but all to no purpose. Politically speaking, Charles was his own worst enemy. He was false to the core, and, as Carlyle has said, "a man whose word will not inform you at all what he means, or will do, is not a man you can bargain with. You must get out of that man's way, or put him out of yours."[1]

499. Pride's Purge. — In 1648, after two years spent in fruitless negotiations, Charles, who had fled to Carisbrooke Castle in the Isle of Wight, made a secret treaty with the Scots, promising to establish the Presbyterian church in England, if they would send an army into the country to restore him to the throne. The Scots marched into England, the Royalists rose to aid them, and civil war again broke out. The army now vowed that if they were victorious they would bring the king to justice. To this neither the Presbyterians in the House of Commons nor the members of the House of Lords would agree.

Colonel Pride then proceeded, as he said, to purge Parliament by driving out all who were opposed to this measure. Cromwell had no part in Pride's expulsion of members, though he afterwards expressed his approval of it. Those who remained were a small body of Independents only. They did not number sixty, and were called in derision the Rump Parliament.

500. Execution of the King. — This legislative remnant next named one hundred and thirty-five persons to constitute a high court of justice to try the king on a charge of treason against the nation, of which the chief judge or presiding officer was John Bradshaw. Out of this number less than half were present throughout the trial. Of those who remained and signed the

---

[1] Carlyle's Past and Present.

death-warrant Cromwell was one. Prince Charles, then a refugee in France, made every effort to save his father. He sent a blank paper bearing his signature and seal to the judges, offering to bind himself to any conditions they might insert, providing his father's life might be spared; but no answer was returned.

On Jan. 20, 1649, the king was brought into court. A week later the judges pronounced sentence of death on "Charles Stuart, king of England," as a "tyrant, traitor, murderer, and public enemy."

Throughout the trial Charles bore himself with dignity and self-possession. The crisis had brought out the best elements of his nature. He was beheaded in London in front of the royal palace of Whitehall. "A great shudder ran through the crowd that saw the deed, then a shriek, then all immediately dispersed."

501. Summary. — The whole of Charles I.'s reign must be regarded as a prolonged struggle between the king and the nation. Under the Tudors and James I. the royal power had been growing more and more despotic, while at the same time the progress of the Protestant Reformation and of Puritanism had encouraged freedom of thought. Between these opposite forces a collision was inevitable, since religious liberty always favors political liberty. Had Charles known how to yield in time, or been sincere in the concessions which he did make, all might have gone well. His duplicity was his ruin. Though his death did not absolutely destroy the theory of the Divine Right of Kings, yet it gave it a blow from which it never recovered.

THE COMMONWEALTH AND PROTECTORATE. — 1649–1660.

502. Establishment of the Commonwealth, or Republic (1649–1660). — On the afternoon of Jan. 30, 1649, while the crowd that had witnessed the execution of Charles was slowly leaving the spot, the House of Commons passed an act prohibiting the proclaiming of any person king of England or Ireland or the dominions thereof.

Less than two months afterward they abolished the House of Lords as both useless and dangerous. England was now a republic, governed, in name at least, by a council of state. Of this council John Bradshaw was president, the poet Milton was foreign secretary, while Fairfax with Cromwell had command of the army. The real power was in the army, and the true head of the army was Cromwell. Without him the so-called republic could not have stood a day.

503. Radical Changes. — All members of the House of Commons, with those who held any civil or military office, were required to swear allegiance to the Commonwealth "without king or House of Lords." The use of the English church service was forbidden, and the statues of Charles in London were pulled down and demolished. The great seal of England was broken, and a new one adopted, having on one side a map of England and Ireland, on the other a representation of the Commons in session, with the words, "In the first year of freedom, by God's blessing restored 1648."*

504. Difficulties of the New Republic. — Shortly after the establishment of the Commonwealth, Fairfax resigned his command, and Cromwell was now the sole leader of the military forces of the country. But the new government, even with his aid, had no easy task before it. It had enemies in the Royalists, who, since the king's execution, had grown stronger; in the Presbyterians, who hated both the Rump Parliament and the army; finally it had enemies in its own ranks in half-crazy fanatics, "Levellers,"[1] "Come-outers,"[2] and other "cattle and creeping things," who would be satisfied with nothing but destruction and confusion. Among them were communists, who, like those of the

---

[1] "Levellers": a name given to certain radical republicans who wished to reduce all ranks and classes to the same level with respect to political power and privileges. * 1648, or 1649, N. S. See p. 318, note.

[2] "Come-outers": this, though a modern term, describes a class who abandoned all established ways, both of government and religion.

present day, wished to abolish private property, and establish "an equal division of unequal earnings," while others declared and acted out their belief in the coming end of the world. Eventually Cromwell had to deal with these enthusiasts in a decided way, especially as some of them threatened to assassinate him in order to hasten the personal reign of Christ and his saints on earth.

505. Risings in Ireland and Scotland; Worcester. — In Ireland the Royalists had proclaimed Prince Charles king. Cromwell was deputed to reduce that country to order. To his invincible army of Independents nothing could have been more congenial than such a crusade. They descended upon the unhappy island, and wiped out the rebellion in such a whirlwind of fire and slaughter, that the horror of the visitation has never been forgotten. To this day the direst imprecation a southern Irishman can utter is, "the curse of Cromwell on ye."

In Scotland also Charles was looked upon as the legitimate sovereign by a strong and influential party. He found in the brave Montrose,[1] who was hanged for treason at Edinburgh, and in other loyal supporters far better friends than he deserved. In 1650 the prince came to Scotland, took the oath of the Covenant, which must have been a bitter pill to him, and rallied a small force, which was completely defeated that year at Dunbar.

Twelve months later, on the anniversary of the victory of Dunbar, Charles made a second attempt to obtain the crown. At the battle of Worcester, Cromwell again routed his forces and brought the war to an end. Charles escaped into Shropshire, where he hid for a day in an oak at Boscobel. After many narrow escapes he at length succeeded in getting out of the country.

506. Cromwell expels Parliament. — Cromwell now urged the necessity of calling a Parliament which should represent the country, reform the laws, and pass a general act of pardon. In his despatch to the House of Commons after the victory of Worcester, he called the battle a "crowning mercy." Some of the

---

[1] See Aytoun's Scottish Ballads: the Execution of Montrose.

republicans in that body took alarm at this phrase, and thought that Cromwell used it to foreshadow a design to place the crown on his own head. For this reason, perhaps, they hesitated to dissolve.

But at last they could not withstand the pressure, and in 1653 a bill was introduced for summoning a new Parliament of four hundred members, but with the provision that all members of the present House were to keep their seats, and have the right to reject newly elected members.

Cromwell, with the army, believed this provision a trick on the part of the Rump to keep themselves in perpetual power.

Sir Harry Vane, who was a leading member of the House, and who had been governor of the colony of Massachusetts, feared that the country was in danger of falling into the hands of Cromwell as military dictator. He therefore urged the immediate passage of the bill as it stood. Cromwell heard that a vote was about to be taken. Putting himself at the head of a squad of soldiers, whom he left at the door, he suddenly entered the House. After listening to the debate for some time, he rose from his seat and charged the Commons with injustice and misgovernment. A member remonstrated. Cromwell grew excited, saying, "You are no Parliament! I say you are no Parliament!" Then he called in the musketeers. The speaker was dragged from his chair, and the members driven after him. As they passed out, Cromwell shouted "drunkard," "glutton," "extortioner," with other opprobrious names. When all were gone, he locked the door and put the key in his pocket. During the night some Royalist wag nailed a placard on the door, bearing the inscription in large letters, "This House to let, unfurnished!"

507. Cromwell becomes Protector (1653). — Cromwell now summoned a new Parliament of his own choosing. It consisted of one hundred and thirty-nine members, and was known as the "Little Parliament."[1] The Royalists nicknamed it "Barebone's

---

[1] A regularly summoned Parliament, elected by the people, would have been much larger. This was chosen from a list furnished by the ministers of the various Independent churches. It was in no true sense a representative body.

Parliament" from one of its members, a London leather merchant named Praise-God Barebone. Notwithstanding the irregularity of its organization and the ridicule cast upon it, the Barebone's Parliament proposed several reforms of great value, which the country afterward adopted.

A council now presented a constitution, entitled the "Instrument of Government,"[1] which made Cromwell Lord Protector of England, Ireland, and Scotland. Up to this time the Commonwealth had been a republic, nominally under the control of the House of Commons, but as a matter of fact governed by Cromwell and the army; now it became a republic under a Protector, or president, who was to hold his office for life.

A few years later, a second constitution was drafted, called the "Humble Petition and Advice,"[2] which offered Cromwell the crown. He would have taken it; but finding the army would not support him in such a step, reluctantly relinquished it. He at the same time endeavored to restore the House of Lords, but could not get them to attend.

508. Emigration of Royalists. — Under the tyranny of the Stuart kings many Puritans had emigrated to Massachusetts and other parts of New England. During the Commonwealth the case was reversed, and numbers of Royalists fled to Virginia. Among them were John Washington, the great-grandfather of George Washington, and the ancestors of Jefferson, Patrick Henry, the Lees, Randolphs, and other prominent families, destined in time to found a republic in the New World much more democratic than anything the old had ever seen.

---

[1] "Instrument of Government": the principal provisions of this constitution were: 1. The government was vested in the Protector and a council appointed for life; 2. Parliament to be summoned every three years, and not to be dissolved under five months; 3. A standing army of 30,000 to be maintained; 4. All taxes to be levied by Parliament; 5. The system of representation was reformed, so that many large places hitherto without representation in Parliament now obtained it; 6. All Roman Catholics, and those concerned in the Irish rebellion, were disfranchised forever.

[2] "The Humble Petition and Advice" was a modification of the "Instrument of Government."

509. Cromwell as a Ruler. — When Cromwell's new Parliament ventured to criticise his course, he dissolved them quite as peremptorily as the late king. Soon after, fear of a Royalist rebellion led him to divide the country into eleven military districts, each governed by a major-general, who ruled by martial law and with despotic power. All Royalist families were heavily taxed to support the standing army; all Catholic priests were banished, and no books or papers could be published without permission of the government.

Cromwell, however, though compelled to resort to severe measures to secure peace, was, in spirit, no oppressor. On the contrary, he proved himself the Protector not only of the realm, but of the Protestants of Europe. When they were threatened with persecution, his influence saved them. He showed, too, that in an age of bigotry he was no bigot. Puritan fanaticism, exasperated by the persecution it had endured under James and Charles, often went to the utmost extremes, even as "Hudibras"[1] said, to "killing of a cat on Monday for catching of a rat on Sunday."

It treated the most innocent customs, if they were in any way associated with Catholicism, or Episcopacy, as serious offences. It closed all places of amusement; it condemned mirth as ungodly; it was a sin to dance round a May-pole, or to eat mince-pie at Christmas. Fox-hunting and horse-racing were forbidden, and bear-baiting prohibited, "not because it gave pain to the bear, but because it gave pleasure to the spectators."

In such an age, when a man could hardly claim to be religious unless he wore sad-colored raiment, talked through his nose, and quoted Scripture at every sentence, Cromwell showed exceptional moderation and good sense.

510. His Religious Toleration. — He favored the toleration of all forms of worship not directly opposed to the govern-

---

[1] "Hudibras": a burlesque poem by Samuel Butler. It was published in 1663, and satirizes all the leading persons and parties of the Commonwealth, but especially the Puritans.

ment. He befriended the Quakers, who were then looked upon as the enemies of every form of worship, and were treated with cruel severity both in England and America. He was instrumental in sending the first Protestant missionaries to Massachusetts to convert the Indians, then supposed by many to be a remnant of the lost tribes of Israel; and after an exclusion of many centuries,[1] he permitted the Jews to return to England, and even to build a synagogue in London.

On the other hand, there are few of the cathedral or parish churches of England which do not continue to testify to the destructive hatred which during the civil wars vented itself on everything savoring of the rule of either pope or bishop. The empty niches, where some gracious image of the Virgin or the figure of some saint once looked down; the patched remnants of brilliantly stained glass, once part of a picture telling some scripture story; the mutilated tombs, broken, hacked, and hewed by pike and sword because on them was some emblem or expression of the old faith — all these still bear witness to the fury of the Puritan soldiers, who did not respect even the graves of their ancestors, if those ancestors had once thought differently from themselves.

511. Victories by Land and Sea. — Yet during Cromwell's rule the country, notwithstanding all the restrictions imposed by a stern military government, grew and prospered. The English forces gained victories by land and sea, and made the name of the Protector respected as that of Charles had never been. At this period the carrying-trade of the world had fallen into the hands of the Dutch, and Amsterdam had become a more important centre of exchange than London. In 1651 the Commonwealth passed measures called Navigation Laws to encourage British commerce by prohibiting the importation or exportation of any goods into England or its colonies in Dutch vessels. Later, war with the Dutch broke out partly on account of questions of trade, and

---

[1] See Paragraph No. 274.

partly because Royalist plotters found protection in Holland. Then Cromwell created such a navy as the country had never before possessed, and, under the command of Blake, the Dutch were beaten so thoroughly that they bound themselves to ever after salute the English flag wherever they should meet it on the seas. A war undertaken in alliance with France against Spain was equally successful. Jamaica was taken as a permanent possession by the British fleet, and France, out of gratitude for assistance, gave the town of Dunkirk to England, so that the flag of the Commonwealth was now planted on the French coast.

512. Cromwell's Death; his Character. — After being king in everything but name for five years, Cromwell died Sept. 3, 1658, on the anniversary of the victories of Dunbar and Worcester. During the latter part of his career he had lived in constant dread of assassination, and wore concealed armor. At the hour of his death one of the most fearful storms was raging that had ever swept over England. To many it seemed a fit accompaniment to the close of such a life.[1]

In one sense, Cromwell was a usurper and a tyrant; but, at heart, his object was his country's welfare. In such cases the motive is all in all. He was a man of rough exterior and hard manner. He cared little for the smooth proprieties of life, yet he had that dignity of bearing which high moral purpose gives. In all that he did he was eminently practical. In an age of isms, theories, and experiments, he was never confused and never faltered in his course.

513. The Times needed Such a Man. — There are emergencies when an ounce of decision is worth a pound of deliberation. When the ship is foundering or on fire, or when the crew have mutinied, it will not avail to sit in the cabin and discuss how it

---

[1] Cromwell was always a lonely man, and had so few real friends that Walter Scott may have expressed his true feeling when he makes him say in "Woodstock": " I would *I* had any creature, were it but a dog, that followed me because it loved me, not for what it could make of me."

happened. Something must be done, and that promptly. Cromwell was the man for such a juncture. He saw clearly that if the country was to be kept together, it must be by decided measures, which no precedent, law, or constitution justified, but which stood justified none the less by the exigencies of the crisis, by his own conscious rectitude of purpose, and by the result.

If there is any truth in Napoleon's maxim, that "the tools belong to him that can use them," then Cromwell had a God-given right to rule; for, first, he had the ability; and, next, if we except his campaign in Ireland, he employed it, all things considered, on the side of order and of justice.

514. Summary. — Cromwell's original purpose appears to have been to establish a government representing the will of the nation more completely than it had ever been before. He favored the restoration of the House of Lords, he endeavored to reform the laws, and he sought to secure religious toleration for the great body of Protestants. Circumstances, however, were often against him; he had many enemies, and in order to secure peace he was obliged to resort to absolute power. Yet the difference in this respect between him and Charles I. was immense; the latter was despotic on his own account, the former for the advantage of those he governed.

RICHARD CROMWELL. — Sept. 3, 1658, to April 22, 1659.[1]

515. Richard Cromwell's Incompetency. — Richard Cromwell, Oliver's eldest son, now succeeded to the Protectorate. He was an amiable individual, as negative in character as his father had been positive. With the extreme Puritans, known as the "godly party," he had no sympathy whatever. "Here," said he to one of them, pointing to a friend of his who stood by, "is a man who can neither preach nor pray, yet I would trust him be-

---

[1] Richard Cromwell continued to reside in the royal palace of Whitehall until July, but he virtually gave up all power in April.

fore you all." Such frankness was not likely to make the new ruler popular with the army made up of men who never lacked a scripture text to justify either a murder or a massacre. Moreover, the times were perilous, and called for a decided hand at the helm. After a brief reign of less than eight months the military leaders requested Richard to resign, and soon after recalled the Rump Parliament.

516. Richard retires. — The Protector retired not only without remonstrance, but apparently with a sense of relief at being so soon eased of a burden too heavy for his weak shoulders to carry. To the people he was hereafter familiarly known as "Tumbledown-Dick," and was caricatured as such on tavern sign-boards. The nation pensioned him off with a moderate allowance, and he lived in obscurity to an advanced age, carrying about with him to the last a trunk filled with the congratulatory addresses and oaths of allegiance which he had received when he became Protector.

Years after his abdication it is reported that he visited Westminster, and when the attendant, who did not recognize him, showed him the throne, he said, "Yes; I have not seen that chair since I sat in it myself in 1659."

517. The Convention Parliament. — The year following Richard's withdrawal was full of anxiety and confusion. The army had dissolved Parliament, there was no longer any regularly organized government, and the country drifted helplessly like a ship without a pilot.

General Monk, then commander-in-chief in Scotland, now marched into England with the determination of calling a new Parliament which should be full, free, and representative of the real political feeling of the nation. When he reached London with his army, the members of the Rump had resumed their sessions. At Monk's invitation the Presbyterian members, whom Colonel Pride had driven from their seats eleven years before, now went back. This assembly issued writs for the summoning of a Convention Parliament (so styled because called without royal authority), and then dissolved by their own consent. Thus ended that memorable Long Parliament which had existed nearly twenty years. About a month later the Convention, including ten members of the House of Lords, met, and at once invited Charles Stuart, then in Holland, to return to his kingdom.[1]

518. Summary. — Richard Cromwell's government existed in name only, never in fact. During his so-called protectorate the country was under the control of the army, or of that Rump Parliament which represented nothing but itself. The period which elapsed after Oliver Cromwell's death was one of waiting and preparation. It ended in the meeting of the free national Parliament, which put an end to the republic, and restored royalty in the person of Charles II.

CHARLES II. — 1660-1685.

519. The Accession of Charles. — The English army heard that Charles was coming, with sullen silence; the ex-members of the Rump, with sullen dread; the rest of the nation, with a feeling of relief. However much they had hated the despotism of the Stuarts, four-fifths of the people welcomed any change which promised to do away with a government maintained by bayonets.

Charles was received at Dover with the wildest demonstrations of joy. Bells pealed, flags waved, bonfires blazed all the way to London, and the king said, with characteristic irony, "It must have been my own fault that I did not come before, for I find no one but declares that he is glad to see me."

The fact that the republic had existed was as far as possible ignored. The new reign was dated, not when it actually began,

---

[1] In anticipation of this event Charles had issued certain promises at Breda, Holland, called the Declaration of Breda, which granted —
1. Free pardon to all those not excepted by Parliament.
2. Liberty of conscience to all whose views did not disturb the peace of the realm.
3. The settlement by Parliament of all claims to landed property.
4. The payment of arrears to Monk's army.

but from the day of Charles I.'s execution twelve years before. The troops of the Commonwealth were speedily disbanded, but the king retained a picked guard of 5000 men, which became the nucleus of a new standing army.

520. The King's Character. — The sovereign who now ascended the throne was in every respect the opposite of Cromwell. Charles had no love of country, no sense of duty, no belief in man, no respect for woman. Evil circumstances and evil companions had made him "a good-humored but hard-hearted voluptuary." For twelve years he had been a wanderer, and at times almost a beggar. Now the sole aim of his life was enjoyment. He desired to be king because he would then have every means for accomplishing that aim.

521. Reaction from Puritanism. — In this purpose Charles had the sympathy of a considerable part of the people. The Puritan faith, represented by such men as Milton and Hampden, was noble indeed; but unfortunately there were many in its ranks who had no like grandeur of soul, but who pushed Puritanism to its most injurious and offensive extreme. That attempt to reduce the whole of life to a narrow system of sour self-denial had at last broken down. Now, under the Restoration, the reaction set in, and the lower and earthly side of human nature — none the less human because it is at the bottom and not at the top — seemed determined to take its full revenge. Butler ridiculed religious zeal in his poem of "Hudibras," which every courtier had by heart. It was an epidemic of immorality. Profligacy became the fashion in both speech and action, and much of the popular literature of that day will not bear the light.

522. The Royal Favorites; the Cabal. — The king surrounded himself with men like himself. They vied with each other in dissipation and in jests on each other. Charles's two chief favorites were the Earl of Rochester, a gifted but ribald poet, and Lord Shaftesbury, who became chancellor. Both have left on record their estimate of their royal master. The first wrote on the door of the king's bed-chamber : —

> " Here lies our sovereign lord, the king,
> Whose word no man relies on;
> He never says a foolish thing,
> Nor ever does a wise one."

To which Charles, on reading it, retorted, " 'Tis true! because while my words are my own, my acts are my ministers'."

A bright repartee tells us what the second favorite thought. "Ah! Shaftesbury," said the king to him one day, "I verily believe you are the wickedest dog in my dominions." "Yes, your Majesty," replied Shaftesbury, "for a *subject* I think perhaps I may be."

The new reign, from a political point of view, began decently and ably with the Earl of Clarendon as leading minister, but in a few years it degenerated into an administration called the Cabal, which was simply a government of debauchees, whose sole object was to advance their own private interests by making the king supreme.[1] Its character and deeds may best be learned from that picture of the council of the "infernal peers," which Milton portrayed in "Paradise Lost," where the five princes of evil, Moloch, Belial, Mammon, Beelzebub, and Satan, meet in the palace of Pandemonium to plot the ruin of the world.[2]

---

[1] This word was originally used to designate the confidential members of the king's private council, and meant perhaps no more than the word *cabinet* does to-day. In 1667 it happened, however, by a singular coincidence, that the initial letters of the five persons comprising it, namely (C)lifford, (A)shley-Cooper [Lord Shaftesbury], (B)uckingham, (A)rlington, and (L)auderdale formed the word CABAL, which henceforth came to have the odious meaning of secret and unscrupulous intrigue that it has ever since retained. It was to Charles II.'s time what the political "ring" is to our own.

[2] Milton's Paradise Lost, Book II. The first edition was published in 1667, the year the Cabal came into power, though its members had long been favorites with the king. It has been supposed by some that the great Puritan poet had them in his mind when he represented the Pandemonic debate. Shaftesbury and Buckingham are also two of the most prominent characters in Dryden's political satire of Absalom and Achitophel, published in 1681.

523. Punishment of the Regicides. — The first act of Charles's first Parliament was to proclaim a pardon to all who had fought against his father in the civil war. The only persons excepted were the members of that High Court of Justice which had sent Charles I. to the block. Of these, ten were executed and nineteen imprisoned for life. Most of the other regicide judges were either already out of the country, or managed to escape soon after. Among these, William Goffe, Edward Whalley, and Col. John Dixwell took refuge in Connecticut, where they remained concealed for several years. Eventually the first two went to Hadley, Massachusetts, where they lived in seclusion in the house of a clergyman until their death. The bodies of Cromwell, Ireton, Bradshaw, and Pride were dug up from their graves in Westminster Abbey, and hanged in chains at Tyburn.[1] They were then buried at the foot of the gallows, along with the mouldering remains of highway robbers and criminals of the lowest sort.

524. Religious Persecution; Covenanters; Bunyan. — The Episcopal form of worship was now restored, and in the course of the next few years severe laws were passed against the Nonconformists, or Dissenters.[2] The Corporation Act ordered all holders of municipal offices to renounce the Puritan covenant,[3] and take the sacrament of the Church of England. Next, the Act of Uniformity enforced the use of the Episcopal Prayer-book upon all clergymen and congregations. This was followed by a law[4] forbidding all

---

[1] Tyburn, near the northeast entrance to Hyde Park, London. It was for several centuries the chief place for the public execution of felons.

[2] The chief Nonconformists, aside from the Roman Catholics, were: 1. The Presbyterians. 2. The Independents, or Congregationalists. 3. The Baptists. 4. The Society of Friends, or Quakers. Originally the name Nonconformist was given to those who refused to conform to the worship of the Church of England, or Episcopacy, and endeavored to change it to suit their views. Later, when the Nonconformists gave up that attempt, and asked only for permission to worship according to their own convictions, they received the milder name of Dissenters.

[3] Covenant: the oath or agreement to maintain the Presbyterian faith and worship. It originated in Scotland. See Paragraph No. 490.

[4] Conventicle Act: from conventicle, a religious meeting of Dissenters.

religious assemblies whatever, except such as worshipped according to the established church. Lastly, the Five-Mile Act forbade all dissenting ministers from teaching in schools, or settling within five miles of an incorporated town.

By these stringent statutes 2000 Presbyterian clergymen were driven from their parishes in a single day, and reduced to the direst distress. The able-bodied among them might indeed pick up a precarious livelihood by hard labor, but the old and the weak soon found their refuge in the grave.

Those who dared to resist these intolerant and inhuman laws were punished with fines, imprisonment, or slavery. The Scottish Parliament — a Parliament, says Bishop Burnet, "mostly drunk " — vied with that of England in persecution of the Dissenters.

The Covenanters were hunted with bugle and bloodhound, like so many deer, by Claverhouse and his men, who hanged and drowned without mercy those who gathered secretly in glens. and caves to worship God. Even when nothing certain was known against those who were seized, there was no trial. The father of a family would be dragged from his cottage by the soldiers, asked if he would take the test of conformity to the Church of England and to Charles's government; if not, then came the order, " Make ready — present — fire !" — and there lay the corpse of the rebel.

Among the multitudes who suffered in England for religion's sake was a poor day-laborer named John Bunyan. He had served against the king in the civil wars, and later had become converted to Puritanism, and turned exhorter and itinerant preacher. He was arrested and convicted of having "devilishly and perniciously abstained from coming to church." The judge sentenced him to Bedford jail, where he remained a prisoner for twelve years. It was, he says, a squalid "Denn."[1] But in his marvellous dream of " A Pilgrimage from this World to the Next," he forgot the misery of his surroundings. Like Milton, in his

---

[1] "As I walk'd through the wilderness of this world, I lighted on a certain place where was a Denn, and I laid me down in that place to sleep: and as I slept I dreamed a dream." The Pilgrim's Progress, edition of 1678.

blindness, loneliness, and poverty, he looked within and found that —

> "The mind is its own place, and in itself
> Can make a heaven of hell."[1]

525. Seizure of a Dutch Colony. — While these things were going on in England, a disgraceful event took place abroad. The Dutch had established a colony in America, and built a town on Manhattan Island at the mouth of the Hudson River, which they called New Amsterdam.

A treaty made by England with Holland under the Commonwealth had recognized the claims of the Dutch in the New World.

Charles, however, had no intention of keeping faith with Holland; and though the two nations were at peace, resolved to seize the territory. He accordingly granted it to his brother James, Duke of York, and sent out a secret expedition to capture the colony in his behalf.

One day an English fleet suddenly appeared in the harbor of the Dutch town, and demanded its immediate and unconditional surrender. The governor was unprepared to make any defence, and the place was given up. Thus, without so much as the firing of a gun, New Amsterdam got the name of New York in honor of the man who, with his royal brother, had with characteristic treachery planned and perpetrated the robbery.

526. The Plague and the Fire. — In 1665 a terrible outbreak of the plague occurred in London, which spread throughout the kingdom. All who could fled from the city. Hundreds of houses were left vacant, while on hundreds more a cross marked on the doors in red chalk, with the words "Lord have mercy on us," written underneath, told where the work of death was going on.[2]

---

[1] Paradise Lost, Book I. 253.

[2] Pepys writes in his diary, describing the beginning of the plague: "The 7th of June, 1665, was the hottest day I ever felt in my life. This day, much against my will, I did in Drury Lane see two or three houses with a red cross upon the door, and 'Lord have mercy upon us' writ there, which was a sad sight." Pepys' Diary, 1660–1669. Defoe wrote a journal of the plague in 1722, based, probably, on the reports of eyewitnesses. It gives a vivid and truthful account of its horrors.

This pestilence swept off over a hundred thousand victims within six months. Among the few brave men who voluntarily remained in the stricken city were the Puritan ministers, who stayed to comfort and console the sick and dying. After the plague was over, they received their reward in those acts of persecution which drove them homeless and helpless from their parishes and friends.

The dead-cart had hardly ceased to go its rounds, when a fire (1666) broke out, of which Evelyn, a courtier, who witnessed it, wrote, that it "was not to be outdone until the final conflagration."[1] By it the city of London proper was reduced to ruins, little more being left than a fringe of houses on the northeast.[2]

The members of the Cabal gloated over the destruction, believing that now that London was destroyed, the king, with the aid of his army, might easily crush out political liberty. But selfish as Charles and his brother James unquestionably were, they were better than the Cabal; for both worked heroically to stop the flames, and gave liberally to feed and shelter the multitudes who had lost everything.

Great as the calamity was, yet from a sanitary point of view it did great good. Nothing short of fire could have effectually cleansed the London of that day, and so put a stop to the periodical ravages of the plague. By sweeping away miles of narrow streets crowded with miserable buildings black with the encrusted filth of ages, the conflagration in the end proved friendly to health and life.

A monument near London Bridge still marks the spot where the flames first burst out. For many years it bore an inscription affirming that the Catholics kindled them in order to be revenged on their persecutors. The poet Pope, at a later period, exposed the falsehood in the lines: —

> "Where London's column pointing towards the skies
> Like a tall bully lifts its head and lies."[3]

---

[1] Evelyn's Diary, 1641-1705, also compare Dryden's Poem, Annus Mirabilis.
[2] See Map in Loftie's London, Vol. I. See also Paragraph No. 64, note 2.
[3] Moral Essays, Epistle iii.

Sir Christopher Wren, the most famous architect of the period, rebuilt the city. The greater part of it had been of wood, but it rose from the ashes brick and stone. One irreparable loss was the old Gothic church of St. Paul. Wren erected the present cathedral on the foundations of the ancient structure. He lies buried under the grand dome of his own grandest work. On a tablet near the tomb of the great master-builder one reads the inscription in Latin, "Reader, if you seek his monument, look around."[1]

527. Invasion by the Dutch.—The new city had not risen from the ruins of the old, when a third calamity overtook it. Charles was at war with Holland. The contest originally grew out of the rivalry of the two countries in their efforts to get the exclusive possession of foreign trade. Parliament granted the king large sums of money to build and equip a navy, but the pleasure-loving monarch wasted it in dissipation. The few ships he had were rotten old hulks, but half provisioned, with crews ready to mutiny because they could not get their pay. A Dutch fleet, manned in part by English sailors who had deserted in disgust, because when they asked for dollars to support their families they got only worthless government tickets, now sailed up the Thames. There was no force to oppose them. They burnt some half-built men-of-war, threatened to blockade London, and made their own terms of peace.

528. Treaty of Dover; the King robs the Exchequer.—But another and still deeper disgrace was at hand. The chief ambition of Charles was to rule without a Parliament; without supplies of money he found this impossible. A way to accomplish the desired end now presented itself.

Louis XIV. of France, then the most powerful monarch in Europe, wished to conquer Holland, with the double object of extending his own kingdom and the power of Romanism. He

---

[1] "Lector, si monumentum requiris, circumspice."

saw in Charles the tool he wanted to gain this end. By the secret treaty of Dover, Louis bribed the English king with a gift of £300,000 to help him carry out his scheme. Thus, without the knowledge of Parliament, Charles deliberately sold himself to the French sovereign in his plot to destroy the political liberty and Protestant faith of Holland. In addition to the above sum, it was furthermore agreed that Louis should pay Charles a pension of £200,000 a year from the date when the latter should openly avow himself a Catholic.

True to his infamous contract, Charles provoked a new war with the Dutch, but found that he needed more money to prosecute it successfully. Not knowing where to borrow, he determined to steal it. Various prominent London merchants and bankers had lent to the government large sums on promise of repayment from the taxes. A part of the revenue amounting to about £1,300,-000, a sum equal to at least $10,000,000 now, had been deposited in the exchequer, or government treasury, to meet the obligation. The king seized this money,[1] partly for his needs, but chiefly for his vices. This act of treachery caused a financial panic which shook London to its foundations and ruined great numbers of people.

529. More Money Schemes. — By declaring war against Holland, Charles had now fulfilled the first part of his secret treaty with Louis, but he was afraid to undertake the second part and openly declare himself a convert to the Church of Rome. He, however, did the next thing to it, by issuing a proclamation of indulgence to all religions, under cover of which he intended to show especial favor to the Catholics.

To offset this proclamation, Parliament at once passed a law requiring every government officer to acknowledge himself a Protestant. Charles became alarmed at this decided stand, and now tried to conciliate Parliament, and coax from them another grant

---

[1] "'Rob me the exchequer, Hal,' said the king to his favorite minister; then 'all went merry as a marriage bell.'" Evelyn's Diary, 10 Oct., 1671.

of money by marrying his niece, the Princess Mary, to William of Orange, president of the Dutch republic, and head of the Protestant party on the continent.

530. The "Popish Plot." — While the king was playing this double part, an infamous scoundrel, named Titus Oates, whose hideous face was but the counterpart of a still more hideous character, pretended that he had discovered a terrible plot. According to his account, the Catholics had formed a conspiracy to burn London, massacre the inhabitants, kill the king, and restore the religion of Rome. The news of this alleged discovery caused an excitement which soon grew into a sort of popular madness. The memory of the great fire was still fresh in people's minds. In their imagination they now saw those scenes of horror repeated, with wholesale murder added. Great numbers of innocent persons were thrown into prison, and many executed. As time went on, the terror seemed to increase. With its increase, Oates grew bolder in his accusations. Chief-Justice Scroggs showed himself an eager abettor of the miserable wretch who swore away men's lives for the sake of the notoriety it gave him. In the extravagance of his presumption Oates dared even to accuse the queen of an attempt to poison Charles. The craze, however, had at last begun to abate somewhat, and no action was taken.

An attempt was now made to pass a law called the "Exclusion Bill," debarring Charles's brother James, the Catholic Duke of York, from succeeding to the crown; but though voted by the Commons, it was defeated by the Lords. A second measure, however, received the sanction of both Houses, by which Catholics were declared incapable of sitting in Parliament; and from this date they remained shut out from all legislative power and from all civil and corporate offices for a period of over a century and a half.

531. Political Parties. — It was about this time that the names "Whig" and "Tory" began to be given to two political parties, which soon became very powerful, and which have ever since divided the Parliamentary government of the country between them.

The term "Whig" was originally given by way of reproach to the Scotch Puritans, or Covenanters, who refused to accept the Episcopacy which Charles I. endeavored to impose upon them.[1] "Tory," on the other hand, was a nickname which appears to have first been applied to the Roman Catholic outlaws of Ireland, who were regarded as both robbers and rebels.

This latter name was now given to those who supported the claims of the king's brother James, the Roman Catholic Duke of York, as successor to the throne; while that of Whig was borne by those who were endeavoring to exclude him, and secure a Protestant successor.[2] The excitement over this question threatened at one period to bring on another civil war. In his fury against the Whigs, Charles revoked the charters of London and many other cities, which were re-granted only on terms agreeable to the Tories. An actual outbreak against the government would probably have occurred had it not been for the discovery of a new conspiracy, which resulted in a reaction favorable to the crown.

532. The Rye House Plot. — This conspiracy, known as the "Rye House Plot," had for its object the murder of Charles and his brother James at a place called the Rye House, in Hertfordshire, not far from London. It was concocted by a number of violent Whigs, who, in their disappointment respecting the passage of the Exclusion Bill, took this method of securing their ends.

It is said that they intended placing on the throne James, Duke of Monmouth, a natural son of Charles, who was popularly

---

[1] See Paragraph No. 490.

[2] Politically, the Whigs and Tories may perhaps be considered as the successors of the Roundheads and Cavaliers of the civil war, the former seeking to limit the power of the crown; the latter, to extend it. At the Restoration (1660), the Cavaliers were all-powerful; but at the time of the dispute on the Exclusion Bill (1679), the Roundhead, or Peoples' party had revived. On account of their petitioning the king to summon a new Parliament, by means of which they hoped to carry the bill shutting out the Duke of York from the throne, they were called "Petitioners," and later, Whigs; while those who expressed their abhorrence of their efforts were called "Abhorrers," and afterward, Tories.

known as the "Protestant Duke." Algernon Sidney, Lord Russell, and the Earl of Essex, who were prominent advocates of the bill, were arrested for participating in the plot. Essex committed suicide in the Tower; Sidney and Russell were tried, convicted, and sentenced to death on insufficient evidence. Both were unquestionably innocent. They died martyrs to the cause of liberty, — Russell, with the fortitude of a Christian; Sidney, with the calmness of a philosopher. The Duke of Monmouth, who was supposed to be implicated in the plot, was banished to Holland.

533. The Royal Society. — During this reign the Royal Society, for the discussion of scientific questions, was organized. In an age when thousands of well-informed people still cherished a lingering belief that lead might be changed into gold; that some medicine might be discovered which would cure every disease, and prevent old age, that worst disease of all; when every cross-grained old woman was suspected of witchcraft, and was liable to be tortured and hanged on that suspicion; the formation of an association to study physical facts was most significant. It showed that the time had come when, instead of guessing what might be, men were at last beginning to resolve to know what actually is. Under the encouragement given by this society, an English mathematician and philosopher published a work which demonstrated the unity of the universe, by proving that the same law governs the falling of an apple and the movements of the planets in their orbits. It was with reference to that wonderful discovery of the all-pervading power of gravitation, which shapes and holds in its control the drop of dew before our eyes, and the farthest star shining in the heavens, that the poet Pope suggested the epitaph which should be graven on the tomb in Westminster Abbey: —

> "Nature and Nature's laws lay hid in night;
> God said, 'Let Newton be!' and all was light."

534. Chief Political Reforms. — As the age did not stand still with respect to progress in knowledge, so it was not wholly unsuccessful in attempts at political reform. The chief measures were, first, the Habeas Corpus Act,[1] which provided that no subject should be detained in prison except by due process of law, thus putting an end to the arbitrary confinement of men for months, and years even, without conviction of guilt or even form of trial. The next reform was the abolition of the king's right to feudal dues and service, by which he was accustomed to extort as much as possible from his subjects,[2] and the substitution of a fixed yearly allowance, raised by tax, of £1,200,000.[3] This change may be considered to have practically abolished the feudal system in England, so far as the crown is concerned, though the law still retains many remnants of it with respect to the relation of landlord and tenant.

535. Death of Charles. — In 1685 the reign came suddenly to an end. Evelyn tells us in his Diary that he was present at the royal court at the Palace of Whitehall on Sunday morning, the last of January of that year. There he saw the king sitting in the grand banqueting-room, chatting gayly with three famous court beauties, "while a crowd of richly dressed nobles were gathered around a gambling-table heaped with gold. Six days after," as he expresses it, "all was in the dust." Charles died a Roman Catholic, his brother James having smuggled a priest into his chamber in time to hear his confession and grant him absolution. Certainly few English rulers have stood in greater need of both.

536. Summary. — The chief events of the period were the persecution of the Puritans, the Plague and Fire of London, the "Popish" and Rye House Plots, and the Dutch Wars. Aside from

---

[1] Habeas Corpus ad subjiciendum (1679) *(that you have the body to answer)*: this writ is addressed by the judge to him who detains another in custody, commanding him to bring him into court and show why he is restrained of his liberty.

[2] See Paragraph No. 200. See also Blackstone's Commentaries, II. 76.

[3] This tax should have been levied on the landed proprietors who had been subject to the feudal dues, but they evaded it, and by getting it assessed as an excise duty on beer and spirits, they compelled the body of the people to bear the burden for them.

these, the reign presents two leading points: 1. The policy of the king; 2. That of the nation. Charles, as we have seen, lived solely to gratify his inordinate love of pleasure. For that, he wasted the revenue, robbed the exchequer, and cheated the navy; for that, he secretly sold himself to France, made war on Holland, and shamefully deceived both Parliament and people. In so far, then, as Charles had an object, it began and ended with himself. Therein, he stood lower than his father, who at least conscientiously believed in the Divine Right of kings and their accountability to the Almighty.

The policy of the nation, on the other hand, was divided. The Whigs were determined to limit the power of the crown, and secure at all hazards a Protestant successor. The Tories were equally resolved to check the growing power of the people, and preserve the hereditary order of succession without any immediate regard to the religious question. Beneath these issues both parties had a common object, which was to maintain the national Episcopal church, and the monarchical system of government, preferring rather to cherish patriotism through loyalty to a personal sovereign, than patriotism alone through devotion to a democratic republic.

JAMES II. — 1685-1689.

537. Accession of James II.; his Two Objects; Oates gets his Deserts. — James, Duke of York, brother of the late king, now came to the throne. His first great ambition was to rule independently of Parliament; in other words, to have his own way in everything; his second, which was, if possible, still nearer his heart, was to restore the Roman Catholic religion in England. He began that restoration at once; and on the Easter Sunday preceding his coronation, "the worship of the church of Rome was once more, after an interval of a hundred and twenty-seven years, performed at Westminster with royal splendor."[1]

Not long after, James had the miscreant Oates brought to trial

---

[1] Macaulay's England.

for the perjuries he had committed in connection with the "Popish Plot." He was found guilty, and the community had the satisfaction of seeing him publicly whipped through London with such terrible severity that "the blood ran in rivulets," and a few more strokes of the lash would have ended his worthless life.

538. Monmouth's Rebellion; Sedgemoor.—At the time of the discovery of the Rye House Plot, a number of Whigs who were implicated in the conspiracy fled to Holland, where the Duke of Monmouth had also gone when banished. Four months after the accession of James, the duke, aided by these refugees and by a small force which he had gathered in the Low Countries, resolved to invade England and demand the crown, in the belief that a large part of the nation would look upon him as representing the cause of Protestantism, and would therefore rally to his support. He landed at Lyme on the coast of Dorsetshire, and there issued an absurd proclamation declaring James to be a usurper, tyrant, and murderer, who had set the great fire of London, cut the throat of Essex,[1] and poisoned Charles II. ! At Taunton, in Somersetshire, a procession of welcome headed by a lady carrying a Bible met the duke, and presented him with the book in behalf of the Protestant faith. He received it, saying, "I come to defend the truths contained in this volume, and to seal them, if it must be so, with my blood." Shortly after, he proclaimed himself sovereign of Great Britain under the title of King Monmouth. Many of the country people now joined him, but the Whig nobles, on whose help he had counted, stood aloof, alienated doubtless by the ridiculous charges he had made against James.

At the battle of Sedgemoor, in Somersetshire (1685), "King Monmouth," with his hastily gathered forces, was utterly routed, and he himself was soon after captured hiding in a ditch. He desired to be taken to the king. His request was granted. When he entered his uncle's presence, he threw himself down and crawled to his feet, weeping and begging piteously for life — only life —

---

[1] See Paragraph No. 532.

on any terms, however hard. He denied that he had issued the lying proclamation published at Lyme; he denied that he had sought the crown of his own free will; finally, in an agony of supplication, he hinted that he would even renounce Protestantism if thereby he might escape death. James told him that he should have the service of a Catholic priest, but would promise nothing more. Monmouth grovelled and pleaded, but the king turned away in silence. Then the duke, seeing that all his efforts were vain, rose to his feet and regained his manhood. He was forthwith sent to the Tower, and shortly after to execution. His headless body was buried under the communion-table of that little chapel of St. Peter within the Tower grounds, where the remains of Anne Boleyn, Lady Jane Grey, Sir Thomas More, and many other royal victims are gathered, and of which, it has been well said, that no sadder spot exists on earth, "since there death is associated with whatever is darkest in human nature and human destiny."[1]

After Monmouth's death there were no further attempts at insurrection, and the struggle at Sedgemoor remains the last encounter worthy of the name of battle fought on English soil.

539. The Bloody Assizes. — The defeat of the insurgents who had rallied under Monmouth's flag was followed by a series of trials known, from their results, as the "Bloody Assizes."[2] They were conducted by Judge Jeffreys, assisted by a band of soldiers under Colonel Kirke, ironically called, from their ferocity, "Kirke's Lambs." But of the two, Jeffreys was the more to be dreaded. He was by nature cruel, and enjoyed the spectacle of mental as well as bodily anguish. As he himself said, he delighted to give those who had the misfortune to appear before him "a lick with the rough side of his tongue," preparatory to roaring out the sentence of torture or death, in which he delighted still more. All who were in the remotest way implicated in the late rising were now hunted

---

[1] Macaulay's England.
[2] Assizes (from the French *asseoir*, to sit or set): sessions of a court; also used in the singular, of a decree or law.

down and brought to a trial which was but a mockery of justice. No one was permitted to defend himself. In fact, defence would nave been useless against the blind fury of such a judge. The threshold of the court was to most that crossed it the threshold of the grave. A gentleman present at one of these scenes of slaughter, touched with pity at the condition of a trembling old man called up for sentence, ventured to put in a word in his behalf. "My Lord," said he to Jeffreys, "this poor creature is dependent on the parish." "Don't trouble yourself," cried the judge; "I will soon ease the parish of the burden," and ordered the officers to execute him at once. Those who escaped death were often still more to be pitied. A young man was sentenced to be imprisoned for seven years, and to be whipped once a year through every market town in the county. In his despair, he petitioned the king to grant him the favor of being hanged. The petition was refused, but a partial remission of the punishment was at length gained by bribing the court; for Jeffreys, though his heart was shut against mercy, always had his pockets open for gain. Alice Lisle, an aged woman, who, out of pity, had concealed two men flying from the king's vengeance, was condemned to be burned alive; and it was with the greatest difficulty that the clergy of Winchester Cathedral succeeded in getting the sentence commuted to beheading.

As the work went on, the spirits of Jeffreys rose higher and higher. He laughed, shouted, joked, and swore like a drunken man. When the court had finished its sittings, more than a thousand persons had been brutally scourged, sold as slaves, hanged, or beheaded. The guide-posts of the highways were converted into gibbets, from which blackened corpses swung in chains, and from every church-tower in Somersetshire ghastly heads looked down on those who gathered there to worship God; in fact, so many bodies were exposed, that the whole air was "tainted with corruption and death."

Not satisfied with vengeance alone, Jeffreys and his friends made these trials a means of speculation. Batches of rebels were given as presents to courtiers, who sold them to be worked and flogged to death on West India plantations; and the queen's maids of honor extorted large sums of money for the pardon of a number of country school-girls who had been convicted of presenting Monmouth with a royal flag at Taunton. On the return of Jeffreys to London after this carnival of blood, his father was so horrified at his cruelty that he forbade him to enter his house. James, on the contrary, testified his approval by making Jeffreys lord chancellor of the realm, at the same time mildly censuring him for not having shown greater severity! The new lord chancellor testified his gratitude to his royal master by procuring the murder, by means of a packed jury, of Alderman Cornish, a prominent London Whig, who was especially hated by the king on account of his support of that Exclusion Bill which was intended to shut James out from the throne. On the same day on which Cornish was executed, Jeffreys also had the satisfaction of having Elizabeth Gaunt burned alive at Tyburn for having assisted one of the Rye House conspirators to escape who had fought for Monmouth at Sedgemoor.

540. The King makes Further Attempts to re-establish Catholicism; Declaration of Indulgence; Oxford. — An event occurred about this time which encouraged James to make a more decided attempt to restore Catholicism. In 1598 Henry IV. of France granted the Protestants of his kingdom liberty of worship, by the Edict of Nantes. In 1685 Louis XIV. deliberately revoked it. By that short-sighted act the Huguenots, or French Protestants, were exposed to cruel persecution, and thousands of them fled to England and America. James now resolved to profit by the example set him by Louis, and if not like the French monarch to drive the Protestants out of Great Britain, at least to restore the country to its allegiance to Rome. He began, contrary to law, by putting Catholics into important offices in both church and state.[2] He furthermore established an army of 13,000 men

---

[1] Nantes (Nantz).   [2] See Paragraph No. 530.

on Hounslow Heath, just outside London, to hold the city in subjection in case there should be a disposition to rebel. He next recalled the Protestant Duke of Ormond, governor of Ireland, and in his place as lord deputy, sent Talbot, Earl of Tyrconnel, a Catholic of notoriously bad character. Tyrconnel had orders to recruit an Irish Roman Catholic army to aid the king in carrying out his designs. He raised some soldiers, but he also raised that famous song of "Lilli Burlero," by which, as its author boasted, James was eventually "sung out of his kingdom."[1] Having, meanwhile, got the courts completely under his control through the appointment of judges in sympathy with Jeffreys and with himself, the king issued a Declaration of Indulgence, suspending all penal laws against both Roman Catholics on the one hand, and Protestant Dissenters on the other. The latter, however, suspecting that this apparently liberal measure was simply a trick to establish Catholicism, refused to avail themselves of it, and denounced it as an open violation of the Constitution.

James next proceeded, by means of the tyrannical High Commission Court, which he had revived,[2] to bring the chief college at Oxford under Catholic control. The president of Magdalen College having died, the Fellows were considering the choice of a successor. The king ordered them to elect a Catholic, and named at first a man of ill repute. The Fellows refused to obey, and elected a Protestant. James ejected the new presi-

---

[1] Lord Wharton, a prominent English Whig, was the author of this satirical political ballad, which, it is said, was sung and whistled from one end of England to the other, in derision of the king's policy. It undoubtedly had a powerful popular influence in bringing on the Revolution of 1688.
The ballad began :—

"Ho, Brother Teague, dost hear de decree ?
Lilli Burlero, bullen a-la,
Dat we shall have a new deputie,
Lilli Burlero, bullen a-la."

The refrain, "Lilli Burlero," etc. (also written "Lillibullero"), is said to have been the watchword used by the Irish Catholics when they rose against the Protestants of Ulster in 1641. See Wilkins's Political Songs, Vol. I.

[2] See Paragraph No. 491.

dent, and drove out the Fellows, leaving them to depend on the charity of the neighboring country gentlemen for their support. But the king, in attacking the rights of the college, had "run his head against a wall,"[1] as he soon discovered to his sorrow. His temporary success, however, emboldened him to issue a second Declaration of Indulgence, of which the real object, like that of the first, was to put Roman Catholics into still higher positions of trust and power.

541. The Petition of the Seven Bishops. — He commanded the clergy throughout the realm to read this declaration on a given Sunday from their pulpits. The Archbishop of Canterbury, accompanied by six bishops, petitioned the king to be excused from reading it in their churches. The king refused to consider the petition. When the day came, hardly a clergyman read the paper, and in the few cases in which they did, the congregation rose and left rather than listen to it.

Furious at such an unexpected result, James ordered the refractory bishops to be sent to the Tower. The whole country now seemed to turn against the king. By his obstinate folly James had succeeded in making enemies of all classes, not only of the Whig Roundheads who had fought against his father in the civil war, but also of the Tory Cavaliers who had fought for him. One of the imprisoned bishops was Trelawney of Bristol. He was a native of Cornwall. The news of his incarceration roused the rough, independent, population of that county. From one end of it to the other the people were now heard singing: —

"And shall Trelawney die, and shall Trelawney die?
There's thirty thousand Cornishmen will know the reason why."

Then the miners took up the words, and beneath the hills and fields the ominous echo was heard : —

---

[1] "What building is that?" asked the Duke of Wellington of his companion, Mr. Croker, pointing, as he spoke, to Magdalen College wall, just as they entered the city in 1834. "That is the wall which James II. ran his head against," was the reply.

"And shall Trelawney die, and shall Trelawney die?
There's twenty thousand underground will know the reason why."

On their trial the popular feeling in favor of the bishops was so strong that not even James's servile judges dared to openly use their influence to convict them. When the case was given to the jury, it is said that the largest and most robust man of the twelve rose and said to the rest: "Look at me! I am bigger than any of you, but before I will bring in a verdict of guilty, I will stay here until I am no thicker than a tobacco-pipe." That decided the matter, and the bishops were acquitted. The news was received in London like the tidings of some great victory, with shouts of joy, illuminations, and bonfires.

542. Birth of a Prince; Invitation to William of Orange.—But just before the acquittal an event took place which changed everything and brought on the memorable Revolution of 1688.

Up to this time the succession to the throne after James rested with his two daughters,—Mary, who had married William, Prince of Orange,[1] and resided in Holland; and her younger sister Anne, who had married George, Prince of Denmark, and was then living in London. Both of the daughters were zealous Protestants, and the expectation that one of them would ascend the English throne on the king's death had kept the people comparatively quiet under the efforts of James to restore Catholicism. But while the bishops were in prison awaiting trial the alarming intelligence was spread that a son had been born to the king. If true, he would now be the next heir to the crown, and would in all probability be educated and come to power a Catholic. This prospect brought matters to a crisis. Great numbers of the people, especially the Whigs, believed the whole matter an imposition, and it was commonly reported that the pretended prince was not the true son of the king and queen, but a child that had been smuggled into the palace to deceive the nation.

On the very day that the bishops were set at liberty, seven of

---

[1] Mary: see Paragraph No. 529.

the leading nobility and gentry, representing both political parties, seconded by the city of London, sent a secret invitation to William, Prince of Orange, urging him to come over with an army to defend his wife Mary's claim to the English throne and to protect the liberty of the English people.

William, after due consideration, decided to accept the invitation, which was probably not unexpected on his part. He was confirmed in his decision not only by the cordial approval of the leading Catholic princes of Europe,* but also by the Pope himself, who had more than once expressed his emphatic disgust at the foolish rashness of King James.[1]

543. The Coming of William, and Flight of James. — William landed with 14,000 troops. It was the fifth and last great landing in the history of England.[2] He declared that he came in Mary's interest and that of the English nation, to secure a free and legal Parliament which should decide the question of the succession. James endeavored to rally a force to resist him, but Lord John Churchill, afterward Duke of Marlborough, and the king's son-in-law, Prince George, both secretly went over to William's side. His troops likewise deserted, and finally even his daughter Anne went over to the enemy. "Now God help me!" exclaimed James, in despair, "for my own children forsake me!" The queen had already fled to France, taking with her her infant son, the unfortunate James Edward, whose birth had caused the revolution, and who, instead of a kingdom, inherited nothing but the nickname of "Pretender," which he in turn transmitted to his son.[3] King James soon followed his wife.

As he crossed the Thames in a boat by night, James threw the great seal of state into the river, in the vain hope that without it a

---

[1] Guizot, Histoire de Charles I. (Discours sur l'Histoire de la Révolution).

[2] The first being that of the Romans, the next that of the Saxons, the third that of St. Augustine, the fourth that of William the Conqueror, the fifth that of the Prince of Orange.

[3] Prince James Edward Stuart, the "Old Pretender," and his son Prince Charles Edward Stuart, the "Young Pretender."   * Except, of course, Louis XIV.

Parliament could not be legally summoned to decide the question which his adversary had raised. The king got as far as the coast, but was discovered by some fishermen and brought back. William reluctantly received him, and purposely allowed him to escape a second time. He now reached France, and found generous welcome and support from Louis XIV., at the court of Versailles.[1] There could be now no reasonable doubt that James's daughter Mary would receive the English crown.

544. Character of the Revolution of 1688. — Never was a revolution of such magnitude and meaning accomplished so peacefully. Not a drop of blood had been shed. There was hardly any excitement or uproar. Even the bronze statue of the runaway king was permitted to stand undisturbed in the rear of the palace of Whitehall, where it remains to this day.

The great change had taken place thus quietly because men's minds were ripe for it. England had entered upon another period of history, in which old institutions, laws and customs were passing away and all was becoming new.

Feudalism had vanished under Charles II.,[2] but political and religious persecution had continued. In future, however, we shall hear no more of the revocation of city charters or of other punishments inflicted because of political opinion,[3] and rarely of any punishment for religious dissent. Courts of justice will undergo reform, and will no longer be "little better than caverns of murderers,"[4] where judges like Scroggs and Jeffreys browbeat the prisoners, took their guilt for granted, insulted and silenced witnesses for their defence, and even cast juries into prison under penalties of heavy fines, for venturing to bring in verdicts contrary to their wishes.[5]

---

[1] For the king's life at Versailles, see Doran's Monarchs retired from Business.
[2] See Paragraph No. 534.
[3] See Paragraph No. 531 and No. 539, the Cornish case.
[4] Hallam's Constitutional History of England.
[5] See Hallam, and also Introduction to Professor Adams' Manual of Historical Literature. For a graphic picture of the times, read, in Bunyan's Pilgrim's Progress, Christian's trial before Lord Hategood

The day, too, had gone by when an English sovereign could cast his subjects into fetid dungeons in the Tower and leave them to die there of lingering disease, in darkness, solitude, and despair; or, like James, sit in the court-room at Edinburgh, and watch with curious delight the agony of the application of the Scotch instruments of torture, the "boot," and the thumbscrew.

For the future, thought and discussion in England were to be in great measure free, as in time they would be wholly so, and perhaps the coward king's heaviest retribution in his secure retreat beyond the sea was the knowledge that all his efforts to prevent the coming of this liberty had absolutely failed.

545. Summary. — The reign of James must be regarded as mainly taken up with the attempt of the king to rule independently of Parliament and law, and to restore the Roman Catholic religion. Monmouth's rebellion, though without real justification, since he could not legitimately claim the crown, was a forerunner of that revolution which invited William of Orange to support Parliament in placing a Protestant sovereign on the throne.

WILLIAM AND MARY (House of Orange-Stuart). — 1689-1702.

546. The Convention; the Declaration of Right. — After the flight of James II., a Convention which was practically a Parliament[1] met, and declared that James having broken "the original contract between king and people," the throne was therefore vacant. During the interregnum,[2] which lasted but a few weeks, the Convention issued a formal statement of principles under the name of the Declaration of Right (1689). That document recited the illegal and arbitrary acts of the late king, proclaimed him no longer sovereign, and resolved that the crown should be tendered to William and Mary.[3] The Declaration having been read to

---

[1] See Paragraph No. 517, and also "Great Seal," Paragraph No. 543.

[2] Interregnum (*inter*, between, and *regnum*, a king or reign). The Convention met Jan. 22, 1689; William and Mary accepted the crown Feb. 13.

[3] William of Orange stood next in order of succession to Mary and Anne (providing the claim of the newly born Prince James, the Pretender, was set aside). See Table, Paragraph No. 581.

them and having received their assent, they were formally invited to accept the joint sovereignty of the realm, with the understanding that the actual administration should be vested in William alone.

547. Jacobites and Non-jurors.—At the accession of the new sovereigns the extreme Tories,[1] who believed the action of the Convention unconstitutional, continued to adhere to James II. as their lawful king. Henceforth this class became known as Jacobites, from *Jacobus*, the Latin name for James. They were especially numerous and determined in the Highlands of Scotland and the South of Ireland. Though they made no open resistance at this time, yet they kept up a secret correspondence with the refugee monarch and were constantly plotting for his restoration. About four hundred of the clergy of the Church of England, including the Archbishop of Canterbury and four more of the famous "Seven Bishops,"[2] with some members of the universities and also some Scotch Presbyterians, refused to take the oath of allegiance to William and Mary. They became known on this account as the Non-jurors,[3] and although they were never harshly treated, they were compelled to resign their positions.

548. The Mutiny and Toleration Acts.— We have seen that one of the chief means of despotism on which James II. relied was the organization of a powerful standing army such as was unknown in England until Cromwell was compelled to rule by military force, but which Charles II. had perpetuated, though in such greatly diminished numbers that the body was no longer formidable. But it was now evident that owing to the abolition of the feudal levies[4] such an army must be maintained at the king's command, especially as war was impending with Louis XIV., who threatened by force of arms and with the help of the Jacobites to restore James to the English throne. To prevent the

---

[1] Tories: see Paragraph No. 531.
[2] See Paragraph No. 541.
[3] Non-juror from *non*, not, and *jurare*, to make oath.
[4] See Paragraphs Nos. 534 and 200.

sovereign from making bad use of such a power, Parliament now passed a law called the Mutiny Act, which practically put the army under the control of the nation,[1] as it has since remained. Thus all danger from that source was taken away.

James's next method for bringing the country under the control of Rome had been to issue spurious measures of toleration granting freedom to all religious beliefs, in order that he might thereby place Catholics in power. As an offset to this measure, Parliament now enacted a statute of toleration which secured freedom of worship to all religious believers except "Papists and such as deny the Trinity." This measure, though one-sided and utterly inconsistent with the broader and juster ideas of toleration which have since prevailed, was nevertheless a most important reform, and put an end at once and forever to the persecution which had disgraced the reigns of the Stuarts, though unfortunately it still left the Catholics and the Unitarians subject to the heavy hand of tyrannical oppression.[2]

549. The Bill of Rights (1689) and Act of Settlement (1701). — Not many months later, Parliament embodied the Declaration of Right, with some slight changes, in the Bill of Rights, which received the signature of the king and became a law. It constitutes the third and last great step which England has taken in constitution-making — the first being the Great Charter of 1215, and the second the Petition of Right of 1628.[3] As the Habeas Corpus Act was contained, in germ at least, in Magna Carta,[4] these three measures sum up the written safeguards of the nation, and constitute, as Lord Chatham, said, "*the Bible of English Liberty.*"

---

[1] The Mutiny Act provides: 1. That the standing army shall be at the king's command — subject to certain rules — for one year only; 2. That no pay shall be issued to troops except by special act of Parliament; 3. That no act of mutiny can be punished except by the annual re-enactment of the Mutiny Bill.

[2] In 1663 Charles II. granted a charter to Rhode Island which secured religious liberty to that colony. It was the first royal charter recognizing the principle of toleration.

[3] See Paragraph No. 484.

[4] See Paragraph No. 313 (3).

With the passage of the Bill of Rights,[1] the doctrine of the Divine Right of kings to govern without being accountable to their subjects, which James I. and his descendants had tried so hard to reduce to practice, came to an end forever. The chief provisions of the bill were: 1. That the king should not maintain a standing army in time of peace, except by consent of Parliament; 2. That no money should be taken from the people save by the consent of Parliament; 3. That every subject has the right to petition the crown for the redress of any grievance; 4. That the election of members of Parliament ought to be free from interference; 5. That Parliament should frequently assemble and enjoy entire freedom of debate; 6. That the king be debarred from interfering in any way with the proper execution of the laws; 7. That a Roman Catholic or a person marrying a Roman Catholic be henceforth incapable of receiving the crown of England. Late in the reign (1701) Parliament reaffirmed and still further extended the provisions of the Bill of Rights by the Act of Settlement, which established a new royal line of Protestant sovereigns.[2] This law practically abolished the principle of hereditary succession and re-established in the clearest and most decided manner the right of the nation to choose its own rulers. According to that measure, "an English sovereign is now as much the creature of an act of Parliament as the pettiest tax-gatherer in his realm;"[3] and he is dependent for his office and power on the will of the people as really, though of course not as directly, as the President of the United States.

---

[1] For full text of the bill, see Taswell-Langmead's Constitutional History of England.
[2] The Act of Settlement provided that after Princess Anne (in default of issue by William or Anne) the crown should descend to the Electress Sophia of Hanover, Germany, and her *Protestant* descendants. The Electress Sophia was the granddaughter of James I. She married Ernest Augustus, Elector (or ruler) of Hanover. As Hallam says, she was " very far removed from any hereditary title," as aside from James II.'s son, whose legitimacy no one now doubted, there were several who stood nearer in right of succession.
[3] Green, History of the English People.

550. Benefits of the Revolution. — Foremost in the list of benefits which England gained by the Revolution should be placed: 1. That Toleration Act already mentioned, which gave to a very large number the right of worshipping God according to the dictates of conscience. 2. Parliament now established the salutary rule that no money should be voted to the king except for specific purposes, and they also limited the royal revenue to a few years' supply instead of granting it for life, as had been done in the case of Charles II. and James.[1] As the Mutiny Act made the army dependent for its existence on the annual meeting and action of the House of Commons, these two measures practically gave the people full control of the two great powers — the purse and the sword,—which they have ever since retained. 3. Parliament next enacted that judges should hold office not as heretofore, at his Majesty's pleasure, but during good behavior, thus taking away that dangerous authority of the king over the courts of justice, which had caused so much oppression and cruelty. 4. But, as Macaulay remarks, of all the reforms produced by the change of government, perhaps none proved more extensively useful than the establishment of the liberty of the press. Up to this time no book or newspaper could be published in England without a license. During the Commonwealth Milton had earnestly labored to get this severe law repealed, declaring that "while he who kills a man kills a reasonable creature . . . he who destroys a good book [by refusing to let it appear] kills reason itself."[2] But under James II. Chief Justice Scroggs had declared it a crime to publish anything whatever concerning the government, whether true or false, without a license, and during that reign there were only four places in England — viz., London, Oxford, Cambridge, and York — where any book, pamphlet, or newspaper could be legally issued, and then only with the sanction of a rigid inspector. Under William and Mary this restriction was removed, and henceforth men were free not only to think, but to print and

---

[1] Later, limited to a single year's supply.
[2] Milton's Areopagitica, or speech in behalf of unlicensed printing.

circulate their thought, and thus to bring the government more directly before that bar of public opinion which judges all men and all institutions:

551. Arrival of James; Act of Attainder; Siege of Londonderry and Battle of the Boyne; Glencoe. — But though William was king of England, and had been accepted as king of Scotland, yet the Irish, like the Scotch Highlanders, refused to recognize him as their lawful sovereign. The great body of Irish population was then, as now, Roman Catholic; but they had been gradually dispossessed of their hold on the land, and by far the larger part of the most desirable portion of the island was owned by a few hundred thousand Protestant colonists. On the other hand James II. had, during his reign, put the civil government and the military power in the hands of the Catholics. Tyrconnel[1] now raised the standard of rebellion in the interest of the Catholics, and invited James to come and regain his throne. The Protestants of the north stood by William, and thus got that name of Orangemen which they have ever since retained. James landed in Ireland in the spring of 1689 with a small French force lent him by Louis XIV.

He established his headquarters at Dublin, and not long after issued that great Act of Attainder which summoned all who were in rebellion against his authority to appear for trial on a given day, or be declared traitors, hanged, drawn and quartered, and their property confiscated.[2] Next, the siege of the Protestant city of Londonderry was begun. For more than three months it held out against shot and shell, famine and fever. The starving inhabitants, exceeding 30,000 in number, were finally reduced to the last extremities. Nothing was left to eat but a few miserable horses and some salted hides. As they looked into each other's

---

[1] See Paragraph No. 540.

[2] Attainder (from the Old French *attaindre*, to accuse, to stain). This act contained between two and three thousand names. It embraced all classes, from half the peerage of Ireland to tradesmen, women, and children. If they failed to appear, they were to be put to death without trial.

hollow eyes, the question came, Must we surrender? Then it was that an aged clergyman, the venerable George Walker, one of the governors of the city, pleaded with them, Bible in hand, to remain firm. That appeal carried the day. They declared that rather than open the gates to the enemy, they would perish of hunger, or, as some voice whispered, that they would fall "first on the horses and the hides, — *then on the prisoners,* — then — *on each other!*" But at this moment, when all hope seemed lost, a shout of triumph was heard. An English force had sailed up the river, broken through all obstructions, and the valiant city was saved. A year later (1690) occurred the decisive battle of the Boyne,[1] at which William commanded in person on the one side, while James was present on the opposite side. William had a somewhat larger force and by far the greater number of well-armed, veteran troops. The contest ended with the utter defeat of James. He stood on a hill at a safe distance, and when he saw that the battle was going against him, turned and fled for France. William, on the other hand, though suffering from a wound, led his own men. The cowardly behavior of James excited the disgust and scorn of both the French and Irish. "Change kings with us," shouted an Irish officer to one of William's men, "change kings with us, and we'll fight you over again." The war was brought to an end by the treaty of Limerick, in 1691, when about 10,000 Irish soldiers who had fought for James, and who no longer cared to remain in their own country after their defeat, were permitted to go to France. "When the wild cry of the women, who stood watching their departure, was hushed, the silence of death settled down upon Ireland. For a hundred years the country remained at peace, but the peace was that of despair."[2] In violation of the treaty, the Catholics were hunted like wild beasts, and terrible vengeance was now taken for that Act of Attainder which James had foolishly been persuaded to issue. Fighting against William

---

[1] Fought in the East of Ireland, on the banks of the river of that name.
[2] Green's English People.

and Mary had also been going on in Scotland, but the Jacobites had been conquered, and a proclamation was sent out commanding all the Highland clans to take the oath of allegiance before Jan. 1, 1692. A chief of the clan of the Macdonalds of Glencoe, through no fault of his own, failed to make submission within the appointed time. Scotch enemies of the clan gave the king to understand that the chief had declined taking the oath, and urged William "to extirpate that set of thieves." The king signed an order to that effect, probably without reading it, or, at any rate, without understanding what was intended. The Scotch authorities managed the rest in their own way. They sent a body of soldiers to Glencoe who were hospitably received by the Macdonalds. After stopping with them a number of days, they rose before light one winter morning, and, suddenly attacking their friendly hosts, murdered all the men who did not escape, and drove the women and children out into the snowdrifts to perish of cold and hunger. They finished their work of destruction by burning the cabins and driving away the cattle. By this act, Glencoe, or the "Glen of Weeping," was changed into the very Valley of the Shadow of Death. The blame which attaches to William is that he did nothing toward punishing those who planned and carried out the horrible massacre.

The English commander, Admiral Russell, like many of William's pretended friends and supporters, had been engaged in treasonable correspondence with James, so that in case the latter succeeded in recovering his crown, he might make sure of the sunshine of royal favor. But at the last he changed his mind and fought so bravely that the French were utterly beaten. The continental wars of William continued, however, for the next five years, until by the Peace of Ryswick,[1] 1697, Louis XIV. bound himself to recognize William as king of England, the Princess Anne as his successor, to withdraw all support from James, and to place the chief fortresses of the Low Countries in

---

[1] Ryswick: a village of Holland, near the Hague.

the hands of the Dutch garrisons. This peace marked the end of the conspiracy between Louis and the Stuarts to turn England into a Roman Catholic country dependent on France. When William went in solemn state to return thanks for the conclusion of the war, it was to the new cathedral of St. Paul's, which Wren had nearly completed, and which was then first used for public worship.

552. The National Debt; the Bank of England. — William had now gained, at least temporarily, the object that he had in view when he accepted the English crown; which was to draw that nation into a close defensive alliance against Louis XIV.,[1] who, as we have seen, was bent on destroying both the political and the religious liberty of the Dutch as a Protestant people. The constant wars which followed William's accession had compelled the king to borrow large sums from the London merchants. Out of these loans sprang, first the National Debt, which was destined to grow, eventually by leaps and bounds, from less than a million of pounds up to so many hundred millions, that all thought of ever paying it is now given up. The second result was the organization of a company for the management of this colossal debt; together the two were destined to become more widely known than any of William's victories.

The building erected by that company stands on Threadneedle Street, in the very heart of London. In one of its courts is a statue of the king set up in 1734, bearing this inscription: "To the memory of the best of princes, William of Orange, founder of the Bank of England" — by far the largest and most important financial institution in the world.

553. William's Death. — William had a brave soul in a feeble body. All his life he was an invalid, but he learned to conquer disease, or at least to hold it in check, as he conquered his enemies. He was never popular in England, and at one time was only kept from returning to his native country through the

---

[1] See Guizot, History of Civilization, chap. XIII.

earnest protestation of his chancellor, Lord Somers, who refused to stamp the king's resignation with the Great Seal. Those who pretended to sustain him were in many cases treacherous, and only wanted a good opportunity to go over to the side of James; others were eager to hear of his death, and when it occurred, through the stumbling of his horse over a mole-hill, drank to "the little gentleman in black velvet," whose underground work caused the accident.

554. Summary. — William's reign was a prolonged battle for Protestantism and for the maintenance of political liberty in both England and Holland. Invalid as he was, he was yet a man of indomitable resolution as well as indomitable courage; and though a foreigner by birth, and caring more for Holland than for any country in the world, yet through his Irish and continental wars with James and Louis, he helped more than any man of the seventeenth century, Cromwell alone excepted, to make England free.

ANNE. — 1702-1714.

555. Accession and Character of Anne. — As William left no children, the Princess Anne, younger sister of the late Queen Mary now came to the throne. She was a negative character, with kindly impulses and little intelligence. "When in good humor she was meekly stupid, and when in ill humor, sulkily stupid;"[1] but if there was any person duller than her majesty, that person was her majesty's husband, Prince George of Denmark. Charles II., who knew him well, said, "I have tried Prince George sober, and I have tried him drunk, and drunk or sober there is nothing in him."

Along with the amiable qualities which gained for the new ruler the title of "Good Queen Anne" her majesty inherited the obstinacy, the prejudices, and the superstitions of the Stuarts. Though a most zealous Protestant and an ardent upholder of

---

[1] Macaulay's England; and compare Stanhope's Reign of Anne.

the Church of England, she declared her faith in the Divine Right of Kings, which had cost her grandfather Charles his head, and she was the last English sovereign who believed that the royal hand could dispel disease. The first theory she never openly proclaimed in any offensive way, but the harmless delusion that she could relieve the sick was a favorite notion with her, and we find in the *London Gazette* of March 12, 1712, an official announcement, stating that on certain days the queen would "touch" for the cure of "king's evil," or scrofula. Among the multitudes who went to test her power was a poor Lichfield bookseller. He carried to her his little half-blind sickly boy, who by virtue either of her majesty's beneficent fingers, or from some other and better reason, grew up to be known as the famous author and lexicographer, Dr. Samuel Johnson.[1]

556. Whig and Tory; High Church and Low. — Politically, the government of the country was divided between the two great parties of the Whigs and the Tories,[2] since succeeded by the Liberals and Conservatives. Though mutually hostile, each believing that its rival's success meant national ruin, yet both were sincerely opposed to despotism on the one hand, and to anarchy on the other. The Whigs, setting Parliament above the throne, were pledged to maintain the Act of Settlement[3] and the Protestant succession; while the Tories, insisting on hereditary sovereignty, were anxious to set aside that act and restore the excluded Stuarts.

The Church of England was likewise divided into two parties, known as High Church and Low Church. The first, who were generally Tories, wished to exalt the power of the bishops and were opposed to the toleration of Dissenters; the second, who were Whigs as a rule, believed it best to curtail the authority of the

---

[1] Johnson told Boswell, his biographer, that he remembered the incident, and that "he had a confused, but somehow a sort of solemn recollection of a lady in diamonds and a long black hood." — BOSWELL'S *Johnson*.

[2] See Paragraph No. 531.

[3] See Paragraph No. 549.

bishops, and to secure to all Trinitarian Protestants entire liberty of worship and all civil and political rights and privileges. Thus to the bitterness of heated political controversy there was added the still more acrid bitterness of theological dispute. Addison tells an amusing story of a boy who was called a "Popish cur" by a Whig, because, having lost his way, he ventured to inquire for Saint Anne's Lane, while he was cuffed for irreverence by a Tory when, correcting himself, he asked bluntly for Anne's Lane.

The queen, although she owed her crown mainly 'to the Whigs, sympathized with the Tories and the High Church, and did all in her power to strengthen both. As for the leaders of the two parties, they seem to have looked out first for themselves, and afterward — often a long way afterward — for their country. During the whole reign they were plotting and counterplotting, mining and undermining, until their subtle schemes to secure office and destroy each other become as incomprehensible and as fathomless as those of the fallen angels in Milton's vision of the Bottomless Pit.

557. The War of the Spanish Succession. — Anne had no sooner come to the throne than war broke out with France. It had its origin in the previous reign. William III. cared little for England compared with his native Holland, whose interests always had the first place in his heart. He had spent his life battling to preserve the independence of the Dutch Republic against the dangers which threatened it, and especially against Louis XIV. of France, who was determined, if possible, to annex the Netherlands, including Holland, to his own dominion. During the latter part of William's reign the French king seemed likely to be able to accomplish his purpose. The king of Spain, who had no children, was in feeble health, and at his death it was probable that Louis XIV.'s grandson, Philip of Anjou, would receive the crown. Louis XIV. was then the most powerful prince in Europe, and should his grandson become king of Spain, it meant that the French monarch would eventually add the Spanish dominions to his own. These dominions comprised not only Spain proper, but a large part of the

Netherlands adjoining Holland,[1] portions of Italy, and immense provinces in both North and South America, including the West Indies. Such an empire, if it came under the control of Louis, would make him irresistible on the continent of Europe, and the little, free Protestant states of Holland could not hope to stand before him. William endeavored to prevent Louis from carrying out his designs respecting Spain, by two secret treaties, and also by an alliance formed between Germany, Holland, and England, all of whom were threatened by the prospective preponderating power of France. Louis had signed these treaties, but had no intention of abiding by them. When, not long after, the king of Spain died and left the crown to Philip of Anjou, the French sovereign openly declared his intention of placing him on the Spanish throne, saying significantly as his grandson left Paris for Madrid, "The Pyrenees no longer exist."[2] Furthermore, Louis now put French garrisons in the border towns of the Spanish Netherlands, showing that he regarded them as practically his own, and he thus had a force ready at any moment to march across the frontier into Holland. Finally, on the death of James II., which occurred shortly before William's, Louis publicly acknowledged the exiled monarch's son, James Edward, the "Old Pretender,"[3] as rightful sovereign of England, Scotland, and Ireland. This, and this only, effectually roused the English people; they were preparing for hostilities when William's sudden death occurred. Immediately after Anne's succession, war was declared, which, since it had grown out of Louis's designs on the crown of Spain, was called the War of the Spanish Succession.

But although the contest was undertaken by England mainly

---

[1] The whole of the Netherlands at one time belonged to Spain, but the northern part, or Holland, had succeeded in establishing its independence, and was protected on the southern frontier by a line of fortified towns.

[2] When Philip went to Spain, Louis XIV., by letters patent, reserved the succession to the Spanish throne to France, thus virtually uniting the two countries, so that the Pyrenees Mountains would no longer have any political meaning as a boundary.

[3] See Paragraphs Nos. 542 and 543.

to prevent the French king from carrying out his threat of placing the "Pretender" on the English throne, — thus restoring the country to the Roman Catholic Stuarts, — yet as it went on it came to have two other important objects. The first of these was the defence of Holland, now a most valuable ally; the second was the protection of the Virginia and New England colonies against the power of France, which threatened through its own American colonies, and through the extensive Spanish possessions it expected to acquire, to get control of the whole of the New World.[1] Thus England had three objects at stake: 1. The maintenance of Protestant government at home; 2. The maintenance of the Protestant power of Holland; 3. The possession of the American continent. For this reason the War of the Spanish Succession may in one sense be regarded as the beginning of a second Hundred Years' War between England and France,[2] destined to decide which was to build up the great empire of the future in the Western Hemisphere.[3]

558. Marlborough; Blenheim and Other Victories. — John Churchill, Duke of Marlborough, commanded the English and Dutch forces, and had for his ally Prince Eugene of Savoy, who led the German armies. The duke, who was known in the enemy's camps by the flattering name of "the handsome Englishman," had risen from obscurity. He owed the beginning of his success to his good looks and a court intrigue. In politics he sympathized chiefly with the Tories, but his interests in the war led him to support the Whigs. He was avaricious, unscrupulous, perfidious. James II. trusted him, and he deceived him and went over to William; William trusted him, and he deceived him and opened a treasonable correspondence with the dethroned

---

[1] At this time England had only the colonies of Virginia and New England, with part of Newfoundland. France and Spain claimed nearly all the rest.

[2] During the next eighty years fighting was going on between England and France, directly or indirectly, for a great part of the time.

[3] See Seeley's Expansion of England.

James; Anne trusted him, and he would undoubtedly have betrayed her if the "Pretender" had only possessed means to bid high enough, or in any way show that his cause was likely to be successful. In his greed for money he hesitated at nothing; he took bribes from army contractors, and robbed his soldiers of their pay; though in this he was perhaps no worse than many other generals of his, and even of later times.[1] As a soldier, Marlborough had no equal. Voltaire says of him with truth that "he never besieged a fortress which he did not take, nor fight a battle which he did not win." This man at once so able and so false, to whom war was a private speculation rather than a contest for right or principle, now opened the campaign by capturing those fortresses in the Spanish Netherlands, which Louis XIV. had garrisoned with French troops to menace Holland; but he could not induce the enemy to risk a battle in the open field. At length, in the summer of 1704, Marlborough, by a brilliant movement, changed the scene of the war from the Netherlands to Bavaria. There, at the little village of Blenheim, he, with Prince Eugene, gained a victory over the French which saved Germany from the power of Louis XIV., and England, out of gratitude for the humiliation of her powerful enemy, presented the duke with the ancient royal Park of Woodstock, and built for him, at the nation's cost, that Palace of Blenheim still occupied by descendants of the duke's family.[2] Gibraltar had been taken a few days before Blenheim by an attack by sea, so that England now had, as she continues still to have, the command of the great inland sea of the Mediterranean.

In the Netherlands, two years later, Marlborough won the battle of Ramillies,[3] by which the whole of that country was recovered from the French. Two years from that time Louis's forces marched back into the Netherlands, and were beaten at Oudenarde, where

---

[1] See Thackeray's Henry Esmond.
[2] Blenheim: a short distance from Oxford. The palace grounds are about twelve miles in circumference.
[3] Ramillies (Ram'e-lēz).

they were trying to recover the territory they had lost. A year afterward, Marlborough carried the war into Northern France, fought his last great fight, and gained his last great victory at Malplaquet,[1] by which the power of Louis was so far broken that both England and Europe could breathe freely, and the English colonies in America felt that for the present there was no danger of their being driven into the Atlantic by either the French or the Spaniards.

559. The Powers behind the Throne; Jennings versus Masham. — While the war was going on, the real power, so far as the crown was concerned, though in Anne's name, was practically in the hands of Sarah Jennings, Duchess of Marlborough, who held the office of Mistress of the Robes. She and the queen had long been inseparable, and it was her influence that caused Anne to desert her father and espouse the cause of William of Orange. The imperious temper of the duchess carried all before it, and in her department she won victories which might be compared with those the duke, her husband, gained on the field of battle. In time, indeed, her sway over her royal companion became so absolute that she decided everything, from questions of state to the cut of a gown or the color of a ribbon, so that it finally grew to be a common saying that "Queen Anne reigns, but Queen Sarah governs."[2] While she continued in power, she used her influence to urge forward the war with France undertaken by England to check the designs of Louis XIV. on Spain and Holland, and also to punish him for his recognition of the claim of the Pretender to the English crown. Her object was to advance her husband, who, as commander-in-chief of the English and Dutch forces on the continent, had won fame and fortune — the first by his splendid ability, the second by his unscrupulous greed.

---

[1] Malplaquet (Măl'plȧ'kā').
[2] For years the queen and the duchess carried on an almost daily correspondence under the names of " Mrs. Morley " (the queen) and " Mrs. Freeman " (the duchess), the latter taking that name because, as she boasted, it suited the frank and bold character of her letters.

After a number of years, the queen and the duchess quarrelled, and the latter was superseded by a Mrs. Masham, who soon got as complete control of Anne as the former favorite had possessed. Mrs. Masham was as sly and supple as the duchess had been dictatorial and violent. She was cousin to Robert Harley, a prominent Tory politician. Through her influence Harley now became prime minister in everything but name. The Whig war policy was abandoned, negotiations for peace were secretly opened, and Marlborough was ordered home in disgrace on a charge of having robbed the government. Mr. Masham, much to his wife's satisfaction, was created a peer of the realm, and finally a treaty was drafted for an inglorious peace. Thus it was, as Hallam remarks, that "the fortunes of Europe were changed by the insolence of one waiting-woman and the cunning of another."[1]

560. Dr. Sacheverell. — An incident occurred at this time which greatly helped the Tories in their schemes. Now that the danger was over, England was growing weary of the continuance of a war which involved a constant drain of both men and money. Dr. Sacheverell, a violent Tory and High Churchman, began preaching a series of sermons in London condemning the war, and the Whigs who were carrying it on. He also endeavored to revive the exploded theory of the Divine Right of kings, and declared that no tyranny on the part of a sovereign could by any possibility justify a subject in resisting the royal will, with much more foolish talk of the same kind, all of which he published. The Whig leaders unwisely brought the preacher to trial for alleged treasonable utterances. He was suspended from his office for three years, and his book of sermons was publicly burned by the common hangman.

This created intense popular excitement; Sacheverell was regarded as a political martyr by all who wished the war ended. A reaction against the government set in; the Whigs were driven from power, the Duchess of Marlborough had to leave her apart-

---

[1] Hallam's Constitutional History of England.

ments in the palace of St. James, and in her spite broke down marble mantels and tore off the locks from doors; Mrs. Masham's friends, the Tories, or peace party, now triumphed, and prepared to put an end to the fighting.

561. The Peace of Utrecht.[1] — Not long after this change a messenger was privately despatched to Louis XIV. to ask if he wished for peace. "It was," says the French minister, "like asking a dying man whether he would wish to be cured."[2] Later, terms were agreed upon between the Tories and the French, though without the knowledge of the English people or their allies; but finally, in 1713, in the quaint Dutch city of Utrecht, the allies, together with France and Spain, signed the treaty bearing that name. By it Louis XIV. bound himself: 1. To acknowledge the Protestant succession in England; 2. To compel the Pretender to quit France; 3. To renounce the union of the crowns of France and Spain;[3] 4. To cede to England all claims to Newfoundland, Acadia, or Nova Scotia, and that vast region known as the Hudson Bay Company's Possessions. Next, Spain was to give up: 1. The Spanish Netherlands to Austria, an ally of Holland, and grant to the Dutch a line of forts to defend their frontier against France; 2. England was to have the exclusive right for thirty-three years of supplying the Spanish-American colonists with negro slaves.[4] This trade had long been coveted by the English, and had been carried on to some extent by them ever since Sir John Hawkins grew so rich through it in Queen Elizabeth's time, that he set up a coat of arms emblazoned with a slave in fetters, that all might see how he had won wealth and distinction.

---

[1] Utrecht (U'trĕkt).
[2] Morris, The Age of Anne.
[3] But Philip was to retain the throne of Spain.
[4] This right had formerly belonged to France. By its transfer England got the privilege of furnishing 4800 "sound, merchantable negroes" annually; "two-thirds to be males" between ten and forty years of age.

562. Union of England and Scotland. — Since the accession of James I., England and Scotland had been ruled by one sovereign, but each country retained its own Parliament and its own forms of worship. In 1707 the two countries were united under the name of Great Britain. The independent Parliament of Scotland was given up, and the Scotch were henceforth represented in the English Parliament by sixteen peers chosen by the House of Lords at the summoning of every Parliament; and by forty-five (now sixty) members returned by Scotland to the House of Commons.

With the consummation of the union Great Britain adopted a new flag, the Union Jack, which was formed by the junction of the red cross of St. George and the white cross of St. Andrew.[1]

563. Literature of the Period; the First Daily Paper. — The reign of Anne has been characterized as one of corruption in high places and of brutality in low, but in literature it takes rank next to that of Elizabeth. There was indeed no great central luminary like Shakespeare, but a constellation of lesser ones — such as Addison, De Foe, and Pope — that shone with a mild splendor peculiarly their own: the lurid brilliancy of the half-mad satirist Dean Swift, who moved in an orbit apart, was also beginning to command attention; while the calm, clear light of John Locke was near its setting. Aside from these great names in letters, it was an age generally of contented dulness, well represented in the good-natured mediocrity of Queen Anne herself. During her reign the first daily newspaper appeared in England — the *Daily Courant;* it was a dingy, badly printed little sheet not much bigger than a man's hand. The publisher said he made it so small "to save the Publick at least one-half the Impertinences of Ordinary News-Papers."

---

[1] St. George: the patron saint of England; St. Andrew: the patron saint of Scotland. In 1801 when Ireland was united to Great Britain, the red cross of St. Patrick was added to the flag. Jack: from *Jacques* (French for James), James I.'s usual signature. The first union flag was his work.

Perhaps it was well this journal made no greater pretensions; for, since it had to compete with swarms of abusive political pamphlets, such as Swift wrote for the Tories and De Foe for the Whigs; since it had also to compete with the gossip and scandal of the coffee-houses and the clubs, the proprietor found it no easy matter to either fill or sell it.

A few years later a new journal appeared of a very different kind, called the *Spectator*, which Addison, its chief contributor, soon made famous. Each number consisted of an essay hitting off the follies and foibles of the age, and was regularly served at the breakfast-tables of people of fashion along with their tea and toast. One of it greatest merits was its happy way of showing that wit and virtue are after all better friends than wit and vice. These two dissimilar sheets, neither of which dared to publish a single line of Parliamentary debate, mark the humble beginning of that vast organized power, represented by the daily press of London, which discusses everything of note or interest throughout the world.

564. Death of the Queen. — With Anne's death in 1714 the Stuart power came to an end. All of her children had died in infancy, except one unfortunate sickly son who lived just long enough to awaken hopes which were buried with him. According to the terms of the Act of Settlement[1] the crown now passed to George, Elector of Hanover, a Protestant descendant of James I. of England; though James Edward, son of James II., believed to the last that his half-sister, the queen, would name him her successor;[2] instead of that it was she who first dubbed him the "Pretender."

565. Summary. — The whole reign of Anne was taken up with the strife of political parties at home, and the War of the Succession abroad. The Whigs were always intriguing through the Duchess of Marlborough and other leaders to keep up the war and to keep out the "Pretender"; the Tories, on the other hand,

---

[1] See Paragraph No. 549.
[2] Anne and the "Pretender" were children of James II. by different mothers.

were just as busy through Mrs. Masham and her coadjutors in endeavoring to establish peace, and with it the Divine Right of Kings, while the extremists among them hoped for the restoration of the Roman Catholic Stuarts in the person of James Edward. The result of the War of the Succession was the defeat of Louis XIV. and the confirmation of that Act of Settlement which secured the English crown to a Protestant prince.

GENERAL VIEW OF THE STUART PERIOD.
1603-1649 (Commonwealth, 1649-1660); 1660-1714.

I. GOVERNMENT. — II. RELIGION. — III. MILITARY AFFAIRS. — IV. LITERATURE, LEARNING, AND ART. — V. GENERAL INDUSTRY AND COMMERCE. — VI. MODE OF LIFE, MANNERS, AND CUSTOMS.

GOVERNMENT.

566. Divine Right of Kings; the Civil War; the Revolution of 1688. — The period began with the attempt of James I. to carry out his theory that the king derives his right to rule directly from God, and in no wise from the people. Charles I. adopted this disastrous theory, and was supported in it by Mainwaring and other clergymen, who declared that the king represents God on earth, and that the subject who resists his will, or refuses a tax or loan to him, does so at the everlasting peril of his soul. Charles's arbitrary methods of government, and levies of illegal taxes, with the imprisonment of those who refused to pay them, led to the meeting of the Long Parliament and the enactment of the statute of the Petition of Right, or second great charter of English liberties.

The same Parliament abolished the despotic court of Star-Chamber and High Commission, which had been used by Strafford and Laud to carry out their tyrannical scheme called "Thorough."

Charles's renewed acts of oppression and open violation of the laws, with his levies of Ship-money, led to the Grand Remonstrance, an appeal to the nation to support Parliament in its struggle with the king. The attempt of the king to arrest five members who had taken a prominent part in drawing up the Remonstrance, brought on the Civil War, and the establishment of a republic which declared, in opposition to the doctrine of the Divine Right of Kings, that "the people are, under God, the origin of all just power." Eventually, Cromwell became Protector of the nation, and ruled by means of a strong military power.

On the restoration of the Stuarts, Charles II. endeavored to rule without Parliament by selling his influence to Louis XIV., by the secret treaty of Dover. During his reign, the Habeas Corpus Act was passed, and feudalism practically abolished.

James II. endeavored to restore the Roman Catholic religion. His treatment of the University of Oxford, and imprisonment of the Seven Bishops, with the birth of a son who would be educated as a Roman Catholic, caused the Revolution of 1688, and placed William and Mary on the throne.

Parliament now passed the Bill of Rights, the third great charter for the protection of the English people, and later confirmed it by the Act of Settlement, which secured the crown to a line of Protestant sovereigns. The Mutiny Bill, passed at the beginning of William III.'s reign, made the army dependent on Parliament. These measures practically put the government in the hands of the House of Commons, where it has ever since remained. William's war caused the beginning of the national debt and the establishment of the Bank of England.

In the reign of Anne, 1707, Scotland and England were united under the name of Great Britain. During her sovereignty the Whig and Tory parties, which came into existence in the time of Charles II., became especially prominent, and they have since (though lately under the name of Liberals and Conservatives) continued to divide the Parliamentary government between them, — the Whigs seeking to extend the power of the people; the Tories, that of the crown and the church.

RELIGION.

567. Religious Parties and Religious Legislation. — At the beginning of this period we find four religious parties in England : 1. The Roman Catholics ; 2. The Episcopalians, or supporters of the National Church of England ; 3. The Puritans, who were seeking to "purify" the church from certain Roman Catholic customs and modes of worship ; 4. The Independents, who were endeavoring to establish independent congregational societies. In Scotland the Puritans established their religion in a church governed by elders, or presbyters, instead of bishops, and on that account got the name of Presbyterians.

James I. persecuted all who dissented from the Church of England; and after the Gunpowder Plot the Roman Catholics were practically deprived of the protection of the law, and subject to terrible oppression. In the same reign two Unitarians were burned at Smithfield for denying the doctrine of the Trinity.

During the period of the Civil War and the Commonwealth, Presbyterianism was established as the national worship of England and Scotland by the Solemn League and Covenant. At the Restoration severe laws against the Scotch Covenanters and other dissenters were enforced, and two thousand clergymen were driven from their parishes to starve; on the other hand, the pretended Popish Plot caused the exclusion of Roman Catholics from both Houses of Parliament, and all persons holding office were obliged to partake of the sacrament according to the Church of England. James II.'s futile attempt to restore Catholicism ended in the Revolution and the passage of the Toleration Act, granting liberty of worship to all Protestant Trinitarians.

MILITARY AFFAIRS.

568. Armor and Arms. — Armor still continued to be worn in some degree during this period, but it consisted chiefly of the helmet with breast and back-plates. Firearms of various kinds were in general use; also hand-grenades, or small bombs, and the bayonet. The chief wars of the period were the Civil War, the wars with the Dutch, William's war with France, and that of the Spanish Succession.

LEARNING, LITERATURE, AND ART.

569. Great Writers. — The most eminent prose writers of this period were Sir Walter Raleigh, Lord Bacon, Sir Isaac Newton, John Bunyan, Jeremy Taylor, John Locke, Hobbes, Dean Swift, De Foe, and Addison; the chief poets, Shakespeare and Jonson (mentioned under the preceding period), Milton, Dryden, Pope, Butler, and Beaumont and Fletcher, with a class of writers known as the "Comic Dramatists of the Restoration," whose works, though not lacking in genius, exhibit many of the worst features of the licentious age in which they were produced. Three other great writers were born in the latter part of this period, — Fielding, the novelist, Hume, the historian, and Butler,[1] the

---

[1] Bishop Butler, author of The Analogy of Religion (1736), a work which gained for him the title of "the Bacon of Theology."

ablest thinker of his time in the English Church, — but their productions belong to the time of the Georges.

570. Progress in Science and Invention. — Sir Isaac Newton revolutionized natural philosophy by his discovery and demonstration of the law of gravitation, and Dr. William Harvey accomplished as great a change in physiological science by his discovery of the circulation of the blood. The most remarkable invention of the age was a rude steam engine, patented in 1698 by Captain Savery, and so far improved by Thomas Newcomen in 1712 that it was used for pumping water in coal mines for many years. Both were destined to be superseded by James Watt's engine, which belongs to a later period (1765).

571. Architecture. — The Gothic style of the preceding periods was followed by the Italian, or classical, represented in the works of Inigo Jones and Sir Christopher Wren. It was a revival, in modified form, of the ancient Greek and Roman architecture. St. Paul's Cathedral, the grandest church ever built in England for Protestant worship, is the best example of this style. Many beautiful manor-houses were built in the early part of this period, which, like the churches of the time, are often ornamented with the exquisite wood-carving of Grinling Gibbons. There were no great artists in England in this age, though Charles I. employed Rubens and other foreign painters to decorate the palace of Whitehall and Windsor Castle.

572. Education. — The higher education of the period was confined almost wholly to the study of Latin and Greek. The discipline of all schools was extremely harsh. Nearly every lesson was emphasized by a liberal application of the rod, and the highest recommendation a teacher could have was that he was known as "a learned and lashing master."

GENERAL INDUSTRY AND COMMERCE.

573. Manufactures. — Woollen goods continued to be a chief article of manufacture. Silks were also produced by thousands of Huguenot weavers, who fled from France to escape the persecutions of Louis XIV. Coal was now extensively mined, and iron and pottery works were giving industrial importance to Birmingham and other growing towns in the midlands.

574. Commerce. — During a great part of this period intense commercial rivalry existed between England and Holland, each of which was anxious to get the monopoly of the colonial import and export trade. Parliament passed stringent navigation laws, under Cromwell and later, to prevent the Dutch from competing with English merchants and shippers. The East India and South Sea companies were means of greatly extending English commercial enterprise, as was also the tobacco culture of Virginia.

575. Roads and Travel. — Good roads were still unknown in England. Stage coaches carried a few passengers at exorbitant rates, requiring an entire day to go a distance which an express train now travels in less than an hour. Goods were carried on pack-horses or in cumbrous wagons, and so great was the expense of transportation that farmers often let their produce rot on the ground rather than attempt to get it to the nearest market town.

In London a few coaches were in use, but covered chairs, carried on poles by two men and called "sedan chairs," were the favorite vehicles. Although London had been in great part rebuilt since the fire of 1666, the streets were still very narrow, without sidewalks, heaped with filth, and miserably lighted.

576. Agriculture; Pauperism. — Agriculture generally made no marked improvement, but gardening did, and many vegetables and fruits were introduced which had not before been cultivated.

Pauperism remained a problem which the government had not yet found a practical method of dealing with. There was little freedom of movement; the poor man's parish was virtually his prison, and if he left it to seek work elsewhere, and required help on the way, he was certain to be sent back to the place where he was legally settled.

MODES OF LIFE, MANNERS, AND CUSTOMS.

577. Dress. — In the time of Charles II. and his successors the dress of the wealthy and fashionable classes was most elaborate and costly. Gentlemen wore their hair long, in ringlets, with an abundance of gold lace and ruffles, and carried long, slender swords, known as rapiers. Later, wigs came into use, and no man of any social standing thought of appearing without one.

In Queen Anne's reign ladies painted their faces and ornamented them with minute black patches, which served not only for "beauty spots," but also showed, by their arrangement, with which political party they sympathized.

578. Coffee-Houses. — Up to the middle of the seventeenth century ale and beer were the common drink of all classes; but about that time coffee was introduced, and coffee-houses became a fashionable resort for gentlemen and for all who wished to learn the news of the day. Tea had not yet come into use; but, in 1660, Pepys says in his diary: "Sept. 25. I did send for a cup of tee (a China drink) of which I never had drank before."

579. The Streets of London. — No efficient police existed in London, and at night the streets were infested with brutal ruffians; and as late as Queen Anne's time, by bands of "fine gentlemen" not less brutal, who amused themselves by overturning sedan chairs, rolling women down hill in barrels, and compelling men to dance jigs, under the stimulus of repeated pricks from a circle of sword points, until they fell fainting from exhaustion. Duels were frequent, on the slightest provocation. Highwaymen abounded both in the city and without, and it was dangerous to travel any distance, even by day, without an armed guard.

580. Brutal Laws. — Hanging was the common punishment for theft and many other crimes. The public whipping of both men and women through the streets was frequent. Debtors were shut up in prison, and left to beg from the passers-by or starve; and ordinary offenders were fastened in a wooden frame called the "pillory" and exposed on a stage where they were pelted by the mob, and their bones not infrequently broken with clubs and brickbats. The pillory continued in use until the accession of Victoria in 1837.

X.

"The history of England is emphatically the history of progress. It is the history of a constant movement of the public mind, of a constant change in the institutions of a great society." — MACAULAY.

INDIA GAINED; AMERICA LOST. — PARLIAMENTARY REFORM. — GOVERNMENT BY THE PEOPLE.

THE HOUSE OF HANOVER, (1714,) TO THE PRESENT TIME.

George I., 1714–1727.
George II., 1727–1760.
George III., 1760–1820.
George IV., 1820–1830.
William IV., 1830–1837.
Victoria, 1837– —

581. Accession of George I. — As Queen Anne died without leaving an heir to the throne, George, Elector of Hanover, now, in accordance with the Act of Settlement,[1] came into possession of the English crown. The new king, however, was in no haste to leave the quiet little German court where he had passed his fifty-fourth birthday, and where he would have gladly spent the rest of his uneventful life. As he owed his new position to Whig legislation, he naturally favored that party and turned his back on the Tories, who, deprived of the sunshine of royal favor, were as unhappy as their rivals were jubilant. In fact, the reaction was so strong that the three Tory leaders were now impeached for treason, on the ground that they had intrigued to restore the fallen house of Stuart, and endeavored to make the Pretender king. Two of the three fled the country, and the third,

---

[1] Act of Settlement: see Paragraph No. 549.

after a term of imprisonment in the Tower, was discharged without further punishment.[1]

582. Character of the New King. — The new sovereign was a selfish, coarse old man, who in private life would, as Lady Montagu said, have passed for an honest blockhead. He neither knew anything about England, nor did he desire to know anything of it. He could not speak a word of the language of the country he was called to govern, and he made no attempt to learn it; even the coronation service had to be explained to him as best it could, in such broken Latin as the ministers could muster. Laboring under these disadvantages, his majesty wisely determined not to try to take any active part in the affairs of the nation. He was a hearty eater and drinker, so that his table exercises took up a considerable portion of his time. Much of the rest he was

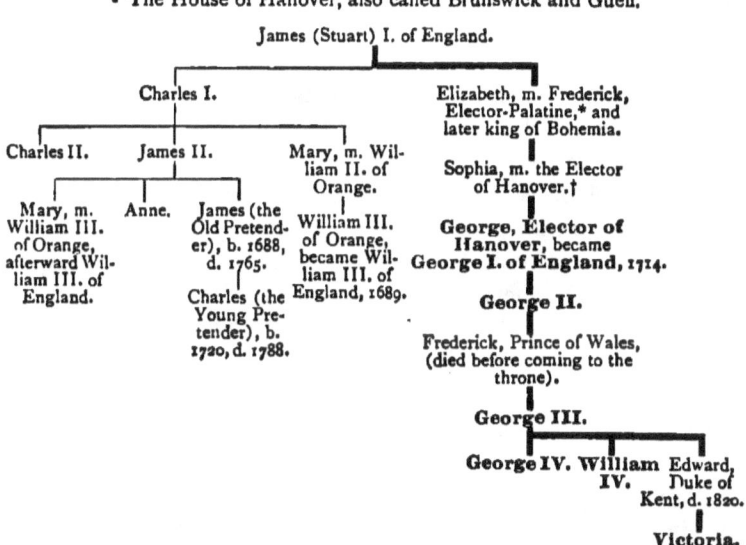

[1] The House of Hanover, also called Brunswick and Guelf.

* Elector-Palatine: a prince ruling over the territory called the Palatinate in Western Germany, on the Rhine.

† Elector of Hanover: a prince ruling over the province of Hanover, a part of the German Empire, lying on the North Sea. The Elector received his title from the fact that he was one of seven princes who had the right of electing the German emperor.

contented to spend quietly smoking his pipe, or playing cards and laughing at the caricature pictures of the English which the German ladies of his court cut out of paper for his amusement. As for politics, he let his Whig friends, with Sir Robert Walpole at the head, manage the country in their own way. Fortunately, the great body of the English people were abundantly able to take care of themselves. Voltaire said of them that they resembled a barrel of their own beer, froth at the top, dregs at the bottom, but thoroughly sound and wholesome in the middle. It was this middle class, with their solid, practical good sense, that kept the nation right. They were by no means enthusiastic worshippers of the German king who had come to reign over them, but they saw one thing clearly: he might be as heavy, dull, and wooden as the figure-head of a ship, yet, like that figure-head, he stood for something greater and better than himself, — for he represented Protestantism, with civil and religious liberty, — and so the people gave him their allegiance.

583. Cabinet Government. — The present method of government dates from this reign. From the earliest period of English history the sovereign was accustomed to have a permanent council composed of some of the chief men of the realm, whom he consulted on all matters of importance. Charles II., either because he found this body inconveniently large for the rapid transaction of business, or else because he believed it inexpedient to discuss his plans with so many, selected a small confidential committee from it. This committee met to consult with the king in his cabinet, or private room, and so came to be called "the cabinet council," or briefly "the cabinet," a name which it has ever since retained.

During Charles II.'s reign and that of his immediate successors the king continued to choose this special council from those whom he believed to be friendly to his measures, often without much regard to party lines, and he was always present at their meetings. With the accession of George I., however, a great change took place. His want of acquaintance with prominent men made it difficult for him to select a cabinet himself, and his ignorance of English rendered his presence at its meetings wholly useless. For these reasons the new king adopted the expedient of appointing a chief adviser, or prime minister, who chose his own cabinet from men of the political party to which he belonged. Thus Sir Robert Walpole, the first prime minister, began that system (though not until the reign was far advanced) by which the executive affairs of the government are managed to-day. The cabinet, or "the government," as it is sometimes called, now generally consists of twelve or fifteen persons chosen by the prime minister, or premier,[1] from the leading members of both Houses of Parliament, but whose political views agree in the main with the majority of the House of Commons.[2] This system, though not fully devel-

---

[1] Now generally called the premier (from the French *premier*, first or chief).

[2] The existence of the Cabinet depends on custom, not law. Its members are never *officially* made known to the public, nor its proceedings recorded. Its meetings, which take place at irregular intervals, according to pressure of business, are entirely secret, and the sovereign is never present. As the Cabinet agrees in its composition with the majority of the House of Commons, it follows that if the Commons are Conservative, the Cabinet will be so likewise; and if Liberal, the reverse. Theoretically, the sovereign chooses the Cabinet; but practically the selection is now always made by the prime minister. If at any time the Cabinet finds that its political policy no longer agrees with that of the House of Commons, it usually resigns, and the sovereign chooses a new prime minister from the opposite party, who forms a new Cabinet in harmony with himself and the Commons. If, however, the prime minister has good reason for believing that a different House of Commons would support him, the sovereign may, by his advice, dissolve Parliament. A new election then takes place, and according to the political character of the members returned, the Cabinet remains in, or goes out of, power. The Cabinet now invariably includes the following officers: —

1. The First Lord of the Treasury (Usually the Prime Minister).
2. The Lord Chancellor.
3. The Lord President of the Council.
4. The Lord Privy Seal.
5. The Chancellor of the Exchequer.
6. The Secretary of State for Home Affairs.
7. The Secretary of State for Foreign Affairs.
8. The Secretary of State for the Colonies.
9. The Secretary of State for India.
10. The Secretary of State for War.
11. The First Lord of the Admiralty.

In addition, a certain number of other officers of the government are frequently included, making the whole number about twelve or fifteen.

oped until the reign of George III., had become so well established when George II. came to the throne, that he said, "In England the ministers are king." If he could have looked forward, he would have seen that the time was coming when the House of Commons would be king, since no ministry or cabinet can now stand which does not have the confidence and support of the Commons.

584. The "Pretender"; "the Fifteen." — The fact that George I. exclusively favored the Whigs exasperated the opposite, or Tory, party, and the Jacobites or extreme members of that party[1] in Scotland, with the secret aid of many in England, now rose, in the hope of placing on the throne the son of James II., James Edward Stuart, called the Chevalier[2] by his friends, but the Pretender by his enemies. The insurrection was led by John, Earl of Mar, who, from his frequent change of politics, had got the nickname of "Bobbing John." Mar encountered the royal forces at Sheriffmuir, in Perthshire, Scotland, where an indecisive battle was fought, which the old ballad thus describes: —

> "There's some say that we won, and some say that they won,
> And some say that none won at a', man;
> But one thing is sure, that at Sheriffmuir
> A battle there was, which I saw, man."

On the same day of the fight at Sheriffmuir, the English Jacobites, with a body of Scotch allies, marched into Preston, Lancashire, and there surrendered, almost without striking a blow. The leaders of the movement, except the Earl of Mar, who, with one or two others, escaped to the continent, were beheaded or hanged, and about a thousand of the rank and file were sold as slaves to the West India and Virginia plantations. The Pretender himself landed in Scotland a few weeks after the defeat of his friends; but

---

[1] See Paragraph No. 547.
[2] The Chevalier de St. George; after the birth of his son Charles in 1720, the former was known by the nickname of the Old Pretender, and the son as the Young Pretender.

finding no encouragement he hurried back to the continent again. Thus ended the rebellion known from the year of its outbreak (1715) as "the Fifteen."

One result of this rising was the passage of an act extending the duration of Parliament from three years, which was the longest time that body could sit, to seven years, a law still in force.[1] The object of this change was to do away with the excitement and tendency to rebellion at that time, resulting from frequent elections, in which party feeling ran to dangerous extremes.

585. The South Sea Bubble. — A few years later a gigantic enterprise was undertaken by the South Sea Company, a body of merchants, originally organized as a company trading in the southern Atlantic and Pacific oceans. A Scotchman named Law had started a similar project in France, known as the Mississippi Company, which proposed to pay off the national debt of France from the profits of its commerce with the West Indies and the country bordering on the Mississippi River. Following his example, the South Sea Company now undertook to pay off the English national debt, mainly, it is said, from the profits of the slave trade between Africa and Brazil.[2] Walpole had no faith in the scheme, and attacked it vigorously; but other influential members of the government gave it their encouragement. The directors now came out with prospectuses promising dividends of fifty per cent on all money invested. Everybody rushed to buy stock, and the shares rapidly advanced from $500 to $5000 a share. A speculative craze followed, the like of which has never since been known. Bubble companies now sprang into existence with objects almost as absurd as those of the philosophers whom Swift

---

[1] The Triennial Act provided that at the end of three years Parliament must be dissolved and a new election held. This was to prevent the sovereign from keeping that body in power indefinitely, contrary, perhaps, to the political feeling of the country, which might prefer a different set of representatives. Under the Septennial Act the time was extended four years, making seven in all, but the sovereign may, of course, dissolve Parliament at any time before that limit is reached.

[2] Loftie's History of London.

ridiculed in "Gulliver's Travels," where one man was trying to make gunpowder out of ice, and another to extract sunbeams from cucumbers. A mere list of these companies would fill several pages. One was to give instruction in astrology, by which every man might be able to foretell his own destiny by examining the stars; a second was to manufacture butter out of beech-trees; a third was for a wheel for driving machinery, which once started would go on forever, thereby furnishing a cheap perpetual motion; a fourth projector, going beyond all the rest in audacity, had the impudence to offer stock for sale in an enterprise "which shall be revealed hereafter." He found the public so gullible and so greedy for gain, that he sold $10,000 worth of the new stock in the course of a single morning, and then prudently disappeared with the cash, though where, as the unfortunate investors found to their sorrow, was not among the things to "be revealed hereafter."

The narrow passage leading to the stock exchange was crowded all day long with struggling fortune hunters, both men and women. Suddenly, when the excitement was at its height, the bubble burst, as Law's scheme in France had a little earlier.

Great numbers of people were hopelessly ruined, and the cry for vengeance was as loud as the bids for stocks had once been. One prominent government official who had helped to blow the bubble was sent to the Tower, and another committed suicide rather than face a parliamentary committee of investigation, one of whose members had suggested that it would be an excellent plan to sew the South Sea directors up in sacks and throw them into the Thames.

586. How a Terrible Disease was conquered. — But among the new things which the people were to try in this century was one which led to most beneficent results. For many generations the great scourge of Europe was the small-pox. Often the disease was as violent as the plague, and carried off nearly as many victims. Medical art seemed powerless to deal with it, and even in years of ordinary health in England about one person out of ten died of this loathsome pestilence. In the early part of George I.'s reign, Lady Mary Montagu, then travelling in Turkey, wrote that the Turks were in the habit of inoculating their children for the disease, which rendered it much milder and less fatal, and that she was about to try the experiment on her own son.

Later, Lady Montagu returned to England, and through her influence and example the practice was introduced there. It was tried first on five criminals in Newgate who had been sentenced to the gallows, but were promised their freedom if they would consent to the operation. As it proved a complete success, the Princess of Wales, with the king's consent, caused it to be tried on her daughter, with equally good results. The medical profession, however, generally refused to sanction the practice, and the clergy in many cases preached against it as an "invention of Satan, intended to counteract the purposes of an all-wise Providence" but through the perseverance and good sense of Lady Montagu, with a few others, the new practice gradually gained ground. Subsequently Dr. Jenner began to make experiments of a different kind which led late in the century to the discovery of vaccination, by which millions of lives have been saved; this, with the discovery of the use of ether in our own time, may justly be called the two greatest triumphs of the art of medicine.

587. How Walpole governed. — Robert Walpole had been a member of the Cabinet during most of the reign down to 1721. He then became premier, and continued in office as head of the government until near the middle of the next reign, or about twenty-one years in all. He was an able financier, and succeeded in reducing the National Debt; he believed in keeping the country out of war, and also, as we have seen, out of bubble speculation, but he was determined at all cost to maintain the Whig party in power, and the Protestant Hanoverian sovereigns on the throne.

In order to accomplish this, he openly bribed members of Parliament to support his party; he bought votes and carried elections by gifts of titles, honors, and bank-notes, thus proving to his own satisfaction the truth of his theory that most men "have their price," and that an appeal to the pocket-book is both quicker and surer than an appeal to principle. But he had to confess before the end of his ministry that he had found in the House of Commons one "boy patriot," as he sneeringly called him, named William Pitt (afterward Earl of Chatham), whom neither his money could buy nor his ridicule move.

Bad as Walpole's policy was in its corrupting influence on the nation, it was an admission that the time had come when the king could no longer venture to rule by force, as in the days of the Stuarts: it meant that the government had been deprived of the arbitrary power it once wielded. Walpole was a fox, not a lion; and "foxes," as Emerson tells us, "are so cunning because they are not strong."

588. Summary. — Though George I. did little for England except keep the Pretender from the throne by occupying it himself, yet that was no small advantage, since it gave the country peace. The establishment of the cabinet system of government under Sir Robert Walpole, the suppression of the Jacobite insurrection, and the disastrous collapse of the South Sea Bubble are the principal events.

GEORGE II. — 1727-1760.

589. Accession and Character. — The second George, who was also of German birth, was much like his father, though he had the advantage of being able to speak broken English readily. His wife, Queen Caroline, was an able woman, who possessed the happy art of ruling her husband without his suspecting it, while she, on the other hand, was ruled by Sir Robert Walpole, whom the king hated, but whom he had to keep as prime minister. George II. was a good soldier, and decidedly preferred war to peace; but Walpole saw clearly that the peace policy was best for the nation, and he and the queen managed to persuade the king not to draw the sword.

590. The War of Jenkins's Ear. — At the end of twelve years, however, trouble arose with Spain. According to the London newspapers of that day, a certain Captain Jenkins, while cruising, or, more probably, smuggling, in the West Indies, had been seized by the Spaniards and barbarously maltreated. They, if we accept his story, accused him of attempting to land English goods contrary to law, and searched his ship. Finding nothing against him, they vented their rage and disappointment by hanging him to the yard-arm of his vessel until he was nearly dead. They then tore off one of his ears, and bade him take it to the king of England with their compliments. Jenkins, it is said, carefully wrapped up his ear and put it in his pocket. When he reached England, he went straight to the House of Commons, drew out the mutilated ear, showed it to the House, and demanded justice. The Spanish restrictions on English trade with the Indies and South America[1] had long been a source of ill feeling. The sight of Jenkins's ear brought matters to a climax; even Walpole could not resist the clamor for vengeance, and contrary to his own judgment he had to vote for war. Though Jenkins was the occasion, the real object of the war was to compel Spain to permit the English to get a larger share in the lucrative commerce of the New World. It was another proof that America was now rapidly becoming an important factor in the politics of Great Britain. The announcement of hostilities with Spain was received in London with delight, and bells pealed from every steeple. "Yes," said Walpole, "they may ring the bells now, but before long they will be wringing their hands," — a prediction which was verified by the heavy losses the English suffered in an expedition against Carthagena, South America, though later Commodore Anson inflicted great damage on the Spanish colonies, and returned to England with large amounts of captured treasure.

---

[1] By the Assiento (contract) Treaty, made at Utrecht in 1713, one English ship of 600 tons burden was allowed to make one trading voyage a year to the colonies of Spanish America.

591. War of the Austrian Succession. — On the death of Charles VI. of the house of Austria, emperor of Germany, his daughter Maria Theresa succeeded to the Austrian dominions. France now united with Spain, Prussia, and other European powers to overturn this arrangement, partly out of jealousy of the Austrian power, and partly from desire to get control of portions of the Austrian possessions. England and Holland, however, both desired to maintain Austria as a check against their old enemy France, and declared war in 1741. During this war George II. went over to the continent to lead the English forces in person. He was not a man of commanding appearance, but he was every inch a soldier, and nothing exhilarated him like the smell of gunpowder. At the battle of Dettingen, in Bavaria, he got down from his horse, and drawing his sword, cried: "Come, boys, now behave like men, and the French will soon run." With that, followed by his troops, he rushed upon the enemy with such impetuosity that they turned and fled. This was the last battle in which an English king took part. It was followed by that of Fontenoy, in the Netherlands, in which the French gained the victory. After nearly eight years' fighting the Treaty of Aix la Chapelle secured a peace advantageous for England.[1]

592. Invasion by the Young Pretender; "the Forty-Five."[2] — While the war of the Austrian Succession was in progress, the French encouraged James II.'s grandson, Charles Edward, the Young Pretender,[3] to make an attempt on the English crown. He landed in 1745 on the northern coast of Scotland with only seven followers, but with the aid of the Scotch Jacobites of the Highlands he gained a battle over the English at Prestonpans, near Edinburgh. Emboldened by his success, he now marched into Derbyshire, England, on his way to London, with the hope, that as he advanced, the country would rise in his

---

[1] Aix la Chapelle (Āks-lă-shă'pel').
[2] So called from the Scotch rising of 1745.
[3] See note to Paragraph No. 584.

favor; but finding no support, he retreated to Scotland. The next year he and his adherents were defeated with great slaughter at Culloden, near Inverness. With the flight of the Pretender from that battle-field, his Scotch sympathizers lost all hope. There were no more ringing Jacobite songs, sung over bowls of steaming punch, of "Who'll be king but Charlie?" and "Over the water to Charlie"; and when in 1788 Charles died in Rome, the unfortunate house of Stuart disappeared from history."[1]

593. War in the East; the Black Hole of Calcutta; Clive's Victories; English Empire of India. — In India the English had long had important trading-posts at Madras, Bombay, Calcutta, and other points, but they had not had control of the country, which was governed by native princes. The French also had established an important trading-post at Pondicherry, south of Madras, and were now secretly planning through alliance with the native rulers to get possession of the entire country. They had met with some success in their efforts, and the times seemed to favor their gaining still greater influence unless some decided measures should be taken to prevent them. At this juncture Robert Clive, a young man who had been employed as clerk in the service of the English East India Company, but who had obtained a humble position in the army, obtained permission to try his hand at driving back the enemy. It was the very work for which he was fitted. He met with success from the first, and he followed it up by the splendid victory of Arcot (1751), which practically gave the English control of Southern India. Shortly after that Clive returned to England. During his absence the native prince of Bengal undertook an expedition against

---

[1] Devoted loyalty to a hopeless cause was never more truly or pathetically expressed than in some of these Jacobite songs, notably in those of Scotland, of which the following lines are an example: —

"Over the water, and over the sea,
And over the water to Charlie;
Come weal, come woe, we'll gather and go,
And live or die with Charlie." — See SCOTT's *Redgauntlet*.

Calcutta, a wealthy British trading-post. He captured the fort which protected it, and seizing the principal English residents, one hundred and forty-six in number, drove them at the point of the sword into a prison called the "Black Hole," less than twenty feet square and having but two small windows. In such a climate, in the fierce heat of midsummer, that dungeon would have been too close for a single European captive; to crowd it with more than seven score persons for a night meant death by all the agonies of heat, thirst, and suffocation. In vain they endeavored to bribe the guard to transfer part of them to another room, in vain they begged for mercy and tried to burst the door. Their jailers only mocked them and would do nothing. Then, says Macaulay, "the prisoners went mad with despair; they trampled each other down, they fought to get at the windows, they fought for the pittance of water which was given them, they raved, prayed, blasphemed, and implored the guards to fire upon them. At length the tumult died away in low gasps and moanings. When daylight came and the dungeon was opened, the floor was heaped with mutilated half-putrescent corpses. Out of the hundred and forty-six, one of whom was a woman, only twenty-three were alive, and they were so changed, so feeble, so ghastly, that their own mothers would not have known them."

When Clive returned he was met with a cry for vengeance. He gathered his troops, recovered Calcutta, and ended by fighting that great battle of Plassey (1757), which was the means of permanently establishing the English empire in India on a firm foundation.[1]

594. The Seven Years' War in Europe and America. — Before the contest had closed by which England won her Asiatic dominions, a new war had broken out. In 1756, the fifth year of the New Style,[2] the aggressive designs of Frederick the Great of

---

[1] See Macaulay's Essay on Clive.

[2] In 1752 the New Style of reckoning time was introduced into Great Britain. Owing to a slight error in the calendar, the year had, in the course of centuries, been gradually losing, so that in 1752 it was eleven days short of what the true computation would make it. Pope Gregory corrected the error in 1582, and his

No. 14.

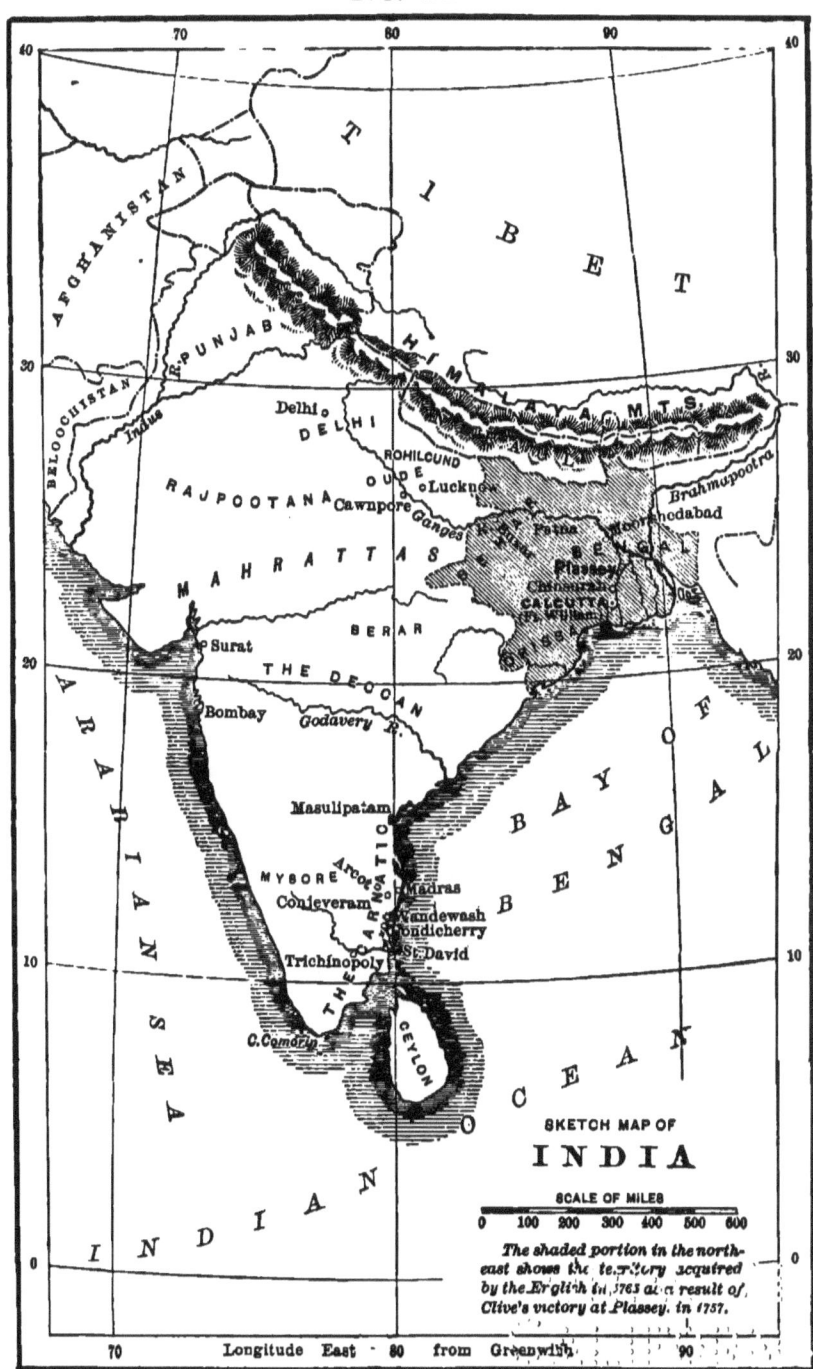

SKETCH MAP OF
INDIA

The shaded portion in the north-east shows the territory acquired by the English in 1765 as a result of Clive's victory at Plassey in 1757.

Prussia caused such alarm that a grand alliance was formed by France, Russia, Austria, and Poland to check his further advance. Great Britain, however, gave her support to Frederick, in the hope of humbling her old enemy France, who, in addition to her attempts to oust the English from India, was also making preparations on a grand scale to get possession of America. Every victory, therefore, which the British forces could gain in Europe would, by crippling the French, make the ultimate victory in America so much the more certain; so that we may look upon the alliance with Frederick as an indirect means employed by England to protect her colonies on the other side of the Atlantic. These had now extended along the entire coast, from the Kennebec River, in Maine, to the borders of Florida.

The French, on the other hand, had planted colonies at Quebec and Montreal, on the St. Lawrence; at Detroit, on the Great Lakes; at New Orleans and other points on the Mississippi. They had also begun to build a line of forts along the Ohio River, which, when completed, would connect their northern and southern colonies, and thus secure to them the whole country west of the Alleghanies. Eventually, they undoubtedly expected to conquer the East also, to erase Virginia, New England, and all other colonial titles from the map, inscribing in their place the name of New France.

During the first part of the war, the English were unsuccessful. In an attempt to take Fort Duquesne,[1] General Braddock met with a crushing defeat from the combined French and Indian forces, which would indeed have proved his utter destruction had not a young Virginian named George Washington saved a rem-

---

calendar was adopted in nearly every country of Europe except Great Britain and Russia, both of which regarded the change as a "popish measure." But in 1751, notwithstanding the popular outcry, Sept. 3, 1752, was made Sept. 14, by an act of Parliament, and by the same act the beginning of the year was altered from March 25 to Jan. 1. The popular clamor against the reform is illustrated in Hogarth's picture of an Election Feast, in which the People's party carry a banner, with the inscription, "Give us back our eleven days."

[1] Duquesne (Doo kane').

nant of his troops by his calmness and courage. Not long after, a second expedition was sent out against the French fort, in which Washington led the advance. The garrison fled at his approach, the English colors were run up, and the place was named Pittsburgh, in honor of William Pitt, then virtually prime minister of England.[1]

About the same time, the English took the forts on the Bay of Fundy, and drove out a number of thousand French settlers from Acadia.[2] This gave them control of Nova Scotia. Other successes followed, by which they obtained possession of important points. Finally, Canada was won from the French by Wolfe's victory over Montcalm, at Quebec (1759), where both gallant soldiers verified the truth of the lines, "The paths of glory lead but to the grave,"[3] which the English general had quoted to some brother-officers the evening before the attack. This ended the war. Spain now ceded Florida to Great Britain, so that in 1763, when peace was made, the English flag waved over the whole eastern half of the American continent, from the Atlantic to the Mississippi. Thus, within a comparatively few years, Great Britain had gained an empire in the East (India), and another in the West (America). A few more such conquests and her "morning drum-beat, following the sun, and keeping company with the hours" would literally "circle the earth with one continuous and unbroken strain of the martial airs of England."[4]

---

[1] He was secretary of state, but in point of influence was head of the Cabinet. See Paragraph No. 587.

[2] See The Leading Facts of American History, page 320, and note.

[3] "The boast of heraldry, the pomp of power,
And all that beauty, all that wealth e'er gave,
Await alike the inevitable hour;
The paths of glory lead but to the grave."
—GRAY'S *Elegy* (1750).

"I would rather be the author of that poem," said Wolfe, "than to have the glory of beating the French to-morrow." Wolfe and Montcalm were both mortally wounded, and died within a few hours of each other.

[4] Daniel Webster, speech of May 7, 1834.

595. Moral Condition of England; Intemperance; Rise of the Methodists. — But grand as were the military successes of the British arms, the reign of George II. was morally torpid. With the exception of a few public men like Pitt, the majority of the Whig party seemed animated by no higher motive than self-interest. It was an age whose want of faith, coarseness, and brutality were well portrayed by Hogarth's pencil and Fielding's pen. For a long time intemperance had been steadily on the increase; strong drink had taken the place of beer, and every attempt to restrict the traffic was met at the elections by the popular cry, "No gin, no king." The London taverns were thronged day and night, and in the windows of those frequented by the lowest class placards were exhibited with the tempting announcement, "Drunk for a penny; dead drunk for twopence; clean straw for nothing." On the straw lay men and women in beastly helplessness. Among the upper classes matters were hardly better. It was a common thing for great statesmen to drink at public dinners until one by one they slid out of their seats and disappeared under the table; and Robert Walpole, the late prime minister of England, said that when he was a young man his father would say to him as he poured out the wine, "Come, Robert, you shall drink twice while I drink once, for I will not permit the son in his sober senses to be witness of the intoxication of his father."[1]

Such was the condition of England when a great religious revival began. Its leader was a student at Oxford, named John Wesley. He, with his brother Charles and a few others, were accustomed to meet at certain hours for devotional exercises. The regularity of their meetings and of their habits generally got for them the name of Methodists, which, like Quaker and many another nickname of the kind, was destined to become a title of respect and honor.

At first Wesley had no intention of separating from the Church

---

[1] See Coxe's Memoirs of Sir Robert Walpole, and Lecky's England in the Eighteenth Century.

of England, but labored only to quicken it to new life; eventually, however, he found it best to begin a more extended and independent movement. The revival swept over England with its regenerating influence, and extended across the sea to America. It was especially powerful among those who had hitherto scoffed at both church and Bible. Rough and hardened men were touched and melted to tears of repentance by the fervor of this Oxford graduate, whom neither threats nor ridicule could turn aside from his one great purpose of saving souls.

Unlike the church, he did not ask the multitude to come to him; he went to them. He rode on horseback from one end of the country to the other, preaching in the fields, under trees, which are still known throughout England by the expressive name of "Gospel Oaks," in cities, at the corners of the streets, on the docks, in the slums; in fact, wherever he could find listening ears and responsive hearts.

If we except the great Puritan movement of the seventeenth century, no such appeal had been heard since the days when Augustine and his band of monks set forth on their mission among the barbarous Saxons. The results answered fully to the zeal that awakened them. Better than the growing prosperity of extending commerce, better than all the conquests in the East or the West, was the new religious spirit which stirred the people of both England and America, and provoked the national church to emulation in good works, — which planted schools, checked intemperance, and brought into vigorous activity all that was best and bravest in a race that when true to itself is excelled by none.

596. Summary. — The history of the reign may be summed up in the movement which has just been described, and in the Asiatic, continental, and American wars with France which ended in the extension of the power of Great Britain in both hemispheres.

GEORGE III. — 1760-1820.

597. Accession and Character; the King's Struggle with the Whigs. — By the death of George II. his grandson,[1] George III., now came to the throne. The new king was a man of excellent character, who prided himself on having been born an Englishman. He had the best interests of his country at heart, but he lacked many of the qualities necessary to a great ruler, and although thoroughly conscientious, he was narrow and stubborn to the last degree. His mother, who had seen how ministers and parties ruled in England, was determined that her son should have the control, and her constant injunction to the young prince was, "Be king, George, be king!" so that when he came to power George was determined to be king if self-will would make him one.

But beneath this spirit of self-will there was moral principle. In being king, George III. intended to carry out a reform such as neither George I. nor II. could have accomplished, providing that either had had the will to undertake it.

The great Whig families of rank and wealth had now held uninterrupted possession of the government for nearly half a century. Their influence was so supreme that the sovereign had practically become a mere cipher, dependent for his authority on the political support which he received. The king was resolved that this state of things should continue no longer. He was determined to reassert the royal authority and secure a government which should reflect his principles, and to have a ministry to whom he could dictate, instead of one that dictated to him.

For a long time he struggled in vain, but at last succeeded, and found in Lord North a premier who bowed to the royal will, and endeavored to carry out George III.'s favorite policy of "governing for, but never by, the people." That policy finally resulted in calling forth the famous resolution of the House of Commons

---

[1] Frederick, Prince of Wales, George II.'s son, died before his father, leaving his son George heir to the throne. See Table, Paragraph No. 581.

that the king's influence "had increased, was increasing, and ought to be diminished";[1] but it had other consequences, which, as we shall presently see, were more far-reaching and disastrous than any one in the House of Commons then imagined.

598. Taxation of the American Colonies. — The wars of the two preceding reigns had largely increased the National Debt, and the government resolved to compel the American colonies to share in a more direct degree than they had yet done, the constantly increasing burden of taxation. England then, like all other European countries, regarded her colonies in a totally different way from what she does at present. It was an open question at that time whether colonial legislative rights existed save as a matter of concession or favor on the part of the home government. It is true that the government had found it expedient to grant or recognize such rights, but they had seldom been very clearly defined, and in many important respects no one knew just what the settlers of Virginia or Massachusetts might or might not do.[2] The general theory of the mother country was that the colonies were convenient receptacles for the surplus population, good or bad, of the British Islands; next, that they were valuable as sources of revenue and profit, politically and commercially; and lastly, that they furnished excellent opportunities for the king's friends to get office and make fortunes. Such was the feeling about India, and such, modified by difference of circumstances, it was respecting America. In consequence of this feeling, the policy pursued toward these settlements was severely restrictive. By the Navigation and other laws of earlier reigns,[3] the American colonies were obliged to confine their trade to England alone, or to such ports as she directed. If they ventured to send a hogshead of tobacco or a bale of produce of any sort to another country, or

---

[1] Resolution moved by Mr. Dunning in 1780.
[2] See Story's Constitution of the United States.
[3] Navigation Laws: see Paragraph No. 511.

by any but an English ship, they forfeited their goods.[1] On the other hand, the colonies were obliged to buy the products of British mills and factories, whether they found it to their advantage or not; the object of the government being to keep the colonies wholly dependent.

They were not permitted to make so much as a horse-shoe nail or print even a copy of the New Testament, but they might, nay, they must, trade with England and pay taxes to her.

It was resistance to these arbitrary measures which first caused trouble. In the reign of Charles II. the colonies endeavored to evade these oppressive laws. To punish them that monarch revoked the New England charters, thus depriving them of whatever degree of self-government they enjoyed, and compelling them to submit to the absolute will of the crown. Under the tyrannical sway of Governor Andros, who was shortly after sent over by James II. to rule, or rather misrule, in the king's name, an explosion of popular wrath occurred which showed that, loyal as the colonies were, they would not continue to endure treatment which no Englishman at home would bear.

599. The Stamp Act. — In accordance with these theories about the colonies, and to meet the pressing needs of the home government, the English ministry, as early as 1764, proceeded to levy a tax on the colonies in return for the protection they had granted them against the French and the Indians. The colonists had paid, however, as they believed, their full proportion of the expense of the war out of their own pockets, and for the future they felt abundantly able to protect themselves. But notwithstanding this plea, a specially obnoxious form of direct tax, called the Stamp Act, was brought forward in 1765. It required that all legal documents, such as deeds, wills, notes, receipts, and the like, should be written upon paper bearing high-priced government stamps. Not only the leading men among the colonists, but the colonists generally, protested

---

[1] This was the case with all produce of any importance; the exceptions need not be enumerated.

against the act, and Benjamin Franklin, with other agents, was sent to England to sustain their protests by argument and remonstrance. But in spite of their efforts the law was passed, and the stamps were duly sent over. The people, however, were determined not to use them, and much tumult ensued. In England strong sympathy with the colonists was expressed by William Pitt (who was shortly after created Earl of Chatham), Burke, Fox, and generally by what was well called "the brains of Parliament." Pitt in particular was extremely indignant. He urged the immediate repeal of the act, saying, "I rejoice that America has resisted." Pitt further declared that any taxation of the colonies without their representation in Parliament was tyranny, that opposition to such taxation was a duty, and that the spirit shown by the Americans was the same that in England had withstood the despotism of the Stuarts, and established the principle once for all that the king cannot take the subject's money without the subject's consent. Against such opposition the law could not stand. The act was accordingly repealed, amid great rejoicing in London; the church bells rang a peal of triumph, and the shipping in the Thames was illuminated; but the good effect on America was lost by the immediate passage of another act which maintained the unconditional right of England to legislate for the colonies, or, in other words, to tax them, if they saw fit, without their consent.

600. The Tea Tax and the "Boston Tea Party," with its Results. — Another plan was now devised for getting money from the colonies. Parliament enacted a law compelling the Americans to pay taxes on a number of imports, such as glass, paper, and tea. In opposition to this law, the colonists formed leagues refusing to use these taxed articles, while at the same time they encouraged smugglers to secretly land them, and the regular trade suffered accordingly. Parliament, finding that this was bad both for the government and for commerce, now abolished all of these duties except that on tea, which was retained for a double purpose: first, and chiefly, to maintain the principle of the right of Great Britain to tax the colonies,[1] and next, to aid the East India Company, which was pleading piteously for help.

In consequence mainly of the refusal of the American colonists to buy tea, the London warehouses of the East India Company were full to overflowing with surplus stock, and the company itself was in a half-bankrupt condition. The custom had been for the company to bring the tea to England, pay a tax on it, and then sell it to be reshipped to America, where the colonists were expected to pay a tax. To aid the company in its embarrassment, the government now agreed to remit this first duty altogether, and to impose a tax of threepence (six cents) a pound on the consumers in America. Such an arrangement would, they argued, be an advantage all around, for first, it would aid the company to dispose of its stock, next, it would enable the colonists to get tea at a cheaper rate than before, and lastly, and most important of all, it would keep the principle of taxation in force. But the colonists did not accept this reasoning. In itself the three-penny tax was a trifle, but underlying it was a principle which seemed to the Americans no trifle; for such principles revolutions had been fought in the past; for such they would be fought in the future.

The colonists resolved not to have the tea at any price. A number of ships laden with the hated taxed herb arrived at the port of Boston. The tea was seized by a band of men disguised as Indians, and thrown into the harbor. The news of that action made the king and ministry furious. Parliament sympathized with the government, and in retaliation passed four acts unparalleled for their severity. The first was the Boston Port Bill, which closed the harbor to all trade; the second was the Massachusetts Bill, which virtually annulled the charter of the colony, took the government away from the people and gave it to the king; the third law ordered that Americans who committed murder in resistance to the law should be sent to England for trial; the fourth declared the country north of the Ohio and east of the

---

[1] "There must be one tax," said the king, "to keep up the right."

Mississippi a part of Canada[1] — the object of this last act being to conciliate the French Canadians, and secure their help against the colonists in case of rebellion.

Even after this unjust action on the part of the government a compromise might have been effected, and peace maintained, if the counsels of the best men had been followed; but George III. would listen to no policy short of coercion: his one idea of *being king* at all hazards had become a monomania. Burke denounced the inexpediency of such oppression, and Fox, another prominent member of Parliament, wrote: "It is intolerable to think that it should be in the power of one blockhead to do so much mischief." For the time, at least, the king was as unreasonable as any of the Stuarts. The obstinacy of Charles I. cost him his head, that of James II., his kingdom, that of George III. resulted in a war which saddled the English tax-payer with an additional debt of six hundred millions of dollars, and ended by Great Britain's losing the fairest and richest dominions that she or any nation ever possessed.

601. The American Revolution; Recognition of the Independence of the United States. — In 1775 war began, and the fighting at Lexington and Bunker Hill showed that the Americans were in earnest. The cry of the colonies had been, "No taxation without representation"; now it had got beyond that, and was, "No legislation without representation." But events moved so fast that even this did not long suffice, and on July 4, 1776, the colonies, in congress assembled, solemnly declared themselves free and independent. As far back as the French war there was at least one man who foresaw this declaration. After the English had taken Quebec, Vergennes,[2] an eminent French statesman, said of the American colonies with respect to Great Britain, "They stand no longer in need of her protection; she will call on them

---

[1] Embracing territory now divided into the five States of Ohio, Indiana, Illinois, Michigan, and Wisconsin.

[2] Vergennes (Věr'zhěn').

to contribute toward supporting the burdens they have helped to bring on her; and they will answer by striking off all dependence."[1]

This prophecy was now fulfilled. Then the English ministry became alarmed, they were ready to make terms, they would in fact grant anything but independence;* but they had opened their eyes to the facts too late, and nothing short of independence would now satisfy the colonists. It is said that attempts were made to open negotiations with General Washington, but the commander-in-chief declined to receive a letter from the English government addressed to him, not in his official capacity, but as "George Washington, Esq.," and so the matter came to nothing. The war went on with varying success through seven heavy years, until, with the aid of the French, the Americans defeated Lord Cornwallis at Yorktown in 1781.[2] By that battle France got her revenge for the loss of Quebec in 1759, and America finally won the cause for which she had spent so much life and treasure.

On a foggy December morning in 1782, George III. entered the House of Lords, and with a faltering voice read a paper in which he acknowledged the independence of the United States of America. He closed his reading with the prayer that neither Great Britain nor America might suffer from the separation; and he expressed the hope that religion, language, interest, and affection might prove an effectual bond of union between the two countries. Eventually the separation proved, as Goldwin Smith says,[3] "a mutual advantage, since it removed to a great extent the arbitrary restrictions on trade, gave a new impetus to commerce, and immensely increased the wealth of both nations."

---

[1] Bancroft's History of the United States.

[2] It is pleasant to know that a hundred years later, in the autumn of 1881, a number of English gentlemen were present at the centennial celebration of the taking of Yorktown to express their hearty good will toward the nation which their ancestors had tried in vain to keep a part of Great Britain.

[3] Goldwin Smith's Lectures on Modern History (the Foundation of the American Colonies).   * This was in 1778, after the French treaty with the U. S.

602. The Lord George Gordon Riots. — While the American war was in progress, England had not been entirely quiet at home. In consequence of the repeal of the most stringent of the unwise and unjust laws against the Roman Catholics, — certainly unwise and unjust in their continuance for so many generations, if not in their origin, — Lord George Gordon, a half-crazed Scotch fanatic, now led an attack upon the government (1780). For six days, London was at the mercy of a furious mob, which set fire to Catholic chapels, pillaged many dwellings, and committed every species of outrage. Newgate prison was broken into, the prisoners released, and the prison burned.[1] No one was safe from attack who did not wear a blue cockade to show that he was a Protestant, and a man's house was not secure unless he chalked "No Popery" on the door in conspicuous letters; or, as one individual did in order to make doubly sure, "No Religion whatever." Before the riot was finally subdued a large amount of property had been destroyed and many lives sacrificed.

603. Impeachment of Warren Hastings. — The same year that the American war came to an end Warren Hastings, governor-general of India, was impeached for corrupt and cruel government, and was tried before the House of Lords, gathered in Westminster Hall. On the side of Hastings was the powerful East India Company, ruling over a territory many times larger than the whole of Great Britain. Against him were arrayed the three ablest and most eloquent men in England, — Burke, Fox, and Sheridan. The trial was continued at intervals for eight years, and resulted in the acquittal of the accused; but it was proved that the chief business of those who went out to India was to wring a fortune from the natives, and then go back to England to spend it in a life of luxury; this fact, and the stupendous corruption that was shown to exist, eventually broke down the gigantic monopoly, and the country was thrown open to the trade of all nations.[2]

---

[1] See Dickens's Barnaby Rudge.
[2] See Burke's Speeches; also Macaulay's Essay on Warren Hastings.

604. Liberty of the Press; Law and Prison Reforms; Abolition of the Slave Trade. — Since the discontinuance of the censorship of the press,[1] though newspapers were nominally free to discuss public affairs, yet the government had no intention of permitting any severe criticism. On the other hand, there were men who were equally determined to speak their minds through the press on political as on all other matters. In the early part of the reign, John Wilkes, an able but scurrilous writer, attacked the policy of the crown in violent terms. A few years later a writer, who signed himself "Junius," began a series of letters in a daily paper, in which he handled the king and the king's friends still more roughly. An attempt was made by the government to punish Wilkes and the publisher of the "Junius" letters, but it signally failed in both cases, and the public feeling was plainly in favor of the right of the freest expression,[2] which was eventually conceded.

Up to this time Parliamentary debates had rarely been reported. In fact, under the Stuarts and the Tudors, members of Parliament would have run the risk of imprisonment if their criticisms of royalty had been made public; but now the papers began to contain the speeches and votes of both Houses on important questions. Every effort was made to suppress these reports, but again the press gained the day; and henceforth the nation learned whether its representatives really represented the will of the people, and so was able to hold them strictly accountable, — a matter of vital importance in every free government.

Another field of reform was also found. The times were brutal. The pillory still stood in the centre of London;[3] and if the unfortunate offender who was put in it escaped with a shower of mud and other unsavory missiles, instead of clubs and brick-

---

[1] See Paragraph No. 550.

[2] Later, during the excitement caused by the French Revolution, there was a reaction from this feeling, but it was only temporary.

[3] The pillory (see Paragraph No. 580) was not abolished until the accession of Queen Victoria.

bats, he was lucky indeed. Gentlemen of fashion arranged pleasure parties to visit the penitentiaries to see the wretched women whipped. The whole code of criminal law was savagely vindictive. Capital punishment was inflicted for upwards of two hundred offences, many of which would now be thought to be sufficiently punished by one or two months' imprisonment in the house of correction. Not only men, but women and children even, were hanged for pilfering goods or food worth a few shillings.[1] The jails were crowded with poor wretches whom want had driven to theft, and who were "worked off," as the saying was, on the gallows every Monday morning in batches of a dozen or twenty, in sight of the jeering, drunken crowds who gathered to witness their death agonies.

Through the efforts of Sir Samuel Romilly, Jeremy Bentham, and others, a reform was effected in this bloody code; and by the labors of the philanthropic John Howard, and forty years later of Elizabeth Fry, the jails were purified of abuses which had made them not only dens of suffering and disease, but schools of crime as well. The laws respecting punishment for debt were also changed for the better, and thousands of miserable beings who were without means to satisfy their creditors were now set free, instead of being kept in useless life-long imprisonment. At the same time Clarkson, Wilberforce, Fox, and Pitt were endeavoring to abolish that relic of barbarism, the African slave trade, which, after twenty years of persistent effort both in Parliament and out, they at last accomplished.

605. War with France; Battle of the Nile; Trafalgar; Spain. — In 1789 the French Revolution broke out. It was a violent and successful attempt to destroy those feudal institutions which the nation had outgrown, and which had, as we have seen, disappeared gradually in England after the Wars of the Roses. At first the revolutionists received the hearty sympathy of many of the

---

[1] Five shillings, or $1.25, was the hanging limit; anything stolen above that sum in money or goods sent the thief to the gallows.

Whig party, but after the execution of Louis XVI. and Queen Marie Antoinette,[1] England became alarmed not only at the horrible scenes of the Reign of Terror, but at the establishment of that democratic Republic which seemed to justify them; and joined an alliance of the principal European powers for the purpose of restoring the French monarchy. Napoleon had now become the real head of the French nation, and seemed bent on making himself master of all Europe. He undertook an expedition against Egypt and the East which was intended as a stepping-stone toward the ultimate conquest of the English empire in India, but his plans were frustrated by Nelson's victory over the French fleet at the battle of the Nile. With the assistance of Spain, Napoleon next prepared to invade England, and was so confident of success that he caused a gold medal to be struck, bearing the inscription, "Descent upon England." "Struck at London, 1804." But the combined French and Spanish fleets on whose co-operation Napoleon was depending were driven by the English into the harbor of Cadiz, and the great expedition was postponed for another year. When, in the autumn of 1805, they left Cadiz harbor, Lord Nelson lay waiting for them off Cape Trafalgar,[2] near by. Two days later he descried the enemy at daybreak. The men on both sides felt that the decisive struggle was at hand. With the exception of a long, heavy swell the sea was calm, with a light breeze, but sufficient to bring the two fleets gradually within range.

> "As they drifted on their path
> There was silence deep as death;
> And the boldest held his breath
> For a time."[3]

Just before the action, Nelson ran up this signal to the masthead of his ship, where all might see it: "ENGLAND EXPECTS EVERY MAN TO DO HIS DUTY." The answer to it was three ringing cheers from the entire fleet, and the fight began. When it

---

[1] See Burke's Reflections on the French Revolution (Death of Marie Antoinette).
[2] Cape Trafalgar (Traf-al'-gar).
[3] Campbell's Battle of the Baltic, but applicable as well to Trafalgar.

ended, Napoleon's boasted navy was no more. Trafalgar Square, in the heart of London, with its tall column bearing aloft a statue of Nelson, commemorates the decisive victory, which was dearly bought with the life of the great admiral. The battle of Trafalgar snuffed out Napoleon's projected invasion of England. He had lost his ships, and their commander had in despair committed suicide; so the French emperor could no longer hope to bridge "the ditch," as he derisively called the boisterous Channel, whose waves rose like a wall between him and the island which he hated. A few years later, Napoleon, who had taken possession of Spain, and placed his brother on the throne, was driven from that country by Sir Arthur Wellesley, destined to be better known as the Duke of Wellington, and the crown was restored to the Spanish nation.

606. Second War with the United States. — The United States waged its first war with Great Britain to gain an independent national existence; in 1812 it declared a second war to secure its personal and maritime rights. During the long and desperate struggle between England and France, each nation had prohibited neutral powers from commercial intercourse with the other, or with any country friendly to the other. Furthermore, the English government had laid down the principle that a person born on British soil could not become a citizen of another nation, but that "once an Englishman always an Englishman" was the only true doctrine. In accordance with that theory, it claimed the right to search American ships and take from them and force into their own service any seamen supposed to be of British birth. In this way Great Britain had seized more than 6000 men, and notwithstanding their protest that they were American citizens, either by birth or by naturalization, had compelled them to enter the English navy. Other points in dispute between the two countries were in a fair way of being settled amicably, but there appeared to be no method of coming to terms in regard to the question of search and impressment, which was the most important of all, since, though the demand of the United States was, in the popular phrase of the day, for "Free Trade and Sailors' Rights," it was the last which was especially emphasized. In 1812 war against Great Britain was declared, and an attack made on Canada which resulted in the American forces being driven back. During the war British troops landed in Maryland, burned the Capitol and other public buildings in Washington, and destroyed the Congressional Library. On the other hand, the American navy had unexpected and extraordinary successes on the ocean and the lakes. Out of sixteen sea combats with approximately equal forces, the Americans gained thirteen.[1] The contest closed with the signal defeat of the English at New Orleans under Sir Edward Pakenham, brother-in-law of the Duke of Wellington, by the Americans under General Andrew Jackson. The right of search was thenceforth dropped, although it was not formally abandoned by Great Britain until 1856.

607. Battle of Waterloo. — On Sunday, June 18, 1815, the English war against Napoleon, which had been carried on almost constantly since his accession to power, culminated in the decisive battle of Waterloo.[2] Napoleon had crossed the Belgian frontier, in order that he might come up with the British before they could form a junction with their Prussian allies. All the previous night the rain had fallen in torrents, and when the soldiers rose from their cheerless bivouac in the trampled and muddy fields of rye, a drizzling rain was still falling. Napoleon planned the battle with the purpose of destroying first the English and then the Prussian forces, but Wellington held his own against the furious attacks of the French. It was evident, however, that even the "Iron Duke," as he was called, could not continue to withstand the terrible assaults many hours longer. As time passed on, and he saw his solid squares melting away under the murderous French fire, as line after line of his soldiers coming forward, silently stepped into the places of their fallen comrades, while the ex-

---

[1] Fiske's Washington and his Country.
[2] Waterloo: near Brussels, Belgium.

pected Prussian reinforcements still delayed their appearance, the English commander exclaimed, "O that night or Blücher[1] would come!" At last Blücher with his Prussians did come, and as Grouchy,[2] the leader of a division on whom Napoleon was counting, did not, Waterloo was finally won by the combined strength of the allies, and not long after, Napoleon was sent to die a prisoner on the desolate rock of St. Helena.

When all was over, Wellington said to Blücher, as he stood by him on a little eminence looking down upon the field covered with the dead and dying, "A great victory is the saddest thing on earth, except a great defeat."

With that victory ended the second Hundred Years' War of England with France, which began with the War of the Spanish Succession in 1704[3] under Marlborough, and which originally had for its double object the humbling of the power that threatened the independence of England, and the protection of those colonies which had now separated from the mother-country, and had become, partly through French help, the republic of the United States of America.

608. Increase of the National Debt; Taxation. — Owing to these hundred years and more of war, the national debt of Great Britain and Ireland, which in 1688 was much less than a million of pounds had now reached the enormous amount of over nine hundred millions (or $4,500,000,000) bearing yearly interest at the rate of more than $160,000,000.[4] So great had been the strain on the finances of the country, that the Bank of England suspended payment, and many heavy failures occurred. In addition to this, a succession of bad harvests sent up the price of wheat to such a point that at one time an ordinary sized loaf of bread cost the farm laborer more than half a day's wages. Taxes had gone on increasing until it seemed as though the people could not endure the burden. As Sydney Smith declared, with entire truth, there

---

[1] Blücher (Bloo'ker).   [2] Grouchy (Grou'she').
[3] See Paragraph No. 557.   [4] Encyclopædia Britannica, "National Debt."

were duties on everything. They began, he said, in childhood with "the boy's taxed top"; they followed to old age, until at last "the dying Englishman pouring his taxed medicine into a taxed spoon, flung himself back on a taxed bed, and died in the arms of an apothecary who had payed a tax of a hundred pounds for the privilege of putting him to death."[1]

609. Union of Great Britain and Ireland. — For a century after the battle of the Boyne Ireland can hardly be said to have had a history.[2] The iron hand of English despotism had crushed the spirit out of the inhabitants, and they suffered in silence. During the first part of the eighteenth century the destitution of the people was so great that Dean Swift, in bitter mockery of the government's neglect, published what he called his "Modest Proposal" for relieving the misery of the half-starved millions by allowing them, as he said, to cook and eat their own children, or else sell them to the butchers. After the French wars broke out an association was formed called the "United Irishmen," which endeavored to secure the aid of France. The rebellion was quelled, and at the beginning of the present century the English government succeeded by the most unscrupulous bribery in buying up a sufficent number of members of the so-called Irish Parliament to secure a vote in favor of union with Great Britain, and in 1800 the two countries were joined — at least in name — under the title of the United Kingdom of Great Britain and Ireland.

William Pitt, son of the late Earl of Chatham, used his influence to obtain for Ireland a fair representation in the united Parliament, urging that it was for the interest of the two countries that both Catholics and Protestants should be eligible for election. His advice, however, was rejected, and although a large majority of the Irish people were zealous Catholics, not a single member of that church was admitted to the House of Commons. To increase if possible the hatred of England, free trade with England had up to

---

[1] Sydney Smith's Essays, Review of Seybert's Annals of the United States.
[2] Green's English People.

this time been withheld from the Irish, greatly to their loss. They were thus treated as a foreign and hostile race, from a commercial as well as a religious point of view.

610. Material Progress; Canals; Steam; Distress of the Working Class; the North of England. — The reign of George III. was, however, in several directions one of marked progress, especially in England. Just after the king's accession a canal was opened in the north for the transportation of goods. It was the first of a system which has since become so widely extended that the canals of England now exceed in length its navigable rivers. The two form such a complete network of water communication that it is said that no place in the realm is more than fifteen miles distant from this means of transportation, which connects all the large towns with each other and with the chief ports.

In 1769 James Watt obtained the first patent for his improved steam engine.[1] The story is told that he took a working model of it to show to the king. His majesty patronizingly asked him, "Well, my man, what have you to sell?" The inventor promptly answered, "What kings covet, may it please your majesty, — *power!*" The story is perhaps too good to be true, but the fact of the "power" could not be denied — power, too, not simply mechanical, but in its results, moral and political as well. In 1811 such was the increase of machinery driven by steam, and such the improvements made by Hargreaves, Arkwright, Crompton, and others in machinery for spinning and weaving, that much distress arose among the working classes. The price of bread was growing higher and higher, while in many districts skilled operatives could not earn by their utmost efforts two dollars a week. They saw their hand-labor supplanted by patent "monsters of iron and fire," which never grew weary, which subsisted on water and coal, and never asked for wages. Led by a man named Ludd, the starving workmen attacked the mills, broke the machinery in pieces, and sometimes burnt the buildings. The

---

[1] See Paragraph No. 570.

riots were at length suppressed, and a number of the leaders executed; but a great change for the better was at hand, and steam was soon to remedy the evils it had seemingly created.

Up to this period the North of England remained the poorest part of the country. The population was sparse, ignorant, and unprosperous. It was in the south that improvements originated. In the reign of Henry VIII. the north fought against the dissolution of the monasteries; in Elizabeth's reign it resisted Protestantism; in that of George I. it sided with the Pretender. But steam wrought a great change. Factories were built, population increased, cities sprang up, and wealth grew apace. Birmingham, Manchester, Leeds, Nottingham, Leicester, Sheffield, and Liverpool made the north a new country. The saying is now current that "what Lancashire thinks to-day, England will think to-morrow." So much for James Watt's "power" and its results.

611. **Discovery of Oxygen; Introduction of Gas; the Safety Lamp; Steam Navigation.** — Notwithstanding the progress that had been made in many departments of knowledge, the science of chemistry remained almost stationary until, in 1774, Dr. Joseph Priestley discovered oxygen, the most abundant, as well as the most important, element in nature. That discovery not only "laid the foundation of modern chemical science,"[1] but, as Professor Liebig remarks, "the knowledge of the composition of the atmosphere, of the solid crust of the earth, of water, and of their influence upon the life of plants and animals was linked with it." It proved, also, of direct practical utility, since the successful pursuit of innumerable trades and manufactures, with the profitable separation of metals from their ores, stands in close connection with the facts which Priestley's experiments made known.

As intellectual light spread, so also did material light. It was not until near the close of the reign of George III. that London could be said to be lighted at night. A few feeble oil lamps were in use, but the streets were dark and dangerous, and highway rob-

---

[1] Professor Youmans's New Chemistry.

beries were frequent. About 1815 a company was formed to light the city with gas. After much opposition from those who were in the whale-oil interest the enterprise succeeded. The new light, as Miss Martineau has said, did more to prevent crime than all that the government had accomplished since the days of Alfred. It changed, too, the whole aspect of the capital, though it was only the forerunner of the electric light, which has since changed it even more. The sight of the great city now, when viewed at night from Highgate archway on the north, or looking down the Thames from Westminster bridge, is something never to be forgotten. It gives one a realizing sense of the immensity of "this province covered with houses," which cannot be got so well in any other way. It brings to mind, too, those lines expressive of the contrasts of wealth and poverty, success and failure, inevitable in such a place: —

"O gleaming lamps of London, that gem the city's crown,
What fortunes lie within you, O lights of London town!
* * * * * * * *
O cruel lamps of London, if tears your light could drown,
Your victims' eyes would weep them, O lights of London town."[1]

The same year in which gas was introduced, Sir Humphry Davy invented the miner's safety lamp. Without seeking a patent, he generously gave his invention to the world, finding his reward in the knowledge that it would be the means of saving thousands of lives wherever men are called to work underground.

Since Watt had demonstrated the value of steam for driving machinery, a number of inventors had been experimenting with the new power, in the hope that they might apply it to propelling vessels. In 1807 Robert Fulton, an American, built the first steamboat, and made the voyage from New York to Albany in it. Shortly after, his vessel began to make regular trips on the Hudson. A number of years later a similar boat began to carry passengers on the Clyde, in Scotland. Finally, in 1819, the bold undertaking was made of crossing the Atlantic by steam. An American steamship, the *Savannah*, of about three hundred tons, set the

---

[1] From the play "The Lights of London."

example by a voyage from the United States to Liverpool. Dr. Lardner, an English scientist, had proved to his own satisfaction that ocean steam navigation was impracticable. The book containing the doctor's demonstration was brought to America by the *Savannah* on her return. Twenty-one years afterward, the Cunard and other great lines, with fleets of vessels ranging from 5,000 to 8,000 tons, were established, making passages from continent to continent in about as many days as the ordinary sailing-vessels formerly required weeks. The fact that during a period of more than forty-five years one of these lines has never lost a passenger is conclusive proof that Providence is on the side of steam, when steam has men that know how to handle it.

612. Literature; Art; Education; Dress.—The reign of George III. is marked by a long list of names eminent in letters and art. First in point of time among these stands Dr. Samuel Johnson, the compiler of the first English dictionary worthy of the name, and that on which those of our own day are based to a considerable extent, the author also of the story of Rasselas — which may be called a satire on discontent and the search after happiness. Next, stands Johnson's friend, Oliver Goldsmith, famous for his genius, his wit, his improvidence, which was always getting him into trouble, and for his novel, the "Vicar of Wakefield," with his poems. Edward Gibbon, David Hume, author of the history of England, and Adam Smith come next in time. In 1776 the first published his "Decline and Fall of the Roman Empire," which after more than a hundred years still stands the ablest history of the subject in any language. In the same year Adam Smith issued "An Inquiry into the Nature and Causes of the Wealth of Nations," which had an immediate and permanent effect on legislation respecting commerce, trade, and finance; during this period, also, Sir William Blackstone became prominent as a writer on law, and Edmund Burke, the distinguished orator and statesman, wrote his "Reflections on the French Revolution." The poets Burns, Byron, and Shelley, with Sheridan, the orator and dramatist, and Sterne, the humorist, belong to this reign; so, too, does the witty satirist, Sydney Smith, and Sir Walter Scott, whose works, like those of Shakespeare, have "made the dead past live again." Maria Edgeworth and Jane Austen have left admirable pictures of the age in their stories of Irish and English life. Coleridge and Wordsworth began to attract attention toward the last of this period, and to be much read by those who loved the poetry of thought and the poetry of nature; while early in the next reign, Charles Lamb published his delightful "Essays of Elia."

In art we have the first English painters and engravers. Hogarth, who died a few years after the beginning of the reign, was celebrated for his coarse but perfect representations of low life and street scenes; and his series of election pictures with his "Beer Lane" and "Gin Alley" are valuable for the insight they give into the history of the times. The chief portrait painters were Reynolds, Lawrence, and Gainsborough, of whom the last afterward became noted for his landscapes. They were followed by Wilkie, whose pictures of "The Rent Day," "The Reading of the Will," with many others, tell a story of interest to every one who looks at them. Last, and greatest, came Turner, who surpassed all former artists in his power of reproducing scenes in nature. At the same time, Bewick, whose cuts used to be the delight of every child that read "Æsop's Fables," gave a new impulse to wood-engraving, while Flaxman rose to be the leading English sculptor, and Wedgewood introduced useful and beautiful articles of pottery.

In common school education little advance had been made for many generations. In the country the great mass of the people were nearly as ignorant as they were in the darkest part of the Middle Ages. Hardly a peasant over forty years of age could be found who could read a verse in the Bible, and not one in ten could write his name. There were no cheap books or newspapers, no railroads, no system of public instruction. The poor scarcely ever left the counties in which they were born, they knew nothing of what was going on in the world, and their education was wholly of that practical kind which comes from work and things, not books and teachers; yet many of them with only these simple helps found out two secrets which the highest culture sometimes misses, — how to be useful and how to be happy.[1]

The close of George III.'s reign marks the beginning of the present age. It was indicated in many ways, and among others by the change in dress. Gentlemen were leaving off the picturesque costumes of the past — the cocked hats, elaborate wigs, silk stockings, ruffles, velvet coats, and swords, — and gradually putting on the plain democratic garb, sober in cut and color, by which we know them to-day.[2]

613. Last Days of George III. — In 1820 George III. died at the age of seventy-eight. During ten years he had been blind, deaf, and insane, having lost his reason not very long after the jubilee, which celebrated the fiftieth year of his reign in 1809. Once, in a lucid interval, he was found by the queen singing a hymn and playing an accompaniment on the harpsichord. He then knelt and prayed aloud for her, for his family, and for the nation; and in closing, for himself, that it might please God to avert his heavy calamity, or grant him resignation to bear it. Then he burst into tears, and his reason again fled.[3] In consequence of the incapacity of the king, his eldest son was appointed Prince Regent, and on the king's death came to the throne.

614. Summary. — The long reign of George III., covering over sixty years, was in every way eventful. During that time England lost her possessions in America. During that period, also, Ireland was united to Great Britain. The wars with France, which lasted more than twenty years, ended in the victory of Trafalgar and the still greater victory of Waterloo. In consequence of these wars, with that of the American revolution, the national debt of Great Britain rose to a height which rendered the burden of taxation

---

[1] See Wordsworth's poem " Resolution and Independence."
[2] See Martin's Civil Costumes of Great Britain.
[3] See Thackeray's Four Georges.

well-nigh insupportable. The second war with the United States in 1812 resulted in completing American independence, and England was forced to relinquish the right of search. The two greatest reforms of the period were the abolition of the slave trade and the mitigation of the laws against debt and crime; the chief material improvement was the application of steam to manufacturing and navigation.

GEORGE IV. — 1820-1830.

615. Accession and Character of George IV. — George IV., eldest son of the late king, came to the throne in his fifty-eighth year; though owing to his father's insanity, he had virtually been king since 1811. His habits of life had made him a selfish, dissolute spendthrift, who, like Charles II., cared only for pleasure. Though while Prince of Wales he had had for many years an income of upwards of half a million of dollars, which was largely increased at a later period, yet he was always hopelessly in debt. In 1795 Parliament appropriated over $3,000,000 to relieve him from his most pressing creditors, but his wild extravagance soon involved him in difficulties again, so that had it not been for help given by the long-suffering tax-payers, his royal highness must have become as bankrupt in purse as he was in character. After his accession matters became worse rather than better. At his coronation, which cost the nation over a million of dollars, he appeared in hired jewels, which he forgot to return, and which Parliament had to pay for. Not only did he waste the nation's money more recklessly than ever, but he used whatever political influence he had to oppose such means of reform as the times demanded.

616. Discontent and Conspiracy; the "Manchester Massacre." — When in 1811 the prince became regent, he desired to form a Whig ministry, not because he cared for Whig principles, but solely for the reason that he should thereby be acting in opposition to his father's wishes. Finding his purpose impracticable, the prince accepted Tory rule, and a government was formed with Lord Liverpool as its nominal head, which had for its main object the exclusion of the Catholics from representation in Parliament.

Liverpool was a dull, well-meaning man, who utterly failed to comprehend the real tendency of the age. He was the son of a commoner who had been raised to the peerage. He had always had a reputation for honest obstinacy, and for little else. After he became premier, Madame de Staël, who was visiting England, asked him one day, "What has become of that *very* stupid man, Mr. Jenkinson?" "Madame," answered the unfortunate minister, "he is now Lord Liverpool."[1]

From such a government, which continued in power for fifteen years, nothing but trouble could be expected. The misery of the country was great. Food was selling at famine prices. Thousands were on the verge of starvation, and tens of thousands did not get enough to eat. Trade was seriously depressed, and multitudes were unable to obtain work. Under these circumstances the suffering masses undertook to hold public meetings to discuss the cause and cure of these evils, but the authorities looked upon these meetings with suspicion, especially as violent speeches against the government were often made, and dispersed them as seditious and tending to riot and rebellion. Many large towns at this period had no voice in legislation. At Birmingham, which was one of this class, the citizens had met and chosen, though without legal authority, a representative to Parliament. Manchester, another important manufacturing town, now determined to do the same. The people were warned not to assemble, but they persisted in doing so, on the ground that peaceful discussion, with the election of a representative, was no violation of law. The meeting was held, and through the blundering of a magistrate, it ended in an attack by a body of troops, by which many people were wounded and a number killed. The bitter feeling caused by the "Manches-

---

[1] Earl's English Premiers, Vol. II. Madame de Staël (Stäl) : a celebrated French writer.

ter Massacre," as it was called, and by the repressive measures of the government generally, led to the "Cato Street Conspiracy." Shortly after the accession of the new king a few desperate men banded together, and meeting in a stable in Cato Street, London, formed a plot to murder Lord Liverpool and the entire Cabinet at a dinner at which all the ministers were to be present. The plot was discovered, and the conspirators speedily disposed of by the gallows or transportation, but nothing was done to relieve the suffering which had provoked the intended crime. No new conspiracy was attempted, but in the course of the next twenty-five years a silent revolution took place, which, as we shall see later, obtained for the people that representation in Parliament which they had hitherto vainly attempted to get.

617. Queen Caroline. — In 1785 Prince George had, contrary to law,[1] married Mrs. Fitzherbert, a Roman Catholic lady of excellent character, and possessed of great beauty. Ten years later, partly through royal compulsion, and partly to get money to pay off some of his numerous debts, the prince married his cousin, Caroline of Brunswick. The union proved a source of unhappiness to both. The princess lacked both discretion and delicacy, and her husband, who disliked her from the first, was reckless and brutal toward her. He separated from her in a year's time, and as soon as she could she withdrew to the continent. On his accession to the throne the king excluded Queen Caroline's name from the Prayer Book, and next applied to Parliament for a divorce on the ground of the queen's unfaithfulness to her marriage vows.

Henry Brougham, afterwards Lord Brougham, acted as the queen's counsel. No sufficient evidence was brought against her, and the ministry declined to take further action. It was decided, however, that she could not claim the honor of coronation, to

---

[1] By the Royal Marriage Act of 1772, no descendant of George II. could make a legal marriage without the consent of the reigning sovereign, unless twenty-five years of age, and the marriage was not objected to by Parliament.

which, as queen-consort, she had a right sanctioned by custom but not secured by law. When the king was crowned, no place was provided for her. By the advice of her counsel, she presented herself at the entrance of Westminster Abbey as the coronation ceremony was about to begin; but, by order of her husband, admission was refused, and she retired to die, heart-broken, a few days after.

618. Three Reforms. — In 1828 the Duke of Wellington, a Tory in politics, became prime minister. His sympathies in all matters of legislation were with the king, but he made a virtue of necessity, and for the time acted with those who demanded reform. The Corporation Act, which was originally passed in the reign of Charles II., and had for its object the exclusion of Dissenters from all town or corporate offices, was now repealed : henceforth a man might become a mayor, alderman, or bank president, and the like, without belonging to the Church of England. At the same time the Test Act, which had also been passed in Charles II.'s reign to keep both Catholics and Dissenters out of government offices, whether civil or military, was repealed. The next year (1829) a still greater reform was carried. For a long period the Roman Catholic Emancipation party had been laboring to obtain the abolition of the unjust laws which had been on the statute books for over a century and a half, by which Catholics were excluded from the right to sit in Parliament — laws which, it will be remembered, were enacted at the time of the alleged "Popish Plot," and in consequence of the perjured evidence given by Titus Oates.[1] After the most strenuous opposition of the king and his party, including the Duke of Wellington, the latter became convinced that further opposition was useless, and he took the lead in securing the success of a measure which he heartily hated, solely, as he declared, to avert civil war.

But at the same time that Catholic emancipation was granted, an act was passed depriving a very large class of small Irish land-

---

[1] See Paragraph No. 530. See also Sydney Smith's "Peter Plymley's Letters."

holders of the right to vote, on the pretext that they would be influenced by either their landlord or their priest.[1]

Under the new order of things, Daniel O'Connell, an Irish gentleman of an old and honorable family, and a man of distinguished ability, came forward as leader of the Catholics. After much difficulty he succeeded in taking his seat in the House of Commons, and henceforth devoted himself, though without avail, to the repeal of the act uniting Ireland with England, and to the restoration of an independent Irish Parliament.

619. The New Police. — Although London had now a population of a million and a half, it still had no effective police. The guardians of the peace at that date were infirm old men who spent their time dozing in sentry-boxes, and had neither the strength nor energy to be of service in any emergency. The young fellows of fashion considered these venerable constables as legitimate game, and often amused themselves by upsetting the sentry-boxes with their occupants, leaving the latter helpless in the street, kicking and struggling like turtles turned on their backs, and as powerless to get on their feet again. During the last year of the reign Sir Robert Peel got a bill passed which organized a new and thoroughly efficient police force, properly equipped and uniformed. Great was the outcry against this innovation, and the "men in blue" were hooted at, not only by London "roughs," but by respectable citizens, as "Bobbies" or "Peelers," in derisive allusion to their founder. But the "Bobbies," who do not carry even a visible club, were not to be jeered out of existence, and they have henceforth continued to do their duty in a way which long since gained for them the good will of all who care for the preservation of law and order.

620. Death of the King. — George IV. died in the summer of 1830. Of him it may well be said, though in a very different sense from that in which the expression was originally used, that

---

[1] The property qualification in Ireland was raised from £2 to £10.

"nothing in his life became him like the leaving it."[1] During his ten years' reign he had squandered enormous sums of money in gambling and dissipation, and had done his utmost to block the wheels of political progress. How far this son of an insane father was responsible, it may not be for us to judge. Walter Scott, who had a kind word for almost every one, and especially for any one of the Tory party, did not fail to say something in praise of the generous good nature of his friend George IV. The sad thing is that his voice is the only one. In a whole nation the rest are silent; or, if they speak, it is neither to commend nor to defend, but to condemn.

621. Summary. — The legislative reforms of George IV.'s reign are its chief features. The repeal of the Test and Corporation acts and Catholic emancipation were tardy measures of justice, for which neither the king nor his ministers deserve any credit, but which, none the less, accomplished great and permanent good.

WILLIAM IV. — 1830-1837.

622. Accession and Character of William IV. — As George IV. left no heir, his brother William, a man of sixty-five, now came to the throne. He had passed most of his life on shipboard, having been placed in the navy when a mere lad. He was somewhat rough in his manner, and cared nothing for the ceremony and etiquette that were so dear to both George III. and IV. His faults, however, were on the surface. He was frank, hearty, and a friend to the people, to whom he was familiarly known as "the Sailor King."

623. Need of Parliamentary Reform; Rotten Boroughs. — From the beginning of this reign it was evident that the great question which must come up for settlement was that of Parliamentary representation. Large numbers of the people of England had now no voice in the government. This unfortunate state of

---

[1] Shakespeare's Macbeth, Act I. Sc. 4.

things was chiefly the result of the great changes which had taken place in the growth of the population of the midlands and the north. Since the introduction of steam the rapid increase of manufactures and commerce had built up many large towns in the iron, coal, pottery, and wool-raising districts, such as Birmingham, Leeds, Sheffield, Manchester, which could not send a member to Parliament; while, on the other hand, many places in the South of England which did send, had long since ceased to be of any importance. Furthermore, the representation was of the most hap-hazard description. In one section no one could vote except substantial property-holders, in another, none but town officers, while in a third, every man who had a tenement big enough to boil a pot in, and hence called a "Potwalloper," possessed the right. To this singular state of things the nation had long been indifferent. During the Middle Ages the inhabitants often had no desire either to go to Parliament themselves or to send others. The expense of the journey was great, the compensation was small, and unless some important matter of special interest to the people was at stake, they preferred staying at home; so that it was often almost as difficult for the sheriff to get a distant county member up to the House of Commons in London as it would have been to carry him there a prisoner to be tried for his life. Now, however, everything was changed; the rise of political parties, the constant and heavy taxation, the jealousy of the increase of royal authority, the influence and honor of the position of a Parliamentary representative, all conspired to make men eager to obtain their full share in the management of the government. This new interest had begun as far back as the civil wars of the seventeenth century, and when Cromwell came to power he effected many much-needed reforms; but after the restoration of the Stuarts the Protector's wise measures were repealed or neglected, the old order, or rather disorder, again asserted itself, and in many cases matters were worse than ever. Thus, for instance, the borough or city of Old Sarum, in Wiltshire, which had once been an important place had, at an early period, gradually declined through the growth of New Sarum, or Salisbury, near by. In the sixteenth century the parent city had so completely decayed that not a single habitation was left on the desolate hill-top where the castle and cathedral once stood. At the foot of the hill was an old tree. In 1830 the owner of that tree and of the field where it grew sent two members to Parliament — that action represented what had been regularly going on for something like three hundred years! In Bath, on the other hand, none of the citizens, out of a large population, might vote except the mayor, aldermen, and common council. These places now got the significant name of "rotten boroughs" from the fact that whether large or small there was no longer any sound political life existing in them.

624. The Reform Bill. — For fifty years after the coming in of the Georges the country had been ruled by a powerful Whig monopoly. Under George III. that monopoly was broken, and the Tories got possession of the government; but whichever party ruled, Parliament, owing to the "rotten borough" system, no longer represented the nation, but simply stood for the will of certain wealthy landholders and town corporations. A loud and determined demand was now made for reform. Among those who helped to urge forward the movement none was more active or influential among the common people than William Cobbett, a self-educated man, but a vigorous and fearless writer, who for years published a small newspaper called the Political Register, which was especially devoted to securing a just and uniform system of representation.

On the accession of William IV. the pressure for reform became so great that Parliament was forced to act. Lord Russell brought in a bill providing for the abolition of the "rotten boroughs" and for a fair system of elections. Those who owned or controlled these boroughs had no intention of giving them up. Their opponents, however, were equally determined, and they knew that they had the support of the nation. In a speech which the Rev.

Sydney Smith made at Taunton, he compared the futile resistance of the House of Lords to the proposed reform, to Mrs. Partington's attempt to drive back the rising tide of the Atlantic with her mop. The ocean rose, and Mrs. Partington, seizing her mop, rose against it; yet, notwithstanding the good lady's efforts, the Atlantic got the best of it; so the speaker prophesied that in this case the people, like the Atlantic, would in the end carry the day.[1]

When the bill came up, the greater part of the lords and bishops, who, so far as they were concerned personally, had all the rights and privileges they wanted, voted against the reform. To them the proposed law seemed, perhaps with good reason, to threaten the stability of the government. The Duke of Wellington was particularly prominent among those who were hostile to it, and wrote: "I don't generally take a gloomy view of things, but I confess that, knowing all that I do, I cannot see what is to save the Church, or property, or colonies, or union with Ireland, or, eventually, monarchy, if the Reform Bill passes."[2]

The king dissolved Parliament; a new one was elected, but it was still more determined to carry the measure. Again the Upper House rejected it. Then a period of wild excitement ensued. The people in many of the towns collected in the public squares, tolled the church bells, built bonfires in which they burned in effigy the bishops, and other leading opponents of the bill, and cried out for the abolition of the House of Lords. In London the rabble smashed the windows of the Duke of Wellington. In Bristol and Derby terrible riots broke out, and at Nottingham the mob fired and destroyed the castle of the Duke of Newcastle, who was noted for his opposition to reform, while all over the country shouts were heard, "The Bill, the whole Bill, and nothing but the Bill!"

625. Passage of the Bill (1832); Results. — In the spring of 1832 the battle began again with greater fierceness than ever.

---

[1] Sydney Smith's Essays and Speeches.
[2] Wellington's Despatches and Letters, Vol. II. 451.

Again the House of Commons voted the bill, and once again the Lords defeated it.

It was evident that matters could not go on in this manner much longer. The ministry, as a final measure, appealed to the king for help. If the Lords would not pass the bill, the sovereign had the power to create a sufficient number of new Whig lords who would. William now yielded to the pressure, and much against his will, gave the following document to his prime minister: "*The King grants permission to Earl Grey, and to his Chancellor, Lord Brougham, to create such a number of Peers as will be sufficient to insure the passing of the Reform Bill—first calling up peers' eldest sons.* WILLIAM R., Windsor, May 17, 1832."[1]

But there was no occasion to make use of this permission. As soon as the peers found that the king had granted it, they yielded. Those who had opposed the bill now stayed away; the measure was carried, received the royal signature, and became law. Its passage brought about a beneficent change. (1) It abolished the "rotten boroughs." (2) It gave every householder who paid rent of fifty dollars in any town a vote, and largely extended the list of county votes as well. (3) It granted two representatives to Birmingham, Leeds, Manchester, and nineteen other large towns, and one representative each to twenty-one other places, all of which had hitherto been unrepresented, besides granting fifteen additional members to the counties. (4) It added in all half a million of voters to the list, and it helped to purify the elections from the violence which had disgraced them. Before the passing of the Reform Bill and the legislation which supplemented it, the election of a member of Parliament was a kind of local reign of terror. The smaller towns were sometimes under the control of drunken ruffians for several weeks. During that time they paraded the streets in bands, assaulting voters of the opposite party with

---

[1] "First calling up peers' eldest sons": that is, in creating new lords, the eldest sons of peers were to have the preference. William R. (*Rex*, King): this is the customary royal signature.

clubs, kidnapping prominent men and confining them until after the election, and perpetrating other outrages which so frightened peaceable citizens that often they did not dare attempt to vote at all.

626. Abolition of Slavery; Factory Reform. — With the new Parliament that came into power the names of Liberal and Conservative began to supplant those of Whig and Tory. The House of Commons now reflected the will of the people better than ever before, and further reforms were accordingly carried.

In 1833 Buxton, Wilberforce, Brougham, and other philanthropists, against the strenuous opposition of the king, secured the passage through Parliament of a bill, for which they, with the younger Pitt, Clarkson, and Zachary Macaulay, had labored in vain for half a century, whereby all negro slaves in British colonies, who now numbered 800,000, were set free, and twenty millions of pounds sterling appropriated to compensate the owners. It was a grand deed grandly done, and could America have followed the noble example, she might thereby have saved a million of human lives and three thousand millions of dollars which were cast into the gulf of civil war, while the corrupting influence of five years of waste and discord would have been avoided.

But negro slaves were not the only slaves in those days. There were white slaves as well, — women and children born in England, but condemned by their necessities to work under ground in the coal mines, or exhaust their strength in the cotton mills.[1] They were driven by brutal masters who cared as little for the welfare of those under them as the overseer of a West India plantation did for his gangs of toilers in the rice swamps. Parliament at length turned its attention to these abuses, and greatly alleviated them by the passage of acts forbidding the employment of women and

---

[1] Children of six and seven years old were kept at work for twelve and thirteen hours continuously in the factories, and were often inhumanly treated. They were also employed in the coal mines at this tender age. All day long they sat in absolute darkness, opening and shutting doors for the passage of coal cars. If, overcome with fatigue, they fell asleep, they were cruelly beaten with a strap.

young children in the collieries and factories, while a later act put an end to the barbarous practice of forcing children to sweep chimneys. In an overcrowded country like England, the lot of the poor must continue to be exceptionally hard, but there is no longer the indifference toward it that once prevailed. Poverty there may still be looked upon as a crime, or something very like it; but it is regarded now as a crime which may possibly have some extenuating circumstances.

627. Inventions; the First Steam Railway; the Friction Match. — Ever since the application of steam to machinery, inventors had been discussing plans for placing the steam engine on wheels and using it as a propelling power in place of horses. Macadam, a Scotch surveyor, had constructed a number of very superior roads made of gravel and broken stone in the South of England, which soon made the name of macadamized turnpike celebrated. The question now was, Might not a still further advance be made by employing steam to draw cars on these roads, or better still, on iron rails? George Stephenson had long been experimenting in that direction, and at length certain capitalists whom he had converted to his views succeeded in getting an act of Parliament for constructing a railway between Liverpool and Manchester, a distance of about thirty miles. When the road was completed by Stephenson, he had great difficulty in getting permission to use an engine instead of horse power on it. Finally his new locomotive, "The Rocket," — which first introduced the tubular boiler, and employed the exhaust or escaping steam to increase the draught of the fire, — was tried with entire success. The road was formally opened in the autumn of 1830, and the Duke of Wellington, then prime minister, was one of the few passengers who ventured on the trial trip.[1] The growth of this new mode of transportation was so rapid that in five years from that

---

[1] "The Rocket," together with Watt's first steam pumping engine, are both preserved in the Patent Office Museum, South Kensington, London.

The tubular boiler is, as its name implies, a boiler traversed by a number of tubes communicating with the smoke-pipe; as the heat passes through these, steam

time London and the principal seaports were connected with the great manufacturing towns, while steam navigation had also nearly doubled its vessels and its tonnage. Ten years later still, the whole country became involved in a speculative craze for building railroads. Hundreds of millions of pounds were invested; for a time Hudson, the "Railway King," as he was called, ruled supreme, and members of Parliament did homage to the man whose schemes promised to cover the whole island with a network of iron roads, every one of which was expected to make its stockholders rich. Eventually these projects ended in a panic, second only to that of the South Sea Bubble, and thousands found that steam could destroy fortunes even faster than it made them.

Toward the close of William's reign, between the years 1829 and 1834, a humble invention was perfected of which little was said at the time, but which contributed in no small degree to the comfort and convenience of every one. Up to this date the two most important of all civilizing agents — fire and light — could only be produced with much difficulty and at considerable expense. Various devices had been contrived to obtain them, but the common method continued to be the primitive one of striking a bit of flint and steel sharply together until a falling spark ignited a piece of tinder or half-burnt rag, which, when it caught, had, with no little expense of breath, to be blown into a flame. The progress of chemistry suggested the use of phosphorus, and after years of experiments the friction match was invented by an English apothecary, who thus gave to the world what is now the commonest, and perhaps at the same time the most useful domestic article in existence.

628. Summary. — William IV.'s short reign of seven years is marked (1) by the great Reform Bill of 1832, which took Parlia-

---

is thereby generated much more rapidly than it could otherwise be. The steam after it has done its work in the cylinders escapes into the smoke-pipe with great force, and of course increases the draught. Without these two improvements of Stephenson's the locomotive would never have attained a greater speed than five or six miles an hour.

ment out of the hands of a moneyed clique and put it under the control of the people; (2) by the abolition of slavery in the British colonies, and factory reform; (3) by the introduction of the friction match, and by the building of the first successful line of railway.

VICTORIA 1837.—

629. The Queen's Descent; Stability of the Government. — As William IV. left no child to inherit the crown, he was succeeded by his niece,[1] the Princess Victoria, daughter of his brother Edward, Duke of Kent. In her lineage the queen represents nearly the whole past sovereignty of the land over which she governs.[2] The blood of both Cerdic, the first Saxon king, and of William the Conqueror,[3] flows in her veins,—a fact which strikingly illustrates the vitality of the hereditary and conservative principles in the history of the English crown.

We see the full force of this when we pause to survey the ground we have passed over. Since the coming of the English to Britain a succession of important changes has taken place.

In 1066 the Normans crossed the Channel, invaded the island, conquered its inhabitants, and seized the throne. Five centuries later the religion of Rome was supplanted by the Protestant faith of Luther.

A hundred years after that event, civil war burst forth, the king was deposed and beheaded, and a republic established. A few years subsequently the monarchy was restored, only to be followed by a revolution, which changed the order of succession, drove one line of sovereigns from the land, and called in another from Germany to take their place. Meanwhile new political parties rose to power, the Reform Bill passed, and Parliament came to represent more perfectly than ever the will of the whole people; yet after all these events, at the end of more than ten centuries from the date

---

[1] See table, Paragraph No. 581.
[2] The only exceptions are the Danish sovereigns and Harold II.
[3] See Genealogical Table, page 402.

when Egbert first assumed the crown, we find England governed by a descendant of her earliest rulers!

630. A New Order of Things; the House of Commons now Supreme. — The new queen was but little over eighteen when called to the throne. At her accession a new order of things began. The Georges, with William IV., had insisted on dismissing their ministers, or chief political advisers, when they pleased, without condescending to give Parliament any reason for the change. That system, which may be considered as the last vestige of "personal government,"[1] that is, of the power of the crown to act without the advice of the nation, died with the late king.

With the coronation of Victoria the principle was established that henceforth the sovereign of the British Empire cannot remove the prime minister or his cabinet without the consent of the House of Commons elected by and directly representing the great body of the people; nor, on the other hand, would the sovereign now venture to retain a ministry which the Commons refused to support.[2]

Custom, too, has decided that the queen must give her sanction to any bill which Parliament approves and desires to make law;[3] so that if the two Houses should agree to draw up and send her own death warrant to the queen, she would be obliged to sign it, or abdicate.[4]

---

[1] See McCarthy, History of Our Own Times.

[2] So carefully does the queen guard herself against any political influence adverse to that of the ministry (and hence of the majority of the House of Commons), that the Mistress of the Robes, or head of her majesty's household, now changes with the ministry, and it is furthermore understood that any ladies under her whose presence might be politically inconvenient to the premier shall retire "of their own accord." In other words, the in-coming ministry have the right to remodel the queen's household — or any other body of offices — in whatever degree they think requisite, and the late Prince Albert could not even appoint his own private secretary, but much to his chagrin had to accept one appointed for him by the prime minister. See May's Constitutional History of England, and Martin's Life of the Prince Consort, vol. 5.

[3] Queen Anne was the last sovereign who vetoed a bill. That was in 1707. During the hundred and eighty years which have followed no English sovereign has ventured to repeat the experiment.

[4] See Bagehot, The English Constitution.

Thus the queen's real position to-day is that of a person who has much indirect influence and but little direct power — far less in fact than that of the President of the United States, who can exercise the right of vetoing a bill, thus preventing a majority of Congress from enacting a law;[1] and may remove the lower class of office-holders at pleasure.

631. Sketch of the Peerage. — A change equally great has taken place with respect to the peers.[2] As that body has played a most important part in the government of England and still retains considerable influence, it may be well to consider their history and present condition. It will be remembered that the peerage originated with the Norman conquest. William rewarded the barons, or chief men, who fought under him at Hastings,[3] with grants of immense estates, which were given on two conditions, one of military service at the call of the sovereign,[4] the other their attendance at the royal council,[5] an advisory and legislative body, which contained the germ of the present parliamentary system. It will thus be seen that the Conqueror made the possession of landed property directly dependent on the discharge of public duties. So that if on the one hand the conquest carried out the principle

>"That they should take who have the power,
>And they should keep who can,"[6]

on the other, it insisted on the higher principle that in return for such *taking* and *keeping* the victors should bind themselves by oath both to defend and to govern the state.

---

[1] Congress may, however, pass a law over the President's veto, providing they can get a two-thirds vote in its favor.

[2] Peers (from the Latin *pares*, equals). The word first occurs in an act of Parliament, 1322, — "Pares et proceres regni Angliæ spirituales et temporales."

[3] The names of the great barons have been preserved in Domesday Book (see Paragraph No. 169), in the roll of Battle Abbey (though that was tampered with by the monks), and on the wall of the twelfth century church at Dives, Normandy, where the Conqueror built his ships.

[4] See Paragraph No. 200.

[5] See Paragraph No. 200.

[6] Wordsworth, Rob Roy's Grave.

In later reigns the king summoned other influential men to attend Parliament, who, to distinguish them from the original barons by land-tenure, were called "barons by writ";[1] and subsequently it became customary for the sovereign to create barons by letters-patent, as is the method at present.[2]

The original baronage continued predominant until the Wars of the Roses[3] so nearly destroyed the ancient nobility, that, as Lord Beaconsfield, says, "A Norman baron was almost as rare a being in England then as a wolf is now."[4] With the coming in of the Tudors a new nobility was created.[5] Even this has become in great measure extinct, and of those who now sit in the House of Lords perhaps not more than a fourth can trace their titles further back than the Georges, who created great numbers of peers in return for political services either rendered or expected.

Politically speaking, the nobility of England, unlike the old nobility of France, is as a rule strictly confined to the male head of the family. None of the children of the most powerful duke or lord have during his life any civil or legal rights or privileges above that of the poorest and obscurest peasant in Great Britain.[6] They are simply commoners. But by courtesy, the eldest son of a nobleman usually receives a part of his father's title, and at his death he enters into possession of his estate[7] and rank, and takes his seat in the House of Lords, having in many cases been a member of the House of Commons by election for a number of years before. The younger sons inherit neither hereditary title, political power, nor landed property, but quite generally obtain offices in the civil service, or positions in the army or the church.

---

[1] See Paragraph No. 315. [2] See Paragraph No. 315. [3] See Paragraph No. 368.
[4] Beaconsfield's Coningsby.   [5] See Paragraph No. 404.
[6] Even the younger children of the sovereign are no exception to this rule. The only one born with a title is the eldest, who is Duke of Cornwall by birth, and is created Prince of Wales. The others are simply commoners. See Freeman's Growth of the English Constitution.

[7] So strictly is property entailed, that there are proprietors of large estates, who cannot so much as cut down a tree without permission of the heir. Badeau's English Aristocracy.

The whole number of peers is, in round numbers, about five hundred.[1] They may be said to own most of the land of England. Their average incomes are estimated at £22,000 ($110,000), or an aggregate of £11,000,000 ($55,000,000), an amount certainly not greater, if indeed it equals, the combined incomes of half a dozen leading American capitalists.

One of the most remarkable things about the peerage in modern times is the fact that its ranks have been constantly recruited from the people ; and just as any boy in America feels himself a possible senator or president, so any one born or naturalized in England may like Pitt, Disraeli, Churchill, Nelson, Wellesley, Brougham, Tennyson, Macaulay, or the American Lord Lyndhurst,[2] hope to win and wear a coronet; for brains and character go to the front in England just as surely as they do elsewhere.

In their legislative action the peers are, with very rare exceptions, ultra conservative. They have seldom granted their assent to any liberal measure except from pressure of the most unmistakable kind. It is for their interest to keep things as they are, and hence they fight against every tendency to give the people a larger measure of power. They opposed the Habeas Corpus Act under Charles II., the Great Reform Bill of 1832, the Education Bill of 1834, the admission of the Jews to Parliament, the repeal of the Corn Laws, and the later extensions of the franchise; but, on the other hand, it was their influence which compelled John to sign Magna Carta ; it was one of their number — Simon de Montfort, Earl of Leicester — who called the House of Commons into being ; and it was the lords as leaders who inaugurated the Revolution of 1688, and established constitutional sovereignty under William and Mary in the place of the arbitrary and despotic self-will of James II.

It is the fashion with impatient radicals to style the Lords "titled obstructionists," privileged to block the way to all improvements ;

---

[1] About four hundred and seventy-five temporal peers and twenty-five spiritual peers (archbishops and bishops).
[2] J. S. Copley, son of the famous artist, (Lord Lyndhurst,) born in Boston, 1772.

but as a matter of fact they have often done the country good service by checking hurried and ill-considered legislation; and though the time may perhaps be not very far distant when a hereditary House of Lords will cease to exist, yet there will always be need in England, as in every other civilized country, of an upper legislative house, composed of men whose motto is to "make haste slowly."

Meanwhile, though England continues to lay strong emphasis on nobility of rank and blood, yet she is never forgetful of the honor due to nobility of character. Perhaps it is the consciousness of this fact which in recent times has led men like Mr. Gladstone to decline a title, content, as not a few of the descendants of the old Saxon families are, with the influence won by an unsullied name and a long and illustrious career. Eight hundred years ago the House of Lords was the only legislative and executive body in the country; now, nearly all the business is done in the House of Commons, and not a penny of money can be voted for any purpose whatever except the Commons first propose it. Thus taxation, the most important of all measures, has passed from the peers to the direct representatives of the people.[1]

632. The Queen's Marriage. — In 1840 the queen, then in her twenty-first year, married her cousin, Prince Albert of Saxe Coburg

---

[1] Other measures may originate in either House, but practically nearly all begin with the Commons, though they require the assent of the Lords to become law. This, however, is now never refused for any great length of time in any important matter in which the people are interested.

The following points are also of interest:—

1. All laws relating to the rights of peers must originate in the House of Lords. Estate and naturalization laws also begin in the Lords.
2. A law directly affecting the House of Commons originates in that House.
3. There is one bill only which the crown has the right of initiating—an Act of General Pardon.

When a bill has passed both Houses, it receives the royal assent in the following words (a form which probably originated with the Norman kings): "La reigne le veult" ("The queen wills it so"); when, in the past, the royal assent was refused, the denial was expressed thus: "La reigne s'avisera" ("The queen will consider it").

The House of Lords is the Supreme Court of Appeal in the kingdom; and it is the tribunal by which persons impeached by the House of Commons are tried.

Gotha, a duchy of Central Germany.[1] The prince was about her own age, of fine personal appearance, and had just graduated from one of the German universities. He was particularly interested in art and education, and throughout his life used his influence to raise the standard of both.

633. Sir Rowland Hill's Postal Reforms. — The same year Sir Rowland Hill introduced a uniform system of cheap postage, by which rates were reduced to a penny for a single letter to any part of the United Kingdom.[3] Since then cheap telegrams and the transportation of parcels by mail (a kind of government express known as parcel-post) have followed, — all, improvements of immense practical benefit.

634. Rise of the Chartists. — The feeling attending the passage of the Reform Bill of 1832 had passed away; but now a

---

[1] **Income of the Queen and Royal Family.** — Up to the accession of George III. the royal income was derived from two sources: 1. Taxation; 2. The rents and profits of the crown lands. George III. surrendered his right to these lands in return for a fixed income granted by Parliament. Since then, every sovereign has done the same. The queen's income is £385,000 ($1,863,400, calling the pound $4.84). The royal family receive in addition, £156,000 ($755,040), or a total of £541,000 ($2,618,440).

The English sovereign has at present the following powers, all of which are *practically* vested in the ministry: —

1. The power of summoning, proroguing (suspending the action of), and dissolving Parliament at pleasure.
2. Of refusing assent to any bill (obsolete).
3. Of making peace, declaring war, and making treaties.
4. Of pardoning convicted offenders; of coining money.
5. Of creating peers, appointing archbishops and bishops, and in general granting all titles of rank and honor.
6. Of the supreme command of the army and navy. The appointment to all offices in the gift of the government, which was formerly in the hands of the sovereign, is now under the control of the prime minister, acting in connection with the civil-service and other commissions.

[3] The postage even within the limits of England proper had been as high as a shilling (twenty-five cents). A poor woman, who wished to hear regularly from her brother, but who could not afford to pay this sum, hit on an ingenious plan for doing so without expense to either side. Sir Rowland Hill happened to learn of it, and was so struck by the circumstance that he at once set to work to devise a reform which should make it possible for the poorest to send and receive letters. See McCarthy's Epoch of Reform, 1830–1850.

popular agitation began, which produced even greater excitement. Although the new law had equalized parliamentary representation and had enlarged the franchise to a very considerable degree, yet the great body of workingmen were still unable to vote. A radical party now arose, which undertook to secure further measures of reform. They embodied their measures in a document called the "People's Charter," which demanded, (1) Universal male suffrage; (2) That the voting at elections should be by ballot; (3) Annual Parliaments; (4) The payment of members of Parliament; (5) The abolition of the property qualification for parliamentary candidates;[1] (6) The division of the whole country into equal electoral districts. The Chartists, as the advocates of these measures called themselves, held public meetings, organized clubs, and published newspapers to disseminate their principles; but for many years little visible progress was made by them. In 1848 the French revolution which dethroned King Louis Philippe imparted fresh impetus to the Chartist movement. The leader of it was Feargus O'Connor. He now formed the plan of sending a monster petition to Parliament, containing, it was claimed, nearly five million signatures, praying for the passage of the charter. It was furthermore arranged that a procession of a million or more of signers should act as an escort to the document, which made a wagon-load in itself. The government became alarmed at the threatened demonstration, and forbade it, on the ground that it was an attempt to coerce legislation. In order that peace might be preserved in London, 250,000 special policemen were sworn in, among whom, it is said, was Louis Napoleon, then a refugee in England.

The Duke of Wellington took command of a large body of

---

[1] Property Qualification: In 1711 an act was passed requiring candidates for election to the House of Commons to have an income of not less than three hundred pounds derived from landed property. The object of this law was to secure members who would be comparatively free from the temptation of receiving bribes from the crown, and also to keep the landed proprietors in power to the exclusion of rich merchants. This law was repealed in 1858.

troops held in reserve to defend the city; and the Bank of England, the Houses of Parliament, the British Museum, and other public buildings were made ready to withstand a siege.

It was now the Chartists' turn to be frightened. When they assembled on Kennington Common they numbered less than 30,000; the procession of a million which was to march across Westminster bridge dwindled to half a dozen; and the huge petition when unrolled and examined was found to contain only about a third of the boasted number of names. Further examination caused still greater shrinkage, for it was discovered that many of the signatures were spurious, having been put down in jest, or copied from grave-stones and old London directories. With that discovery the whole movement collapsed, and the House of Commons rang with "inextinguishable laughter" over the national scare.

Still the demands of the Chartists had a solid foundation of good sense, which not even the blustering braggadocio of the leaders of the movement could wholly destroy. The reforms asked for were needed, and since then they have been in great part accomplished by the steady, quiet influence of reason and of time.

The printed or written ballot has been substituted for the old method of electing candidates by a show of hands or by shouting yes or no — a method by which it was easy to make blunders, and equally easy to commit frauds. The property qualification has been abolished, so that the poorest day-laborer may now run for Parliament. The right of "manhood suffrage" has been, as we shall see, greatly extended, and before the century closes, it is safe to say that every man in England will have a voice in the elections.

635. The Corn Laws. — At the accession of the queen protective duties or taxes existed in Great Britain on all imported breadstuffs and on many manufactured articles. Sir Robert Peel, who became prime minister in 1841, favored a reduction in the last class of duties, but believed it necessary to maintain the former in order to keep up the price of grain and thus encourage the English farmers. The result of this mistaken policy was great distress among workingmen, who could not afford out of their miserable wages to pay high prices for bread. A number of philanthropists led by Richard Cobden and John Bright organized an Anti-Corn Law League[1] to obtain the repeal of the grain duties.

On the other hand, Ebenezer Elliott, the "Corn Law Rhymer," as he was popularly called, gave voice to the sufferings of the poor in rude but vigorous verse, which appealed to the excited feelings of thousands in such words as these: —

> "England! what for mine and me,
> What hath bread-tax done for thee?
> * * * *
> Cursed thy harvests, cursed thy land,
> Hunger-stung thy skill'd right hand."

When, however, session after session of Parliament passed and nothing was done for the relief of the perishing multitudes, many were in despair, and at meetings held to discuss measures, crowds joined in singing Elliott's new national anthem: —

> "When wilt Thou save the people?
> O God of mercy! when?
> Not kings and lords, but nations!
> Not thrones and crowns, but men!
> Flowers of thy heart, O God, are they!
> Let them not pass, like weeds, away!
> Their heritage a sunless day!
> God save the people!"

Still the government was not convinced; the corn laws were enforced, and the situation grew daily more desperate and more threatening.

636. The Irish Famine; Repeal of the Corn Laws; Free Trade. — At last the Irish famine opened the premier's eyes.

---

[1] Corn is the name given in England to wheat or other grain used for food. Indian corn, called maize, is seldom eaten.

When in Elizabeth's reign, Sir Walter Raleigh introduced the cheap but precarious potato into Ireland, his motive was one of pure good will. He could not foresee that it would in time become in that country an almost universal food, that through its very abundance the population would rapidly increase, and that then by the sudden failure of the crop terrible destitution would ensue. Such was the case in the summer of 1845. It is said by eye-witnesses that in a single night the entire potato crop was destroyed by blight, and that the healthy plants were transformed into a mass of putrefying vegetation. Thus at one fell stroke the food of nearly a whole nation was cut off.[1]

In the years that followed, the famine became appalling. The starving peasants left their miserable huts and streamed into the towns for relief, only to die of hunger in the streets.

Parliament responded nobly to the piteous calls for help, and voted in all no less than $50,000,000 to relieve the distress.[2] Subscriptions were also taken up in London and the chief towns by which large sums were obtained, and America contributed ship-loads of provisions and a good deal of money; but the misery was so great that even these measures failed to accomplish what was hoped, and when the famine was over, and its results came to be estimated, it was found that Ireland had lost about 2,000,000 (or one-fourth) of her population.[3] This was the combined effect of starvation, of the various diseases that followed in its path, and of emigration.[4] In the face of such appalling facts, and of the bad harvests and distress in England, the prime minister could hold out no longer, and by a gradual process, extending from 1846 to 1849, the obnoxious corn laws were gradually repealed with the exception of a trifling duty, which was finally removed in 1869.

---

[1] O'Connor, The Parnell Movement (The Famine).
[2] Molesworth's History of England from 1830, Vol. II.
[3] The actual number of deaths from starvation, or fever caused by insufficient food, was estimated at from 200,000 to 300,000. See Encyclopædia Britannica, "Ireland."
[4] McCarthy, History of Our Own Times, vol. I.

The beginning once made, free trade in nearly everything, except wine, spirits, and tobacco, followed. They were, and still are, subject to a heavy duty, perhaps because the government believes, as Napoleon did, that the vices have broad backs and can comfortably carry the heaviest taxes. But, by a singular contrast, while nearly all goods and products now enter England free, yet Australia and several other colonies continue to impose duties on imports from the mother country.

637. The World's Fair; Repeal of the Window and the Newspaper Tax; the Atlantic Cable. — In 1851 the great industrial exhibition known as the "World's Fair" was opened in Hyde Park, London. The original plan of it was conceived by Prince Albert; and it proved to be not only a complete success in itself, but it led to many similar fairs on the part of different nations. For the first time in history, the products and inventions of all countries on the globe were brought together under one roof, in a gigantic structure of glass and iron called the "Crystal Palace," which is still in use for exhibition purposes at Sydenham, a suburb of London.

The same year, the barbarous tax on light and air, known as the "Window Tax," was repealed; and from that date the Englishman, whether in London or out, might enjoy his sunshine, — when he could get it, — without having to pay for every beam: a luxury, which only the rich could afford. A little later, a stamp tax on newspapers, which had been devised in Queen Anne's time in the avowed hope of crushing them out, was repealed; and the result was that henceforth the workingman, as he sat by his fireside, could inform himself of what the world was doing and thinking, — two things of which he had before known almost nothing, and cared, perhaps, even less.

To get this news of the world's life more speedily, the first Atlantic cable, connecting England with America, was laid in 1858. Since then, a large part of the globe has been joined in like manner; and all the great cities of every civilized land are practically one in their knowledge of events. So many improvements have also been made in the use of electricity, not only for the transmission of intelligence, but as an illuminator, and more recently still as a motive power, that it now seems probable that "the age of steam" is soon to be superseded by the higher "age of electricity."

638. The Opium War; the War in the Crimea; the Rebellion in India. — Up to 1854 no wars occurred in this reign worthy of mention, with the exception of that with China in 1839. At that time the Chinese emperor, either from a desire to put a stop to the consumption of opium in his dominions, or because he wished to encourage the home production of the drug,[1] prohibited its importation. As the English in India were largely engaged in the production of opium for the Chinese market, — the people of that country smoking it instead of tobacco, — the British government insisted that the emperor should not interfere with so lucrative a trade. War ensued. The Chinese, being unable to contend against English gunboats, were soon forced to withdraw their prohibition of the foreign opium traffic; and the English government, with the planters of India, reaped a golden reward of many millions for their deliberate violation of the rights of a heathen and half-civilized people. The war opened five important ports to British trade, and subsequent wars opened a number more on the rivers in the interior.

In 1853 Turkey declared war against Russia. The latter power had insisted on protecting all Christians in the Turkish dominions against the oppression of the sultan. England and France considered the czar's championship of the Christians as a mere pretext for occupying Turkish territory. To prevent this

---

[1] By far the greater part of the opium consumed in China is now raised, either with or without the full consent of the government, by the Chinese themselves. The probability is that before many years the home production will supply the entire demand, and thus exclude importations of the drug from India. It is estimated that about one hundred millions of the population of China are addicted to opium-smoking.

aggression they formed an alliance with the sultan, which resulted in the Russo-Turkish war, and ended by the taking of Sebastopol by the allied forces. Russia was obliged to retract her demands; and peace was declared in the spring of 1856.

The following year was memorable for the outbreak of the Sepoy rebellion in India. The real cause of the revolt was probably a long-smothered feeling of resentment on the part of the Sepoy, or native, troops against English rule, — a feeling that dates back to the extortion and misgovernment of Warren Hastings. The immediate cause of the uprising was the introduction of an improved rifle using a greased cartridge, which had to be bitten off before being rammed down. To the Hindoo the fat of cattle or swine is an abomination; and his religion forbids his tasting it. An attempt on the part of the government to enforce the use of the new cartridge brought on a general mutiny. During the revolt, the native troops perpetrated the most horrible atrocities on the English women and children who fell into their hands. When the insurrection was finally quelled under Havelock and Campbell, the English soldiers retaliated by binding numbers of prisoners to the mouths of cannon and blowing them to shreds. At the close of the rebellion, the government of India was wholly transferred to the crown; and in 1876 the queen received the title of Empress of India.

639. Death of Prince Albert; the American Civil War. — Late in 1861 the prince consort died suddenly. In him the nation lost an earnest promoter of social, educational, and industrial reforms; and the United States, a true and judicious friend, who at a most critical period in the Civil War used his influence to maintain peace between the two countries.

Since his death the queen has held no court; and so complete has been her seclusion that in 1868 a radical member of Parliament moved that her majesty be invited to abdicate or choose a regent. The motion was indignantly rejected; but it revealed the feeling which quite generally exists, that "the real queen died with her husband, and that only her shadow remains."

In the spring of the year (1861) in which Prince Albert died, civil war broke out between the Northern and Southern States of the American Union. A few weeks later, the queen issued a proclamation declaring her "determination to maintain a strict and impartial neutrality in the contest between the said contending parties." The rights of belligerents — in other words, all the rights of war according to the law of nations — were granted to the South equally with the North; and her majesty's subjects were warned against aiding either side in the conflict.

The progress of the war caused terrible distress in Lancashire, owing to the cutting-off of supplies of cotton for the mills through the blockade of the ports of the Confederate States. The starving weavers, however, gave their moral support to the North, and continued steadfast to the cause of the Union even in the sorest period of their suffering. The great majority of the manufacturers and business classes generally, the Liverpool merchants, the nobility, with a few exceptions, and most of the distinguished political and social leaders, in Parliament and out, with nearly all the influential journals, sympathized with the efforts of the South to establish an independent confederacy.[1] Late in the autumn of 1861 Captain Wilkes, of the United States Navy, boarded the British mail-steamer *Trent*, and seized Messrs. Mason and Slidell, Confederate commissioners, on their way to England. When intelligence of the act was conveyed to President Lincoln, he expressed his unqualified disapproval of it, saying: "This is the very thing the British captains used to do. They claimed the right of searching

---

[1] Lord John Russell (Foreign Secretary), Lord Brougham, Sir John Bowring, Carlyle, Ruskin, the London *Times* and *Punch*, espoused the cause of the South more or less openly; while others, like Mr. Gladstone, declared their full belief in the ultimate success of the Confederacy.

On the other hand, Prince Albert, John Bright, John Stuart Mill, Professor Newman, and the London *Daily News* defended the cause of the North.

After the death of President Lincoln, *Punch* manfully acknowledged (see issue of May 6, 1865), that it had been altogether wrong in its estimate of him and his measures; and Mr. Gladstone, in his "Kin beyond Sea" in "Gleanings of Past Years," paid a noble tribute to the course pursued by America since the close of the war.

American ships, and carrying men out of them. That was the cause of the War of 1812. Now, we cannot abandon our own principles; we shall have to give up these men, and apologize for what we have done."

Accordingly, on a demand made by the British government,— a demand which, through the influence of the prince consort, and with the approval of the queen, was couched in most conciliatory language,— the commissioners were given up, and an apology made by Secretary Seward.

During the progress of the war, a number of fast-sailing vessels were fitted out in Great Britain, and employed in running the blockade of the Southern ports, for the purpose of supplying them with arms, ammunition, and manufactured goods of various kinds. Later, several gunboats were built in British shipyards by agents of the Confederate government, for the purpose of attacking the commerce of the United States. The most famous of these privateers was the *Alabama*, built expressly for the Confederate service by Laird, of Liverpool, armed with British cannon, and manned chiefly by British sailors. Though notified of her true character, Lord Palmerston, then prime minister, allowed her to leave port, satisfied with the pretext that she was going on a trial trip.[1] She set sail on her career of destruction, and soon drove nearly every American merchant vessel from the seas. In the summer of 1864 she was defeated and sunk by the United States gunboat *Kearsarge*. After the war the government of the United States demanded damages from Great Britain for losses caused by the *Alabama* and other English-built privateers. A treaty was agreed to by the two nations; and by its provisions an international court was held at Geneva, Switzerland, which awarded $15,500,000 in gold as compensation to the United States, which was duly paid. The most important result of this treaty and tribunal was that they established a precedent

---

[1] The queen's advocate gave his opinion that the *Alabama* should be detained; but it reached the Foreign Secretary (Lord Russell) just after she had put to sea.

for settling by arbitration on equitable and amicable terms whatever questions might arise in future between the two nations.¹

640. The Second Reform Bill; Woman Suffrage; Admission of Jews to Parliament. — Excellent as was the Reform Bill of 1832,² many thoughtful men felt that it did not go far enough. There was also great need of municipal reform, since in many cities the tax-payers had no voice in the management of local affairs, and the city officers spent the income of large charitable funds in feasting and merry-making while the poor got little or nothing. In 1835 a law was passed giving tax-payers in such cities³ control of municipal elections. By a subsequent amendment, the ballot in such cases was extended to women,⁴ and for the first time perhaps in modern history woman suffrage was formally granted by supreme legislative act. A number of years later, the political restrictions imposed on the Jews were removed. Up to this time (1858) this class of citizens, though very wealthy and influential in London and some other cities, and although entitled to vote and hold municipal office, were yet debarred from Parliament by a law which required them to make oath "on the faith of a Christian." This law was now so modified that Baron Rothschild took his seat among the legislators of the country.⁵

In 1867 Mr. Disraeli (afterward Earl of Beaconsfield), the leader of the Tory, or Conservative, party, brought in a second Reform Bill, which became a law. This provided what is called "household suffrage," or, in other words, gave the right to vote to

---

¹ This treaty imposed duties on neutral governments of a far more stringent sort than Great Britain had hitherto been willing to concede. It resulted, furthermore, in the passage of an act of Parliament, punishing with severe penalties such illegal ship-building as that of the *Alabama*. See Sheldon Amos, Fifty Years of the English Constitution, 1830-1880.

² See Paragraph No. 625.

³ This municipal act did not include the city of London.

⁴ Woman suffrage was granted to single women and widows (householders) in 1869. In 1870 an act was passed enabling them to vote at school-board elections, and also to become members of such boards.

⁵ See Macaulay's Essays, "Civil Disabilities of the Jews."

every householder in all the towns of the kingdom who paid a tax for the support of the poor, and to all lodgers paying a rental of £10 ($50) yearly; it also increased the number of voters among small property-holders in counties.

There still, however, remained a large class in the country districts for whom nothing had been done. The men who tilled the soil were miserably poor and miserably ignorant. Joseph Arch, a Warwickshire farm laborer, who had been educated by hunger and toil, succeeded in establishing a national union among men of his class, of which he became president, and eventually, mainly through his efforts, they secured the ballot. Since then, under the Liberal ministry of Mr. Gladstone, a third Reform Bill has been passed,[1] which went into operation in 1886, by which all residents of counties throughout the United Kingdom have the right to vote on the same condition as those of towns.

It is estimated that this law added about two and a half millions of voters, and that there is now one voter to every six persons of the total population, whereas, before the passing of the first Reform Bill (1832), there was not over one in fifty. In the first "People's Parliament," in 1886, Joseph Arch, and several others, were returned as representatives of classes of the population who, up to that date, had had no voice in the legislation of the country. One step more, and a short one, and Great Britain, like America, will have universal "manhood suffrage."

641. Abolition of Compulsory Church Rates; Disestablishment of the Irish Episcopal Church; the Education Act.—While these reforms were taking place with respect to elections, others of great importance were also being effected. Since its establishment the Church of England had compelled all persons, of whatever belief, to pay taxes for the maintenance of the church of the parish where they resided. Methodists, Baptists, and other Dissenters, objected to this law as unjust, since in addition to the expense of supporting their own form of worship, they were obliged to contribute

---

[1] The Representation Act.

toward maintaining one with which they had no sympathy. So great had the opposition become to paying their "church rates," that in 1859 there were over fifteen hundred parishes in England in which the authorities could not collect them. After much agitation a law was finally passed abolishing this mode of tax, and making the payment of rates purely voluntary.[1] A similar act of justice was soon after granted to Ireland.[2] At the time of the union of the two countries in 1800,[3] the maintenance of the Protestant Episcopal Church continued to remain obligatory upon the Irish people, although only a very small part of them were of that faith. Mr. Gladstone's law disestablishing this branch of the national church left all religious denominations in Ireland to the voluntary support of those who belonged to them, so that henceforth the English resident in that country can no longer claim the privilege of worshipping God at the expense of his Roman Catholic neighbor.

In 1870 a system of common schools was established throughout the kingdom under the direction of a government board, and hence popularly known as "Board Schools." Up to this date most of the children of the poor had been educated in schools maintained by the Church of England, the various dissenting denominations, and by charitable associations, or such endowments as those of Edward VI.[4] It was found, however, that more than half of the children of the country were not reached by these institutions, but were growing up in such a state of dense ignorance, that in the agricultural districts a large proportion could neither read nor write. By the "Board Schools" elementary unsectarian instruction is made compulsory, and though not wholly free, it is so nearly so that it is brought within the means of the poorest. A year later the universities and colleges, with most of the offices

---

[1] Church rates were levied on all occupiers of land or houses within the parish. They were abolished in 1868. The Church of England is now mainly supported by a tax on landowners, and by its endowments.

[2] The Disestablishment Bill was passed in 1869, and took effect in 1871.

[3] See Paragraph No. 609.   [4] See Paragraph No. 417.

and professorships connected with them, were thrown open to all persons without regard to religious belief; whereas, formerly, no one could graduate from Oxford or Cambridge without subscribing to the doctrines of the Church of England.

642. The First Irish Land Act. — The same year (1870) that the government undertook to provide for the education of the masses, Mr. Gladstone, then prime minister and head of the Liberal party, brought in a bill for the relief of the Irish peasantry. The circumstances under which land was held in Ireland were peculiar. A very large part — in fact about all the best of that island — was, and still is, owned by Englishmen whose ancestors obtained it through the wholesale confiscations of Cromwell, James I., and later sovereigns, in punishment for rebellion. Very few English landlords have cared to live in the country or to do anything for its improvement. Their overseers believed they did their whole duty when they forced the farm tenants to pay the largest amount of rent that could be wrung from them, and they had it in their power to dispossess a tenant of his land whenever they saw fit, without giving a reason for the act. If by his labor the tenant made the land more fertile, he reaped no profit from his industry, for the rent was at once increased, and swallowed up all that he raised. Such a system of extortion was destructive to the peasant farmer, and produced nothing for him but misery and discontent. The new law endeavored to remedy these evils by providing that if a landlord ejected a rent-paying tenant, he should pay him damages, and also allow him a fair sum for whatever improvements he had made. In addition, provision was made for a ready means of arbitration between landlord and tenant, and the tenant who failed to pay an exorbitant rate was not to be hastily or unjustly driven from the land.

643. Distress in Ireland; the Land League. — It was hoped by the friends of the measure that the new law would be productive of relief; but from 1876 to 1879 the potato crop failed in Ireland, and the country seemed threatened with a famine like that of 1845. Thousands who could not get the means to pay even a moderate rent, much less the amounts demanded, were now forced to leave their cabins and seek shelter in the bogs, with the prospect of dying there of starvation. This state of things led a number of influential Irishmen to form a Land League, which had for its object the abolition of the present landlord system, and the securing of such legislation as should eventually result in giving the Irish peasantry possession of the soil they cultivated.

Later, the League came to have a membership of several hundred thousand persons, extending over the greater part of Ireland. Finding that it was difficult to get parliamentary help for their grievances, the League resolved to try a different kind of tactics. Accordingly they formed a compact not to work for, buy from, sell to, or have any intercourse with, such landlords, or their agents, or with any other person, who extorted exorbitant rent, ejected tenants unable to pay, or took possession of land from which tenants had been unjustly driven. This process of social excommunication was first tried on an English agent, or overseer, named Boycott, and soon became famous under the name of "boycotting." As the struggle went on, many of the suffering poor became desperate. Farm buildings, belonging to landlords and their agents, were burned, cattle horribly mutilated, and a number of the agents shot. At the same time the cry rose of No Rent, Death to the Landlords! Hundreds of tenants now refused to pay for the places they held, and even attacked those who did. Eventually the lawlessness of the country provoked the government to take severe measures; the Land League, which was believed to be responsible for the refusal to pay rent, and for the accompanying outrages, was suppressed; but the feeling which gave rise to it could not be extinguished, and it soon burst forth more violently than ever.

644. The Second Irish Land Act; Fenian and Communist Outrages. — In 1881 Mr. Gladstone succeeded in carrying through a second land law, which it was hoped might be more effective in relieving the Irish peasants than the first had been. This measure is familiarly known as the "Three F's,"— Fair-rent, Fixity-of-tenure, and Free-sale. By the provisions of this act the tenant may appeal to a board of land commissioners appointed by the law to fix the rate of his rent in case the demands made by the landlord seem to him excessive. Next, he can continue to hold his farm, provided he pays the rate determined on, for a period of fifteen years, during which time the rent cannot be raised nor the tenant evicted except for violation of agreement or persistent neglect or waste of the land; lastly, he may sell his tenancy when he sees fit to the highest bidder.

After the passage of this second Land Act, Lord Frederick Cavendish, chief secretary of Ireland, and Mr. Burke, a prominent government official, were murdered in Phœnix Park, Dublin. Later, members of various secret and communistic societies perpetrated dynamite outrages in London and other parts of England for the purpose of intimidating the government. These dastardly plots for destruction and murder have been denounced with horror by the leaders of the Irish National Party, who declare that "the cause of Ireland is not to be served by the knife of the assassin or the infernal machine." Notwithstanding the vindictive feeling which these rash acts have caused, despite also of the passage of the coercion bill of 1887, the majority of the more intelligent and thoughtful of the Irish people have faith that the logic of events will ultimately obtain for them the full enjoyment of those political rights which England so fully possesses, and which she cannot, without being false to herself, deny to her sister-island.

645. The Leading Names in Science, Literature, and Art. — In the progress of science the present age has had no equal in the past history of England, except in the discovery of the law of gravitation by Sir Isaac Newton. That great thinker demonstrated that all forms of matter, great or small, near or distant, are governed by one universal law. In like manner the researches of the past fifty years have virtually established the belief that all material forms, whether living or not, obey an equally universal law of development, by which the higher are derived from the lower through a succession of gradual but progressive changes.

This conception originated long before the beginning of the Victorian era, but it lacked the acknowledged support of carefully examined facts, and was regarded by most sensible men as a plausible but untenable idea. The thinker who did more than any other to supply the facts, and to put the theory, so far as it relates to natural history, on a solid and lasting foundation, was the distinguished English naturalist, Charles Darwin,[1] who died in 1882, and found an honored resting-place in Westminster Abbey, near the graves of the well-known geologist, Sir Charles Lyell, and Livingstone, the African explorer.

On his return in 1837 from a voyage of scientific discovery round the world, he began to examine and classify the facts which he had collected, and continued to collect, relating to natural history. After twenty-two years of uninterrupted labor he published a work ("The Origin of Species") in 1859 in which he showed that animal life owes its course of development to the struggle for existence and "the survival of the fittest." Darwin's work may truthfully be said to have wrought a revolution in the study of nature as great as that accomplished by Newton in the seventeenth century. Though calling forth the most heated and prolonged discussion, the Darwinian theory has gradually made its way, and is now generally received, though sometimes in a modified form, by nearly every eminent man of science throughout the world. A little later than the date at which Mr. Darwin began his researches, Sir William Grove, an eminent electrician, commenced a series of experiments which have led to a great change in our conceptions of matter and force. He showed that heat, light, and electricity are mutually convertible; that they must be regarded as

---

[1] Alfred Russell Wallace, also noted as a naturalist, worked out the theory of evolution by "natural selection" about the same time, though not so fully with respect to details, as Darwin: as each of these investigators arrived at his conclusions independently of the other, the theory was thus doubly confirmed.

modes of motion; and, finally, that all force is persistent and indestructible,[1] thus proving, as Professor Tyndall says, that "To nature, nothing can be added; from nature, nothing can be taken away." Together, these, with kindred discoveries, have resulted in the theory of evolution, or development, which Herbert Spencer and others have endeavored to make the basis of a system of philosophy embracing the whole field of nature and life.

In literature so many names of note are found that the mere enumeration of them would be impracticable here. It will be sufficient to mention the novelists, Dickens, Thackeray, Brontë, and "George Eliot"; the historians, Hallam, Arnold, Grote, Macaulay, Alison, Buckle, Froude, and Freeman; the essayists, Carlyle, Landor, and De Quincey; the poets, Browning and Tennyson; the philosophical writers, Hamilton, Mill, and Spencer; with Lyell, Faraday, Carpenter, Tyndall, Huxley, and Wallace in science; the eminent art-critic and writer on political economy, John Ruskin; and in addition, the chief artists of the period, Millais, Rossetti, Burne-Jones, Watts, and Hunt.

646. Progress in England.—The legislation of the last twenty-five years offers abundant evidence that Macaulay was right when he declared that "the history of England is the history of a great and progressive nation." Merely to read the records of the statute-book during that time would convince any person not hopelessly prejudiced that no people of Europe have made greater advancement than the people of Great Britain. Nor has this progress been confined to political reform. On the contrary, it is found in every department of thought and action. Since the beginning of the century, and, in fact, to a great degree since the accession of the present queen, the systems of law and judicature have been in large measure reconstructed.[2] This is especially evident in the

---

[1] An Essay on the Correlation of Physical Forces, by W. R. Grove.

[2] Twenty-five years ago the Parliamentary Statutes filled forty-four huge folio volumes, and the Common Law, as contained in judicial decisions dating from the time of Edward II., filled about twelve hundred more. The work of examining, digesting, and consolidating this enormous mass of legal lore was begun in 1863, and is still in progress.

Court of Chancery[1] and the criminal courts. In 1825 the property belonging to suitors in the former court amounted to nearly two hundred millions of dollars.[2] The simplest case required a dozen years for its settlement, while difficult ones consumed a lifetime, or more, and were handed down from father to son — a legacy of baffled hopes, of increasing expense, of mental suffering worse than that of hereditary disease. Much has been done to remedy these evils, which Dickens set forth with such power in his novel, "Bleak House," and which at one time seemed so utterly hopeless that it was customary for a prize-fighter, when he had got his opponent wholly at his mercy, to declare that he had his head "in chancery"!

In criminal courts an equal reform has taken place, and men accused of burglary and murder are now allowed to have counsel to defend them; whereas, up to the era of the coronation of Victoria, they were obliged to plead their own cases as best they might against skilled public prosecutors, who used every resource known to the law to convict them.

Great changes for the better have also taken place in the treatment of the insane. Until near the close of the last century, this unfortunate class was quite generally regarded as possessed by demons, and dealt with accordingly. In 1792 William Tuke, a member of the Society of Friends, inaugurated a better system; but the old method continued for many years longer. In fact, we have the highest authority for saying, that down to a late period in the present century the inmates of many asylums were worse off than the most desperate criminals. They were shut up in dark, and often filthy, cells, where "they were chained to the wall, flogged, starved, and not infrequently killed."[3] Since then, all mechanical restraint has been abolished, and the patients are, as a rule, treated with the care and kindness which their condition demands.

---

[1] See Paragraph No. 195.
[2] See Walpole's History of England, Vol. III.
[3] Encyclopædia Britannica, 9th ed., "Insanity."

Immense improvement has likewise been made in the social condition of the people. Not only has the average wealth of the country greatly increased, but deposits in savings banks prove that the workingmen are laying away large sums which were formerly spent in drink. Statistics show[1] that crime, drunkenness, and pauperism have materially diminished. On the other hand, free libraries, reading-rooms, and art-galleries have been opened in all the large towns. Liverpool is no longer "that black spot on the Mersey" which its cellar population of 40,000, and its hideous slums, with a population of nearly 70,000 more, once made it. Sanitary regulations, with house-to-house inspection, have done away with filth and disease, which were formerly accepted as a matter of course, and new safeguards now protect the health and life of classes of the population who were once simply miserable outcasts. Hospitals and charitable associations, with bands of trained nurses, provide for the sick and suffering poor. Prison discipline has ceased to be the terrible thing it was when Charles Reade wrote "Never too Late to Mend," and the convict in his cell no longer feels that he is utterly helpless and friendless.

It is no exaggeration to say that the best men and the best minds in England, without distinction of rank or class, are now laboring for the advancement of the people. They see, what has never been so clearly seen before, that the nation is a unit, that the welfare of each depends ultimately on the welfare of all, and that the higher a man stands, and the greater his wealth and privileges, so much the more is he bound to extend a helping hand to those less favored than himself. Undoubtedly the weak point in England is the fact that a few thousand of her population own all the land which thirty millions live upon,[2] and here lies the great danger of the future. Yet aside from that hot-headed socialism which insists alike on the abolition of rank and of private property in land, there has thus far been little disposition to violent action. England, by nature conservative, is slow to break the bond of historic

---

[1] See Ward, Reign of Queen Victoria.   [2] See Statistics, page 409.

No. 15.

THE BRITISH EMPIRE AT THE PRESENT TIME.

To face page 382.

continuity which connects her present with her past. "Do you think we shall ever have a second revolution?" the Duke of Wellington was once asked. "We may," answered the great general, "but if we do, it will come by act of Parliament." That reply probably expresses the general temper of the people, who believe that they can gain by the ballot more than they can by an appeal to force, knowing that theirs is —

> "A land of settled government,
> A land of just and old renown,
> Where freedom broadens slowly down,
> From precedent to precedent." [1]

647. General Summary of the Rise of the English People. — Such is the condition of England near the close of the nineteenth century, in the jubilee year of the Victorian era.[2] If we pause now and look back to the time when the island of Britain first became inhabited, we shall see the successive steps which have transformed a few thousand barbarians into a great and powerful empire.[3]

1. Judging from the remains of their flint implements and weapons, we have every reason to suppose that the original population of Britain was in no respect superior to the American Indians that Columbus found in the New World. They had the equality which everywhere prevails among savages, where all are alike ignorant, alike poor, and alike miserable. The tribal unity which bound them together in hostile clans resembled that found among a pack of wolves or a herd of buffalo — it was instinctive rather than intelligent, and sprang from necessity rather

---

[1] Tennyson's "You ask me why."

[2] The queen celebrated her jubilee year on the 21st of June, 1887, by services held in Westminster Abbey. It is to be regretted that the occasion could not also have been celebrated by the beginning of some national work for the welfare of the people, such as might have given her majesty an opportunity to commemorate her long and prosperous reign in the glad remembrance of thousands of grateful hearts.

[3] See Map No. 14, page 382.

than from independent choice. Gradually these tribes learned to make tools and weapons of bronze, and to some extent even of iron; then they ceased the wandering life of men who live by hunting and fishing, and began to cultivate the soil, raise herds of cattle, and live in rudely fortified towns. Such was their condition when Cæsar invaded the island, and when the power of Roman armies and Roman civilization reduced the aborigines to a state but little better than that of the most abject slavery. When, after several centuries of occupation, the Roman power was withdrawn, we find that the race they had subjugated had gained nothing from their conquerors, but that, on the other hand, they had lost much of their native courage and man hood.

2. With the Saxon invasion the true history of the country may be said to begin. The fierce blue-eyed German race living on the shores of the Baltic and of the North Sea, brought with them a love of liberty and a power to defend it which even the Romans in their continental campaigns had not been able to subdue. They laid the foundations of a new nation; their speech, their laws, their customs, became permanent, and by them the Britain of the Celts and the Romans was baptized with that name of England which it has ever since retained.

3. Five hundred years later came the Norman Conquest. By it the Saxons were temporarily brought into subjection to a people who, though they spoke a different language, sprang originally from the same Germanic stock as themselves.

This conquest introduced higher elements of civilization, the life of England was to a certain extent united with the broader and more cultivated life of the continent, and the feudal or military tenure of the land, which had begun among the Saxons, was fully organized and developed. At the same time the king became the real head of the government, which before was practically in the hands of the nobles, who threatened to split it up into a self-destructive anarchy.

The most striking feature of this period was the fact that political liberty depended wholly on the possession of the soil. The landless man was a slave or a serf; in either case, so far as the state was concerned, his rank was simply zero. Above him there was, properly speaking, no English people; that is, no great body of inhabitants united by common descent, by participation in the government, by common interests, by pride of nationality and love of country. On the contrary, there were only classes separated by strongly marked lines — ranks of clergy, or ranks of nobles, with their dependents. Those who owned and ruled the country were Normans, speaking a different tongue from those below, and looking upon them with that contempt with which the victor regards the vanquished, while those below returned the feeling with sullen hate and fear.

4. The rise of the people was obscure and gradual. It began in the conflicts between the barons and the crown. In those contests both parties needed the help of the working classes. To get it each side made haste to grant some privilege to those whose assistance they required. Next, the foreign wars had no small influence, since friendly relations naturally sprang up between those who fought side by side, and the Saxon yeoman and the Norman knight henceforth felt that England was their common home, and that in her cause they must forget differences of rank and blood.

It was, however, in the provisions of the Great Charter that the people first gained legal recognition. When the barons forced King John to issue that document, they found it expedient to protect the rights of all. For that reason, the great nobles and the clergy made common cause with peasants, tradesmen, and serfs. Finally, the rise of the free cities secured to their inhabitants many of the privileges of self-government, while the Wat Tyler insurrection of a later period led eventually to the emancipation of that numerous class which was bound to the soil.

5. But the real unity of the people first showed itself unmistakably in consequence of a new system of taxation, levied on persons of small property as well as on the wealthy landholders. The moment the government laid hands on the tradesman's and the laborer's pockets, they demanded to have a share in legislation.

Out of that demand sprang the House of Commons, a body, as its name implies, made up of representatives chosen mainly from the people and by the people.

The great contest now was for the power to levy taxes — if the king could do it he might take the subject's money when he pleased; if Parliament alone had the control in this matter, then it would be as they pleased. Little by little not only did Parliament obtain the coveted power, but that part of Parliament which directly represented the people got it, and it was finally settled that no tax could be demanded save by their vote. This victory, however, was not gained except by a long and bitter conflict, in which sometimes one and sometimes the other of the contestants got the best of it, and in which also Jack Cade's insurrection in behalf of free elections had its full influence. But though temporarily beaten, the people never quite gave up the struggle; thus "the murmuring Parliament of Mary became the grumbling Parliament of Elizabeth, and finally the rebellious and victorious Parliament of Charles I.," when the executioner's axe settled the question who was to rule, set up a short-lived but vigorous republic.

6. Meanwhile a great change had taken place in the condition of the aristocracy. The wars of the Roses had destroyed the power of the Norman barons, and the Tudors — especially Henry VIII. by his action in suppressing the monasteries, and granting the lands to his favorites — virtually created a new aristocracy, many of whom sprang from the ranks of the people.

Under Cromwell, the republic practically became a monarchy, — though Cromwell was at heart no monarchist; all power was in the hands of the Army, with the Protector at its head. After the restoration of the monarchy, the government of the country was carried on mainly by the two great political parties, the Whigs and the Tories, representing the Cavaliers and Roundheads, or the aristocratic and people's parties of the civil war. With the flight of James II., the passage of the Bill of Rights and the Act of Settlement, Parliament set aside the regular hereditary order of succession, and established a new order, in which the sovereign was made dependent on the people for his right to rule. Next, the Mutiny Bill put the power of the army practically into the hands of Parliament, which already held full control of the purse. The Toleration Act granted liberty of worship, and the abolition of the censorship of the press gave freedom to expression. With the coming in of George I., the king ceased to appoint his cabinet, leaving its formation to his prime minister. Hereafter the cabinet no longer met with the king, and the executive functions of the government were conducted, to a constantly increasing extent, without his taking any active part in them. Still, though the people through Parliament claimed to rule, yet the great landholders, and especially the Whig nobility, held the chief power; the sovereign, it is true, no longer tried to govern in spite of Parliament, but by controlling elections and legislation he managed to govern through it.

7. With the invention of the steam-engine, and the growth of great manufacturing towns in the central and northern counties of England, many thousands of the population were left without representation. Their demands to have this inequality righted resulted in the Reform Bill of 1832, which broke up in great measure the political monopoly hitherto enjoyed by the landholders and aristocracy, and distributed the power among the middle classes. The accession of Queen Victoria established the principle that the cabinet should be held directly responsible to the majority of the House of Commons, and that they should not be appointed contrary to the wish, or dismissed contrary to the consent, of that majority. By the Reform Bills of 1867 and 1884, the suffrage has been greatly extended, so that, practically, the centre of political gravity which was formerly among the wealthy and privileged classes, and which passed from them to the manufacturing and mercantile population, has shifted to the working classes, who now possess the balance of power in England almost as completely as they do in America. Thus we see that by gradual steps those who once had few or no rights, have come

to be the masters; and though England continues to be a monarchy in name, yet it is well-nigh a republic in fact.

In feudal times the motto of knighthood was *Noblesse oblige* — or, nobility of rank demands nobility of character. To-day the motto of every free nation should be, Liberty is Responsibility, for henceforth both in England and America the people who govern are bound, by their own history and their own declared principles, to use their opportunities to govern well.

The danger of the past lay in the tyranny of the minority, that of the present is the tyranny of the majority. The great problem of our time is to learn how to reconcile the interests of each with the welfare of all. To do that, whether on an island or on a continent, in England or America, is to build up the kingdom of justice and good will upon the earth.

648. Characteristics of English History; the Unity of the English-Speaking Race; Conclusion. — This rapid and imperfect sketch shows what has been accomplished by the people of Britain. Other European peoples may have developed earlier, and made perhaps more rapid advances in certain forms of civilization, but none have surpassed, nay, none have equalled, the English-speaking race in the practical character and permanence of their progress. Guizot says[1] the true order of national development in free government is, first, to convert the natural liberties of man into clearly defined political rights; and, next, to guarantee the security of those rights by the establishment of forces capable of maintaining them. Nowhere do we find better illustrations of this law of progress than in the history of England, and of the colonies which England has planted. Trial by jury,[2] the legal right to resist oppression,[3] legislative representation,[4] religious freedom,[5] and, finally, the principle that all political power is a trust held for the public good[6] — these are the assured results of Anglo-

---

[1] Guizot's History of Representative Government, Lecture VI.
[2] See Paragraph No. 227.   [3] See Paragraph No. 313.
[4] See Paragraph No. 265.   [5] See Paragraph No. 548, and note 2.
[6] See Macaulay's Essay on Walpole.

Saxon growth, and the legitimate heritage of every nation of Anglo-Saxon descent.

Here, in America, we sometimes lose sight of what those have done for us who occupied the world before we came into it. We forget that English history is in a very large degree our history, and that England is, as Hawthorne liked to call it, "our old home." In fact, if we go back less than three centuries, the record of America becomes one with that of the mother country, which first discovered[1] and first permanently settled this, and which gave us for leaders and educators Washington, Franklin, the Adamses, and John Harvard. In descent, by far the greater part of us are of English blood;[2] while in language, literature, law, legislative forms of government, and the essential features of civilization, we all owe to England a greater debt than to any other country; and without a knowledge of her history we cannot rightly understand our own. Standing on her soil we possess practically the same personal rights that we do here; we speak the same tongue, we meet with the same familiar names. We feel that whatever is glorious in her past is ours also; that Westminster Abbey belongs as much to us as to her, for our ancestors helped to build its walls, and their dust is gathered in its tombs; that Shakespeare and Milton belong to us in like manner, for they wrote in the language we speak, for the instruction and delight of our fathers' fathers, who beat back the Spanish Armada, and gave their lives for liberty on the fields of Marston Moor and Naseby.

Let it be granted that grave issues have arisen in the past to separate us; yet, after all, our interests and our sympathies, like

---

[1] See Paragraphs No. 387 and No. 473.

[2] In 1840 the population of the United States, in round numbers, was 17,000,000, of whom the greater part were probably of English descent. Since then there has been an enormous immigration, forty per cent of which was from the British Islands; but it is perhaps safe to say that three-quarters of our present population of 60,000,000 are those who were living here in 1840, with their descendants. Of the immigrants coming from non-English-speaking races, the Germans predominate, and it is to them, as we have seen, that the English owe their origin, they being in fact but a modification of the Teutonic race.

our national histories, have more in common than they have apart. The progress of each country now reacts for good on the other. If we consider the total combined population of the United States and of the British Empire, we find that to-day upwards of one hundred millions of people speak the English tongue, and are governed by the fundamental principles of English constitutional law. They hold possession of over twelve millions of square miles of the earth's surface — an area nearly equal to the united continents of North America and Europe. By far the greater part of the wealth and power of the globe is theirs. They have expanded by their territorial and colonial growth as no other people have. They have absorbed and assimilated the millions of emigrants from every race and of every tongue which have poured into their dominions. The result is, that the inhabitants of the British islands, of Australia, New Zealand, the United States and Canada, practically form one great Anglo-Saxon race, diverse in origin, separated by distance, but everywhere exhibiting the same spirit of intelligent enterprise and of steady, resistless growth. Thus considered, America and England are necessary one to the other. Their interests now and in the future are essentially the same.

In view of these facts let us say, with an eminent thinker,[1] whose intellectual home is on both sides the Atlantic, "Whatever there be between the two nations to forget and forgive, is forgotten and forgiven. If the two peoples, which are one, be true to their duty, who can doubt that the destinies of the world are in their hands?"

---

[1] Archdeacon Farrar, Address on General Grant, Westminster Abbey, 1885.

GENERAL SUMMARY OF ENGLISH CONSTITUTIONAL HISTORY.[1]

1. Origin and Primitive Government of the English People. — The main body of the English people did not originate in Britain, but in Northwestern Germany. The Jutes, Saxons, and Angles were independent, kindred tribes living on the banks of the Elbe and its vicinity.

They had no written laws, but obeyed time-honored customs which had all the force of laws. All matters of public importance were decided by each tribe at meetings held in the open air. There every freeman had an equal voice in the decision. There the people chose their rulers and military leaders; they discussed questions of peace and war; finally, acting as a high court of justice, they tried criminals and settled disputes about property.

In these rude methods we see the beginning of the English Constitution. Its growth has been the slow work of centuries, but the great principles underlying it have never changed. At every stage of their progress the English people and their descendants throughout the globe have claimed the right of self-government; and, if we except the period of the Norman Conquest, whenever that right has been persistently withheld or denied the people have risen in arms and regained it.

2. Conquest of Britain; Origin and Power of the King. — After the Romans abandoned Britain the English invaded the island, and in the course of a hundred and fifty years (449-600) conquered it and established a number of rival settlements. The native Britons were, in great part, killed off or driven to take refuge in Wales and Cornwall.

The conquerors brought to their new home the methods of government and modes of life to which they had been accustomed in Germany. A cluster of towns — that is, a small number of enclosed [2] habitations — formed a hundred (a district having either a hundred families or able to furnish a hundred warriors); a cluster of hundreds formed a shire or county. Each of these divisions had its public meeting, composed of all its freemen or their representatives, for the management of its own affairs. But a state of war — for the English tribes fought each other as well as fought the Britons — made a strong central government necessary. For this reason the leader of each tribe was made king. At first he was chosen, at large, by the entire tribe; later, unless there was some good reason for a different choice, the king's eldest son was selected as his successor. Thus the right to rule was practically fixed in the line of a certain family descent.

The ruler of each of these petty kingdoms was (1) the commander-in-chief in war; (2) he was the supreme judge.

---

[1] This Summary is inserted for the benefit of those who desire a compact, connected view of the development of the English Constitution, such as may be conveniently used either for reference, for a general review of the subject, or for purposes of special study. — D. H. M.

For authorities, see Stubbs (449-1485); Hallam (1485-1760); May (1760-1870); Amos (1870-1880); see also Hansard's and Cobbett's Parliamentary History, the works of Freeman, Taswell-Langmead (the best one-volume Constitutional History), Feilden (as a convenient reference-book this manual has no equal), and Ransome, in the List of Books on page 404.

The references at the bottom of the page are to the body of the History unless otherwise stated.

[2] See page 56, Paragraph 139.

3. The Witenagemot, or General Council. — In all other respects the king's authority was limited — except when he was strong enough to get his own way — by the Witenagemot, or General Council. This body consisted of the chief men of each kingdom acting in behalf of its people.[1] It exercised the following powers: (1) it elected the king, and if the people confirmed the choice, he was crowned. (2) If the king proved unsatisfactory, the council might depose him and choose a successor. (3) The king, with the consent of the council, made the laws — that is, he declared the customs of the tribe. (4) The king, with the council, appointed the chief officers of the kingdom (after the introduction of Christianity this included the bishops); but the king alone appointed the sheriff, to represent him, and collect the revenue in each shire. (5) The council confirmed or denied grants of portions of the public lands made by the king to private persons. (6) The council acted as the high court of justice, the king sitting as supreme judge. (7) The council, with the king, discussed all questions of importance — such as the levying of taxes, the making of treaties; smaller matters were left to the towns, hundreds, and shires to settle for themselves. After the consolidation of the different English kingdoms into one, the Witenagemot expanded into the National Council. In it we see "the true beginning of the Parliament of England."

4. How England became a United Kingdom; Influence of the Church and of the Danish Invasions. — For a number of centuries Britain consisted of a number of little rival kingdoms, almost constantly at war with each other. Meanwhile missionaries from Rome had introduced Christianity (597). Through the influence of Theodore of Tarsus, archbishop of Canterbury (668), the clergy of the different hostile kingdoms met in general Church councils.[2] This religious unity of action prepared the way for political unity. The Catholic Church — the only Christian Church then existing — made men feel that their highest interests were one; it "created the nation."

This was the first cause of the union of the kingdoms. The second was the invasions of the Danes. These fierce marauders forced the people south of the Thames to join in common defence, under the leadership of Alfred, king of the West Saxons. By the treaty of Wedmore (878), the Danes were compelled to give up Southwestern England, but they retained the whole of the Northeast. About the middle of the tenth century, one of Alfred's grandsons conquered the Danes, and took the title of "King of all England."[3] Later, the Danes, reinforced by fresh invasions of their countrymen, made themselves masters of the land; yet Canute, the most powerful of these Danish kings, ruled according to English methods. At length the great body of the people

---

[1] The Witenagemot, says Stubbs (*Select Charters*), represented the people, although it was not a collection of representatives.
[2] This movement began several years earlier, — see page 38, — but Theodore of Tarsus was its first great organizer.
[3] Some authorities consider Edgar (959) as the first "King of all England." In 828 Egbert, King of the West Saxons, once, though but once, took the lesser title of "King of the English." See page 39.

united in choosing Edward the Confessor king (1042-1066). He was English by birth, but Norman by education. Under him the unity of the English kingdom was, in name at least, fully restored.

5. Beginning of the Feudal System; its Results. — Meantime a great change had taken place in England with respect to holding land. We shall see clearly to what that change was tending if we look at the condition of France. There a system of government and of land tenure existed known as the Feudal System. Under it the king was regarded as the owner of the entire realm. He granted, with his royal protection, the use of portions of the land to his chief men or nobles, with the privilege of building castles and of establishing private courts of justice on these estates. Such grants were made on two conditions: (1) that the tenants should take part in the king's council; (2) that they should do military service in the king's behalf, and furnish besides a certain number of fully armed horsemen in proportion to the amount of land they had received. So long as they fulfilled these conditions — made under oath — they could retain their estates, and hand them down to their children; but if they failed to keep their oath, they forfeited the land to the king.

These great military barons or lords let out parts of their immense manors,[1] or estates, on similar conditions — namely, (1) that their vassals or tenants should pay rent to them by doing military or other service; and (2) that they should agree that all questions concerning their rights and duties should be tried in the lord's private court.[2] On the other hand, the lord of the manor pledged himself to protect his vassals.

On every manor there were usually three classes of these tenants: (1) those who discharged their rent by doing military duty; (2) those who paid by a certain fixed amount of labor — or, if they preferred, in produce or in money; (3) the villeins, or common laborers, who were bound to remain on the estate and work for the lord, and whose condition, although they were not wholly destitute of legal rights, was practically not very much above that of slaves.

But there was another way by which men might enter the Feudal System; for while it was growing up there were many small free landholders, who owned their farms, and owed no man any service whatever. In those times of constant civil war such men would be in almost daily peril of losing, not only their property, but their lives. To escape this danger, they would hasten to "commend" themselves to some powerful neighboring lord. To do this, they pledged themselves to become "his men," surrendered their farms to him, and received them

---

[1] Manor: — see Plan of a Manor on page 80 — (Old French *manoir*, a mansion), the estate of a feudal lord. Every manor had two courts. The most important of these was the "*court baron*." It was composed of all the free tenants of the manor, with the lord (or his representative) presiding. It dealt with civil cases only. The second court was the "*court customary*," which dealt with cases connected with villeinage. The manors held by the greater barons had a third court, the "*court leet*," which dealt with criminal cases, and could inflict the death penalty. In all cases the decisions of the manorial courts would be pretty sure to be in the lord's favor. In England, however, these courts never acquired the degree of power which they did on the continent.

[2] See Note above, on the Manor.

again as feudal vassals. That is, the lord bound himself to protect them against their enemies, and they bound themselves to do "suit and service"[1] like the other tenants of the manor; *for "suit and service" on the one side, and "protection" on the other, made up the threefold foundation of the Feudal System.*

Thus in time all classes of society became bound together. At the top stood the king, who was no man's tenant, but, in name at least, every man's master; at the bottom crouched the villein, who was no man's master, but was, in fact, the most servile and helpless of tenants.

Such was the condition of things in France. In England, however, this system of land tenure was never completely established until after the Norman Conquest (1066). For in England the tie which bound men to the king and to each other was originally one of pure choice, and had nothing directly to do with land. Gradually, however, this changed; and by the time of Edward the Confessor land in England had come to be held on conditions so closely resembling those of France that one step more — and that a very short one — would have made England a kingdom exhibiting all the most dangerous features of French feudalism.

For, notwithstanding certain advantages,[2] feudalism had this great evil: that the chief nobles often became in time more powerful than the king. This danger now menaced England. For convenience Canute the Dane had divided the realm into four earldoms. The holders of these vast estates had grown so mighty that they scorned royal authority. Edward the Confessor did not dare resist them. The ambition of each earl was to get the supreme mastery. This threatened to bring on civil war, and to split the kingdom into fragments. Fortunately for the welfare of the nation, William of Normandy, by his invasion and conquest of England (1066), put an effectual stop to the selfish schemes of these four rival nobles.

6. **William the Conqueror and his Work.** — After William's victory at Hastings and march on London, the National Council chose him sovereign, — they would not have dared to refuse, — and he was crowned by the archbishop of York in Westminster Abbey. This coronation made him the legal successor of the line of English kings. In form, therefore, there was no break in the order of government; for though William had forced himself upon the throne, he had done so according to law and custom, and not directly by the sword.

Great changes followed the conquest, but they were not violent. The king abolished the four great earldoms, and restored national unity. He gradually dispossessed the chief English landholders of their lands, and bestowed them, under strict feudal laws, on his Norman followers. He likewise gave all the highest positions in the Church to Norman bishops and abbots. The National Council now changed its character. It became simply a body of Norman barons, who were

---

[1] That is, they pledged themselves to do suit in the lord's private court, and to do service in his army.
[2] On the Advantages of Feudalism, see page 51.

bound by feudal custom to meet with the king. But they did not restrain his authority; for William would brook no interference with his will from any one, not even from the Pope himself.

But though the Conqueror had a tyrant's power, he rarely used it like a tyrant. We have seen[1] that the great excellence of the early English government lay in the fact that the towns, hundreds, and shires were self-governing in all local matters; the drawback to this system was its lack of unity and of a strong central power that could make itself respected and obeyed. William supplied this power, — without which there could be no true national strength, — yet at the same time he was careful to encourage the local system of self-government. He gave London a liberal charter to protect its rights and liberties. He began the organization of a royal court of justice; he checked the rapacious Norman barons in their efforts to get control of the people's courts.

Furthermore, side by side with the feudal cavalry army, he maintained the old English county militia of foot-soldiers, in which every freeman was bound to serve. He used this militia, when necessary, to prevent the barons from getting the upperhand, and so destroying those liberties which were protected by the crown as its own best safeguard against the plots of the nobles.

Next, William had a census, survey, and valuation made of all the estates in the kingdom outside London which were worth examination. The result of this great work was recorded in Domesday Book. By means of that book — still preserved — the king knew what no English ruler had known before him; that was, the property-holding population and resources of the kingdom. Thus a solid foundation was laid on which to establish the feudal revenue and the military power of the crown.

Finally, just before his death, the Conqueror completed the organization of his government. Hitherto the vassals of the great barons had been bound to them alone. They were sworn to fight for their masters, even if those masters rose in open rebellion against the sovereign. William changed all that. At a meeting held at Salisbury (1086) he compelled every landholder in England, from the greatest to the smallest, — 60,000, it is said, — to swear to be "faithful to him against all others." By that oath he "broke the neck of the Feudal System" *as a form of government*, though he retained and developed the principle of feudal land tenure. Thus at one stroke he made the crown the supreme power in England; had he not done so, the nation would soon have been a prey to civil war.

7. **William's Norman Successors.** — William Rufus has a bad name in history, and he fully deserves it. But he had this merit: he held the Norman barons in check with a stiff hand, and so, in one way, gave the country comparative peace.

His successor, Henry I., granted (1100) a charter of liberties[2] to his

---

[1] See Paragraphs 2, 3, of this Summary.
[2] For Henry I.'s charter, see Note 1, on page 73.

people, by which he recognized the sacredness of the old English laws for the protection of life and property. Somewhat more than a century later this document became, as we shall see, the basis of the most celebrated charter known in English history. Henry attempted important reforms in the administration of the laws, and laid the foundation of that system which his grandson, Henry II., was to develop and establish. By these measures he gained the title of the "Lion of Justice," who "made peace for both man and beast." Furthermore, in an important controversy with the Pope respecting the appointment of bishops,[1] Henry obtained the right (1107) to require that both bishops and abbots, after taking possession of their Church estates, should be obliged like the barons to furnish troops for the defence of the kingdom.

But in the next reign — that of Stephen — the barons got the upper hand, and the king was powerless to control them. They built castles without royal license, and from these private fortresses they sallied forth to ravage, rob, and murder in all directions. Had that period of terror continued much longer, England would have been torn to pieces by a multitude of greedy tyrants.

8. Reforms of Henry II.; Scutage; Assize of Clarendon; Juries; Institutions of Clarendon. — With Henry II. the true reign of law begins. To carry out the reforms begun by his grandfather, Henry I., the king fought both barons and clergy. Over the first he won a complete and final victory; over the second he gained a partial one.

Henry began his work by pulling down the unlicensed castles built by the "robber barons." But, according to feudal usage, the king was dependent on these very barons for his cavalry — his chief armed force. He resolved to make himself independent of their reluctant aid. To do this he offered to release them from military service, providing they would pay a tax, called scutage, or shield-money (1159).[2] The barons gladly accepted the offer. With the money Henry was able to hire "mercenaries," or foreign troops, to fight for him abroad, and, if need be, in England as well. Thus he struck a great blow at the power of the barons, since they, through disuse of arms, grew weaker, while the king grew steadily stronger. To complete the work, Henry, many years later (1181), reorganized the old English national militia,[3] and made it thoroughly effective for the defence of the royal authority. For just a hundred years (1074-1174) the barons had been trying to overthrow the government; under Henry II. the long struggle came to an end, and the royal power triumphed.

But in getting the military control of the kingdom, Henry had won only half of the victory he was seeking; to complete his supremacy

---

[1] See page 73, Paragraph 186.
[2] Scutage (see page 89): the demand for scutage seems to show that the feudal tenure was now fully organized, and that the whole realm was by this time divided into knights' fees, — that is, into portions of land yielding £20 annually, — each of which was obliged to furnish one fully armed, well-mounted knight to serve the King (if called on) for forty days annually.
[3] National militia: see page 50, Paragraph 121.

over the powerful nobles, the king must obtain control of the administration of justice.

In order to do this more effectually, Henry issued the Assize of Clarendon (1166). It was the first true national code of law ever put forth by an English king, since previous codes had been little more than summaries of old "customs." The realm had already been divided into six circuits, having three judges for each circuit. The Assize of Clarendon gave these judges power not only to enter and preside over every county court, but also over every court held by a baron on his manor. This put a pretty decisive check to the hitherto uncontrolled baronial system of justice — or injustice — with its private dungeons and its private gibbets. It brought everything under the eye of the king's judges, so that those who wished to appeal to them could now do so without the expense, trouble, and danger of a journey to the royal palace.

Again, it had been the practice among the Norman barons to settle disputes about land by the barbarous method of trial by battle;[1] Henry gave tenants the right to have the case decided by a body of twelve knights acquainted with the facts.

In criminal cases a great change was likewise effected. Henceforth twelve men from each hundred, with four from each township, — sixteen at least, — acting as a grand jury, were to present all suspected criminals to the circuit judges.[2] The judges sent them to the ordeal;[3] if they failed to pass it, they were then punished by law as convicted felons; if they did pass it, they were banished from the kingdom as persons of evil repute. After the abolition of the ordeal (1215), a petty jury of witnesses was allowed to testify in favor of the accused, and clear them if they could from the charges brought by the grand jury. If their testimony was not decisive, more witnesses were added until twelve were obtained who could unanimously decide one way or the other. In the course of time[4] this smaller body became judges of the evidence for or against the accused, and thus the modern system of trial by jury was established.

These reforms had three important results: (1) they greatly diminished the power of the barons by taking the administration of justice, in large measure, out of their hands; (2) they established a more uniform system of law; (3) they brought large sums of money, in the way of court-fees and fines, into the king's treasury, and so made him stronger than ever.

But meanwhile Henry was carrying on a still sharper battle in his attempt to bring the Church courts — which William I. had separated from the ordinary courts — under control of the same system of justice. In these Church courts any person claiming to belong to the clergy had a right to be tried. Such courts had no power to inflict death, even

---

[1] See page 79, Paragraph 198.
[2] See the Assize of Clarendon (1166) in Stubbs's Select Charters.
[3] See page 52, Paragraph 127.
[4] Certainly by 1450. But as late as the reign of George I. juries were accustomed to bring in verdicts determined partly by their own personal knowledge of the facts. See Taswell-Langmead (revised ed.), page 179.

for murder. In Stephen's reign many notorious criminals had managed to get themselves enrolled among the clergy, and had thus escaped the hanging they deserved. Henry was determined to have all men — in the circle of clergy or out of it — stand equal before the law. Instead of two kinds of justice, he would have but one; this would not only secure a still higher uniformity of law, but it would sweep into the king's treasury many fat fees and fines which the Church courts were then getting for themselves.

By the laws entitled the Constitutions of Clarendon (1164), the common courts were empowered to decide whether a man claiming to belong to the clergy should be tried by the Church courts or not. If they granted him the privilege of a Church court trial, they kept a sharp watch on the progress of the case; if the accused was convicted, he must then be handed over to the judges of the ordinary courts, and they took especial pains to convince him of the Bible truth, that "the way of the transgressor is hard." For a time the Constitutions were rigidly enforced, but in the end Henry was forced to renounce them. Later, however, the principle he had endeavored to set up was fully established.[1]

The greatest result springing from Henry's efforts was the training of the people in public affairs, and the definitive establishment of that system of Common Law which regards the people as the supreme source of both law and government, and which is directly and vitally connected with the principle of representation and of trial by jury.[2]

9. Rise of Free Towns. — While these important changes were taking place, the towns were growing in population and wealth. But as these towns occupied land belonging either directly to the king or to some baron, they were subject to the authority of one or the other, and so possessed no real freedom. In the reign of Richard I. many towns purchased certain rights of self-government from the king. This power of controlling their own affairs greatly increased their prosperity, and in time, as we shall see, secured them a voice in the management of the affairs of the nation.

10. John's Loss of Normandy; Magna Carta. — Up to John's reign many barons continued to hold large estates in Normandy, in addition to those they had acquired in England; hence their interests were divided between the two countries. Through war John lost his French possessions. Henceforth the barons shut out from Normandy came to look upon England as their true home. From Henry II.'s reign the Normans and the English had been gradually mingling; from this time they became practically one people. John's tyranny and cruelty brought their union into sharp, decisive action. The result of his greed for money, and his defiance of all law, was a tremendous insurrection. Before this time the people had always taken the side of

---

[1] Edward I. limited the jurisdiction of the Church courts to purely spiritual cases, such as heresy and the like; but the work which he, following the example of Henry II., had undertaken, was not fully accomplished until the fifteenth century.
[2] See, on this point, Green's Henry II., in the "English Statesmen" Series.

the king against the barons; now, with equal reason, they turned about and rose with the barons against the king.

Under the guidance of Archbishop Langton, barons, clergy, and people demanded reform. The archbishop brought out the half-forgotten charter of Henry I. This now furnished a model for Magna Carta, or the "Great Charter of the Liberties of England."[1]

It contained nothing that was new in principle. It was simply a clearer, fuller, stronger statement of those "rights of Englishmen which were already old."

John, though wild with rage, did not dare refuse to affix his royal seal to the Great Charter of 1215. By doing so he solemnly guaranteed: (1) the rights of the Church; (2) those of the barons; (3) those of all freemen; (4) those of the villeins, or farm-laborers. The value of this charter to the people at large is shown by the fact that nearly one-third of its sixty-three articles were inserted in their behalf. Of these articles, the most important was that which declared that no man should be deprived of liberty or property, or injured in body or estate, save by the judgment of his equals or by the law of the land.

In regard to taxation, the Charter provided that, except the customary feudal "aids,"[2] none should be levied unless by the consent of the National Council. Finally, the Charter expressly provided that twenty-five barons — one of whom was mayor of London — should be appointed to compel the king to carry out his agreement.

11. Henry III. and the Great Charter; the Forest Charter; Provisions of Oxford; Rise of the House of Commons; Important Land Laws. — Under Henry III. the Great Charter was reissued. But the important articles which forbade the king to levy taxes except by consent of the National Council, together with some others restricting his power to increase his revenue, were dropped, and never again restored.[3]

On the other hand, Henry was obliged to issue a Forest Charter, based on certain articles of Magna Carta, which declared that no man should lose life or limb for hunting in the royal forests.

Though the Great Charter was now shorn of some of its safeguards to liberty, yet it was still so highly prized that its confirmation was purchased at a high price from successive sovereigns. Down to the second year of Henry VI.'s reign (1423), we find that it had been confirmed no less than thirty-seven times.

Notwithstanding his solemn oath,[4] the vain and worthless Henry III. deliberately violated the provisions of the Charter, in order to raise money to waste in his foolish foreign wars or on his court circle of French favorites.

Finally (1258), a body of armed barons, led by Simon de Montfort, earl of Leicester, forced the king to summon a Parliament at Oxford.

---

[1] Magna Carta: see Constitutional Documents, page 443.
[2] For the three customary Feudal Aids, see page 80, Paragraph 200.
[3] See Stubbs's Select Charters (Edward I.), page 484; but compare Note 1 on page 443.
[4] See page 112, Paragraph 262.

There a scheme of reform, called the Provisions of Oxford, was adopted. By these Provisions, which Henry swore to observe, the government was practically taken out of the king's hands, — at least as far as he had power to do mischief, — and entrusted to certain councils or committees of state.

A few years later, Henry refused to abide by the Provisions of Oxford, and civil war broke out. De Montfort, earl of Leicester, gained a decisive victory at Lewes, and captured the king. The earl then summoned a National Council, made up of those who favored his policy of reform. This was the famous Parliament of 1265. To it De Montfort summoned: (1) a small number of barons; (2) a large number of the higher clergy; (3) two knights, or country gentlemen, from each shire; (4) two burghers, or citizens, from every town.

The knights of the shire had been summoned to Parliament before;[1] but this was the first time that the towns had been invited to send representatives. By that act the earl set the example of giving the people at large a fuller share in the government than they had yet had. To De Montfort, therefore, justly belongs the glory of being "the founder of the House of Commons"; though owing, perhaps, to his death shortly afterward at the battle of Evesham (1265), the regular and continuous representation of the towns did not begin until thirty years later.

Meanwhile (1279-1290), three land laws of great importance were enacted. The first limited the acquisition of landed property by the Church;[2] the second encouraged the transmission of land by will to the eldest son, thus keeping estates together instead of breaking them up among several heirs;[3] the third made purchasers of estates the direct feudal tenants of the king.[4] The object of these three laws was to prevent landholders from evading their feudal obligations; hence they decidedly strengthened the royal power.[5]

12. Edward I.'s "Model Parliament"; Confirmation of the Charters. — In 1295, Edward I., one of the ablest men that ever sat on the English throne, adopted De Montfort's scheme of representation. The king was greatly pressed for money, and his object was to get the help of the towns, and thus secure a system of taxation which should include all classes. With the significant words, "that which toucheth all should be approved by all," he summoned to Westminster the first really complete, or "Model Parliament,"[6] consisting of King, Lords

---

[1] They were first summoned by John, in 1213.
[2] Statute of Mortmain (1279): see page 120, Paragraph 278. It was especially directed against the acquisition of land by monasteries.
[3] Statute De Donis Conditionalibus (or of Westminster II.) (1285): see page 119, Paragraph 277.
[4] Statute of Quia Emptores (1290): see page 119, Paragraph 277.
[5] During the same period the Statute of Winchester (1285) reorganized the national militia and the police system. See page 119, Paragraph 276.
[6] De Montfort's Parliament was not wholly lawful and regular, because not voluntarily summoned by the King himself. Parliament must be summoned by the sovereign, opened by the sovereign (in person or by commission); all laws require the sovereign's signature to complete them; and finally, Parliament can be suspended or dissolved by the sovereign only.

CONSTITUTIONAL SUMMARY. 401

(temporal and spiritual), and Commons.[1] The form Parliament then received it has kept substantially ever since. We shall see how from this time the Commons gradually grew in influence, — though with periods of relapse, — until at length they have become the controlling power in legislation.

Ten years after the meeting of the "Model Parliament," in order to get money to carry on a war with France, Edward levied a tax on the barons, and seized a large quantity of wool belonging to the merchants. So determined was the resistance to these acts that civil war was threatened. In order to avert it, the king was obliged to summon a Parliament (1297), and to sign a confirmation of both the Great Charter and the Forest Charter. He furthermore bound himself in the most solemn manner not to tax his subjects or seize their goods without their consent. Henceforth Parliament alone was considered to hold control of the nation's purse; and although this principle was afterward evaded, no king openly denied its binding force.

13. **Division of Parliament into Two Houses; Growth of the Power of the Commons; Legislation by Statute; Impeachment; Power over the Purse.** — In Edward's reign a great change occurred in Parliament. The knights of the shire (about 1343)[2] joined the representatives from the towns, and began to sit apart from the Lords as a distinct House of Commons. This union gave that house a new character, and invested it with a power in Parliament which the representation from the towns alone could not have exerted. But though thus strengthened, the Commons did not venture to claim an equal part with the Lords in framing laws. Their attitude was that of humble petitioners. When they had voted the supplies of money which the king asked for, the Commons might then meekly beg for legislation. Even when the king and the lords assented to their petitions, the Commons often found to their disappointment that the laws which had been promised did not correspond to those for which they had asked. Henry V. pledged his word (1414) that the petitions, when accepted, should be made into laws without any alteration. But, as a matter of fact, this was not effectually done until near the close of the reign of Henry VI. (about 1461).[3] Then the Commons succeeded in obtaining the right to present proposed laws in the form of regular bills instead of petitions. These bills when enacted became statutes or acts of Parliament, as we know them to-day. This change was a most important one, since it made it impossible for the king with the lords to fraudulently defeat the expressed will of the Commons after they had once assented to the legislation the Commons desired.

Meanwhile the Commons gained, for the first time (1376), the right of impeaching such ministers of the crown as they had reason to believe

---
[1] The lower clergy were summoned to send representatives; but their representatives came very irregularly, and in the fourteenth century ceased coming altogether. From that time they voted their supplies for the Crown in Convocation, until 1663, when Convocation ceased to meet. The higher clergy — bishops and abbots — met with the House of Lords.
[2] The exact date cannot be determined. Sir T. E. May thinks it was about 1343.
[3] Exact date cannot be determined.

were unfaithful to the interests of the people. This of course put an immense restraining power in their hands, since they could now make the ministers responsible, in great measure, for the king.[1]

Next (1406), the Commons insisted on having an account rendered of the money spent by the king; and at times they even limited[2] their appropriations of money to particular purposes. Finally, in 1407, the Commons took the most decided step of all. They boldly demanded and obtained *the exclusive right of making all grants of money* required by the crown.[3]

In future the king — unless he violated the law — had to look to the Commons — that is, to the direct representation of the mass of the people — for his chief supplies. This made the will of the Commons more powerful than it had ever been.

14. Religious Legislation; Emancipation of the Villeins; Disfranchisement of County Electors. — While these reforms were taking place, two statutes had been enacted, — that of Provisors (1350)[4] and of Præmunire (1353 and 1393),[5] — limiting the power of the Pope over the English Church. On the other hand, the rise of the Lollards had caused a statute to be passed (1401) against heretics, and under it the first martyr had been burned in England. During this period the villeins had risen in insurrection (1381), and were gradually gaining their liberty. Thus a very large body of people who had been practically excluded from political rights now began to slowly acquire them.[6] But, on the other hand, a statute was enacted (1430) which prohibited all persons having an income of less than forty shillings a year — or what would be equal to forty pounds at the present value of money — from voting for knights of the shire. The consequence was that the poorer and humbler classes in the country were no longer directly represented in the House of Commons.

15. Wars of the Roses; Decline of Parliament; Partial Revival of its Power under Elizabeth. — The Civil Wars of the Roses (1455-1485) gave a decided check to the further development of parliamentary power. Many noble families were ruined by the protracted struggle, and the new nobles created by the king were pledged to uphold the interests of the crown. Furthermore, numerous towns absorbed in their own local affairs ceased to elect members to the Commons. Thus, with a House of Lords on the side of royal authority, and with a House of Commons diminished in numbers and in influence, the decline of the independent attitude of Parliament was inevitable.

---

[1] But after 1450 the Commons ceased to exercise the right of impeachment until 1621, when they impeached Lord Bacon and others.
[2] The Commons dropped the right of appropriating money for specific objects, — except in a single instance under Henry VI., — and did not revive it until 1624.
[3] This right the Commons never surrendered.
[4] Provisors: this was a law forbidding the Pope to provide any person (by a..ticipation) with a position in the English Church until the death of the incumbent.
[5] Præmunire: see Constitutional Documents, page 446. Practically, neither the law of Provisors nor of Præmunire was strictly enforced until Henry VIII.'s reign.
[6] Villeins appear, however, to have had the right of voting for knights of the shire until the statute of 1430 disfranchised them.

The result of these changes was very marked. From the reign of Henry VI. to that of Elizabeth — a period of about two hundred years — "the voice of Parliament was rarely heard." The Tudors practically set up a new or "personal monarchy," in which their will rose above both Parliament and the constitution;[1] and Henry VII., instead of asking the Commons for money, extorted it in fines enforced by his Court of Star Chamber, or compelled his wealthy subjects to grant it to him in "benevolences"[2] — those "loving contributions," as the king called them, "lovingly advanced."

During this period England laid claim to a new continent, and Henry VIII., repudiating the authority of the Pope, declared himself the "supreme head" (1535) of the English Catholic Church. In the next reign (Edward VI.) the Catholic worship, which had existed in England for nearly a thousand years, was abolished (1540), and the Protestant faith became henceforth — except during Mary's short reign — the established religion of the kingdom. It was enforced by two Acts of Uniformity (1549, 1552). One effect of the overthrow of Catholicism was to change the character of the House of Lords, by reducing the number of spiritual lords from a majority to a minority, as they have ever since remained.[3]

At the beginning of Elizabeth's reign the Second Act of Supremacy (1559) shut out all Catholics from the House of Commons.[4] Protestantism was fully and finally established as the state religion,[5] embodied in the creed known as the Thirty-nine Articles (1563); and by the Third Act of Uniformity (1559) very severe measures were taken against all — whether Catholics or Puritans — who refused to conform to the Episcopal mode of worship. The High Commission Court was organized (1583) to try and punish heretics — whether Catholics or Puritans. The great number of paupers caused by the destruction of the monasteries under Henry VIII., and the gradual decay of relations of feudal service, caused the passage of the first Poor Law (1601), and so brought the government face to face with a problem which has never yet been satisfactorily settled; namely, what to do with habitual paupers and tramps.

The closing part of Elizabeth's reign marks the revival of parliamentary power. The House of Commons now had many Puritan members, and they did not hesitate to assert their right to advise the queen on all questions of national importance. Elizabeth sharply rebuked them for presuming to meddle with questions of religion, or for urging her either to take a husband or to name a successor to the throne; but even she did not venture to run directly counter to the will of the people. When the Commons demanded (1601) that she should put

---

[1] Theoretically Henry VII.'s power was restrained by certain checks (see page 181, Note 1); and even Henry VIII. generally ruled according to the letter of the law, however much he may have violated its spirit. It is noticeable, too, that it was under Henry VIII. (1541) that Parliament first formally claimed freedom of speech as one of its "undoubted privileges."
[2] Benevolence: see pages 169, 182.   [3] See page 224, Note 2.   [4] See pages 211, 212.
[5] By the Third Act of Uniformity and the establishment of the High Commission Court; see page 211. The First and Second Acts of Uniformity were enacted under Edward VI.

a stop to the pernicious practice of granting trading monopolies[1] to her favorites, she was obliged to yield her assent.

16. James I.; the "Divine Right of Kings"; Struggle with Parliament. — James began his reign by declaring that kings rule not by the will of the people, but by "divine right." "God makes the king," said he, "and the king makes the law." For this reason he demanded that his proclamations should have all the force of acts of Parliament. Furthermore, since he appointed the judges, he could generally get their decisions to support him; thus he made even the courts of justice serve as instruments of his will. In his arrogance he declared that neither Parliament nor the people had any right to discuss matters of state, whether foreign or domestic, since he was resolved to reserve such questions for the royal intellect to deal with. By his religious intolerance he maddened both Puritans and Catholics, and the Pilgrim Fathers fled from England to escape his tyranny.

But there was a limit set to his overbearing conceit. When he dictated to the Commons (1604) what persons should sit in that body, they indignantly refused to submit to any interference on his part, and their refusal was so emphatic that James never brought up the matter again.

The king, however, was so determined to shut out members whom he did not like that he attempted to gain his ends by having such persons seized on charge of debt and thrown into prison. The Commons, on the other hand, not only insisted that their ancient privilege of exemption from arrest in such cases should be respected, but they passed a special law (1604) to clinch the privilege.

Ten years later (1614) James, pressed for money, called a Parliament to get supplies. He had taken precautions to get a majority of members elected who would, he hoped, vote him what he wanted. But to his dismay the Commons declined to grant him a penny unless he would promise to cease imposing illegal duties on merchandise. The king angrily refused, and dissolved the Parliament.[2]

Finally, in order to show James that it would not be trifled with, a later Parliament (1621) revived the right of impeachment, which had not been resorted to since 1450.[3] The Commons now charged Lord Chancellor Bacon, judge of the High Court of Chancery, and "keeper of the king's conscience," with accepting bribes. Bacon held the highest office in the gift of the crown, and the real object of the impeachment was to strike the king through the person of his chief official and supporter. Bacon confessed his crime, saying: "I was the justest judge that was in England these fifty years, but it was the justest censure in Parliament that was these two hundred years."

James tried his best to save his servile favorite, but it was useless, and Bacon was convicted, disgraced, and punished.

---

[1] Monopolies: see pages 214, 215.
[2] This Parliament was nicknamed the "Addled Parliament," because it did not enact a single law, though it most effectually "addled" the King's plans.
[3] See Paragraph 13 of this Summary.

The Commons of the same Parliament petitioned the king against the alleged growth of the Catholic religion in the kingdom, and especially against the proposed marriage of the Prince of Wales to a Spanish Catholic princess. James ordered the Commons to let mysteries of state alone. They claimed liberty of speech. The king asserted that they had no liberties except such as the royal power saw fit to grant. Then the Commons drew up their famous Protest, in which they declared that their liberties were not derived from the king, but were " the ancient and undoubted birthright and inheritance of the people of England." In his rage James ordered the journal of the Commons to be brought to him, tore out the Protest with his own hand, and sent five of the members of the House to prison. This rash act made the Commons more determined than ever not to yield to arbitrary power. James died three years later, leaving his unfortunate son Charles to settle the angry controversy he had raised.

17. Charles I.; Forced Loans; the Petition of Right. — Charles I. came to the throne full of his father's lofty ideas of the Divine Right of Kings to govern as they pleased. In private life he was conscientious, but in his public policy he was a man " of dark and crooked ways."

He had married a French Catholic princess, and the Puritans, who were now very strong in the House of Commons, believed that the king secretly sympathized with the queen's religion. This was not the case; for Charles, after his peculiar fashion, was a sincere Protestant, though he favored the introduction into the English Church of some of the ceremonies peculiar to Catholic worship.

The Commons showed their distrust of the king by voting him the tax of tonnage and poundage[1] for a single year only, instead of for life, as had been their custom. The Lords refused to assent to such a limited grant,[2] and Charles deliberately collected the tax without the authority of Parliament. Failing, however, to get a sufficient supply in that way, the king forced men of property to grant him "benevolences," and to loan him large sums of money with no hope of its return. Those who dared to refuse were thrown into prison on some pretended charge, or had squads of brutal soldiers quartered in their houses.

When even these measures failed to supply his wants, Charles was forced to summon a Parliament, and ask for help. Instead of granting it, the Commons drew up the Petition of Right[3] of 1628, as an indignant remonstrance, and as a safeguard against further acts of tyranny. This petition has been called " the Second Great Charter of the Liberties of England." It declared: 1, That no one should be compelled to pay any tax or to supply the king with money, except by order of act of Parliament; 2, that neither soldiers nor sailors should be quartered in private houses;[4] 3, that no one should be imprisoned or punished contrary to law. Charles was forced by his need of money to assent to

---

[1] Tonnage and poundage: certain duties levied on wine and merchandise.
[2] See Taswell-Langmead (revised ed.), page 557, Note.
[3] Petition of Right: see Constitutional Documents, page 417.
[4] The King was also deprived of the power to press citizens into the army and navy.

this petition, which thus became a most important part of the English constitution. But the king did not keep his word. When Parliament next met (1629), it refused to grant money unless Charles would renew his pledge not to violate the law. The king made some concessions, but finally resolved to adjourn Parliament. Several members of the Commons held the Speaker in the chair, by force — thus preventing the adjournment of the House — until resolutions offered by Sir John Eliot were passed. These resolutions were aimed directly at the king. They declared: 1. That he is a traitor who attempts any change in the established religion of the kingdom;[1] 2, who levies any tax not voted by Parliament; 3, or who voluntarily pays such a tax. Parliament then adjourned.

18. "Thorough"; Ship-Money; the Short Parliament. — The king swore that "the vipers" who opposed him should have their reward. Eliot was thrown into prison, and kept there till he died. Charles made up his mind that, with the help of Archbishop Laud in Church matters, and of Lord Strafford in affairs of state, he would rule without Parliaments. Strafford urged the king to adopt the policy of "Thorough";[2] in other words, to follow the bent of his own will without consulting the will of the nation. This, of course, practically meant the overthrow of parliamentary and constitutional government. Charles heartily approved of this plan for setting up what he called a "beneficent despotism" based on "Divine Right."

The king now resorted to various illegal means to obtain supplies. The last device he hit upon was that of raising ship-money. To do this, he levied a tax on all the counties of England — inland as well as seaboard, — on the pretext that he purposed building a navy for the defence of the kingdom. John Hampden refused to pay the tax, but Charles's servile judges decided against him, when the case was brought into court.

Charles ruled without a Parliament for eleven years. He might, perhaps, have gone on in this way for as many more, had he not provoked the Scots to rebel by attempting to force a modified form of the English Prayer-Book on the Church of that country. The necessities of the war with the Scots compelled the king to call a Parliament. It declined to grant the king money to carry on the war unless he would give some satisfactory guarantee of governing according to the will of the people. Charles refused to do this, and after a three weeks' session he dissolved what was known as the "Short Parliament."

19. The "Long Parliament"; the Civil War. — But the war gave Charles no choice, and before the year was out he was obliged to call the famous "Long Parliament" of 1640.[3] That body met, with

---

[1] The Puritans generally believed that the King wished to restore the Catholic religion as the established Church of England, but in this idea they were mistaken.

[2] "Thorough": Strafford wrote to Laud, "You may govern as you please. . . . I am confident that the King is able to carry any just and honorable action thorough [*i.e.* through or against] all imaginable opposition." Both Strafford and Laud used this word "thorough," in this sense, to designate their tyrannical policy.

[3] The Long Parliament: it sat from 1640 to 1653, and was not finally dissolved until 1660.

the firm determination to restore the liberties of Englishmen or to perish in the attempt. 1. It impeached Strafford and Laud, and sent them to the scaffold as traitors.[1] 2. It swept away those instruments of royal oppression, the Court of Star Chamber and the High Commission Court.[2] 3. It expelled the bishops from the House of Lords. 4. It passed the Triennial Bill, compelling the king to summon a Parliament at least once in three years.[3] 5. It also passed a law declaring that the king could not suspend or dissolve Parliament without its consent. 6. Last of all, the Commons drew up the Grand Remonstrance, enunciating at great length the grievances of the last sixteen years, and vehemently appealing to the people to support them in their attempts at reform. The Remonstrance was printed and distributed throughout England.[4]

About a month later (1642), the king, at the head of an armed force, undertook to seize Hampden, Pym, and three other of the most active members of the Commons on a charge of treason. The attempt failed. Soon afterward the Commons passed the Militia Bill, and thus took the command of the national militia and of the chief fortresses of the realm, "to hold," as they said, "for king and Parliament." The act was unconstitutional; but, after the attempted seizure of the five members, the Commons felt certain that if they left the command of the militia in the king's hands, they would simply sign their own death-warrant.

In resentment at this action, Charles now (1642) began the civil war. It resulted in the execution of the king, and in the temporary overthrow of the monarchy, the House of Lords, and the established Episcopal Church. In place of the monarchy, the party in power set up a short-lived Puritan Republic. This was followed by the Protectorate of Oliver Cromwell and that of his son Richard.

20. Charles II.; Abolition of Feudal Tenure; Establishment of a Standing Army. — In 1660 the people, weary of the Protectorate form of government, welcomed the return of Charles II. His coming marks the restoration of the monarchy, of the House of Lords, and of the National Episcopal Church.

A great change was now effected in the source of the king's revenue. Hitherto it had sprung largely from feudal dues. These had long been difficult to collect, because the feudal system had practically died out. The feudal land tenure with its dues was now abolished, — a reform, says Blackstone, greater even than that of Magna Carta, — and in their place a tax was levied for a fixed sum. This tax should in justice have fallen on the landowners, who profited by the change; but they managed to evade it, in great measure, and by getting it levied on beer

---

[1] Charles assured Strafford that Parliament should not touch "a hair of his head"; but to save himself the King signed the Bill of Attainder (see p. 446), which sent his ablest and most faithful servant to the block. Well might Strafford exclaim, "Put not your trust in princes."

[2] On the Court of Star Chamber and the High Commission Court, see pages 183, 211 (Note 1), and 224.

[3] The Triennial Act was repealed in 1664, and re-enacted in 1694. In 1716 the Septennial Act increased the limit of three years to seven. This act is still in force.

[4] The press soon became, for the first time, a most active agent of political agitation, both for and against the King. See page 244, Paragraph 495.

and some other liquors, they forced the working classes to shoulder the chief part of the burden, which they still continue to carry.

Parliament now restored the command of the militia to the king;[1] and, for the first time in English history, it also gave him the command of a standing army of 5000 men — thus, in one way, making him more powerful than ever before.

On the other hand, Parliament revived the practice of limiting its appropriations of money to specific purposes.[2] It furthermore began to require an exact account of how the king spent the money — a most embarrassing question for Charles to answer. Again, Parliament did not hesitate to impeach and remove the king's ministers whenever they forfeited the confidence of that body.[3]

The religious legislation of this period marks the strong reaction from Puritanism which had set in. 1. The Corporation Act (1661) excluded all persons who did not renounce the Puritan Covenant, and partake of the Sacrament according to the Church of England, from holding municipal or other corporate offices. 2. The Fourth Act of Uniformity[4] required all clergymen to accept the Book of Common Prayer of (1662) the Church of England. The result of this law was that no less than 2000 Puritan ministers were driven from their pulpits in a single day. 3. A third act of Parliament followed[5] which forbade the preaching or hearing of Puritan doctrines, under severe penalties. 4. A later act[6] prohibited nonconforming clergymen from teaching, or from coming within five miles of any corporate town (except when travelling).

21. Origin of Cabinet Government; the Secret Treaty of Dover; the Test Act; the Habeas Corpus Act. — Charles made a great and most important change with respect to the Privy Council. Instead of consulting the entire council on matters of state, he established the custom of inviting a few only to meet with him in his cabinet or private room. This limited body of confidential advisers was called the Cabal or secret council.

Charles's great ambition was to increase his standing army, to rule independently of Parliament, and to get an abundance of money to spend on his extravagant pleasures and vices.

In order to accomplish these three ends he made a secret and shameful treaty with Louis XIV. of France (1670). Louis wished to crush the Dutch Protestant Republic of Holland, to get possession of Spain, and to secure, if possible, the ascendency of Catholicism in England as well as throughout Europe. Charles, who was destitute of any religious principle, — or, in fact, of any sense of honor, — agreed to publicly declare himself a Catholic, to favor the propagation of that faith in England, and to make war on Holland in return for very liberal grants of money, and for the loan of 6000 French troops by Louis, to help him put down

---

[1] See Militia Bill, Paragraph 19 of this Summary.   [2] See Paragraph 13 of this Summary.
[3] See Paragraph 13 of this Summary (Impeachment).
[4] The first and second Acts of Uniformity date from Edward VI. (1549, 1552); the third from Elizabeth (1559).   [5] The Conventicle Act (1664).
[6] The Five Mile Act (1665). It excepted those clergymen who took the oath of non-resistance to the King, and who swore not to attempt to alter the constitution of Church or State. See Hallam.

any opposition in England. Two members of the Cabal were acquainted with the terms of this secret treaty of Dover.[1]

Charles did not dare to openly avow himself a convert — or pretended convert — to the Catholic religion; but he issued a Declaration of Indulgence (1672) suspending the harsh and unjust statute against the English Catholics.

Parliament took the alarm and passed the Test Act (1673), by which all Catholics were shut out from holding any government office or position. This act broke up the Cabal, by compelling a Catholic nobleman, who was one of its leading members, to resign. Later, Parliament further showed its power by compelling the king to sign the Act of Habeas Corpus (1679), which put an end to his arbitrarily throwing men into prison, and keeping them there, in order to stop their free discussion of his plots against the constitution.[2]

But though the Cabal had been broken up, the principle of a limited private council survived, and, after the Revolution of 1688, it was revived, and took the name of the Cabinet. Under the leadership of the prime minister, who is its head, the Cabinet has become responsible for the policy of the sovereign.[3] Should Parliament decidedly oppose that policy, the prime minister, with his cabinet, either resigns, and a new cabinet is chosen, or the minister appeals to the people for support, and a new parliamentary election is held, by which the nation decides the question. This method renders the old, and never desirable, remedy of the impeachment of the ministers of the sovereign no longer necessary. The prime minister — who answers for the acts of the sovereign and for his policy — is more directly responsible to the people than is the President of the United States.

22. The Pretended "Popish Plot"; Rise of the Whigs and the Tories; Revocation of Town Charters. — The pretended "Popish Plot" (1678) to kill the king, in order to place his brother James — a Catholic convert — on the throne, caused the rise of a strong movement (1680) to exclude James from the right of succession. The Exclusion Bill failed, but henceforward two prominent political parties appear in Parliament, — one, that of the Whigs or Liberals, bent on extending the power of the people; the other, that of the Tories or Conservatives, resolved to maintain the power of the crown.

Charles, of course, did all in his power to encourage the latter party. In order to strengthen their numbers in the Commons, he found pretexts for revoking the charters of many Whig towns. He then issued new charters to these towns, giving the power of election to the Tories.[4] While engaged in this congenial work the king died, and his brother James came to the throne.

---

[1] Charles signed a second secret treaty of Dover in 1678.
[2] See Habeas Corpus Act in Constitutional Documents, p. 446.
[3] The real efficiency of the Cabinet system of government was not fully developed until after the Reform Act of 1832 had widely extended the right of suffrage, and thus made the government more directly responsible to the people. See, too, page 309, Note 2.
[4] The right of election in many towns was then confined to the town-officers or to a few influential inhabitants. This continued to be the case until the passage of the Reform Bill in 1832.

23. James II.; the Dispensing Power; Declaration of Indulgence; the Revolution of 1688. — James II. was a zealous Catholic, and therefore naturally desired to secure freedom of worship in England for people of his own faith. In his zeal he went too far, and the Pope expressed his disgust at the king's foolish rashness. By the exercise of the dispensing power [1] he suspended the Test Act and the Act of Uniformity, in order that Catholics might be relieved from the penalties imposed by these laws, and also for the purpose of giving them civil and military offices, from which the Test Act excluded them. James also established a new High Commission Court,[2] and made the infamous Judge Jeffreys the head of this despotic tribunal. This court had the supervision of all churches and institutions of education. Its main object was to further the spread of Catholicism, and to silence those clergymen who preached against that faith. The king appointed a Catholic president of Magdalen College, Oxford, and expelled from the college all who opposed the appointment. Later he issued two Declarations of Indulgence (1687, 1688), in which he proclaimed universal religious toleration. It was generally believed that under cover of these declarations the king intended to favor the ascendancy of Catholicism. Seven bishops, who petitioned for the privilege of declining to read the declarations from their pulpits, were imprisoned, but on their trial were acquitted by a jury in full sympathy with them.

These acts of the king, together with the fact that he had greatly increased the standing army, and had stationed it just outside of London, caused great alarm throughout England. The majority of the people of both parties believed that James was plotting ' to subvert and extirpate the Protestant religion and the laws and liberties of the kingdom.'[3]

Still, so long as the king remained childless, the nation was encouraged by the hope that James's daughter Mary might succeed him. She was known to be a decided Protestant, and she had married William, prince of Orange, the head of the Protestant Republic of Holland. But the birth of a son to James (1688) put an end to that hope. Immediately a number of leading Whigs and Tories [4] united in sending an invitation to the prince of Orange to come over to England with an army to protect Parliament against the king backed by his standing army.

24. William and Mary; Declaration of Right; Results of the Revolution. — William came; James fled to France. A Convention Parliament [5] drew up a Declaration of Right which declared that the

---

[1] This was the exercise of the right, claimed by the King as one of his prerogatives, of exempting individuals from the penalty of certain laws. The King also claimed the right of suspending entirely (as in the case of the Declaration of Indulgence) one or more statutes. Both these rights had been exercised, at times, from a very early date.

[2] New High Commission Court: see Note 2, on Paragraph 19 of this Summary.

[3] See the language of the Bill of Rights (Constitutional Documents), page 445.

[4] Seven in all; viz. the Earl of Derby, the Earl of Devonshire, the Earl of Shrewsbury, Lord Lumley, Bishop Compton (bishop of London), Admiral Edward Russell, and Henry Sydney.

[5] Convention Parliament: it was so called because it was not regularly summoned by the King — he having fled the country.

king had abdicated, and which therefore offered the crown to William and Mary. They accepted. Thus by the bloodless Revolution of 1688 the English nation transferred the sovereignty to those who had no direct legal claim to it so long as James and his son were living. Hence by this act the people deliberately set aside hereditary succession, as a binding rule, and revived the primitive English custom of choosing such a sovereign as they deemed best. In this sense the uprising of 1688 was most emphatically a revolution. It made, as Green has said, an English monarch as much the creature of an act of Parliament as the pettiest tax-gatherer in his realm. But it was a still greater revolution in another way, since it gave a death-blow to the direct "personal monarchy," which began with the Tudors two hundred years before. It is true that in George III.'s reign we shall see that power temporarily revived, but we shall never hear anything more of that Divine Right of Kings, for which one Stuart "lost his head, and another, his crown." Henceforth the House of Commons will govern England, although, as we shall see, it will be nearly a hundred and fifty years before that House will be able to free itself from the control of either a few powerful families on the one hand, or that of the crown on the other.

25. Bill of Rights; the Commons by the Revenue and the Mutiny Act obtain Complete Control over the Purse and the Sword. — In order to make the constitutional rights of the people unmistakably clear, the Bill of Rights (1689) — an expansion of the Declaration of Right — was drawn up. The Bill of Rights [1] declared: (1) That there should be no suspension or change in the laws, and no taxation except by act of Parliament; (2) that there should be freedom of election to Parliament and freedom of speech in Parliament (both rights that the Stuarts had attempted to control); (3) that the sovereign should not keep a standing army, in time of peace, except by consent of Parliament; (4) that in future no Roman Catholic should sit on the English throne.[2]

This most important bill, having received the signature of William and Mary, became law. It constitutes the third great written charter or safeguard of English liberty. Taken in connection with Magna Carta and the Petition of Right, it forms, according to Lord Chatham, "the Bible of the English Constitution."

But Parliament had not yet finished the work of reform it had taken in hand. The executive strength of every government depends on its control of two powers, — the purse and the sword. Parliament had, as we have seen, got a tight grasp on the first, for the Commons, and the Commons alone, could levy taxes; but within certain very wide limits, the personal expenditure of the sovereign still practically remained unchecked. Parliament now (1689) took the decisive step of voting by the Revenue Act, (1) a specific sum for the maintenance of the crown, and (2) of voting this supply, not for the life of the sovereign, as had

---
[1] Bill of Rights: see Constitutional Documents, page 445.
[2] This last clause was reaffirmed by the Act of Settlement. See page 283, Note 2, and page 446.

been the custom, but for four years. A little later this supply was fixed for a single year only. This action gave to the Commons final and complete control of the purse.[1]

Next, Parliament passed the Mutiny Act (1689),[2] which granted the king power to enforce martial law — in other words, to maintain a standing army — for one year at a time, and no longer save by renewal of the law. This act gave Parliament complete control of the sword, and thus finished the great work; for without the annual meeting and the annual vote of that body, an English sovereign would at the end of a twelvemonth stand penniless and helpless.

26. Reforms in the Courts; the Toleration Act; the Press made Free. — The same year (1689) Parliament effected great and sorely needed reforms in the administration of justice.[3]

Next, Parliament passed the Toleration Act (1689). This measure granted liberty of worship to all Protestant dissenters except those who denied the doctrine of the Trinity.[4] The Toleration Act, however, did not abolish the Corporation Act or the Test Act,[5] and it granted no religious freedom to Catholics.[6] Still, the Toleration Act was a step forward, and it prepared the way for that absolute liberty of worship and of religious belief which now exists in England.

In finance, the reign of William and Mary was marked by the practical beginning of the permanent national debt and by the establishment of the Bank of England.[7]

Now, too (1695), the English press, for the first time in its history, became permanently free,[8] though hampered by a very severe law of libel and by stamp duties.[9] From this period the influence of newspapers continued to increase, until the final abolition of the stamp duty (1855) made it possible to issue penny and even half-penny papers at a profit. These cheap newspapers sprang at once into an immense circulation among all classes, and thus they became the power for good or evil, according to their character, which they are to-day. So that it would be no exaggeration to say that back of the power of Parliament now stands the greater power of the press.

27. The House of Commons no longer a Representative Body; the First Two Georges and their Ministers. — But now that the Revolution of 1688 had done its work, and transferred the power of the crown to the House of Commons, a new difficulty arose. That was the fact that the Commons did not represent the people, but stood simply as the representatives of a small number of rich Whig land-

---

[1] See page 363, Note 1. [2] See page 282, Note 1. [3] See page 279 and Notes 4 and 5.
[4] Freedom of worship was granted to Unitarians in 1812.
[5] The Act of Indemnity of 1727 suspended the penalties of the Test and the Corporation Act; they were both repealed in 1828.
[6] Later, very severe laws were enacted against the Catholics; and in the next reign (Anne's) the Act of Occasional Conformity and the Schism Act were directed against Protestant Dissenters.
[7] On the National Debt and the Bank of England, see page 288.
[8] See page 284.
[9] Furthermore, the Corresponding Societies' Acts (1793, 1799) operated for a time as a decided check on the freedom of the press. See May's Constitutional History.

owners.[1] In many towns the right to vote was confined to the town-officers or to the well-to-do citizens. In other cases, towns which had dwindled in population to a very few inhabitants, continued to have the right to send two members to Parliament, while on the other hand large and flourishing cities had grown up which had no power to send even a single member. The result of this state of things was that the wealthy Whig families bought up the votes of electors, and so regularly controlled the elections.

Under the first two Georges, both of whom were foreigners, the ministers — especially Robert Walpole, who was the first real prime minister of England, and who held his place for twenty years (1722-1742) — naturally stood in the foreground. They understood the ins and outs of English politics, while the two German sovereigns, the first of whom never learned to speak English, neither knew nor cared anything about them. When men wanted favors or offices, they went to the ministers for them. This made men like Walpole so powerful that George II. said bitterly, "In this country the ministers are kings."

28. George III.'s Revival of "Personal Monarchy"; the "King's Friends." — George III. was born in England, and prided himself on being an Englishman. He came to the throne fully resolved, as Walpole said, "to make his power shine out," and to carry out his mother's constant injunction of, "George, be king!" To do this, he set himself to work to trample on the power of the ministers, to take the distribution of offices and honors out of their hands, and furthermore to break down the influence of the great Whig families in Parliament. He had no intention of reforming the House of Commons, or of securing the representation of the people in it; his purpose was to gain the control of the House, and use it for his own ends. In this he was thoroughly conscientious, according to his idea of right, — for he believed with all his heart in promoting the welfare of England, — only he thought that welfare depended on the will of the king much more than on that of the nation. His maxim was "everything for, but nothing by, the people." By liberal gifts of money, — he spent £25,000 in a single day (1762) in bribes,[2] — by gifts of offices and of honors to those who favored him, and by taking away offices, honors, and pensions from those who opposed him, George III. succeeded in his purpose. He raised up a body of men in Parliament, known by the significant name of the "King's Friends," who stood ready at all times to vote for his measures. In this way he actually revived "personal monarchy"[3] for a time, and by using his "Friends" in the House of Commons and in the Lords as his tools, he made himself quite independent of the checks imposed by the constitution.

---

[1] The influence of the Whigs had secured the passage of the Act of Settlement which brought in the Georges; for this reason the Whigs had gained the chief political power.
[2] Pitt (Lord Chatham) was one of the few public men of that day who would neither give nor take a bribe; Walpole declared with entire truth that the great majority of politicians could be bought — it was only a question of price. The King appears to have economized in his living, in order to get more money to use as a corruption fund. See May's Constitutional History. [3] "Personal Monarchy": see Paragraph 15 of this Summary.

29. The American Revolution. — The king's power reached its greatest height between 1770-1782. He made most disastrous use of it, not only at home, but abroad. He insisted that the English colonists in America should pay taxes without representation in Parliament, even of that imperfect kind which then existed in Great Britain. This determination brought on the American Revolution — called in England the "King's War." The war, in spite of its ardent support by the "King's Friends," roused a powerful opposition in Parliament. Chatham, Burke, Fox, and other able men protested against the king's arbitrary course. Finally Dunning moved and carried this resolution (1780) in the Commons: "Resolved, that the power of the crown has increased, is increasing, and ought to be diminished." This vigorous proposition came too late to affect the conduct of the war, and England lost the most valuable of her colonial possessions. The struggle, which ended successfully for the patriots in America, was in reality part of the same battle fought in England by other patriots in the halls of Parliament. On the western side of the Atlantic it resulted in the establishment of national independence; on the eastern side, in the final overthrow of royal tyranny and the triumph of the constitution. It furthermore laid the foundation of that just and generous policy on the part of England toward her other colonies, which has made her mistress of the largest and most prosperous empire on the globe.

30. John Wilkes and the Middlesex Elections; Publication of Parliamentary Debates. — Meanwhile John Wilkes, a member of the House of Commons, had gained the recognition of a most important principle. He was a coarse and violent opponent of the royal policy, and had been expelled from the House on account of his bitter personal attack on the king.[1] Several years later (1768) he was re-elected to Parliament, but was again expelled for seditious libel;[2] he was three times re-elected by the people of London and Middlesex, who looked upon him as the champion of their cause; each time the House refused to permit him to take his seat, but at the fourth election he was successful. A few years later (1782) he induced the House to strike out from its journal the resolution there recorded against him.[3] Thus Wilkes, by his indomitable persistency, succeeded in establishing the right of the people to elect the candidate of their choice to Parliament. During the same period the people gained another great victory over Parliament. That body had utterly refused to permit the debates to be reported in the newspapers. But the redoubtable Wilkes was determined to obtain and publish such reports; rather than have another prolonged battle with him, Parliament conceded the privilege (1771). The result was that the public now, for the first time, began to know what business Parliament actually transacted, and how it was done. This fact of course rendered the members of both houses far more

---

[1] In No. 45 of the *North Briton* (1763) Wilkes rudely accused the King of having deliberately uttered a falsehood in his speech to Parliament.
[2] The libel was contained in a letter written to the newspapers by Wilkes.
[3] The resolution was finally stricken out, on the ground that it was "subversive of the rights of the whole body of electors."

directly responsible to the will of the people than they had ever been before.[1]

31. The Reform Bills of 1832, 1867, 1885; Demand for "Manhood Suffrage." — But notwithstanding this decided political progress, still the greatest reform of all — that of the system of electing members of Parliament — still remained to be accomplished. Cromwell had attempted it (1654), but the Restoration put an end to the work which the Protector had so wisely begun. Lord Chatham felt the necessity so strongly that he had not hesitated to declare (1766) that the system of representation — or rather misrepresentation — which then existed was the "rotten part of the constitution." "If it does not drop," said he, "it must be amputated." Later (1770) he became so alarmed at the prospect that he declared that "before the end of the century either the Parliament will reform itself from within, or be reformed from without with a vengeance."

But the excitement caused by the French Revolution and the wars with Napoleon, not only prevented any general movement of reform, but made it possible to enact stringent laws against agitation in that direction.[2] Finally, however, the unrepresented millions refused to endure their condition any longer. They rose in their might,[3] and by terrible riots made it evident that it would be dangerous for Parliament to postpone action on their demands. The Reform Bill — "the Great Charter of 1832" — was passed. It swept away the "rotten boroughs," which had so long been a disgrace to the country. It granted the right of election to many large towns in the midlands and the north which had hitherto been unable to send members to Parliament, and it placed representation on a broader, healthier, and more equitable basis than had ever existed before. It was a significant fact that when the first reformed Parliament met, composed largely of Liberals, it showed its true spirit by abolishing slavery in the West Indies. Later (1848) the Chartists advocated further reforms,[4] most of which have since been adopted.

In 1867 an act,[5] scarcely less important than that of 1832, broadened representation still further; and in 1888 the franchise was again extended. A little later (1888) the County Council Act reconstructed the local self-government of the country in great measure.[6] The cry is now for unrestricted "manhood suffrage," — woman suffrage in a limited degree already exists,[7] — and the demand is also for the recognition of the principle of "one man one vote."[8]

32. Extension of Religious Liberty; Admission of Catholics and Jews to Parliament; Free Trade. — Meanwhile immense prog-

---

[1] The publication of Division Lists (equivalent to Yeas and Nays) by the House of Commons in 1836 and by the Lords in 1857 completed this work. Since then the public have known how each member of Parliament votes on every important question.

[2] See pages 345, 346. [3] See pages 349–354. [4] See pages 363, 364. [5] See pages 373, 374.

[6] The Local Government or County Council Act: this gives to counties the management of their local affairs and secures uniformity of method and of administration. See Chambers' Encyclopædia (revised ed.) "County Councils." [7] See page 373 and Note 4.

[8] That is, the abolition of certain franchise privileges springing from the possession of landed property in different counties or Parliamentary districts, by which the owner of such property is entitled to cast more than one vote for a candidate for Parliament.

ress was made in extending the principles of religious liberty to all bodies of believers. After nearly three hundred years (or since the Second Act of Supremacy, 1559), Catholics were (1830) admitted to the House of Commons; and in the next generation (1858) Jews were likewise admitted. Recent legislation (the Oaths' Act of 1888) makes it impossible to exclude any one on account of his religious belief or unbelief.

Commercially the nation has made equal progress. The barbarous corn-laws [1] were repealed in 1848, the narrow protective policy of centuries abandoned; and since that period England has practically taken its stand on unlimited free trade with all countries.

33. Condition of Ireland; Reform in the Land and the Church Laws; Civil Service Reform; Education; Conclusion. — In one direction, however, there had been no advance. Ireland was politically united to Great Britain [2] at the beginning of the century (1801); but long after the Irish Catholics had obtained the right of representation in Parliament, they were compelled to submit to unjust land laws, and also to contribute to the support of the Established (Protestant) Church in Ireland. Finally, through the efforts of Mr. Gladstone and others, this branch of the Church was disestablished (1869); [3] later (1870 and 1881) important reforms were effected in the Irish land laws.[4]

To supplement the great electoral reforms which had so widely extended the power of the popular vote, two other measures were now carried. One was that of Civil Service Reform (1870), which opened all clerkships and similar positions in the gift of the government to the free competition of candidates, without regard to their political opinions. This did away with most of that demoralizing system of favoritism which makes government offices the spoils by which successful political parties reward "little men for little services."

The same year (1870) England, chiefly through Mr. Forster's efforts, took up the second measure, the question of national education. The conviction gained ground that if the working-classes are to vote, then they must not be allowed to remain in ignorance — the nation declared "we must educate our future masters." In this spirit a system of elementary government schools was established, which gives instruction to tens of thousands of children who hitherto were forced to grow up without its advantages.[5] These schools are not yet wholly free, although recent legislation [6] practically puts most of them on that basis.

Thus England stands to-day on a strong and broad foundation of liberal political suffrage and of national education. The tendencies now indicate that before many years both will become absolutely free and absolutely universal.

This brief sketch of English Constitutional History shows conclusively that the nation's record is one of slow but certain progress. To-day England stands a monarchy in name, but a republic in fact; a sovereign reigns, but the people rule. The future is in their hands.

---

[1] Corn Laws: see pages 365-368. [2] On the union of Scotland with England, see page 298.
[3] See page 375. [4] See pages 376, 377. [5] See page 375.
[6] The Assisted Education Act of 1891. This gives such a degree of government assistance to elementary schools that the instruction in them is now virtually rendered free.

CONSTITUTIONAL DOCUMENTS.

Abstract of the Articles of Magna Carta (1215). — 1. "The Church of England shall be free, and have her whole rights, and her liberties inviolable." The freedom of elections of ecclesiastics by the Church is confirmed. 2–8. Feudal rights guaranteed, and abuses remedied. 9–11. Treatment of debtors alleviated. 12. "*No scutage or aid [except the three customary feudal aids] shall be imposed in our kingdom, unless by the Common Council of the realm.*"[1] 13. London, and all towns, to have their ancient liberties. 14. *The King binds himself to summon the Common Council of the realm respecting the assessing of an aid (except as provided in 12) or a scutage.*[1] 15, 16. Guarantee of feudal rights to tenants. 17–19. Provisions respecting holding certain courts. 20, 21. *Of amercements. They are to be proportionate to the offence, and imposed according to the oath of honest men in the neighborhood. No amercement to touch the necessary means of subsistence of a free man, the merchandise of a merchant, or the agricultural tools of a villein; earls and barons to be amerced by their equals.* 23–34. Miscellaneous, minor articles. 35. Weights and measures to be uniform. 36. *Nothing shall be given or taken, for the future, for the Writ of Inquisition of life or limb, but it shall be freely granted, and not denied.*[2] 37, 38. Provisions respecting land tenure and trials at law. 39. "No FREEMAN SHALL BE TAKEN OR IMPRISONED, OR DISSEIZED, OR OUTLAWED, OR BANISHED, OR ANY WAYS DESTROYED, NOR WILL WE PASS UPON HIM, NOR WILL WE SEND UPON HIM, UNLESS BY THE LAWFUL JUDGMENT OF HIS PEERS, OR BY THE LAW OF THE LAND." 40. "WE WILL SELL TO NO MAN, WE WILL NOT DENY TO ANY MAN, EITHER JUSTICE OR RIGHT." 41, 42. Provisions respecting merchants, and freedom of entering and quitting the realm, except in war time. 43–46. Minor provisions. 47, 48. Provisions disafforesting all forests seized by John, and guaranteeing forest rights to subjects. 49–60. Various minor provisions. 62. Provision for carrying out the charter by the barons in case the King fails in the performance of his agreement. 63. The freedom of the Church reaffirmed. Every one in the kingdom to have and hold his liberties and rights.

"Given under our hand, in the presence of the witnesses above named, and many others, in the meadow called Runnymede between Windsor and Staines, the 15th day of June, in the 17th of our reign." [Here is appended the King's seal.]

Confirmation of the Charters by Edward I. (1297). — In 1297 Edward I. confirmed Magna Carta and the Forest Charter granted by Henry III. in 1217 by letters patent. The document consists of seven articles, of which the following, namely, the sixth and seventh, are the most important.

6. Moreover we have granted for us and our heirs, as well to archbishops, bishops, abbots, priors, and other folk of holy Church, as also to earls, barons, and to all the commonalty of the land, that *for no business from henceforth will we take such manner of aids, tasks, nor prises but by the common consent of the realm*, and for the common profit thereof, saving the ancient aids and prises due and accustomed.

7. And for so much as the more part of the commonalty of the realm find themselves sore grieved with the maletote [*i.e.* an unjust tax or duty] of wools, that is to wit, a toll of forty shillings for every sack of wool, and have made petition to us to release the same; we, at their requests, have clearly released it, and have granted for us and our heirs that we shall not take such thing nor any other without their common assent and good will; saving to us and our heirs the custom of wools, skins, and leather, granted before by the commonalty aforesaid. In witness of which things we have caused these our letters to be made patents. Witness Edward our son, at London, the 10th day of October, the five-and-twentieth of our reign.

And be it remembered that this same Charter, in the same terms, word for word, was sealed in Flanders under the King's Great Seal, that is to say, at Ghent, the 5th day of November, in the 25th year of the reign of our aforesaid Lord the King, and sent into England.

THE PETITION OF RIGHT.

JUNE 7, 1628.

The Petition exhibited to His Majesty by the Lords Spiritual and Temporal, and Commons in this present Parliament assembled, concerning divers Rights and Liberties of the Subjects, with the King's Majesty's Royal Answer thereunto in full Parliament.

To THE KING'S MOST EXCELLENT MAJESTY: Humbly show unto our Sovereign Lord the King, the Lords Spiritual and Temporal, and Commons in Parliament assembled, that whereas it is declared and enacted by a statute made in the time of the reign of King Edward

---

[1] These important articles were omitted when Magna Carta was reissued in 1216 by Henry III. Stubbs says they were never restored; but Edward I., in his Confirmation of the Charters, seems to reaffirm them. See the Confirmation; see also Gneist's Eng. Const., II, 9.

[2] This article is regarded by some authorities as the prototype of the statute of *Habeas Corpus;* others consider that it is implied in Articles 39–40.

the First, commonly called *Statutum de Tallagio non concedendo*,[1] that no tallage [here, a tax levied by the King upon the lands of the crown, and upon all royal towns] or aid shall be laid or levied by the King or his heirs in this realm, without the goodwill and assent of the Archbishops, Bishops, Earls, Barons, Knights, Burgesses, and other the freemen of the commonalty of this realm: and by authority of Parliament holden in the five and twentieth year of the reign of King Edward the Third, it is declared and enacted, that from thenceforth no person shall be compelled to make any loans to the King against his will, because such loans were against reason and the franchise of the land; and by other laws of this realm it is provided, that none should be charged by any charge or imposition, called a Benevolence, or by such like charge, by which the statutes before-mentioned, and other the good laws and statutes of this realm, your subjects have inherited this freedom, that they should not be compelled to contribute to any tax, tallage, aid, or other like charge, nor set by common consent in Parliament.

Yet nevertheless, of late divers commissions directed to sundry Commissioners in several counties with instructions have issued; by means whereof your people have been in divers places assembled, and required to lend certain sums of money unto your Majesty, and many of them upon their refusal so to do, have had an oath administered unto them, not warrantable by the laws or statutes of this realm, and have been constrained to become bound to make appearance and give attendance before your Privy Council, and in other places, and others of them have been therefore imprisoned, confined, and sundry other ways molested and disquieted: and divers other charges have been laid and levied upon your people in several counties, by Lords Lieutenants, Deputy Lieutenants, Commissioners for Musters, Justices of Peace and others, by command or direction from your Majesty or your Privy Council, against the laws and free customs of this realm:

And where also by the statute called, "The Great Charter of the Liberties of England," it is declared and enacted, that no freeman may be taken or imprisoned or be disseised of his freeholds or liberties, or his free customs, or be outlawed or exiled; or in any manner destroyed, but by the lawful judgment of his peers, or by the law of the land:

And in the eight and twentieth year of the reign of King Edward the Third, it was declared and enacted by authority of Parliament, that no man of what estate or condition that he be, should be put out of his lands or tenements, nor taken, nor imprisoned, nor disherited, nor put to death, without being brought to answer by due process of law:

Nevertheless, against the tenor of the said statutes, and other the good laws and statutes of your realm, to that end provided, divers of your subjects have of late been imprisoned without any cause showed, and when for their deliverance they were brought before your Justices, by your Majesty's writs of Habeas Corpus, there to undergo and receive as the Court should order, and their keepers commanded to certify the causes of their detainer; no cause was certified, but that they were detained by your Majesty's special command, signified by the Lords of your Privy Council, and yet were returned back to several prisons, without being charged with anything to which they might make answer according to law:

And whereas of late great companies of soldiers and mariners have been dispersed into divers counties of the realm, and the inhabitants against their wills have been compelled to receive them into their houses, and there to suffer them to sojourn, against the laws and customs of this realm, and to the great grievance and vexation of the people:

And whereas also by authority of Parliament, in the 25th year of the reign of King Edward the Third, it is declared and enacted, that no man shall be forejudged of life or limb against the form of the Great Charter, and the law of the land: and by the said Great Charter and other the laws and statutes of this your realm, no man ought to be adjudged to death; but by the laws established in this your realm, either by the customs of the same realm or by Acts of Parliament: and whereas no offender of what kind soever is exempted from the proceedings to be used, and punishments to be inflicted by the laws and statutes of this your realm: nevertheless of late divers commissions under your Majesty's Great Seal have issued forth, by which certain persons have been assigned and appointed Commissioners with power and authority to proceed within the land, according to the justice of martial law against such soldiers and mariners, or other dissolute persons joining with them, as should commit any murder, robbery, felony, mutiny, or other outrage or misdemeanour whatsoever, and by such summary course and order, as is agreeable to martial law, and is used in armies in time of war, to proceed to the trial and condemnation of such offenders, and them to cause to be executed and put to death, according to the law martial:

By pretext whereof, some of your Majesty's subjects have been by some of the said Commissioners put to death, when and where, if by the laws and statutes of the land they had deserved death, by the same laws and statutes also they might, and by no other ought to have been, adjudged and executed.

---

[1] A Statute concerning Tallage not granted by Parliament. This is now held not to have been a statute. See Gardiner's *Documents of the Puritan Revolution*, page 1. It is considered by Stubbs an unauthorized and imperfect abstract of Edward I.'s Confirmation of the Charters — which see.

And also sundry grievous offenders by colour thereof, claiming an exemption, have escaped the punishments due to them by the laws and statutes of this your realm, by reason that divers of your officers and ministers of justice have unjustly refused, or forborne to proceed against such offenders according to the same laws and statutes, upon pretence that the said offenders were punishable only by martial law, and by authority of such commissions as aforesaid, which commissions, and all other of like nature, are wholly and directly contrary to the said laws and statutes of this your realm:

They do therefore humbly pray your Most Excellent Majesty, that no man hereafter be compelled to make or yield any gift, loan, benevolence, tax, or such like charge, without common consent by Act of Parliament; and that none be called to make answer, or take such oath, or to give attendance, or be confined, or otherwise molested or disquieted concerning the same, or for refusal thereof; and that no freeman, in any such manner as is before-mentioned, be imprisoned or detained; and that your Majesty will be pleased to remove the said soldiers and mariners, and that your people may not be so burdened in time to come; and that the foresaid commissions for proceeding by martial law, may be revoked and annulled; and that hereafter no commissions of like nature may issue forth to any person or persons whatsoever, to be executed as aforesaid, lest by colour of them any of your Majesty's subjects be destroyed or put to death, contrary to the laws and franchise of the land.

All which they most humbly pray of your Most Excellent Majesty, as their rights and liberties according to the laws and statutes of this realm: and that your Majesty would also vouchsafe to declare, that the awards, doings, and proceedings to the prejudice of your people, in any of the premises, shall not be drawn hereafter into consequence or example: and that your Majesty would be also graciously pleased, for the further comfort and safety of your people, to declare your royal will and pleasure, that in the things aforesaid all your officers and ministers shall serve you, according to the laws and statutes of this realm, as they tender the honour of your Majesty, and the prosperity of this kingdom.

[Which Petition being read the 2nd of June 1628, the King gave the following evasive and unsatisfactory answer, instead of the usual one, given below.]

The King willeth that right be done according to the laws and customs of the realm; and that the statutes be put in due execution, that his subjects may have no cause to complain of any wrong or oppressions, contrary to their just rights and liberties, to the preservation whereof he holds himself as well obliged as of his prerogative.

On June 7 the King decided to make answer in the accustomed form, *Soit droit fait comme est désiré.* [Equivalent to the form of royal assent, " le roi (or la reigne) le veult." See page 362, Note 3. On the Petition of Right see Hallam and compare Gardiner's England and his *Documents of the Puritan Revolution.*

The Bill of Rights (1689). — This Bill consists of thirteen Articles, of which the following is an abstract. It begins by stating that " *Whereas the late King James II., by the advice of divers evil counsellors, judges, and ministers employed by him, did endeavor to subvert and extirpate the Protestant religion, and the laws and liberties of this Kingdom;*" 1. By dispensing with and suspending the laws without consent of Parliament. 2. By prosecuting worthy bishops for humbly petitioning him to be excused for concurring in the same assumed power. 3. By erecting a High Commission Court. 4. By levying money without consent of Parliament. 5. By keeping a standing army in time of peace without consent of Parliament. 6. By disarming Protestants and arming Papists. 7. By violating the freedom of elections. 8. By arbitrary and illegal prosecutions. 9. By putting corrupt and unqualified persons on juries. 10. By requiring excessive bail. 11. By imposing excessive fines and cruel punishments. 12. By granting fines and forfeiture against persons before their conviction.

It is then declared that " the late King James the Second having abdicated the government, and the throne being thereby vacant," therefore the Prince of Orange (" whom it hath pleased Almighty God to make the glorious instrument of delivering their kingdom from Popery and arbitrary power ") did by the advice of " the Lords Spiritual and Temporal, and divers principal persons of the Commons " summon in Convention Parliament.

This Convention Parliament declares, that the acts above enumerated are contrary to law. They then bestow the Crown on William and Mary — the sole regal power to be vested only in the Prince of Orange — and provide that after the decease of William and Mary the Crown shall descend " to the heirs of the body of the said Princess; and, for default of such issue, to the Princess Anne of Denmark [1] and the heirs of her body; and for default of such issue, to the heirs of the body of the said Prince of Orange."

Here follows new oaths of allegiance and supremacy in lieu of those formerly required.

The subsequent articles are as follows: IV. Recites the acceptance of the Crown by William and Mary. V. The Convention Parliament to provide for " the settlement of the religion,

---

[1] The Princess Anne, sister of the Princess Mary, married Prince George of Denmark in 1683; hence she is here styled " the Princess of Denmark."

laws and liberties of the Kingdom." VI. All the clauses in the Bill of Rights are "the true, ancient, and indubitable rights and liberties of the people of this Kingdom." VII. Recognition and declaration of William and Mary as King and Queen. VIII. Repetition of the settlement of the Crown and limitations of the succession. IX. Exclusion from the Crown of all persons holding communion with the "Church of Rome" or who "profess the Popish religion" or who "shall marry a Papist." X. Every King or Queen hereafter succeeding to the Crown to assent to the Act [*i.e.* the Test Act of 1673] "disabling Papists from sitting in either House of Parliament." XI. The King and Queen assent to all the articles of the Bill of Rights. XII. The Dispensing Power abolished. XIII. Exception made in favor of charters, grants, and pardons made before October 23, 1689.

The Act of Settlement (1700–1701).[1] — Excludes Roman Catholics from succession to the Crown; and declares that if a Roman Catholic obtains the Crown, "the people of these realms shall be and are thereby absolved of their allegiance." Settles the Crown on the Electress Sophia,[2] and " the heirs of her body being Protestants." Requires the sovereign to join in communion with the Church of England. No war to be undertaken in defence of any territories not belonging to the English Crown except with the consent of Parliament. Judges to hold their office during good behavior. No pardon by the Crown to be pleadable against an impeachment by the House of Commons.

MISCELLANEOUS ACTS AND LAWS.

I. **Bill of Attainder.** — This was a bill (which might in itself decree sentence of death) passed by Parliament, by which, originally, the blood of a person held to be convicted of treason or felony was declared to be *attainted* or corrupted so that his power to inherit, transmit, or hold property was destroyed. After Henry VIII.'s reign the law was modified so as not to work "corruption of blood" in the case of new felonies. Under the Stuarts, Bills of Attainder were generally brought only in cases where the Commons believed that impeachment would fail — as in the cases of Strafford and Laud. It should be noticed that in an Impeachment the Commons bring the accusation, and the Lords alone act as judges; but that in a Bill of Attainder the Commons — that is, the accusers — themselves act as judges, as well as the Lords.

II. **Statute of Præmunire (1393).** — This statute was enacted to check the power claimed by the Pope in England in cases which interfered with power claimed by the King, as in appeals made to the Court of Rome respecting Church matters, over which the King's court had jurisdiction. The statute received its name from the writ served on the party who had broken the law: "*Præmunire facias* A. B."; that is, "Cause A. B. to be forewarned" that he appear before us to answer the contempt with which he stands charged. Henry VIII. made use of this statute in order to compel the clergy to accept his supremacy over the English Church.

III. **Habeas Corpus Act (1679).** — The name of this celebrated statute is derived from its referring to the opening words of the writ: "*Habeas corpus ad subjiciendum*" (see page 269, Note 1). Sir James Mackintosh declares that the essence of the statute is contained in clauses 39, 40 of Magna Carta — which see. The right to habeas corpus was conceded by the Petition of Right and also by the Statute of 1640. But in order to better secure the liberty of the subject and for prevention of imprisonments beyond the seas, the Habeas Corpus Act of 1679 was enacted, regulating the issue and return of writs of habeas corpus.

The principal provisions of the Act are: 1. Jailers (except in cases of commitment for treason or felony) must within three days of the reception of the writ produce the prisoner in court, unless the court is at a distance, when the time may be extended to twenty days at the most. 2. A jailer, refusing to do this, forfeits £100 for the first offence, and £200 for the second. 3. No one set at liberty upon any Habeas Corpus to be re-committed for the same offence except by the court having jurisdiction of the case. 4. The Act not to apply to cases of debt.

---

[1] This act, says Taswell Langmead, is "the Title Deed of the reigning Dynasty, and a veritable original contract between the Crown and the People."

[2] The Electress Sophia was the granddaughter of James I.; she married the Elector of Hanover, and became mother of George I. See page 403.

SUMMARY OF THE PRINCIPAL DATES IN ENGLISH HISTORY.[1]

[The * marks the most important dates.]

I. THE PREHISTORIC PERIOD.

Britain part of the continent of Europe.
The Rough-Stone Age.
The Polished-Stone Age.
Age of Bronze begins, 1500 B.C.?
Britain mentioned (?) by the name of the "Tin Islands" by Herodotus, B.C. 450.
Britain mentioned by the name of "Albion" by Aristotle? B.C. 350?
Pytheas visits and describes Britain, B.C. 330?
Introduction of Iron, B.C. 250?

II. THE ROMAN PERIOD, B.C. 55, 54; A.D. 43–410.

*Cæsar lands in Britain, B.C. 55 and 54.
Claudius begins the conquest of Britain, A.D. 43.
Caractacus taken prisoner, 50.
Slaughter of the Druids, '1.
Revolt of Boadicea, 61.
Establishment of the Roman power by Agricola, 78–84.
Agricola builds a line of forts, 81.
Hadrian's Wall, 121?
*Britain abandoned by the Romans, 410.

III. THE SAXON, OR EARLY ENGLISH, PERIOD, 449–1013; 1042–1066.

*The Jutes settle in Kent, 449.
Ella and Cissa found the kingdom of Sussex, 477.
Cerdic founds the kingdom of Wessex, 495.
Arthur defeats the Saxons, 520?
The Angles settle Northumbria, 547.
Gildas writes his history of Britain, 550?
*Landing of Augustine; conversion of Kent, 597.
Cædmon, first English poet, 664.
Church council at Whitby, 664.

Conversion of Northumbria, 667.
Church bells first mentioned by Bede, 680.
Bede, the historian, dies, 735.
Egbert takes refuge at the court of Charlemagne, 786.
First landing of the Danes in England, 789.
*Egbert (king of Wessex, conquers a large part of the country (827) and takes the title of "King of the English"), 828.
Alfred the Great, 871.
The Anglo-Saxon Chronicle becomes important from about this time, 871.
*Treaty of Wedmore, 879.
Alfred issues his code of laws, 890.
Alfred builds a fleet, 897.
Frithguilds (for mutual defence, etc.) mentioned about 930?
Dunstan, Archbishop of Canterbury, 960.
*Britain is called England, 960?
Struggle between the regular and secular clergy, 975.
Invasion of the Danes — Danegeld paid by decree of the Witan for the first time, 991.

IV. DANISH PERIOD, 1013–1042.

Sweyn, the Dane, is acknowledged king of the English, 1013.
Edward (afterward King Edward the Confessor) is taken to Normandy, where he remains until 1042, 1013.
Canute, the Dane, chosen king, 1017.
Divides England into four great earldoms, 1017.
Godwin made Earl of Wessex, 1020.

V. THE SAXON, OR EARLY ENGLISH, PERIOD (RESTORED), 1042–1066.

Edward the Confessor, 1042.
Edward begins building Westminster Abbey, 1049.

---

[1] Many early dates are approximate only.

William, Duke of Normandy, visits Edward, 1052.
Harold, last of the Saxon kings, 1066.
William of Normandy claims the throne, 1066.
Invasion from Norway; battle of Stamford Bridge, Sept. 25, 1066.
William of Normandy lands at Pevensey, Sept. 28, 1066.
*Battle of Senlac, or Hastings — Harold killed — Oct. 14, 1066.

VI. THE NORMAN PERIOD, 1066-1154.

William (crowned in Westminster Abbey on Christmas Day), 1066.
System of feudal land-tenure begins to be regularly organized, 1066?
*William grants a charter to London, 1066?
Begins building Tower of London, 1066?
Beginning of Norman architecture, 1066?
Curfew introduced, about 1068?
William harries the North, 1069.
Law of Englishry, 1069?
Reorganizes the church, 1070.
Creates the Palatine earldoms, 1070?
Establishes separate ecclesiastical courts, 1070?
Trial by battle introduced, 1070?
The English, under Hereward, finally defeated at Ely, 1071.
William invades Scotland, and compels the king to do him homage, 1072.
William refuses to become subject to the Pope, 1076.
*Domesday Book completed, 1086. — Reports: Tenants-in-chief (barons, bishops, abbots), about 1500; Under-tenants (chiefly English dispossessed of their estates, about 8000; Yeomen, north of Watling St., about 35,000; Yeomen, sunk to a condition bordering on serfdom (south of Watling St.), about 90,000; Villeins, or serfs, about 109,000; Slaves, about 25,000; Citizens, monks, nuns, priests, etc., about 1;732,000; Total population, about 2,000,000.
*All the landholders of England swear allegiance to William, at Salisbury, 1086.
William Rufus, 1087.
Suppresses rebellion of the barons, 1088.
Makes war on Normandy, 1090.
Quarrel with Anselm — robs church of its revenue, 1094.
Suppresses second rebellion of the barons, 1095.
Builds Westminster Hall, London Bridge, 1097?
Henry I., 1100.
*First charter of liberties, 1100.
Expels Robert of Belesme, 1102.
Quarrels with Anselm about investitures, 1103.
Battle of Tinchebrai — Normandy conquered, 1106.
Henry and Anselm come to terms, 1106.
Matilda, d. of the king, marries Geoffrey of Anjou, 1128.
Barons swear to make Matilda successor to the throne, 1133.
Stephen, 1135.
Charter of liberties, 1135.
Tournaments begin, 1135?
Matilda, d. of Henry I., claims the crown, 1135.
Battle of the Standard, 1138.
Civil war begins, 1139.
William of Malmesbury's Chronicle closes, 1142.
Knights Hospitallers established in England, 1150?
Matilda's son (Henry II.) marries Eleanor of France, and acquires her provinces, 1152.
Treaty of Wallingford, 1153.

VII. THE ANGEVIN, OR PLANTAGENET, PERIOD, 1154-1399.

Henry II., 1154.
*Merchant and craft guilds become prominent, 1154?
*Payment of scutage regularly established, 1160 (see 1385).
*Constitutions of Clarendon, 1164.
Quarrel with Becket, 1164.
Coats of Arms, 1165?
*Assize of Clarendon, 1166.
Becket murdered, 1170.
*Partial conquest of Ireland, 1171.
Henry's wife and sons rebel, 1173.
Henry does penance at Becket's tomb, 1174.
Rebellion of barons suppressed, 1174.
Assize of Northampton (divides England into judicial circuits), 1176.
Five judges appointed to hear all cases, 1178.
Knights Templars established in England, 1180?
Assize of Arms (regulates national militia), 1181.
Henry's sons again rebel, 1183.
Assize of the Forest, 1184.

*Saladin Tithe (first tax on personal property), 1188.
*Great Assize (substitutes trial by jury in civil cases for trial by battle), 1188?
Richard I., 1189.
Richard persecutes the Jews, sells offices, extorts money, 1189.
*Richard grants many town charters, 1189.
Joins the third crusade, 1190.
*Legal recognition of the corporation of London marks the triumph of the mercantile element, 1191.
Richard taken prisoner, 1192.
England ransoms the king, 1194.
Returns to England, and is re-crowned; extorts money, 1194.
Builds Château Gaillard, near Rouen, 1197.
John, 1199.
Introduction of the mariner's compass, 1200?
Gothic, or Pointed, architecture, begins in England, 1200?
Layamon's "Brut," 1200?
Murder (?) of Arthur, 1203.
*Loss of Normandy, 1204.
John refuses to receive Archbishop Langton, 1208.
The kingdom placed under an interdict, 1208.
The Pope excommunicates John, 1209.
Threatens to depose him, 1211.
John becomes the Pope's vassal, 1213.
*The meeting at St. Albans (first representative assembly on record) to consider measures of reform, 1213.
*The Great Charter, June 15, 1215.
The Pope refuses to recognize the charter, and excommunicates the leaders of the barons, 1215.
The barons invite Louis, son of the king of France, to take the crown, 1215.
War between John and the barons, 1216.
Henry III., 1216.
Louis goes back to France, 1217.
Charter of the Forests, 1217.
Henry begins rebuilding Westminster Abbey, 1220?
The Mendicant Friars land in England, 1221.
Coal mines opened, 1234?
*Parliament of Merton rejects the Canon Law, 1236.
All persons having an income of £20 a year from landed property forced to receive knighthood, 1256.
The Pope first claims "annates" from England, 1256.
"The Mad Parliament" draws up the Provisions of Oxford, 1258.

Matthew Paris, greatest of the mediæval chroniclers, dies, 1259.
The Barons' War; battle of Lewes, 1264.
*Walter de Merton founds Merton College, Oxford (beginning of the collegiate system), 1264.
*Rise of the House of Commons under Earl Simon de Montfort, 1265.
Battle of Evesham; Earl Simon killed, 1265.
*Roger Bacon issues his "Opus Majus," 1267.
Roger Bacon describes gunpowder? 1267.
Courts of Exchequer, King's Bench, and Common Pleas fully organized, 1272?
Edward I., 1272.
The groat (four pence) first coined, 1272. Up to this date the only coin issued was the silver penny.
*Statute of Mortmain, 1279.
Conquest of Wales, 1284.
First Prince of Wales, 1284?
*The Statute of De Donis, or Entail, 1285.
Customs (on wine, wool, etc.) first levied, 1290?
The Jews expelled from England, 1290.
Statute of Quia Emptores (increases number of small freeholders holding directly from the crown or great lords), 1290.
Alliance between Scotland and France against England, 1294.
*First complete Parliament (Lords, Clergy, and Commons: subsequently the clergy usually met by themselves in convocation), 1295.
War with Scotland, 1295-6.
Edward seizes the wool of the merchants (Maltote, or "evil tax"), 1297.
Edward confirms the charters, 1297.
Consent of Parliament established as necessary to taxation (by the confirmation of the charters), 1297.
Chimneys begin to come into use, 1300?
Renewed war with Scotland; execution of Wallace; defeat of Bruce, 1303-6.
Edward II., 1307.
Seizure of the property of the Knights Templars, 1308.
Gaveston dismissed, 1308.
Torture first employed in England, 1310?
The Lords Ordainers (to regulate the king's household), 1310.
Gaveston executed, 1312.
Battle of Bannockburn, 1314.
*House of Commons gains a share in legislation, 1322.
Roger Mortimer and the queen conspire against Edward, 1326.

The Despensers (king's favorites) hanged, 1326.
The king deposed and murdered, 1327.
Edward III., 1327.
Mixed armor (plate and mail), 1327?
Many brilliant tournaments held, 1327?
Independence of Scotland recognized, 1328.
*Woollen manufacture introduced from Flanders, 1331?
*House of Commons (Knights of the Shire and Commons united) begin to sit by themselves as a distinct body, 1333.
Edward takes the title of King of France, 1337.
The first gold coins struck, 1337?
Creates his son Edward Duke of Cornwall (title of duke first used), 1337.
*Beginning of the Hundred Years' War with France, 1338 (see 1453).
Talliage (tax on towns and lands held by the crown) abolished, 1340.
*Victory of Crécy (cannon first used?), 1346.
*Capture of Calais, 1347.
Court of Chancery finally established, 1348.
*The Black Death, 1349.
*First Statute of Laborers (regulates price of labor, etc.), 1349.
First Statute of Provisors (limits power of Pope in England), 1351.
First Statute of Treasons, 1352.
First Statute of Præmunire (limits power of the Pope in England), 1353 (see 1393).
Many Staples (market or custom towns) established, 1354?
Great increase of the woollen trade with the continent, 1354?
*Victory of Poitiers, 1356.
*Mandeville writes his Travels, 1360?
Exportation of corn forbidden, 1360 (see 1846).
*Treaty of Bretigny, 1360.
No tax to be levied on wool without consent of Parliament, 1362; renewed, 1371.
First iron foundries, 1370?
*Wykeham founds Winchester College (first great public school), 1373; completes C., 1393.
Parliament first grants tonnage and poundage (a tax on merchandise) to the king, 1373.
*The House of Commons gains the right of impeaching the king's ministers, 1376.
*Wycliffe begins the Reformation (rise of the Lollards), 1377?
Richard II., 1377.
*Wycliffe translates the Bible, 1380?

*Peasant revolts led by Wat Tyler, 1381.
Langland writes "Piers Ploughman," 1381.
*Chaucer begins the "Canterbury Tales," 1384?
Scutage given up, 1385? (see 1160).
The title of Marquis created, 1386.
*The Great Statute of Præmunire (see 1353), 1393.
Richard banishes the Duke of Hereford (son of John of Gaunt, Duke of Lancaster) and the Duke of Norfolk, 1398.
Death of John of Gaunt; Richard seizes his estate, 1399.
The Duke of Hereford (now Duke of Lancaster) returns to England, claims his estate and the crown, 1399.
Richard deposed (and, later, murdered), 1399.
*Parliament sets aside the order of succession and chooses Henry king, 1399.

VIII. THE LANCASTRIAN PERIOD (RED ROSE), 1399–1461.

Henry IV., 1399.
Complete plate armor, 1400?
Rebellion of Glendower, 1400.
Fortescue writes on government, 1400?
*First statute punishing heretics with death, 1401.
First martyr (William Sawtre) under the new law), 1401.
Revolt of the Percies; battle of Shrewsbury, 1403.
*The House of Commons obtains the exclusive right to make grants of money, 1407.
Henry V., 1413.
*Statutes to be made by Parliament without alteration by the king, 1414.
Lollard conspiracies, 1414–1415.
*Battle of Agincourt, 1415.
*Treaty of Troyes, 1420.
Henry VI., 1422 (crowned king of England and France).
Dukes of Bedford and Gloucester Protectors during the king's minority, 1422.
The Paston Letters, 1424–1509.
Siege of Orleans, 1428.
*County suffrage restricted, 1430.
Joan of Arc burned, 1431.
Title of Viscount created, 1440.
*Cade's insurrection, 1450.
*End of the Hundred Years' War; loss of France, 1453 (see 1338).
*Wars of the Roses, 1455–1485.
Henry dethroned, 1461.

IX. THE YORKIST PERIOD (WHITE ROSE), 1461-1485.

Edward IV., 1461.
Henry (the late king) captured and imprisoned, 1465.
Warwick, "the king-maker," restores Henry VI., 1470.
Queen Margaret's son killed at Tewksbury and the queen imprisoned, 1471.
Henry dies a prisoner in the Tower, 1471.
Edward exacts "benevolences," 1475.
Queen Margaret ransomed and leaves England, 1476.
*Caxton prints the first book in England, 1477.
Edward V., 1483.
Richard, Duke of Gloucester, appointed Protector, 1483.
Murders Edward in the Tower (?), 1483.
Richard III., 1483.
Suppresses rebellion, 1483.
College of Heralds established, 1483.
Benevolences abolished, 1484 (see 1475).
*Battle of Bosworth Field, 1485.

X. THE TUDOR PERIOD, 1485-1603.

Henry VII., 1485.
Sovereigns first coined, 1485?
Henry marries Elizabeth of York, thus uniting the Houses of Lancaster and York, 1486.
Court of Star-Chamber, 1487.
The Pretenders Simnel and Warbeck, 1487 and 1492.
Statutes of Livery and Maintenance enforced by Empson and Dudley, 1487.
Poynings' Act (puts an end to the legislative power of the English colony in Ireland), 1494.
The Great Intercourse (commercial treaty between England and the Netherlands), 1496.
*The Cabots discover the American continent, 1497.
*Beginning of "the New Learning" (Colet, Erasmus, More), 1499.
Henry VIII., 1509.
Colet founds St. Paul's School, 1512.
Battle of Flodden, 1513.
Wolsey becomes cardinal and lord chancellor, 1515.
More writes "Utopia," 1516.
Rude firearms begin to come into use, 1517?
Field of the Cloth of Gold, 1520.

The Pope confers on Henry the title of "Defender of the Faith," 1521.
Tyndall and Coverdale translate the Bible, 1525-30.
Henry begins divorce suit against Catharine of Aragon, 1528.
Fall of Wolsey, 1529.
Cranmer obtains the opinions of the Universities, 1530.
Clergy compelled to acknowledge Henry the Head of the English Church, 1531.
Appeals to Rome forbidden, 1532.
Henry privately marries Anne Boleyn, 1532.
Cranmer pronounces Henry's marriage with Catharine void, 1533.
London paved, 1533?
Payment of "annates" to Rome forbidden, 1534.
The authority of the Pope in England abolished, 1534.
*Act of Supremacy declares the king Supreme Head of the Church of England, 1535.
Fisher and More executed, 1535.
Pope threatens to excommunicate Henry, 1535.
Cromwell comes to power, 1535.
England and Wales finally united, 1536.
Benefit of clergy restricted, 1536.
*Dissolution of the monasteries begins, 1536.
Much distress among the poor; great increase of vagrants, 1536?
The Bible translated and placed in the churches, 1536.
Stringent vagrant laws, 1536?
Insurrection in the North ("Pilgrimage of Grace"), 1536.
Many new nobles created, 1536?
Parish registers begin, 1538.
The king's Proclamations to have the force of law, 1539 (repealed, 1547).
The abbots cease to sit in the House of Lords, 1539.
The Six Articles, 1539.
Cromwell executed, 1540.
Hall's Chronicle, 1540?
Statute punishing witchcraft with death, 1541.
First cannon cast in England, 1543.
Edward VI., 1547.
Duke of Somerset made Protector during Edward's minority, 1547.
Bethlehem Hospital (first for the insane), 1547.
Battle of Pinkie, 1547.
Trades-unions formed, 1548?
First English Prayer-Book, 1549.

Latimer preaches, 1549.
*Act of Uniformity (virtually establishes Protestantism), 1549.
First Huguenot emigration to England, 1550?
The Forty-Two Articles of Religion (afterward reduced to thirty-nine), 1552.
Second Act of Uniformity, and Second Prayer-Book, 1552.
Great seizure of unenclosed lands by the nobles, 1552?
*Many Protestant grammar schools and several hospitals founded by the king, 1552-3.
Mary, 1553.
Lady Jane Grey proclaimed queen, 1553.
Edward's laws, establishing Protestantism, repealed, 1553.
Wyatt's rebellion, 1554.
Lady Jane Grey executed, 1554.
Mary marries Philip II. of Spain, 1554.
Statutes against the Pope (since 1529) repealed; Catholicism re-established, 1554.
Coaches introduced into England, 1555?
Severe persecution of the Protestants (Cranmer, Ridley, and Latimer burned), 1555-6.
Watches begin to come into use in England, 1557?
Loss of Calais, 1558.
Elizabeth, 1558.
Acts of Supremacy and Uniformity re-enacted (Protestantism restored), 1559.
Glass manufactured in England, 1559?
John Knox preaches in Edinburgh, 1559.
Hawkins begins the slave trade, 1562.
The Thirty-Nine Articles established, 1563.
Insurrections in behalf of Romanism, 1569.
Ascham publishes "The Schoolmaster," 1570.
The English Puritans begin to be prominent, 1571?
Holinshed's Chronicle, 1577.
Drake sails round the globe, 1577.
Lyly publishes his "Euphues," 1579.
Manufacture of paper in England, 1580?
Jesuit missionaries land in England, 1580.
High Commission Court established, 1583.
Raleigh attempts to colonize Virginia, 1584.
*Shakespeare at the Blackfriars and Globe Theatres in London, 1586?
Raleigh introduces tobacco, 1586?
Raleigh introduces the potato into Ireland, 1586?
Execution of Mary Queen of Scots, 1587.
*Defeat of the Armada, 1588.
Spenser publishes "The Faërie Queene," 1590.
Sidney writes his "Arcadia," 1590?

Marlowe and Jonson write, 1590?
Hooker writes, 1594?
Establishment of the East India Company, 1600.
First regular Poor-Law, 1601.
Completion of the conquest of Ireland, 1603.

XI. THE STUART PERIOD (FIRST PART), 1603-1649.

James I., 1603 (king of Scotland and England).
The Millenary Petition, 1603.
Plot against the king; Raleigh imprisoned, 1603.
New laws punishing witchcraft, 1603?
Hampton Court Conference, 1604.
James proclaims the Divine Right of Kings, 1604?
Right of the Commons to control their elections established, 1604.
The Gunpowder Plot, 1605.
Severe laws against the Catholics, 1606.
*Colony founded at Jamestown, Virginia, 1607.
The Baptists establish a society in London, 1608?
Protestant colonies planted in Ulster, Ireland, 1610.
James creates baronets, 1611.
*Authorized translation of the Bible completed, 1611.
Beaumont and Fletcher write, 1613?
Execution of Raleigh, 1618.
Post-office regularly established throughout the country, 1619?
*Bacon publishes his New System of Philosophy, 1620.
*Harvey discovers the circulation of the blood, 1620.
*The Pilgrims land at Plymouth, New England, 1620.
Massinger writes, 1620.
Impeachment of Lord Bacon, 1621.
The Commons protest against the king's violation of their liberties, 1621.
James tears up the protest, 1621.
Imprisons members of Parliament, 1622.
*First regular newspaper in England, 1622.
First patent for inventions granted, 1623?
Right of sanctuary abolished, 1624.
Charles I., 1625.
Italian architecture begins in England, 1625?
Parliament demands reforms, and refuses grants of money unless they are conceded, 1625.

Hackney coaches introduced, 1625?
Coal comes into general use, 1625?
Sir John Eliot sent to the Tower, 1626.
The king raises money illegally, 1626.
John Hampden imprisoned for refusing to lend money to the king, 1627.
*The Petition of Right, 1628.
Wentworth (Strafford) and Laud with the policy of "Thorough," 1635.
Sedan chairs come into use, 1635?
Hampden refuses to pay ship-money, 1637.
The king tries to force a liturgy on the Scottish Church, 1637.   [1638.
Scottish National (Presbyterian) Covenant,
The Short Parliament, 1640.
*The Long Parliament meets, 1640.
Torture last used in England, 1640?
Laud imprisoned (later executed), 1640.
Baker publishes his Chronicle, 1641.
Execution of Strafford, 1641.
The Triennial Act (for summoning a new Parliament every three years), 1641.
Parliament resolves not to be adjourned or dissolved except by its own consent, 1641.
Abolishes the Star-Chamber and High Commission Courts, 1641.
Passes statutes against ship-money and other illegal measures of the king, 1641.
The Grand Remonstrance, 1641.
Hobbes writes, 1642?
The king attempts to seize the five members, 1642.
*Beginning of the Civil War (battle of Edgehill), 1642.
Cromwell organizes his "Ironsides," 1642.
*The Solemn League and Covenant, 1643.
The Excise Act, 1643.
The Independents become prominent, 1643?
The Westminster Assembly of Divines (draws up the Presbyterian creed, etc.), 1643-7.
Stringent restrictions on the Press, 1644.
Milton's Areopagitica, 1644.
Battle of Marston Moor, 1644.
The Self-Denying Ordinance, 1645.
The "New Model" army, 1645.
Battle of Naseby, 1645.
Charles a prisoner, 1647.
Charles makes a secret treaty with the Scots, 1647.
Royalist revolt, 1648.
Pride's Purge, 1648.
The Rump Parliament, 1648.
*Execution of the king, 1649.

XII. THE COMMONWEALTH AND PROTECTORATE PERIOD, 1649–1660.

House of Lords abolished, 1649; meets next, 1660.
The Commonwealth, or Republic, declared, 1649.
Charles II. proclaimed king in Scotland, 1649.
Many Cavaliers emigrate to Virginia, 1649?
Cromwell's campaign in Ireland, 1649-50.
Rise of the Quakers, 1650?
Iron (and other metal) rolling-mills, 1650?
Battle of Dunbar, 1650.
Cotton begins to be largely imported, 1650?
Battle of Worcester (flight of Charles II.), 1651.
The Navigation Act (modified, 1823; repealed, 1849), 1651.
War with the Dutch, 1652.
Coffee-houses opened, 1652?
Izaak Walton's "Complete Angler," 1653.
Cromwell expels Parliament, 1653.
"Barebone's Parliament," 1653.
The Instrument of Government, 1653.
*Cromwell, Protector, 1653.
War with Spain, 1655.
England divided into eleven military districts, 1655.
The Humble Petition and Advice, 1657.
Richard Cromwell, Protector, 1658.
Fuller's Church History, 1658.
The army compels Richard to abdicate, 1659.
General Monk calls a "Free Parliament," 1660.
Charles II. sends the Declaration of Breda, 1660.
*The Convention Parliament invites Charles II. to return, 1660.

XIII. THE STUART PERIOD (SECOND PART), 1660–1714.

Charles II., 1660.
Standing army established, 1660.
Regicides executed, 1660.
Board of Trade organized, 1660.
Feudal dues and services abolished, 1660.
Tea introduced, 1660?
Corporation Act, 1661 (repealed, 1828).
Act of Uniformity re-enacted, 1662.
Presbyterian clergy driven out, 1662.
Press licensing act, 1662 (see 1695).
Royal Society founded in London, 1662.
Butler writes "Hudibras," 1663.
Hearth Tax, 1663 (repealed, 1689)

Convocation surrenders its right of self-taxation, 1663.
Conventicle Act, 1664.
Repeal of Triennial Act, 1664 (see 1641).
Seizure of New Amsterdam (New York), 1664.
War with the Dutch, 1665.
The Plague in London, 1665.
The Five-Mile Act, 1665.
Great fire of London, 1666.
The Dutch sail up the Thames, 1667.
The Cabal comes into power, 1667.
Milton publishes "Paradise Lost," 1667.
*Secret Treaty of Dover, 1670.
Bunyan writes "Pilgrim's Progress," 1670.
Clarendon's History of the Rebellion, 1670?
The king robs the Exchequer, 1672.
Declaration of Indulgence, 1672.
The Test Act, 1673 (repealed, 1828).
Wren begins to rebuild St. Paul's (Italian style), 1675.
*The so-called Popish Plot, 1678.
*The Disabling Act (excludes Catholics),1678.
*The Habeas Corpus Act passed, 1679.
The Exclusion Bill introduced, 1679.
*Rise of Whigs and Tories, 1680?
Dryden writes "Absalom and Achitophel," 1681.
The Rye House Plot, 1683.
Execution of Russell and Sydney, 1683.
Town charters revoked, 1684.
New England charters revoked, 1684.
James II., 1685.
Monmouth's rebellion; Battle of Sedgemoor, 1685.
The Bloody Assizes, 1685.
Many Huguenots settle in England, 1685.
Huguenots begin silk manufacture in England, 1685?
*Newton demonstrates the law of gravitation, 1687.
Tyrconnel made Lord Deputy of Ireland, 1687.
"Lilli Burlero," 1687.
Expulsion of the Fellows of Magdalen College, 1687.
Declaration of Indulgence, 1687-8.
Imprisonment of the Seven Bishops; trial and acquittal, 1688.
Birth of Prince James, "the Pretender," 1688.
William of Orange invited to England, 1688.
Arrival of William; his Declaration, 1688.
Flight of James, 1688.
The Convention Parliament, 1689.
The Declaration of Right, 1689.

William and Mary (Orange-Stuart), 1689.
Grand Alliance against Louis XIV., 1689.
Jacobite rebellion in Scotland (Killiecrankie), 1689.
The bayonet begins to be used, 1689?
Siege of Londonderry, 1689.
*Mutiny Bill passes, 1689.
*Toleration Act, 1689.
*Bill of Rights, 1689.
Secession of the non-jurors, 1689.
Act of Grace, 1690.
Battle of Beachy Head, 1690.
*Battle of the Boyne, 1690.
Chelsea army hospital, 1690.
Treaty of Limerick, 1691.
Severe laws against Irish Catholics, 1692.
Massacre of Glencoe, 1692.
Lord Churchill (Duke of Marlborough) deprived of office, 1692.
Battle of La Hogue, 1692.
Flint-lock muskets come into use, 1692?
*Beginning of the national debt, 1693.
*Bank of England established, 1694.
Tax on paper, 1694 (repealed, 1861).
Death of Queen Mary, 1694.
Triennial Act restored, 1694 (see 1664).
*The press made free, 1695.
Greenwich Hospital, for seamen, established, 1696.
Window tax imposed, 1696 (see 1851).
Trials for Treason Act (reforms political trials), 1696.
Peace of Ryswick, 1697.
The Partition Treaties (an attempt to settle the question of the Spanish Succession), 1698 and 1700.
London clubs begin, 1700?
Severe Act against Roman Catholics, 1700 (repealed, 1778).
*Act of Settlement, 1701.
Abjuration Act, 1702.
Anne, 1702 (last of the Stuart sovereigns).
War with France, 1702.
Great power of the Duchess of Marlborough, 1702.
Judges to hold office during good behavior, 1702.
High and Low Church parties, 1703.
First daily newspaper in England, 1703.
*Battle of Blenheim, 1704.
*Gibraltar taken, 1704.
John Locke dies, 1704.
Battle of Ramillies, 1706.
*Union of England and Scotland (Great Britain), 1707.

Union Jack adopted, 1707.
Mrs. Masham comes into power, 1710.
Trial of Dr. Sacheverell, 1710.
Marlborough disgraced, 1711.
Property qualification for members of the House of Commons established, 1711 (repealed, 1858).
Act against Occasional Conformity, 1711 (repealed, 1718).
Addison writes for the "Spectator," 1711.
Pope writes, 1712.
Newcomen invents his steam-engine (for pumping mines), 1712.
*Treaty of Utrecht, 1713.
The Schism Act, 1714 (repealed, 1718).

XIV. THE HANOVERIAN PERIOD, 1714 TO THE PRESENT TIME.

George I., 1714.
Jacobite rebellion in Scotland, in favor of the Old Pretender, 1715.
Septennial Act, 1716.
Convocation suspended, 1717-1850.
Repeal of Occasional Conformity, 1718 (see 1711).
The Triple and Quadruple Alliance, 1717, 1718.
De Foe writes "Robinson Crusoe," 1719.
*The South Sea Bubble, 1720.
Inoculation for small-pox introduced, 1721.
Sir Robert Walpole first prime minister, 1721.
*Modern cabinet system begins, 1721.
Swift writes "Gulliver's Travels," 1726.
War with Austria and Spain, 1727.
George II., 1727.
Laws punishing witchcraft with death repealed, 1736.
Bishop Butler writes his "Analogy," 1736.
John Wesley — Rise of the Methodists, 1738.
Hogarth's pictures, 1738?
War of "Jenkins's Ear," 1739.
War of the Austrian Succession, 1741.
The Place Act (limits the number of offices to be held by members of Parliament), 1742.
Battle of Dettingen, 1743.
Jacobite rebellion in Scotland, in favor of the Young Pretender, 1745.
The Pretender defeated at Culloden, 1746.
Peace of Aix-la-Chapelle, 1748.
Fielding writes "Tom Jones," 1749.
Gray's Elegy, 1751.
Clive takes Arcot, 1751.
Introduction of the New Style, 1752.

British Museum founded, 1753.
Hume begins his History of England, 1754.
Seven Years' War with France, 1756.
"The Black Hole" of Calcutta, 1756.
*Clive wins the battle of Plassey; foundation of England's Indian empire, 1757.
*Victory of Quebec, 1759 (England gains Canada).
George III., 1760.
Johnson, Goldsmith, and Sterne write, 1760?
Wedgwood establishes his potteries, 1760.
Bribery Act (to punish bribery of voters), 1762.
Canada ceded to Great Britain, 1763.
Wilkes attacks the government ("North Briton"), 1763.
Hargreaves invents the spinning-jenny, 1764.
*Stamp Act, 1765 (repealed, 1766).
Blackstone's Commentaries, 1765.
*Watt's steam-engine, 1765.
Arkwright's spinning-machine, 1768.
Letters of "Junius," 1769.
Umbrellas introduced, 1770?
*Debates in Parliament regularly reported, 1771.
Pressing to death abolished, 1772.
Royal Marriage Act, 1772.
*"The Boston Tea Party," 1773.
The four "Intolerable Acts," 1774.
*Prison reforms by John Howard, 1774.
Priestley discovers oxygen gas, 1774.
The American Revolution begins, 1775.
*Declaration of American Independence, 1776.
Gibbon begins his History of Rome, 1776.
Smith's "Wealth of Nations," 1776.
Roman Catholic Relief Act (repeals Act of 1700), 1778.
Act relieving Dissenting ministers and schoolmasters, 1779.
Free trade granted to Ireland, 1780.
Jeremy Bentham writes, 1780?
Ducking-stool last used, 1780?
Robert Raikes opens Sunday-schools, 1780?
Lord George Gordon riots, 1780.
Defeat of Cornwallis at Yorktown, 1781.
Poynings' Law repealed, 1782 (see 1494).
Great improvement in the manufacture of iron (puddling), 1784?
Treaties of Paris and Versailles, 1783.
*Recognition of the independence of the United States, 1783.
*Mail coaches established, 1784.
Board of Control for India, 1784.
The London "Times" established, 1785.
Trial of Warren Hastings, 1786.
West Africa colonized, 1787?

Gainsborough dies, 1788.
Burke's "Reflections on the French Revolution," 1790.
Robert Burns writes, 1790?
Formation of the "United Irishmen," 1792.
Sir J. Reynolds dies, 1792.
War with France, 1793.
Fire-engine patented, 1793.
Bank of England suspends payment, 1797.
Battle of the Nile, 1798.
*Vaccination introduced, 1799?
Reform in care of the insane, 1800?
*Union of Great Britain and Ireland, 1800.
First Census of Great Britain, 1801.
Colonization of Australia, 1802.
Paley's "Natural Theology," 1803.
Malthus writes on Population, 1803.
Chimney-sweeping machine, 1805.
*Battle of Trafalgar, 1805.
Abolition of the slave-trade, 1807.
Many trades-unions formed, 1807?
The Orders in Council, 1807.
The Peninsula War, 1808-14.
Luddite riots, 1811.
George III. becomes insane; Prince of Wales appointed regent, 1811.
Dissenters' Relief Bill, 1812.
Debtors' Act (releases "poor debtors"), 1812.
*First steamboat in Great Britain, 1812.
*Second War with America, 1812.
Sheridan and Coleridge, 1812?
Toleration granted to Unitarians, 1813.
Walter Scott's "Waverley Novels," 1814.
London lighted with gas, 1815?
Davy invents the miner's safety-lamp, 1815.
*Battle of Waterloo, 1815.
South Africa acquired, 1815.
Wager of battle abolished, 1819.
Macadamized roads, 1819?
The Six Acts (relating to seditious meetings, etc.), 1819.
*First Atlantic steamship, 1819.
George IV., 1820.
Bill for the queen's divorce, 1820.
Byron, Shelley, Wordsworth, Scott, Southey, Lamb, Moore, 1820?
Cabs introduced, 1822.
Society for the prevention of cruelty to animals, 1824.
Capital punishment greatly restricted, 1824.
First temperance society, 1826.
Flaxman, the sculptor, dies, 1826.
Benefit of clergy abolished, 1827.
*Repeal of the Corporation Act, 1828, (see 1661).

*Repeal of the Test Act, 1828 (see 1673).
*Catholic emancipation (repeals act of 1678), 1829.
Irish property qualification for franchise increased, 1829.
Omnibuses introduced, 1829.
*Friction matches, 1829?
The new police, 1829.
William IV., 1830.
Stephenson invents the first successful locomotive (the "Rocket"), 1830.
*Opening of the Liverpool and Manchester Railway, 1830.
Cobbett edits the Political Register, 1830?
First iron vessels built, 1830?
*Passage of the Reform Bill, 1832.
Party names of Liberal and Conservative begin to come into use, 1832.
*Emancipation of slaves in British colonies, 1833.
First Factory Act (regulates the employment of women and children), 1833.
East India trade thrown open, 1833.
New Poor-Law, 1834.
Government grant to "British" and "National" (Dissenting and Church of England) schools, 1834.
Municipal Corporation Act, 1835.
All trades in towns declared free, 1835.
Virtual abolition of the Press Gang, 1835.
Civil Marriage Act (permits Dissenters to be married in their own chapels), 1836.
Commutation of Tithes Act, 1836.
Sydney Smith writes.
Victoria, 1837.
Criminal law reforms, 1837.
Abolition of the pillory, 1837.
The electric telegraph in England, 1838?
The Opium War, 1839.
Union of Upper and Lower Canada, 1840.
National Sanitary Commission, 1840, 1843.
*Penny postage established, 1840.
Photography introduced, 1841?
Privilege of peerage (equivalent to benefit of clergy) abolished, 1841.
Chimney Sweep Act (forbids employment of children), 1842.
China compelled to open a number of ports to trade, 1842.
*Grove discovers the law of the indestructibility of force, 1842.
Percussion-lock muskets adopted, 1842.
Thames Tunnel completed, 1842.
Revolvers introduced, 1845?
India rubber begins to be extensively used, 1845?

Jews admitted to municipal offices, 1846.
*Famine in Ireland, 1846.
Railway speculation and panic, 1846.
*Repeal of the Corn Laws; beginning of free trade, 1846 (see 1360).
*Ether begins to be used in surgery, 1846.
Sewing-machines, 1846?
Government grants $50,000,000 for relief of the Irish famine, 1847.
Chartist agitation, 1848.
First government board of health, 1848.
Repeal of the Navigation Act, 1849 (see 1651).
*First "World's Fair," 1851.
Reaping and mowing machines, 1851?
Repeal of window tax, 1851 (see 1696).
Tenement House Act (one of a series for relief of working classes), 1851.
Colonization of New Zealand, 1852.
Reform of Court of Chancery begins, 1852.
The Crimean War, 1854.
Hallam, Macaulay, Arnold, Froude, Freeman, Carlyle, Thackeray, Brontë, Dickens, "George Eliot," Mill, Darwin, Spencer, Faraday, Tyndall, Huxley, Ruskin, Tennyson, Browning, 1855?
First large iron steamer built, 1855?
Abolition of the newspaper tax, 1855.
*Rise of cheap newspapers, 1855.
Bessemer's iron and steel process, 1856.
Right of search abandoned, 1856.
The Indian Mutiny, 1857.
Sovereignty of India given to the crown, 1858.
*First Atlantic cable, 1858; relaid, 1866.
*Jews admitted to Parliament, 1858.
Abolition of property qualification for members of Parliament, 1858 (see 1711).
*Darwin publishes "The Origin of Species," 1859.
Flogging virtually abolished in the army, 1859.
Weather predictions begin, 1860?
*The first English iron-clad built, 1861.
Imprisonment for debt (except fraudulent) abolished, 1861.
England recognizes the Confederates as "belligerents," 1861.
The *Trent* Affair, 1861.
Repeal of the paper tax, 1861 (see 1694).
*The escape of the *Alabama*, 1862.
*Herbert Spencer publishes his "First Principles," setting forth the philosophy of Evolution, 1862.
London underground railway opened, 1863.
Steam fire engines introduced, 1863?

*Reform Act, extending the franchise, 1867.
Establishment of the Dominion of Canada, 1867.
Compulsory church rates abolished, 1868.
Public executions abolished, 1868.
*Disestablishment of the Irish branch of the Church of England, 1869.
*Woman suffrage (to single women and widows who are householders), 1869.
*Government ("Board") schools established, 1870.
Street railways, 1870?
Women allowed to vote at school-board elections and serve on school boards, 1870.
Revision and consolidation of the statutes, 1870.
*Civil service examinations established, 1870.
Married Woman's Property Act, 1870, 1882.
*First Irish Land Bill, 1870.
Purchase of commissions in the army abolished, 1871.
Trades-unions recognized, 1871, 1875.
*Abolition of religious tests in the universities, 1871.
*The Ballot Act, 1872.
*Joseph Arch organizes the Agricultural Union, 1872.
*Geneva Tribunal (allows damages in the *Alabama* case), 1872.
National Federation of Employers, 1873.
England purchases nearly half of the Suez Canal, 1875.
The queen made Empress of India, 1877.
*Electric lighting in London, 1878?
*Telephone introduced, 1878?
*The Irish Land League, 1879.
Anti-rent agitation in Ireland, 1879.
Boycotting begins, 1880.
Burial Bill (gives Dissenters right to bury in public churchyards with their own religious services), 1880.
Irish Coercion Act, 1881.
Flogging abolished in the navy, 1881.
*Second Irish Land Act, 1881.
Act facilitating free trade in land, 1882.
Suppression of the Land League, 1882.
*Reform of Elections Act, 1884.
*Reform Act (extending suffrage to counties), "1884.
*Over 2,500,000 new voters admitted under Reform Act of 1884, 1885.
First "People's Parliament" (Peers, 549; H. of C., 670), 1886.
The Queen's Jubilee, June 21, 1887.
New Irish Crimes Act, 1887.

DESCENT OF THE ENGLISH SOVEREIGNS FROM EGBERT TO QUEEN VICTORIA.*

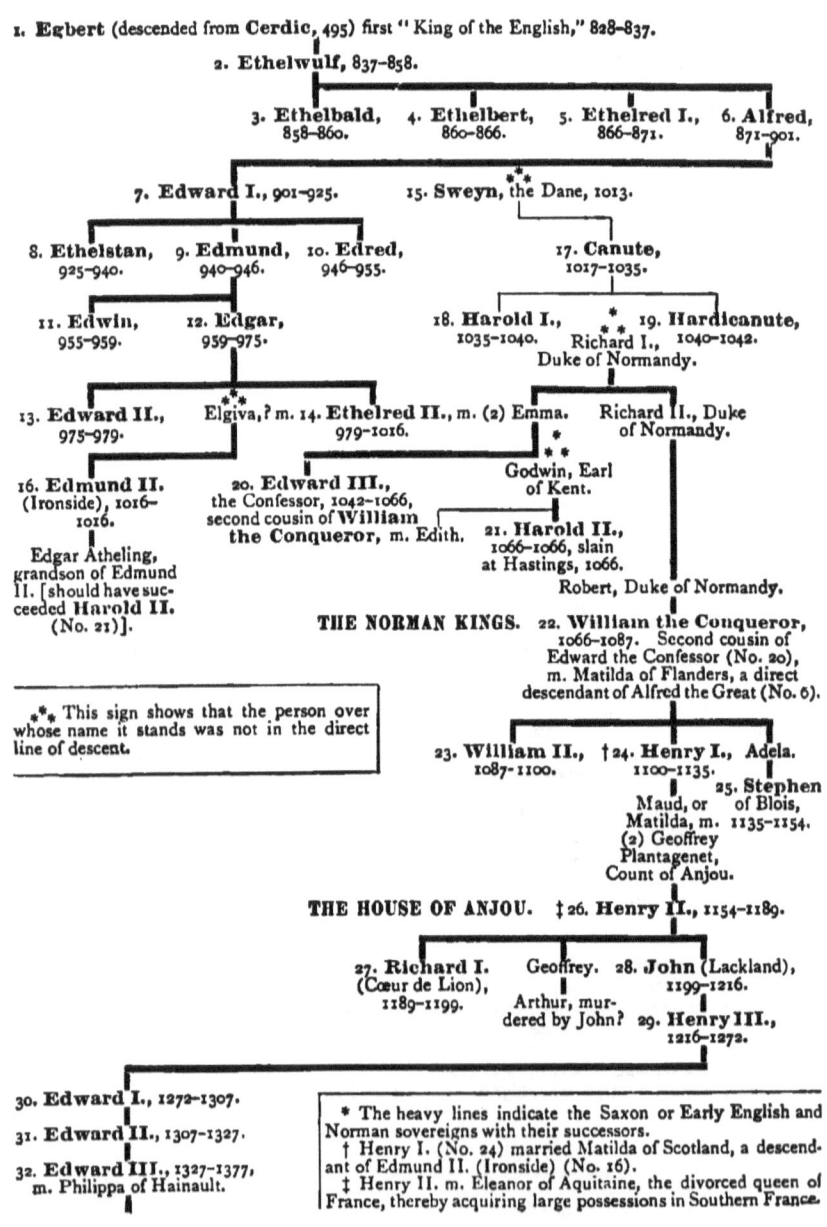

* The heavy lines indicate the Saxon or Early English and Norman sovereigns with their successors.
† Henry I. (No. 24) married Matilda of Scotland, a descendant of Edmund II. (Ironside) (No. 16).
‡ Henry II. m. Eleanor of Aquitaine, the divorced queen of France, thereby acquiring large possessions in Southern France.

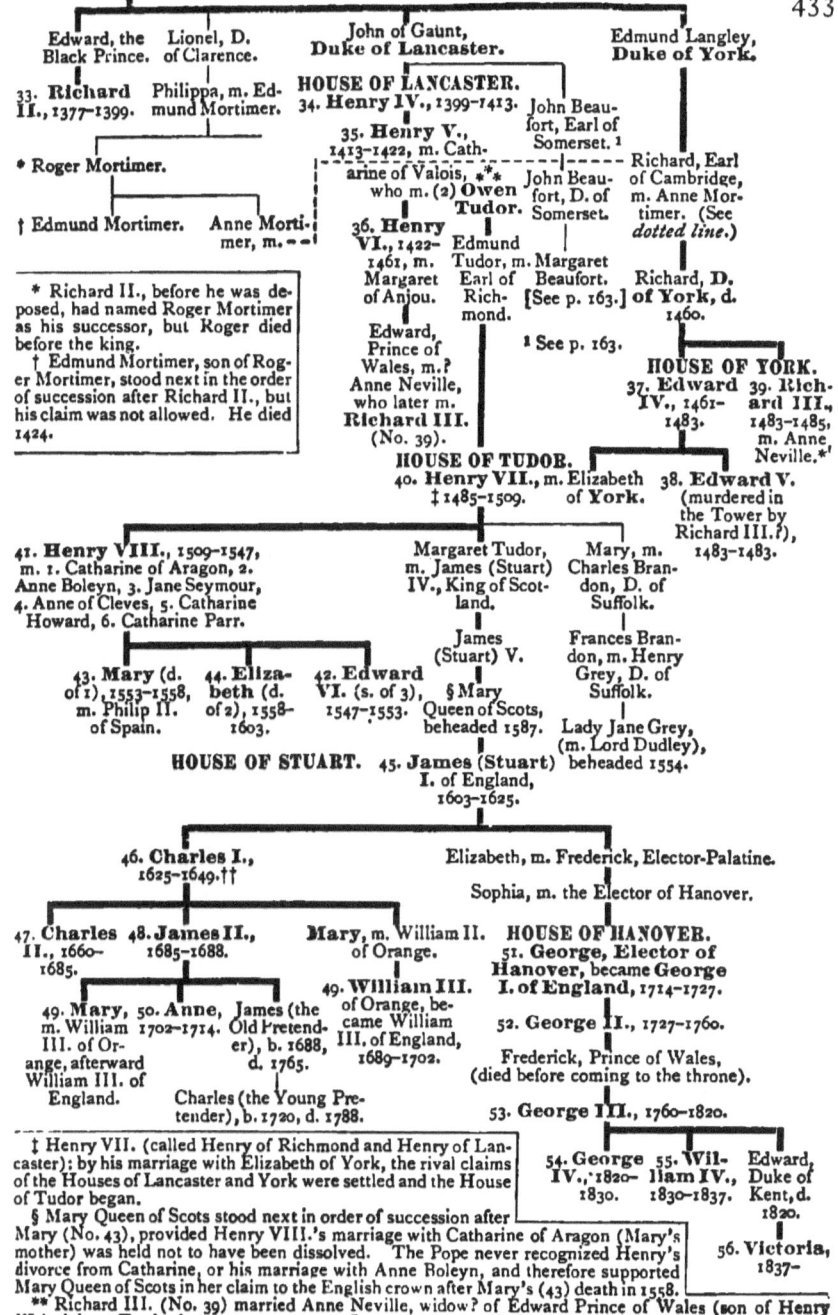

A SHORT LIST OF BOOKS ON ENGLISH HISTORY.

[The * marks contemporary or early history.]

I. THE PREHISTORIC PERIOD.

Dawkins's Early Man in Britain.
Geikie's Prehistoric Europe.
Keary's Dawn of History.
Wright's The Celt, the Roman, and the Saxon.
Elton's Origins of English History.
Rhys's Celtic Britain.
Geoffrey of Monmouth's Chronicle (legendary).
Geikie's Influence of Geology on English History, in Macmillan's Magazine, 1882.

II. THE ROMAN PERIOD, 55, 54 B.C.; 43-410 A.D.

*Cæsar's Commentaries on the Gallic War (Books IV. and V., chiefly 55, 54 B.C.).
*Tacitus's Agricola and Annals (chiefly from 78-84).
*Gildas's History of Britain (whole period).
*Bede's Ecclesiastical History of Britain (whole period).
Wright's The Celt, the Roman, and the Saxon.
Elton's Origins of English History.
Pearson's England during the Early and Middle Ages.
¹ Scarth's Roman Britain.

III. THE SAXON, OR EARLY ENGLISH, PERIOD, 449-1066.

*The Anglo-Saxon Chronicle (whole period).
*Gildas's History of Britain (Roman Conquest to 560).
*Bede's Ecclesiastical History of Britain (earliest times to 731).
*Nennius's History of Britain (earliest times to 642).
*Geoffrey of Monmouth's Chronicle (legendary) (earliest times to 689).
*Asser's Life of Alfred the Great.

Elton's Origins of English History.
Pauli's Life of Alfred.
Green's Making of England.
Green's Conquest of England.
Freeman's Norman Conquest, vols. I.-II.
Lappenberg's England under the Anglo-Saxon Kings.
Pearson's History of England during the Early and Middle Ages.
Pearson's Historical Atlas.
Freeman's Origin of the English Nation.
Stubbs's Constitutional History of England.
Taine's History of English Literature.
Church's Beginning of the Middle Ages.
² Armitage's Childhood of the English Nation.
² Grant Allen's Anglo-Saxon Britain.
² York-Powell's Early England.
² Freeman's Early English History.

IV. THE NORMAN PERIOD, 1066-1154.

*The Anglo-Saxon Chronicle (Peterborough continuation) (whole period).
*Ordericus Vitalis's Ecclesiastical History (to 1141).
*Wace's Roman de Rou (Taylor's translation) (to 1106).
*Bruce's Bayeux Tapestry Elucidated (with plates).
*William of Malmesbury's Chronicle (to 1142).
*Roger of Hoveden's Chronicle (whole period).
Freeman's Norman Conquest.
Church's Life of Anselm.
Taine's History of English Literature.
Stubbs's Constitutional History of England.
² Freeman's Short History of the Norman Conquest.
² Armitage's Childhood of the English Nation.
² Johnson's Normans in Europe.
² Creighton's England a Continental Power.

---

¹ The best short history.   ² The four best short histories.

V. The Angevin Period, 1154–1399.

*Matthew Paris's Chronicle (1067–1253).
⁴Richard of Devizes' Chronicle (1189–1192).
*Froissart's Chronicles (1325–1400).
Walsingham's Historia Brevis (1272–1422) (not translated).
*Jocelin of Brakelonde's Chronicle (1173–1202) (see Carlyle's Past and Present, Book II.).
Norgate's Angevin Kings.
Taine's History of English Literature.
Anstey's William of Wykeham.
Pearson's England in the Early and Middle Ages.
Maurice's Stephen Langton.
Creighton's Life of Simon de Montfort.
Stubbs's Constitutional History of England.
Bémont's Vie de Simon de Montfort.
Gairdner and Spedding's Studies in English History (the Lollards).
Knight's Life of Caxton.
Seebohm's Essay on the Black Death (Fortnightly Review, 1865).
Maurice's Wat Tyler, et al.
Charles's Vie de Roger Bacon.
Buddensieg's Life of Wiclif.
Burrows's Wiclif's Place in History.
Pauli's Pictures of Old England.
[1] Stubbs's Early Plantagenets.
[1] Rowley's Rise of the People.
[1] Warburton's Edward III.
Shakespeare's John and Richard (Hudson's edition).
Scott's Ivanhoe and the Talisman (Richard I. and John).

VI. The Lancastrian Period, 1399–1461.

*The Paston Letters (Gairdner's edition) (1424–1506).
*Fortescue's Governance of England (Plummer's edition) (1460?).
*Walsingham's Historia Brevis (not translated) (1272–1422).
*Hall's Chronicle (1398–1509).
Brougham's England under the House of Lancaster.
Besant's Life of Sir Richard Whittington.
Taine's English Literature.
Rand's Chaucer's England.

Stubbs's Constitutional History of England.
Strickland's Queens of England (Margaret of Anjou).
Reed's English History in Shakespeare.
[2] Gairdner's Houses of Lancaster and York.
[2] Rowley's Rise of the People.
Shakespeare's Henry IV., V., and VI. (Hudson's edition).

VII. The Yorkist Period, 1461–1485.

*The Paston Letters (Gairdner's edition) (1424–1506).
*Sir Thomas More's Edward V. and Richard III.
*Hall's Chronicle (1398–1509).
Hallam's Middle Ages.
Gairdner's Richard III.
Taine's English Literature.
Stubbs's Constitutional History of England.
[2] Gairdner's Houses of Lancaster and York.
[2] Rowley's Rise of the People.
Shakespeare's Richard III. (Hudson's edition).

VIII. The Tudor Period, 1485–1603.

*Holinshed's History of England (from earliest times to 1577).
*Lord Bacon's Life of Henry VII.
*Latimer's 1st and 6th Sermons before Edward VI. and "The Ploughers" (1549).
*Hall's Chronicle (1398–1509).
Hallam's Constitutional History of England.
Lingard's History of England (Roman Catholic).
Froude's History of England.
Strickland's Queens of England (Catharine of Aragon, Anne Boleyn, Mary, Elizabeth).
Demaus's Life of Latimer.
Froude's Short Studies.
Nicholls's Life of Cabot.
Dixon's History of the Church of England.
Hall's Society in the Age of Elizabeth.
Thornbury's Shakespeare's England.
Macaulay's Essay on Lord Burleigh.
Barrows's Life of Drake.
Creighton's Life of Raleigh.
Taine's English Literature.

---

[1] The three best short histories.   [2] The two best short histories.

[1] Creighton's The Tudors and the Reformation.
[1] Seebohm's Era of the Protestant Revolution.
[1] Moberly's Early Tudors.
[1] Creighton's Age of Elizabeth.
Shakespeare's Henry VIII. (Hudson's edition).
Scott's Kenilworth, Abbot, Monastery (Elizabeth, and Mary Queen of Scots).

IX. THE STUART PERIOD (FIRST PART), 1603–1649.

*The Prose Works of James I. (1599–1625).
*Fuller's Church History of Britain (earliest times to 1648).
*Clarendon's History of the Rebellion (1625–1660).
*Memoirs of Col. Hutchinson (1616–1664).
*May's History of the Long Parliament (1640–1643).
Taine's History of English Literature.
Speddings's Lord Bacon and his Times.
Gardiner's History of England (1603–1642).
Church's Life of Lord Bacon.
Hallam's Constitutional History of England.
Hume's History of England (Tory).
Macaulay's History of England (Whig).
Lingard's History of England (Roman Catholic).
Strickland's Queens of England.
Ranke's History of England in the XVII. Century.
Guizot's Histoire[2] de Charles I.
Bancroft's History of the United States.
Macaulay's Essays (Bacon, Hampden, Hallam's History).
Goldwin Smith's Three English Statesmen (Cromwell, Pym, Hampden).
[3] Cordery's Struggle against Absolute Monarchy.
[3] Cordery and Phillpott's King and Commonwealth.
[3] Gardiner's Puritan Revolution.
Scott's Fortunes of Nigel (James I.).

X. THE COMMONWEALTH AND PROTECTORATE, 1649–1660 (SEE PRECEDING PERIOD).

*Ludlow's Memoirs (1640–1668).
*Carlyle's Life and Letters of Oliver Cromwell.
Carlyle's Hero Worship (Cromwell).
Guizot's Cromwell and the Commonwealth.
Guizot's Richard Cromwell.
Guizot's Life of Monk.
Masson's Life and Times of Milton.
Bisset's Omitted Chapters in the History of England.
Pattison's Life of Milton.
Scott's Woodstock (Cromwell).

XI. STUART PERIOD (SECOND PART), 1660–1714.

*Evelyn's Diary (1641–1706).
*Pepys's Diary (1659–1669).
*Burnet's History of His Own Time (1660–1713).
Macaulay's History of England (Whig).
Hallam's Constitutional History of England.
Taine's History of English Literature.
Strickland's Queens of England.
Ranke's History of England in the Seventeenth Century.
Hume's History of England (Tory).
Brewster's Life of Newton.
Lingard's History of England (Roman Catholic).
Green's History of the English People.
Stanhope's History of England.
Lecky's History of England in the Eighteenth Century.
Macaulay's Essays (Milton, Mackintosh's History, War of the Spanish Succession, and The Comic Dramatists of the Restoration).
Creighton's Life of Marlborough.
Guizot's History of Civilization (Chapter XIII).
[3] Morris's Age of Anne.
[3] Hale's Fall of the Stuarts.
[3] Cordery's Struggle against Absolute Monarchy.
Scott's Peveril of the Peak, and Old Mortality (Charles II.).
Thackeray's Henry Esmond (Anne).

XII. THE HANOVERIAN PERIOD, 1714 TO THE PRESENT TIME.

*Memoirs of Robert Walpole.
*Horace Walpole's Memoirs and Journals.

---

[1] The four best short histories.
[2] See Guizot's History of the Revolution for translation of all but introduction of 120 pages.
[3] The three best short histories.

BOOKS ON ENGLISH HISTORY. 437

Hallam's Constitutional History of England (to death of George II., 1760).
May's Constitutional History (1760-1870).
Amos's English Constitution (1830-1880).
Amos's Primer of the English Constitution.
Bagehot's English Constitution.
Lecky's History of England in the XVIII. Century.
Walpole's History of England (1815-1860).
Molesworth's History of England (1830-1870).
Martineau's History of England (1816-1846).
Taine's History of English Literature.
Bancroft's History of the United States.
Bryant's History of the United States.
Stanhope's History of England (1713-1783).
Green's Causes of the Revolution.
Seeley's Expansion of England.
Frothingham's Rise of the Republic.
McCarthy's History of Our Own Times (1837-1880).
McCarthy's England under Gladstone (1880-1884).
Ward's Reign of Victoria (1837-1887).
Southey's Life of Wesley.
Southey's Life of Nelson.
Wharton's Wits and Beaux of Society.
Waite's Life of Wellington.

Massey's Life of George III.
Goldwin Smith's Lectures (Foundation of the American Colonies).
Macaulay's Essays (Warren Hastings, Clive, Pitt, Walpole, Chatham, Johnson, Madame D'Arblay).
Smiles's Life of James Watt.
Sydney Smith's Peter Plymley's Letters.
Smiles's Life of Stephenson.
Thackeray's Four Georges.
Smiles's Industrial Biography.
Grant Allen's Life of Darwin.
Ashton's Dawn of the XIX. Century in England.
[1] Ludlow's American Revolution.
[1] Rowley's Settlement of the Constitution (1689-1784).
[1] Morris's Early Hanoverians (George I. and II.).
[1] McCarthy's Epoch of Reform (1830-1850).
[1] Tancock's England during the American and European Wars (1765-1820).
[1] Browning's Modern England (1820-1874).
Scott's Rob Roy, Waverley, and Redgauntlet (the Old and the Young Pretender, 1715, 1745-53).
Thackeray's Virginians (Washington).
Dickens's Barnaby Rudge (1780).

For fuller information in regard to authorities, see Professor Allen's Reader's Guide to English History; or, where a critical estimate of the author is desired, consult Professor Adams's Manual of Historical Literature, and Professor Mullinger's Authorities. For review articles, see Poole's Index to Reviews.

In addition to the above list, the following general histories will be found excellent: —

Hume's England (Brewer's Student's edition), 1 vol.
Green's Short History of the English People, 1 vol.
Bright's History of England, 3 vols.
Burt's Synoptical History of England, 1 vol.
On the Constitutional History of England: Taswell-Langmead's Constitutional History, 1 vol.; Creasy's, 1 vol.: Ransome's, 1 vol.
Rogers's British Citizen, 1 vol.

Works of Reference.

Gneist's Constitutional History of England.
Knight's Pictorial History of England.
Taylor's Words and Places.
P. V. Smith's English Institutions.
Hallam's Middle Ages.
Edmunds's Names of Places.

Cassell's Dictionary of English History.
Feilden's Short Constitutional History of England.
Freeman's Rise of the English Constitution.
Digby's History of the Law of Real Property.
Blackstone's Commentaries.
Mackay's History of Popular Delusions.
Cunningham's Growth of English Industry and Commerce.
Dowell's History of Taxation in England.
J. E. T. Rogers's Work and Wages.
Ackland and Ransome's Handbook of English Political History.
Spencer's Sociological Tables (England).
Cutts's Scenes and Characters of the Middle Ages.
Eccleston's English Antiquities.
Jessopp's Life in Norfolk Six Hundred Years Ago (Nineteenth Century, 1883).

---

[1] The six best short histories.

Wright's Domestic Manners in England in the Middle Ages.
Godwin's Archæologist's Handbook.
Parker's Our English Home (Oxford, 1860).
Bohn's Cyclopedia of Political Knowledge.
Bevans's Statistical Map of England.
Parker's Elements of Gothic Architecture.
Johnston's Historical Atlas.
Wilkins's Political Ballads.
Bailey's Succession to the Crown.

On Modern England and English Life, see

Irving's Bracebridge Hall, and Sketch-Book.
Emerson's English Traits.
Colman's European Life and Manners.
Hawthorne's Our Old Home, and Note Books.
Howitt's Visits to Remarkable Places, and Rural Life.

Timbs's Abbeys and Castles of England and Wales.
Heath's English Peasantry.
Taine's Notes on England.
Nadal's London Society.
Hoppins's Old England.
Higginson's English Statesmen.
R. G. White's England Without and Within.
Escott's England.
Society in London, by a Foreign Resident (Harper).
Patten's England as seen by an American Banker.
O. W. Holmes's One Hundred Days in Europe.
R. L. Collier's English Home Life.
Laugel's L'Angleterre.
Daryl's La Vie Publique en Angleterre.
Max O'Rell's John Bull et son Ile.
Badeau's English Aristocracy.

STATISTICS FOR 1887.

Area of England and Wales, 58,310 square miles.
Extreme length, 365 miles; extreme width, 311 miles.
No part more than about 120 miles from the sea.
Mean temperature during the year in Great Britain, 49.06°.
Population of England and Wales, 27,870,586.
Population to square mile, 482 (the most densely populated country in Europe, except Belgium).
Area of Great Britain, 88,006 square miles.
Population of Great Britain, 31,819,979.
Area of Great Britain and Ireland, 120,832 square miles.
Population of Great Britain and Ireland, 37,020,000.
Population of London, about 4,250,000.
About one-third of the entire population of England and Wales is in the cities.
Area of British Empire, 9,079,711 square miles.
Population of British Empire, 320,676,000.
National debt of Great Britain and Ireland, £748,750,000 ($3,623,950,000).[1]
Average rate of taxation per head, £2.1.1 ($9.94).[1]
Church of England (membership), 13,500,000.[2]
Dissenting churches, 12,500,000.[2]
Roman Catholics, 2,500,000.
Number of paupers in receipt of relief, 807,639.
Total number of children of school age (5–15), 5,426,490.
Total attendance (not including private schools), 3,273,124.
Total British army, 676,156.
Total effective force, 200,785.
Total navy, 60,632.
Total number of vessels in navy, 258.
Iron-clads (ranging from 1230 to 11,800 tons each), 76.

---

[1] Calling the pound $4.84.   [2] Some estimates make them about equal.

Of the cultivated land of England and Wales, something over one-fourth, is held by 874 persons, while about 10,000 persons hold two-thirds of the whole.
Number of men in army and navy, 1 out of 26.
National debt per capita, $127.
Total wealth of Great Britain and Ireland, $45,000,000,000 (the wealthiest nation on the globe).
Annual increase of wealth, $375,000,000
Average annual income, $165.
Death rate (England and Wales), 19.3 per 1000.

Statistics of the United States (for Comparison).

Area (including Alaska), 3,611,849 square miles.
Population, about 60,000,000.
National debt, $1,380,087,279.
Total wealth, $35,000,000,000.
Annual increase of wealth, $825,000,000.
Average annual income, $165.
Taxation per capita, $6.00.
Standing army, 26,000.
Navy, 10,340.
Number of men in army and navy, 1 out of 322.
From 1840–1880 the wealth of Great Britain doubled; that of the United States increased tenfold.
AUTHORITIES: — Encyclopædia Britannica; Scribner's Statistical Atlas; Mulhall's Balance-Sheet of the World; Atkinson's Strength of Nations; Jean's Supremacy of England; The Statesman's Year-Book.

INDEX.

Abolition of the slave trade, 331.
    slavery, 354.
Acadia, villagers expelled, 320.
Act of Attainder, 285.
    Settlement, 282, 299, 301, 306.
    Supremacy, 211.
    Toleration, 282.
    Uniformity, 260.
Addison, Joseph, 299.
Agincourt, battle of, 156.
Agricola, Roman governor, 23.
Aix la Chapelle, treaty of, 316.
Alabama, privateer, 372.
Albert, Prince Consort, 362.
    his death, 370.
Albion, derivation of the name, 9.
Alfred the Great, 40.
    his laws and translations, 42.
    his navy, 42; his victories, 41.
America discovered, 186.
American colonies taxed, 324.
    Revolution, 328.
    civil war, 370, 371.
Anderida, siege of, 33.
Andros, Sir Edmund, 325.
Angevins, or Plantagenets, 87.
Angles, invasion by, 34.
Anne Boleyn, 191, 194, 198.
    of Cleves, 198.
    Queen, 289, 299.
Anselm, Archbishop, 72, 73.
Arch, Joseph, 374.
Architecture, 56, 84, 147, 226, 303.
Arthur, King, 34.
    Prince, murdered, 103.
Articles of Faith, 202.
Artillery introduced, 184.
Atlantic cable laid, 368.
Augustine reaches England, 35.
Austrian Succession, War of, 316.

Bacon, Lord Francis, 218.
    his impeachment, 236, 302.
    Friar Roger, 111, 128.

Bacon, Sir Nicholas, 216.
Baliol, awarded Scotch crown, 117.
    owns allegiance to Edward, 117.
    rebels, and is overthrown, 117.
Bank of England, 288.
Barebones's Parliament, 250.
Baronage, sketch of, 359.
Battle of Agincourt, 156.
    Blenheim, 294.
    Bosworth Field, 172.
    the Boyne, 286.
    Bunker Hill, 328.
    Crecy, 127.
    Culloden, 317.
    Dettingen, 316.
    Edgehill, 244.
    Flodden Field, 190.
    Fontenoy, 316.
    Hastings, 60.
    Lewes, 113.
    Marston Moor, 245.
    Naseby, 245.
    New Orleans, 335.
    the Nile, 333.
    Plassey, 318.
    Ramillies, 294.
    St. Albans, 165.
    Sedgemoor, 271.
    Sheriffmuir, 310.
    Shrewsbury, 152.
    the Standard, 76.
    Tewkesbury, 167.
    Tinchebrai, 74.
    Towton, 165.
    Trafalgar, 333.
    Wakefield, 165.
    Waterloo, 335.
    Yorktown, 329.
Bayeux Tapestry, 61, 84.
Becket, Thomas, chancellor, 89.
    leaves England, 91.
    returns, 93; is murdered, 93.
Benevolences, 169, 175.
Bible, the first English, 138.

INDEX. 441

Bill of Rights, 282, 301.
Black Death, the, 132.
    Hole of Calcutta, 317.
    Prince, 128, 130, 131.
Bloody Assizes, the, 272.
Boadicea, her revolt, 21.
    her death, 22.
Board schools, 375.
Boleyn, Anne, 191; executed, 198.
Books, the earliest, 55.
Boston Tea Party, 327.
Bretigny, peace of, 130.
Bright, John, 366.
Britain, primitive, its climate, etc., 1.
    becomes England, 39.
Britons, their bravery, 34.
Bronze Age, 7.
    men, Greek account of, 8.
Brougham, Lord Henry, 346, 353, 361.
Bruce, Robert, his revolt, 120.
    king of Scots, 123.
Buckingham, Duke of, 171.
Bunyan, John, 261, 302.
Butler, Bishop, 302.

Cabal, the, 258.
Cabinet government, rise of, 308.
Cabot, John and Sebastian, 185, 226.
Cade, Jack, his rebellion, 161.
Cæsar, his campaigns, 18, 19, 20.
Calais taken, 129.
Calendar, correction of, 318.
Canal system begun, 338.
Cannon, first use of, 128.
Canute (Knut) succeeds his father, 45.
    divides England into four earldoms, 45.
Caractacus, captive, his dignity, 20.
Caroline, Queen, 314.
    of Brunswick, Queen, 346.
Catharine of Aragon, 191.
Catholic emancipation, 347.
Cato Street conspiracy, 346.
Caxton introduces printing, 167, 168.
Cecil, Sir William, 210.
Celts, early, their condition, 8.
Channel, the British, in history, 15.
Charles I., King, 238–247.
    II., King, 257–269.
Charter, the Great, 105, 108, 109, 112, 142.
Charter, Henry I.'s, 73.
Chartists, the, 363.
Chaucer, 133, 137, 141.
Christianity introduced, 22.
    its effects, 53.
Christ's Hospital, 203.

Church property confiscated, 195, 203.
    rates abolished, 374.
Churchill, John, Duke of Marlborough, 278, 293, 361.
Clarkson, Thomas, 332.
Climate of England, 16.
Clive, Lord, his victories, 317.
Cobden, Richard, 366.
Columbus, his discoveries, 185, 187, 226.
Commercial position of England, 16.
Common law, 53.
Commons, House of, supreme, 358.
    rise of the House of, 114.
Commonwealth, protectorate, 247.
Compurgation, 52.
Constitutions of Clarendon, 91.
Corn Laws, the, 365; repealed, 366.
Cornwallis, Lord, his defeat, 329.
Corporation Act, 260, 347.
Counties palatine, 64.
Courts, reformed, 381.
Covenanters, the, 241, 261.
Cranmer, Dr. Thomas, 193.
Crimea, war in the, 369.
Cromwell, Oliver, 241, 248, 250, 252, 254.
    Richard, 255, 256.
    Thomas, 194; beheaded, 198.
Crosby Hall, London, 178.
Crusades, 102.
Cuthbert, monk and missionary, 36.

"Danegeld," tribute to Northmen, 44.
Danish names, 14; invasion, 40.
Darwin, Charles, 379.
David I., of Scotland, invades England, 76.
Davy, Sir Humphry, 340.
Declaration of Right, 280.
De Foe, Daniel, 302.
De Montfort, Earl Simon, 112, 143, 361.
    defeats Henry III., 113.
    summons a parliament, 114.
    his monument still unbuilt, 114.
Despenser, Hugh, and his son, 123.
Disraeli, Lord Beaconsfield, 361, 373.
Dissenters relieved, 375.
"Divine Right of Kings," 232, 238, 290, 296, 300.
Domesday Book, 67.
Dover, treaty of, 264.
Drake, Sir Francis, 220.
Druids, their abode, teaching, etc., 10.
    expedition against, 21.
Dryden, John, 302.
Dudley, Lord Gulford, 205; beheaded, 206.
Dunstan, Archbishop of Canterbury, 43.

Education Bill, 361, 374.
Edward, Prince, 45; Confessor, 46.
　I., King, summons Parliament, 115.
　　builds Conway and other castles, 116.
　II., his incapacity, 123.
　　deposed and murdered, 124.
　III., king at fourteen, 124; his death, 134.
　IV., King, 167.
　V., Prince, 170.
　VI., King, 201.
　　(Black Prince), 128, 130, 131.
Egbert, King, 39.
Eleanor, Queen, her heroism, 115.
　her death, 118; crosses, 118.
　her tomb, 119.
Eliot, Sir John, 240.
Elizabeth, Queen, 206, 208–222.
　of York, 172.
Elliott, Ebenezer, corn-law poet, 366.
England, early, its geography, etc., 12.
　its commercial situation, 16.
English people, their progress, 380–388.
　history, its characteristics, 388.
　-speaking race, its unity, 388.
Entail, 119, 143.

Factory reform, 354.
Fairfax, Lord Thomas, 248.
Fair Rosamond, 94.
Feudal System, 50, 80, 269.
Field of the Cloth of Gold, 190.
Fielding, Henry, 302.
Fire, great, of London, 262.
Fisher, Bishop John, executed, 195.
Five Members, attempted arrest of the, 242.
Folkland, 50.
Fox, Charles James, 332.
Franklin, Benjamin, 326.
Frederick the Great, of Prussia, 318.
Freemen their duties, 50.
Free trade, 366.
French Revolution, 332.
Friction match, the, 355.
Frobisher, Sir Martin, his voyages, 217.
Fry, Elizabeth, philanthropist, 332.
Fulton, Robert, his steamboat, 340.

Gas, burning, first used, 339.
Gaveston, Piers, banished, 122.
　returns, 122; beheaded, 122.
Geneva, international court at, 372.
George, of Denmark, Prince, 289.
　I., King, 306–314.
　II., King, 314–322.
　III., King, 323–343.
　IV., King, 344–348.

Gibraltar taken, 294.
Gladstone, William Ewart, 362, 371.
Glencoe, massacre of, 287.
Glendower, Owen, 151.
Gloucester, appointed Protector, 169.
Gordon, Lord George, riots, 330.
"Gospel Oaks," 322.
Government, its stability, 357.
Gregory I. and English slaves in Rome, 35
　Pope, sends missionaries, 35.
　VII., his appeal to William, 65.
Grey, Earl, 353.
　Lady Jane, 204; beheaded, 206.
Grove, Sir William, 379.
Guilds, 57, 147.
Gunpowder plot, 232.

Habeas Corpus Act, 269, 361.
Hampden, John, 238, 241.
Hampton Court Conference, 231.
Harold, King, 47, 58.
　his death, 60; his grave, 60.
Hastings, Warren, impeached, 330.
Henry I., issues a charter, 73.
　seizes Normandy, 74.
　II., his charter and reforms, 88.
　quarrels with Becket, 90, 93.
　III., King, 109; his extravagance, 110.
　rebuilds Westminster Abbey, 110.
　IV., Duke of Lancaster, king, 150.
　his death, 154.
　V., Prince, 154; king, 155.
　conquest of France, 155, 157.
　VI., King, 158.
　marries Margaret of Anjou, 160.
　dies a prisoner in the Tower, 166.
　VII., marries Elizabeth of York, 179.
　his chapel, 186.
　VIII., King, 187; his death, 200.
　his marriages, 190, 194, 198, 199.
Hereward, 62.
High Commission Court, 211, 242, 275.
Hildebrand (Pope Gregory VII.), 65.
Hill, Sir Rowland, 363.
Howard, Catharine, 199.
　John, philanthropist, 332.
Hume, David, 302.
Hundred Years' War, 126, 131.

India, rebellion in, 369.
　Clive in, 317.
　English Empire in, 317.
Insane, improved treatment of, 381.
Intemperance in the eighteenth century, 321.
Ireland, colonization of, 235.
　famine in, 366.

INDEX. 443

Irish Church disestablished, 374.
    Land Act, 376, 378.
    Land League, 377.
Iron, its early use, 9.
Isabelle of France, Queen, 123.
    her infidelity, 123.
    murders her husband, 124.
    prisoner for life, 125.

Jacobites, 281.
James I., King, 229–237.
    II., King, 270–280.
Jeffreys, Judge George, 272.
Jenkins's ear, war of, 315.
Jenner, Dr. Edward, 313.
Jews, robbed and expelled, 118.
    admitted to Parliament, 361, 373.
Joan of Arc, 159.
John (Lackland), King, his quarrels, 103.
    murders Prince Arthur, 103.
    grants Magna Carta, 106.
    his evasions; his death, 108.
    of Gaunt (Ghent), 134.
Johnson, Dr. Samuel, 290, 302.
Jonson, Ben, 218, 302.
"Junius," his letters, 331.
Jutes, their invasion, 32.

Knighthood, 83.
Knights of St. John (Hospitallers), 144.
    Templars, 144.

Land League, 377.
Law reform, 331, 380.
Lewes, battle of, 113.
Lincoln, President Abraham, 371.
Literature, rise of English, 133, 137.
    of Anne's reign, 298.
    of Elizabeth's, 216, 218.
    of George III.'s, 341.
    of present age, 380.
Livingstone, David, African explorer, 379.
Locke, John, 302.
Lollards, 139; persecuted, 153.
    outbreak of, 155.
London (Llyn-din), its origin, 21.
    police, 348.
    William's charter, 61.
Londonderry, siege of, 285.
Long Parliament, 241.
Lords Ordainers, 122.
Luther, 187, 189.
Lyell, Sir Charles, 379.

Macaulay, Lord Thomas Babington, 361.
Magellan, Ferdinand de, navigator, 226.

Magna Carta, 105, 107, 142.
Man, primitive, his condition, 2.
    what we owe to him, 10.
Manchester massacre, 344.
Mandeville, Sir John, his travels, 133.
Mar, John Erskine, Earl of, 310.
Margaret, Queen, her bravery, 165.
    flight to Scotland, 166.
    prisoner; released; died in France, 167.
Marlborough, John Churchill, Duke of, 278, 293.
    Sarah Jennings, Duchess of, 295.
Martin Luther, 187, 189.
Mary (Bloody), Queen, 204.
    marries Philip II. of Spain, 206.
    her persecutions, 206; her death, 207.
    "Queen of Scots," 202, 218, 219.
Masham, Mrs. Abigail, 296.
Matilda (Maud), queen of Henry I., 73.
    claims the crown, 75.
Methodists, their rise, 321.
Milton, John, 248, 302.
Miner's safety lamp, by Davy, 340.
Monasteries suppressed, 195.
Monk, General (Duke of Albemarle), 256.
Monks, their literary work, 37.
Monmouth, Duke of, 271.
Monopolies, 215, 237.
Montcalm, Marquis de, his defence of Quebec; his death, 320.
Montrose, James Graham, Marquis, 249.
More, Sir Thomas, chancellor, executed, 195.
    his "Utopia," 216.
Mortimer, Roger (Earl of March), 123.
Mortmain, 120, 144.
Mutiny Act, 282.

Names: Celtic, Roman, 13.
    Saxon, Danish, Norman, 14.
Nantes, edict of, 274.
Napoleon Bonaparte, 333.
National council, 77.
    debt, 288, 336.
Nelson, Lord Horatio, Admiral, 333, 361.
New Amsterdam seized, 262.
    Forest, 66.
"New Learning," the, 188.
"New Style," correction of the calendar, 318.
Newspaper, first, 244, 298.
    tax, 368.
Newton, Sir Isaac, 268, 303, 379.
Nobility, the, 80, 160, 360.
Non-jurors, 281.
Norman Conquest, 58; its results, 69, 357.
Normandy, loss of, 104.
North, Lord, premier, 323

Northmen, the, invade France, 44.
or Normans, settle Normandy, 44.

Oates, Titus, 266, 270.
O'Connell, Daniel, 348.
O'Connor, Feargus, 364.
Oldcastle, Sir John, 155.
Opium War, the, 369.
Ordeal, the, 52.
Oxygen, discovery of, 339.

"Parliament, the Mad," 112.
 expelled, 249.
 convention, 256, 280.
 debates of, published, 331.
Parliamentary reform, 349.
Parr, Catharine, 199.
Peel, Sir Robert, premier, 348.
Peerage, sketch of, 359.
Peers, their number and influence, 361.
"Petition of Right," 239.
Philip II., of Spain, 206.
"Pilgrims, the," 233.
Pillory, the, 331.
Pitt, William, Earl of Chatham, 314, 326.
 the younger, premier, 332, 337, 361.
Plague, the, 132, 262.
Plantagenet, 87.
Poitiers, victory of, 130.
Police, the new, 348.
Political progress, 358.
Poor-law, the first, 222.
Pope, the, and William I., 65.
 and John, 105.
 and Henry VIII., 194.
 Alexander, 302.
Popish plot, 266.
Postal reform, 363.
Post-office begun, 224.
Prehistoric man, 10.
President of United States, his powers, 359.
Press, the, 284, 331.
"Pretender," the (James Edward), 278, 292, 310.
 the Young" (Charles Edward), 310, 316.
"Pride's Purge," 246.
Priestley, Dr. Joseph, scientist, 339.
Prince Rupert, 243.
Printing, introduction of, 167, 177.
Protestantism established, 202.
 effects of, 204.
Purveyance, 176.

Quebec, capture of, 320.
Queen, the, her powers, 358.
 Victoria, her lineage, 357.
 her marriage, 362.

Railway, steam, the first, 355.
Raleigh, Sir Walter, 217; beheaded, 237.
Reform Bill, 351, 361.
 the second, 373.
 the third, 374.
"Regicides," the, 260.
Revolution of 1688, 279, 284.
 American, 328.
 French, 332.
Richard I. (Cœur de Lion), King, 97.
 in third crusade, 99; prisoner, 101
 II., King, 134.
 deposed and murdered, 140.
 III. (Duke of Gloucester), King, 170
 his death, 173.
Robert invades England and retires, 74.
 prisoner; his death, 74.
Roman Catholicism, 199, 204, 206, 270, 274, 283.
 invasion, 12, 19.
 first colony, 20; cities, 24.
 system of government, 24.
 paved roads, 24; forts and walls, 25.
 taxation and cruelty, 27.
 remains still existing, 28.
Rotten boroughs, 349.
Royal Society, the, 268.
Rump Parliament, 246.
Runes, 54.
Rye House Plot, 267.
Ryswick, peace of, 200.

Sacheverell, Dr Henry, 296.
Saint Albans, council held there, 106.
 Bartholomew's Day (massacre), 219.
 Paul's Cathedral, 288, 303.
Saxon invasion, 33, 47.
 names, 14.
Schools, government, 375.
Scroggs, Sir William, Chief Justice, 266, 284
Scutage, 89, 144.
Seven Bishops, petition of, 276.
 Years' War, 318.
Seymour, Jane, 198.
Shakespeare, 218, 226, 302.
Ship money, 240.
Siege of Londonderry, 285.
Slave trade abolished, 331.
Slavery abolished, 354.
Small-pox conquered, 312.
Smith, John, Captain, 233.
Solemn League and Covenant, the, 244.
South Sea Bubble, 311.
Spanish Armada, 220.
 Succession, War of, 291.
Spectator, the (Addison's), 299.

INDEX.

Spenser, Edmund, poet, 218.
Stamp Act, the, 325.
Star-Chamber Court, 183, 240, 242.
Statistics, 408, 409.
Statutes of Winchester, 119.
Steam-engine, 303; perfected, 338.
    navigation, 340.
Stephen, last of Norman kings, 75, 77.
Stone Age, rough, 2; polished, 5.
    of Scone, 116.
Stonehenge, 10, 68.
Strike, the great, 132, 148.
Supremacy, Act of, 194, 211.
Survey, the great, 67.
Sweyn, the Dane, conquers England, 45.
Swift, Jonathan, Dean, 302, 311.
Sydney, Sir Philip, 217.

Talbot, Richard (Earl of Tyrconnel), 275, 285.
Taylor, Jeremy, Bishop, 302.
Tea tax, 326.
Tennyson, Lord, poet, 361.
Test Act, 347.
Thirty-nine Articles, the, 212.
Tin, early found in Cornwall, 9.
Toleration Act, 281, 284.
Tower of London, 63, 85.
Towns, rise of free, 99.
Treaty of Dover, 264.
    Troyes, 157.
    Utrecht, 297.
    Wedmore, 41.
Trelawney, Jonathan, Bishop, 276.
Trial by battle, 79.
    by jury, 96.
Tudor, House of, 179.
Tyler, Wat, 135.
Tyndall, John, scientist, 380.

Union of England and Scotland, 298.
    of Great Britain and Ireland, 337.
Unitarians burned, 302.
United States, independence of, 328.
    war with, 328-329.
    second war, 334.
Utrecht, treaty of, 297.

Vaccination introduced, 313.
Vane, Sir Henry, 250.
Victoria, Queen, 357.
Virginia colonized, 233.
Vortigern's advice, 32.

Wales, Prince of, the first, 116.
Wallace, Sir William, rebels, 117.
    captured and executed, 118.
Walpole, Sir Robert, premier, 308, 313, 321.
Walsingham, Sir Francis, 210.
Walworth, mayor of London, 136.
Wars of the Roses, 162-164, 173.
Washington, George, 251, 319, 329.
Watt, James, inventor, 338, 339, 340.
Wat Tyler, his rebellion, 135; killed, 136.
Wellington, Duke of, 334, 335, 336, 347, 352, 361.
Wentworth, Thomas, Earl of Strafford, 240.
Wesley, Rev. John, 321.
Westminster Abbey built, 46; rebuilt, 110.
White Horse, the, Alfred's standard, 41.
Wilberforce, William, philanthropist, 332.
Wilkes, John, political writer, 331.
William, the Norman, invades England, 58.
    grants charter to London, 61.
    builds Tower of London, 63.
    his character, 66; his death, 68.
    his grave, how paid for, 69.
    his bequest, 70.
    Prince of Orange, 277, 289,
    and Mary crowned, 280-289.
    Rufus, King, his violence and fraud, 71.
    his merits; his death, 72.
    IV., King, 349-356.
Window tax, 368.
Witan (council), 49.
Wolfe, Gen. James, captures Quebec, 320.
Wolsey, Cardinal Thomas, 191-193.
Woman suffrage, 373.
Wool, its production and manufacture, 125, 148, 227.
World's Fair, 368.
Wren, Sir Christopher, architect, 264, 288, 303.
Wyatt, Sir Thomas, his rebellion, 205.
Wycliffe, John, reformer and martyr, 133, 138, 139.

www.ingramcontent.com/pod-product-compliance
Lightning Source LLC
Chambersburg PA
CBHW051847300426
44117CB00006B/302